Ukulele Chord

ENCYCLOPEDIA

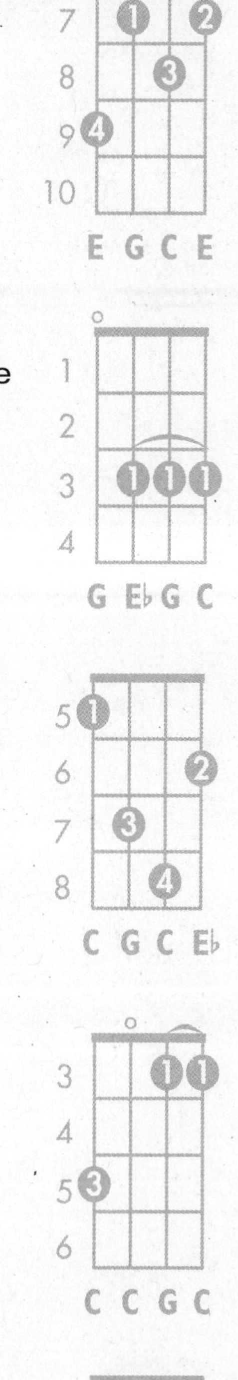

Ukulele Chord Encyclopedia is a practical, easy-to-use chord dictionary. Chords are listed alphabetically and chromatically for quick reference. On each page, chord variations (different fingerings and positions of each chord) are arranged in a logical order—beginning at the bottom of the ukulele neck and progressing to the top of the neck. This helps facilitate locating the chords in different positions over the entire fretboard. The Chord Theory chapter makes it easy to understand intervals and how chords are constructed. A complete fingerboard chart is included, along with a listing of major and minor scales in every key. This book gives you everything you need to expand your ever-growing chord vocabulary, and also helps you understand chord theory and construction.

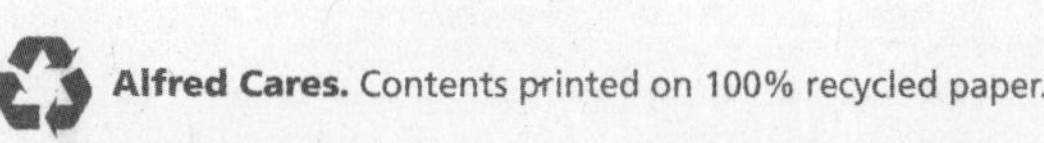

Alfred Music
P.O. Box 10003
Van Nuys, CA 91410-0003
alfred.com

ISBN-10: 0-7390-8925-0
ISBN-13: 978-0-7390-8925-5

Cover photographs: Martin Ukulele courtesyof the Martin Guitar Company
Chocolate Heart Mango Concert Classic Ukulele courtesy of Gordon and Char Mayer, of Mya-Moe Ukuleles

Current printing last digit:
10 9 8 7 6 5 4 3 2 1

Alfred Cares. Contents printed on 100% recycled paper.

CONTENTS

CHORD THEORY

Intervals 4
Basic Triads 6
Building Chords 7
Incomplete Voicings 9
A Note About Keys 9

READING CHORDS

Chord Symbol Variations 10
Chord Frames 11

CHORDS

Enharmonic Equivalents	A♭ (G♯)	A	B♭ (A♯)	B	C	C♯ (D♭)	D	E♭ (D♯)	E	F	F♯ (G♭)	G
Major	12	22	32	42	52	62	72	82	92	102	112	122
Minor	12	22	32	42	52	62	72	82	92	102	112	122
Diminished	12	22	32	42	52	62	72	82	92	102	112	122
Augmented	13	23	33	43	53	63	73	83	93	103	113	123
Fifth	13	23	33	43	53	63	73	83	93	103	113	123
Major Suspended Fourth	13	23	33	43	53	63	73	83	93	103	113	123
Major Sixth	14	24	34	44	54	64	74	84	94	104	114	124
Minor Sixth	14	24	34	44	54	64	74	84	94	104	114	124
Major Seventh	14	24	34	44	54	64	74	84	94	104	114	124
Seventh	14	24	34	44	54	64	74	84	94	104	114	124
Minor Seventh	15	25	35	45	55	65	75	85	95	105	115	125
Minor Seventh Flat Fifth	15	25	35	45	55	65	75	85	95	105	115	125
Diminished Seventh	15	25	35	45	55	65	75	85	95	105	115	125
Seventh Suspended Fourth	15	25	35	45	55	65	75	85	95	105	115	125
Major Add Ninth	16	26	36	46	56	66	76	86	96	106	116	126
Major Ninth	16	26	36	46	56	66	76	86	96	106	116	126
Ninth	16	26	36	46	56	66	76	86	96	106	116	126
Minor Ninth	16	26	36	46	56	66	76	86	96	106	116	126
Sixth Add Ninth	17	27	37	47	57	67	77	87	97	107	117	127
Minor Sixth Add Ninth	17	27	37	47	57	67	77	87	97	107	117	127
Minor Major Seventh	17	27	37	47	57	67	77	87	97	107	117	127
Minor Ninth Major Seventh	17	27	37	47	57	67	77	87	97	107	117	127
Eleventh	18	28	38	48	58	68	78	88	98	108	118	128
Minor Eleventh	18	28	38	48	58	68	78	88	98	108	118	128
Thirteenth	18	28	38	48	58	68	78	88	98	108	118	128
Flat Fifth	18	28	38	48	58	68	78	88	98	108	118	128
Seventh Flat Fifth	19	29	39	49	59	69	79	89	99	109	119	129
Seventh Augmented Fifth	19	29	39	49	59	69	79	89	99	109	119	129
Major Seventh Flat Fifth	19	29	39	49	59	69	79	89	99	109	119	129
Seventh Flat Ninth	19	29	39	49	59	69	79	89	99	109	119	129
Seventh Sharp Ninth	20	30	40	50	60	70	80	90	100	110	120	130
Seventh Flat Ninth Augmented Fifth	20	30	40	50	60	70	80	90	100	110	120	130
Ninth Augmented Fifth	20	30	40	50	60	70	80	90	100	110	120	130
Ninth Flat Fifth	20	30	40	50	60	70	80	90	100	110	120	130
Ninth Sharp Eleventh	21	31	41	51	61	71	81	91	101	111	121	131
Thirteenth Flat Ninth	21	31	41	51	61	71	81	91	101	111	121	131
Thirteenth Flat Ninth Flat Fifth	21	31	41	51	61	71	81	91	101	111	121	131

SCALES

Major 132
Natural Minor 133
Harmonic Minor 134
Melodic Minor 135

UKULELE FINGERBOARD CHART 136

CHORD THEORY

Intervals

Play any note on the ukulele, then play a note one fret above it. The distance between these two notes is a *half step*. Play another note followed by a note two frets above it. The distance between these two notes is a *whole step* (two half steps). The distance between any two notes is referred to as an *interval*.

A *scale* is a series notes in a specific arrangement of whole and half steps. In the example of the C major scale below, the letter names are shown above the notes and the *scale degrees* (numbers) of the notes are written below. Notice that C is the first degree of the scale, D is the second, etc.

The name of an interval is determined by counting the number of scale degrees from one note to the next. For example, an interval of a 3rd, starting on C, would be determined by counting up three scale degrees, or C-D-E (1-2-3). C to E is a 3rd. An interval of a 4th, starting on C, would be determined by counting up four scale degrees, or C-D-E-F (1-2-3-4). C to F is a 4th.

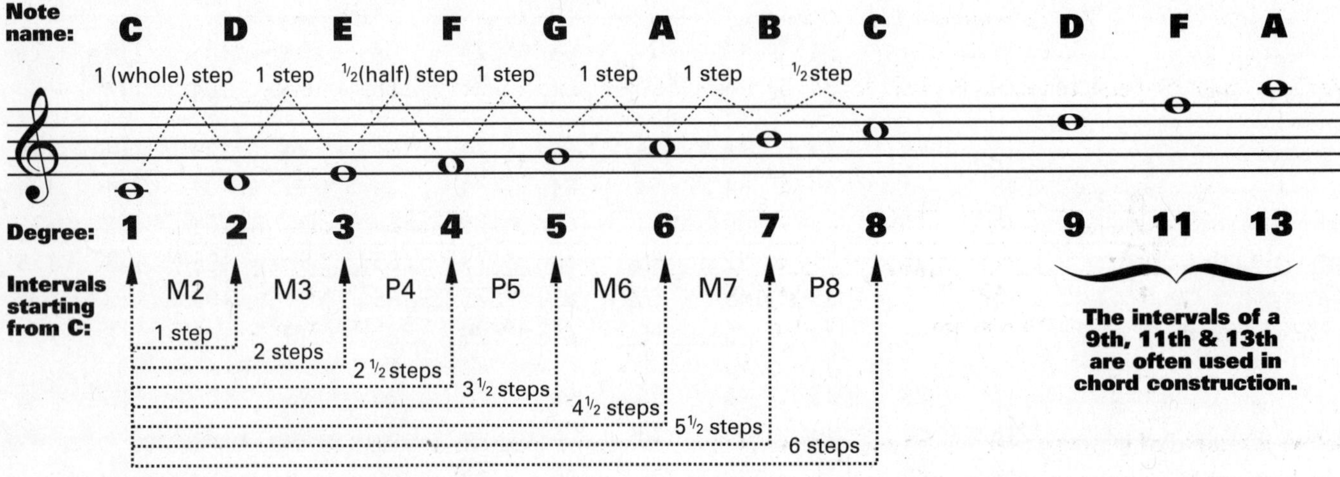

Intervals are not only labeled by the distance between scale degrees, but by the quality of the interval. An interval's quality is determined by counting the number of whole steps and half steps between the two notes of an interval. For example, C to E is a 3rd. C to E is also a major third because there are 2 whole steps between C and E. Likewise, C to E♭ is a 3rd. C to E♭ is also a minor third because there are 1½ steps between C and E♭. There are five qualities used to describe intervals: major, minor, perfect, diminished, and augmented.

M = Major **o = Diminished (dim)** **m = Minor** **+ = Augmented (aug)** **P = Perfect**

Particular intervals are associated with certain qualities:

2nds, 9ths	=	Major, Minor & Augmented
3rds, 6ths, 13ths	=	Major, Minor, Augmented & Diminished
4ths, 5ths, 11ths	=	Perfect, Augmented & Diminished
7ths	=	Major, Minor & Diminished

Intervals

When a *major* interval is made **smaller** by a half step it becomes a *minor* interval.

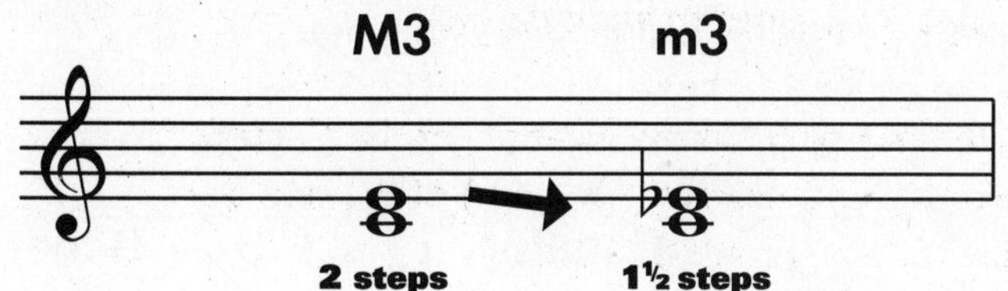

When a *minor* interval is made **larger** by a half step it becomes a *major* interval.

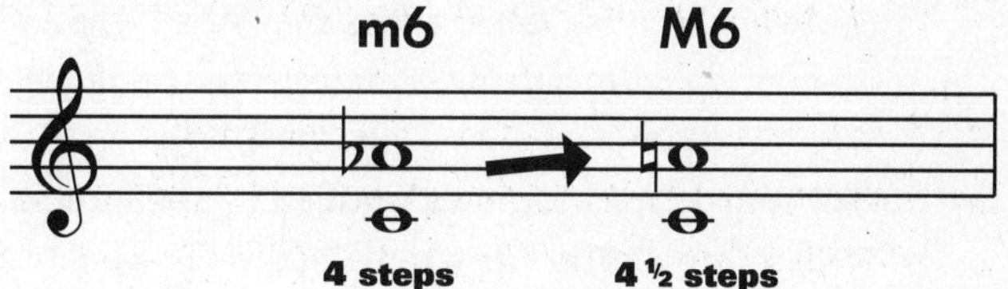

When a *minor* or *perfect* interval is made **smaller** by a half step it becomes a *diminished* interval.

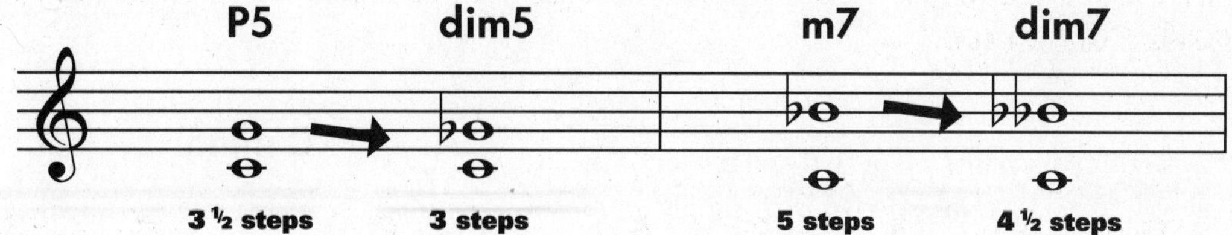

When a *major* or *perfect* interval is made **larger** by a half step it becomes an *augmented* interval.

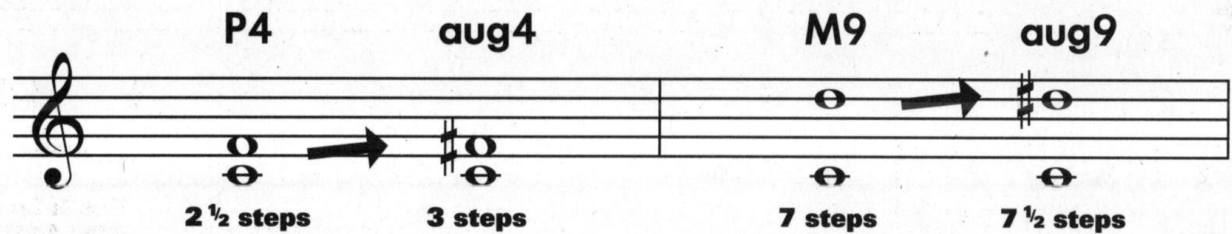

Below is a table of intervals starting on the note C. Notice that some intervals are labeled *enharmonic*, which means that they are written differently but sound the same (see **aug2** & **m3**).

TABLE OF INTERVALS

CHORD THEORY

Basic Triads

Two or more notes played together is called a *chord*. Most commonly, a chord will consist of three or more notes. A three-note chord is called a *triad*. The *root* of a triad (or any other chord) is the note from which a chord is constructed. The relationship of the intervals from the root to the other notes of a chord determines the chord *type*. Triads are most frequently identified as one of four chord types: *major, minor, diminished* and *augmented.*

All chord types can be identified by the intervals used to create the chord. For example, the C major triad is built beginning with C as the root, adding a major 3rd (E) and adding a perfect 5th (G). All major triads contain a root, M3 and P5.

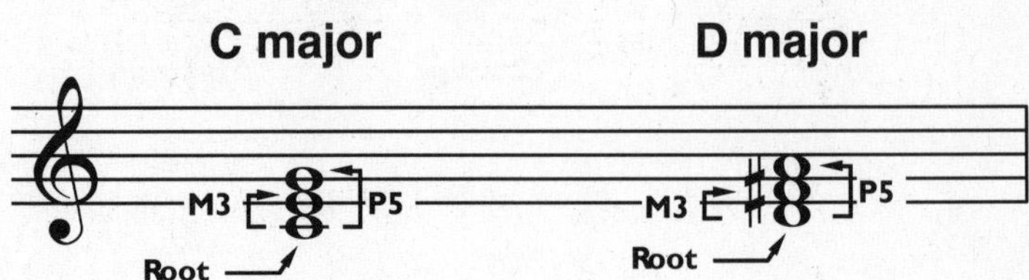

Minor triads contain a root, minor 3rd and perfect 5th. (An easier way to build a minor triad is to simply lower the 3rd of a major triad.) All minor triads contain a root, m3 and P5.

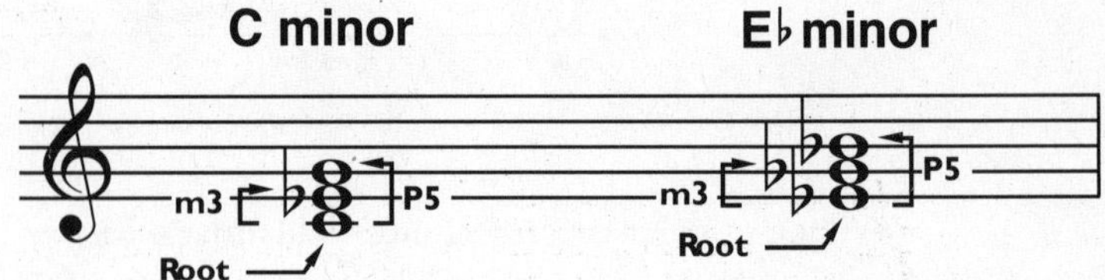

Diminished triads contain a root, minor 3rd and diminished 5th. If the perfect 5th of a minor triad is made smaller by a half step (to become a diminished 5th), the result is a diminished triad. All diminished triads contain a root, m3 and dim5.

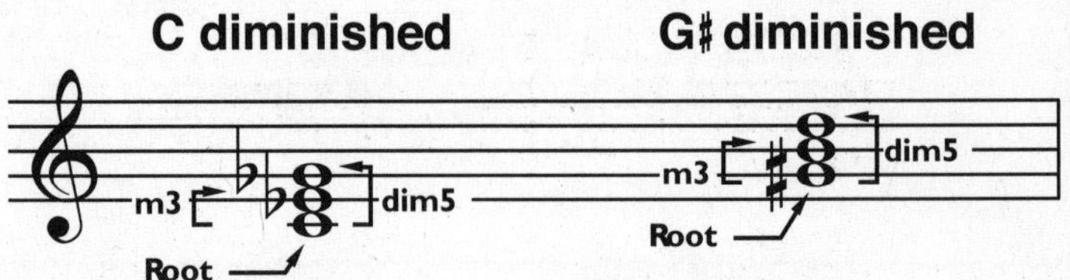

Augmented triads contain a root, major 3rd and augmented 5th. If the perfect 5th of a major triad is made larger by a half step (to become an augmented 5th), the result is an augmented triad. All augmented triads contain a root, M3 and aug5.

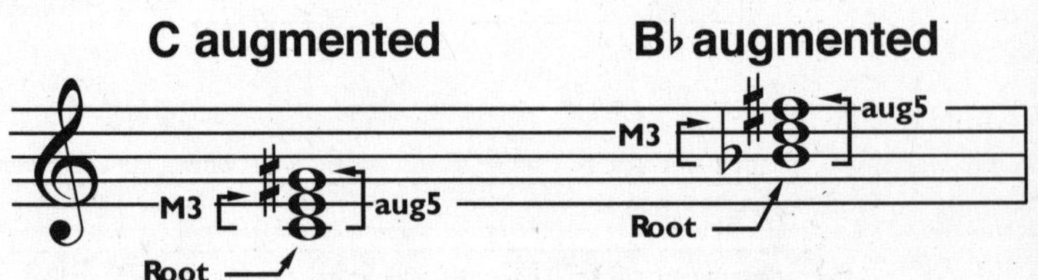

An important concept to remember about chords is that the bottom note of a chord will not always be the root. If the root of a triad, for instance, is moved above the 5th so that the 3rd is the bottom note of the chord, it is said to be in the *first inversion*. If the root and 3rd are moved above the 5th, the chord is in the *second inversion*. The number of inversions that a chord can have is related to the number of notes in the chord: a three-note chord can have two inversions, a four-note chord can have three inversions, etc.

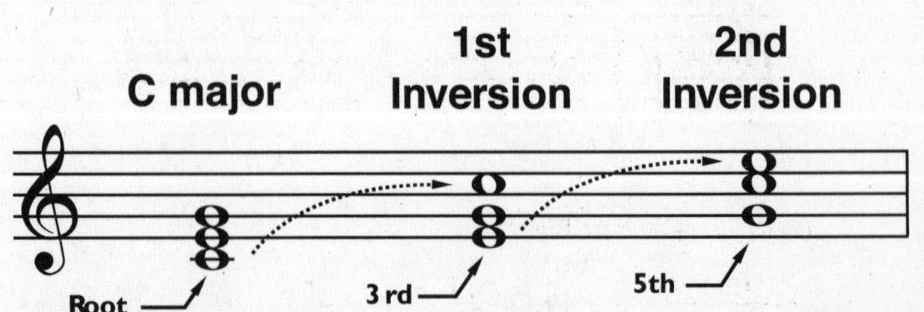

Building Chords

By using the four chord types as basic building blocks, it is possible to create a variety of chords by adding 6ths, 7ths, 9ths, 11ths, etc. The following are examples of some of the many variations.

* The *suspended fourth* chord does not contain a third. An assumption is made that the 4th degree of the chord will harmonically be inclined to *resolve* to the 3rd degree. In other words, the 4th is *suspended* until it moves to the 3rd.

CHORD THEORY

Building Chords

Up until now, the examples have shown intervals and chord construction based on C. Until you are familiar with all the chords, the C chord examples on the previous page can serve as a reference guide when building chords based on other notes: For instance, locate C7(♭9). To construct a G7(♭9) chord, first determine what intervals are contained in C7(♭9), then follow the steps outlined below.

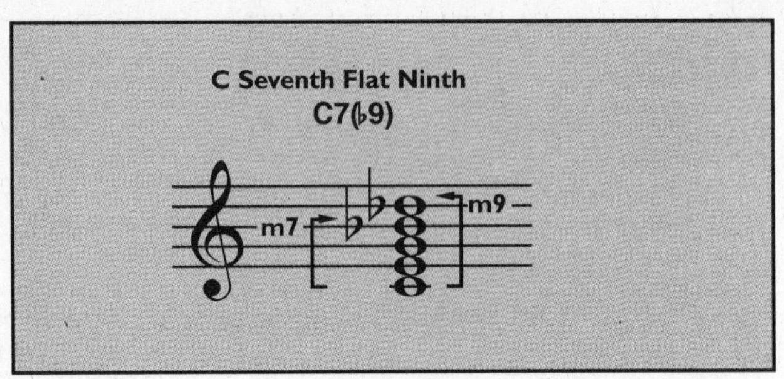

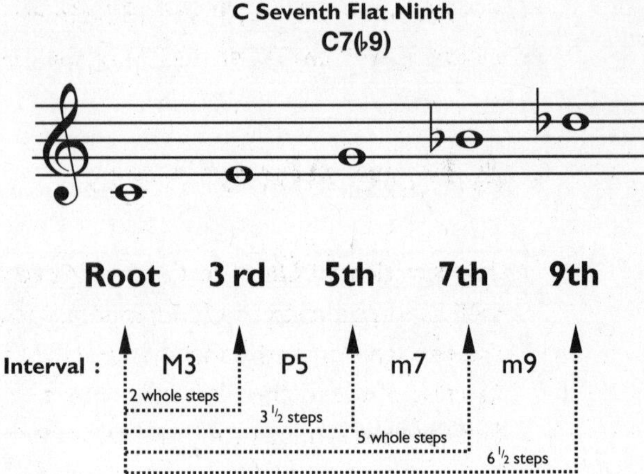

- Determine the *root* of the chord. A chord is always named for its root—in this case, G is the root of G7(♭9).
- Count *letter* names up from the *letter name of the root* (G), as we did when building intervals on page 169, to determine the intervals of the chord. Counting three letter names up from G to B (G–A–B, 1–2–3) is a 3rd, G to D (G–A–B–C–D) is a 5th, G to F is a 7th, and G to A is a 9th.
- Determine the *quality* of the intervals by counting whole steps and half steps up from the root; G to B (2 whole steps) is a major 3rd, G to D (3½ steps) is a perfect 5th, G to F (5 whole steps) is a minor 7th, and G to A♭ (6½ steps) is a minor 9th.

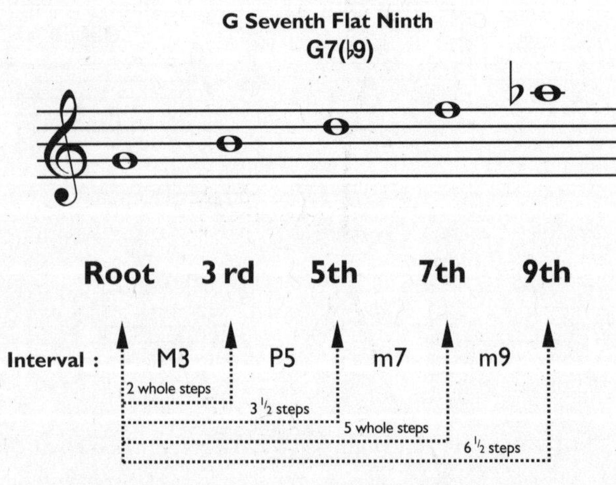

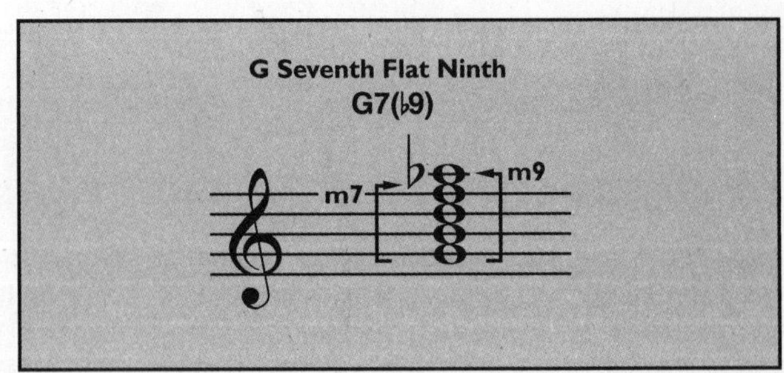

Follow this general guideline to figure out the notes of any chord. As interval and chord construction become more familiar, it will become possible to create your own original fingerings on the ukulele. Feel free to experiment!

Incomplete Voicings

A *voicing* is an arrangement of the notes in a chord. Since your ukulele has only four strings, you can play only three- or four-note voicings, but it is not uncommon to omit the root from a voicing. In this book, a *rootless voicing* is indicated with a single asterisk (*) to the right of the chord diagram.

Sometimes, the 7th is omitted from an *extended chord*, which is a chord with tones that extend beyond the 7th, such as 9th, 11th, and 13th chords. In this book, extended chords with the 7th omitted are indicated with two asterisks (**) to the right of the chord diagram.

A Note About Keys

The function of ***Ukulele Chord Encyclopedia*** is to provide access to fingerings of thousands of ukulele chords as well as introducing the fundamentals of chord construction. As the beginning ukulelist becomes accomplished in the recognition and construction of intervals and chords, the next natural step is to seek an understanding of the *function* of these chords within *keys* or *chord progressions*. Although it is not fundamental to playing chord changes, further study in harmony and chord progressions can only enrich the musical experience of the advancing ukulelist and is therefore highly recommended.

Ukulele Chord Encyclopedia is organized to provide the fingerings of chords in all keys. The *Circle of Fifths* below will help to clarify which chords are enharmonic equivalents (notice that chords can be written enharmonically as well as notes-see page 5). The Circle of Fifths also serves as a quick reference guide to the relationship of the keys and how key signatures can be figured out in a logical manner. Clockwise movement (up a P5) provides all of the sharp keys by adding one sharp to the key signature progressively. Counter-clockwise (down a P5) provides the flat keys by adding one flat similarly.

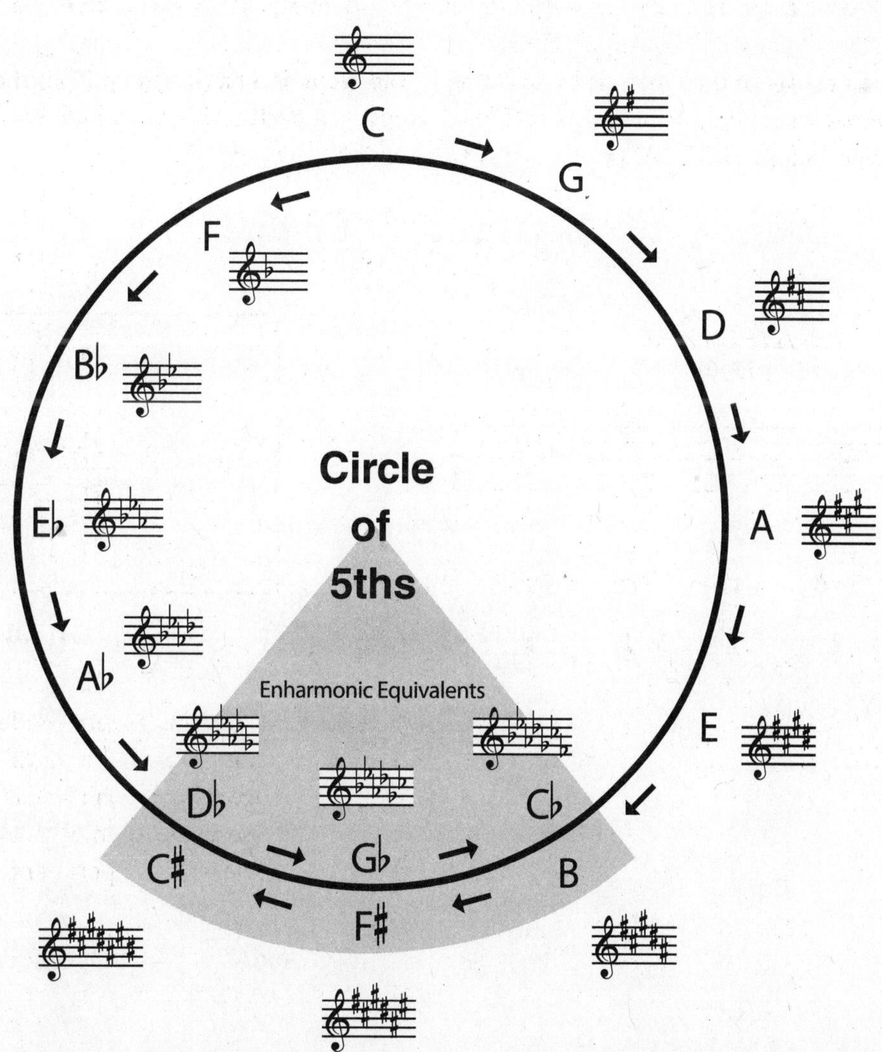

Chord Symbol Variations

Chord symbols are a form of musical shorthand that give the ukulelist as much information about a chord as quickly as possible. Since chord symbols are not universally standardized, they are often written in many different ways—some are understandable, others are confusing. To illustrate this point, below is a listing of some of the ways copyists, composers and arrangers have created variations on the more common chord symbols.

C	**Csus**	**C(♭5)**	**C(add9)**	**C5**	**Cm**
C major	Csus4	C-5	C(9)	C(no3)	Cmin
Cmaj	C(addF)	C(5-)	C(add2)	C(omit3)	Cmi
CM	C4	C(♯4)	C(+9)		C-
			C(+D)		

C+	**C°**	**C6**	**C6/9**	**Cm6/9**	**Cm6**
C+5	Cdim	Cmaj6	C6(add9)	C-6/9	C-6
Caug	Cdim7	C(addA)	C6(addD)	Cm6(+9)	Cm(addA)
Caug5	C7dim	C(A)	C9(no7)	Cm6(add9)	Cm(+6)
C(♯5)			C9/6	Cm6(+D)	

C7	**C7sus**	**Cm7**	**Cm7(♭5)**	**C7+**	**C7(♭5)**
C(addB♭)	C7sus4	Cmi7	Cmi7-5	C7+5	C7-5
C7̸	Csus7	Cmin7	C-7(5-)	C7aug	C7(5-)
C(-7)	C7(+4)	C-7	Cø	C7aug5	C7̸-5
C(+7)		C7mi	C½dim	C7(♯5)	C7(♯4)

Cmaj7	**Cmaj7(♭5)**	**Cm(maj7)**	**C7(♭9)**	**C7(♯9)**	**C7+(♭9)**
Cma7	Cmaj7(-5)	C-maj7	C7(-9)	C7(+9)	Caug7-9
C7	C7̸(-5)	C-7̸	C9♭	C9♯	C+7(♭9)
C△	C△(♭5)	Cmi7̸	C9-	C9+	C+9♭
C△7					C7+(-9)

Cm9	**C9**	**C9+**	**C9(♭5)**	**Cmaj9**	**C9(♯11)**
Cm7(9)	C$^{9}_{7}$	C9(+5)	C9(-5)	C7̸(9)	C9(+11)
Cm7(+9)	C7add9	Caug9	C7$^{9}_{-5}$	C7̸(+9)	C(♯11)
C-9	C7(addD)	C(♯9♯5)	C9(5♭)	C9(maj7)	C11+
Cmi7(9+)	C7(+9)	C+9		C9̸	C11♯

Cm9(maj7)	**C11**	**Cm11**	**C13**	**C13(♭9)**	**C13($^{\flat 9}_{\flat 5}$)**
C-9(♯7)	C9(11)	C-11	C9addA	C13(-9)	C13(-9-5)
C(-9)7̸	C9addF	Cm(♭11)	C9(6)	C$^{13}_{\flat 9}$	C(♭9♭5)addA
Cmi9(♯7)	C9+11	Cmi7$^{11}_{9}$	C7addA	C(♭9)addA	
	C7$^{9}_{11}$	C-7($^{9}_{11}$)	C7+A		

Chord Frames

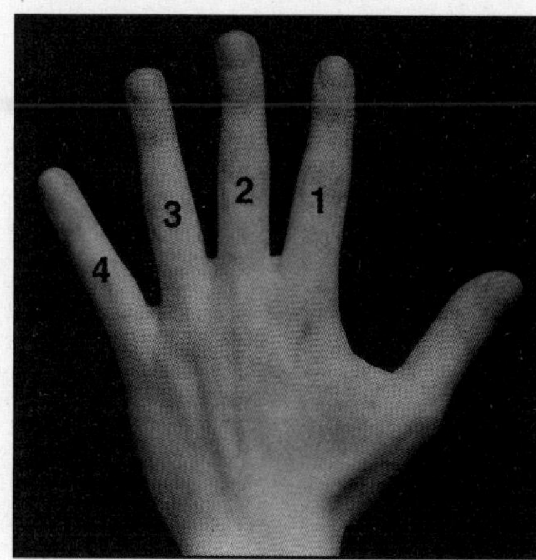

Ukulele chord frames are diagrams that contain all the information necessary to play a particular chord. The fingerings, note names and position of the chord on the neck are all provided on the chord frame (see below). The photo at the left shows which finger number corresponds to which finger.

Choose chord positions that require the least motion from one chord to the next; select fingerings that are in approximately the same location on the ukulele neck. This will provide smoother and more comfortable transitions between chords in a progression.

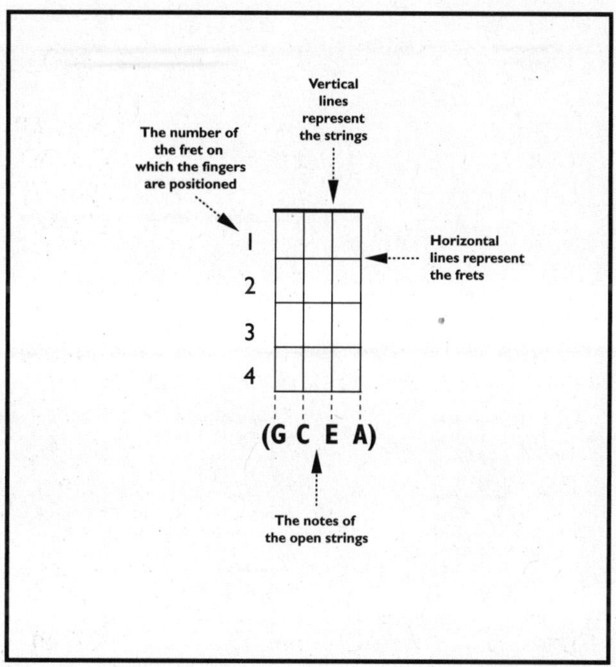

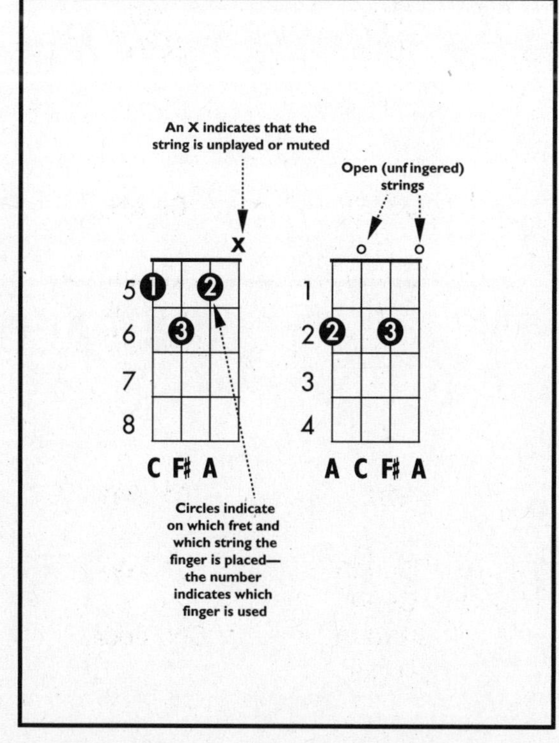

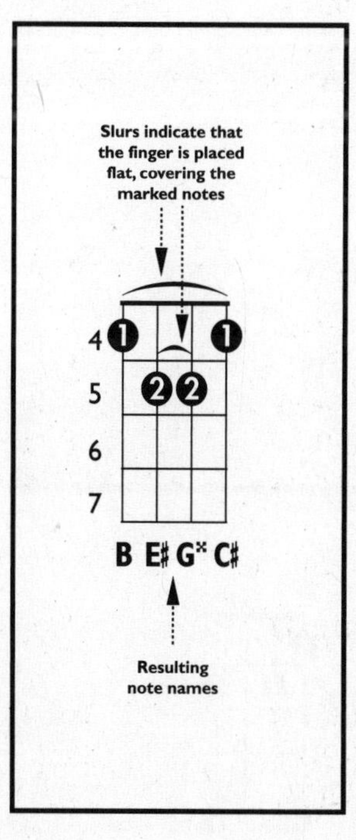

A♭

A♭ Major

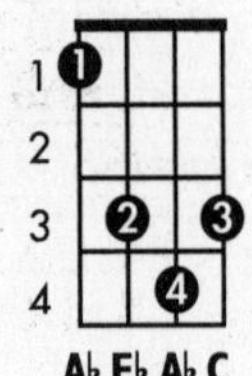

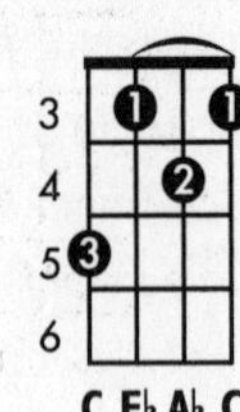

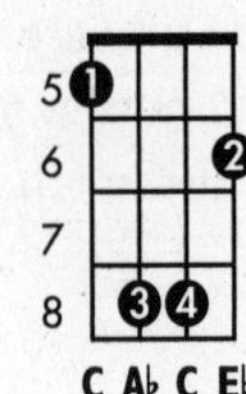

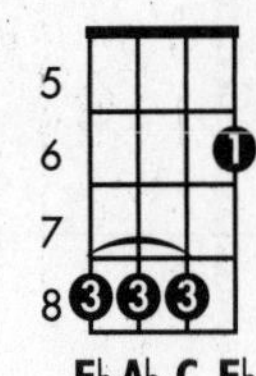

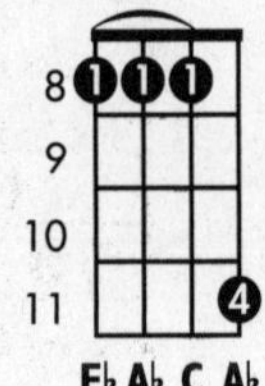

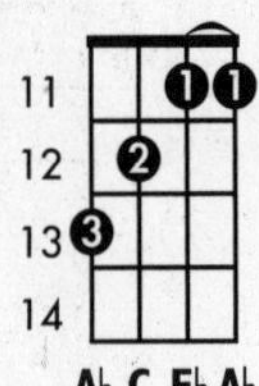

A♭m

A♭ Minor

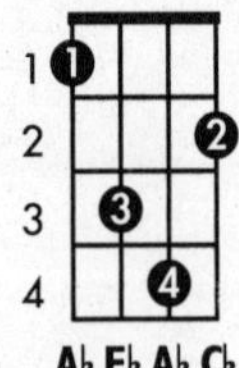

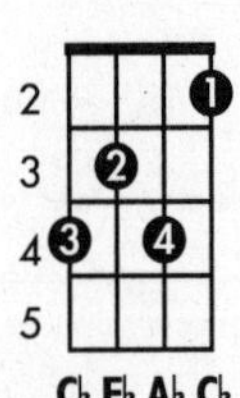

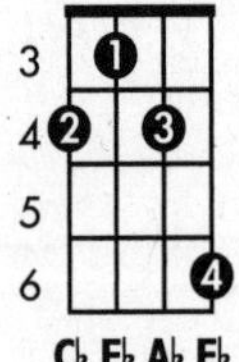

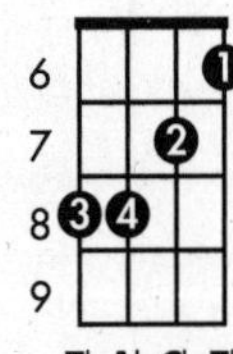

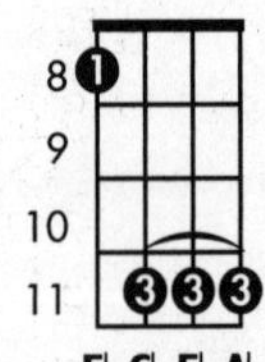

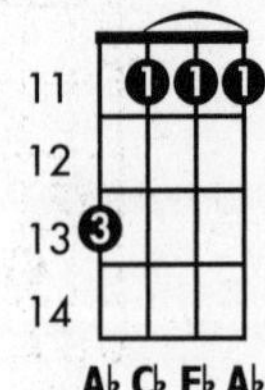

A♭°

A♭ Diminished

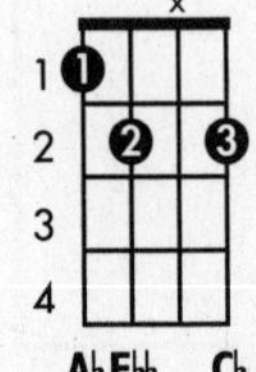

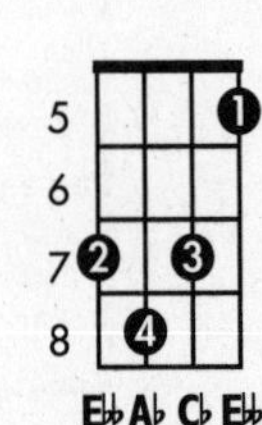

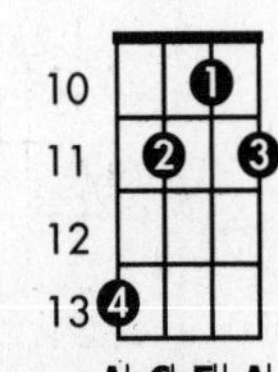

A♭ Augmented

A♭+

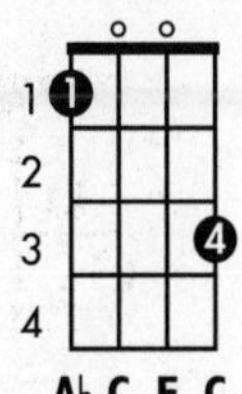

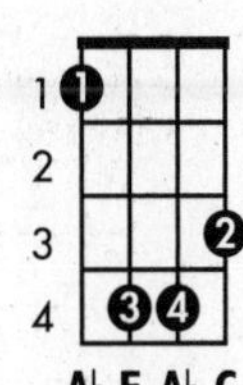

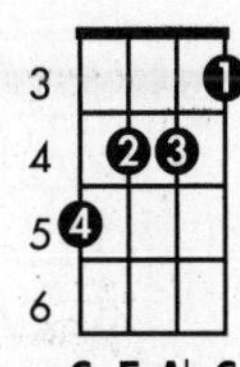

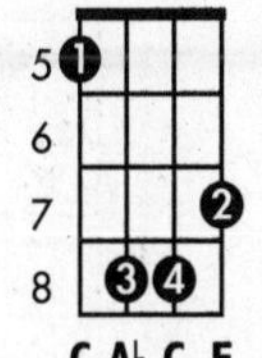

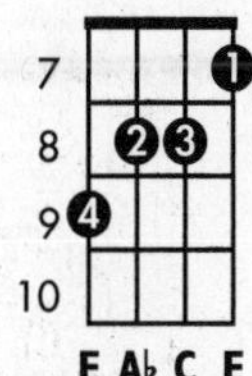

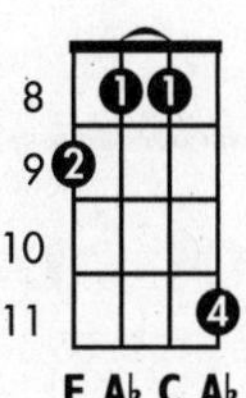

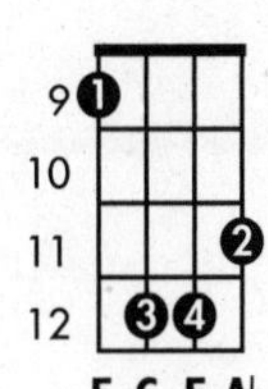

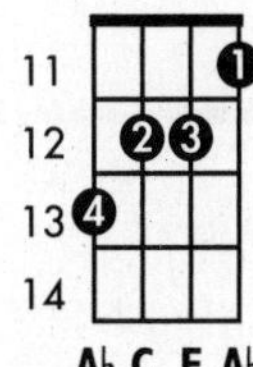

A♭ Fifth

A♭5

Sometimes written **A♭(omit 3)**

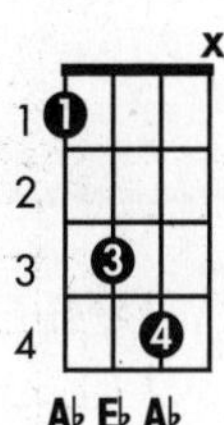

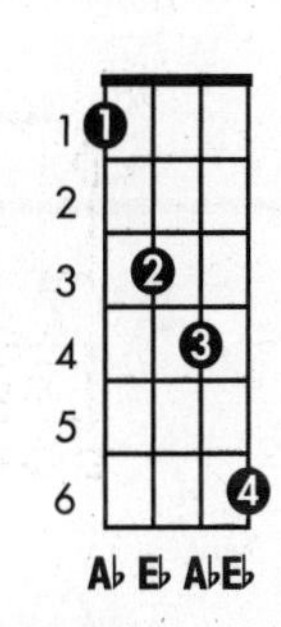

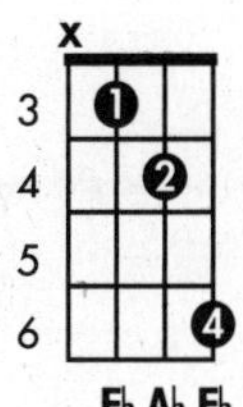

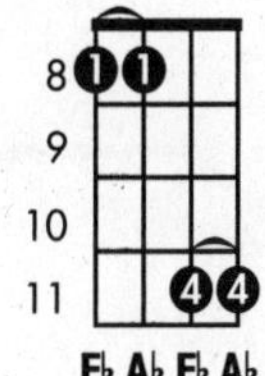

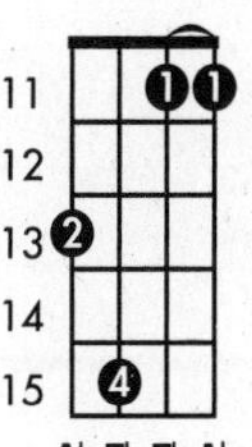

A♭ Major Suspended Fourth

A♭sus

Sometimes written **A♭sus4**

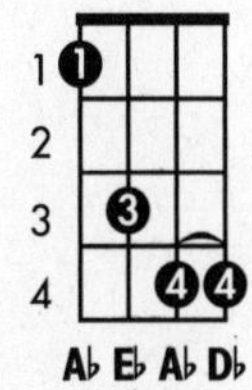

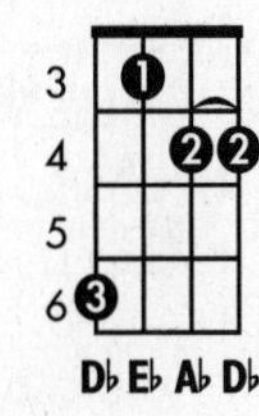

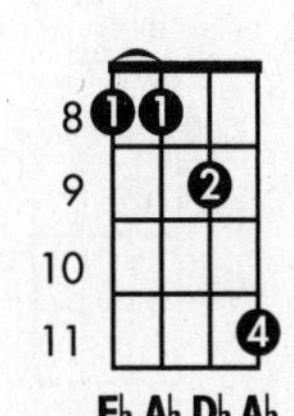

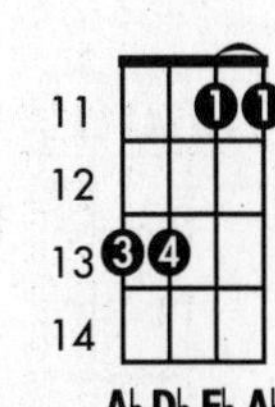

A♭6 — A♭ Major 6th

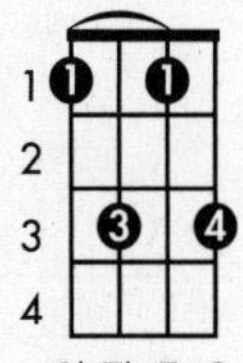

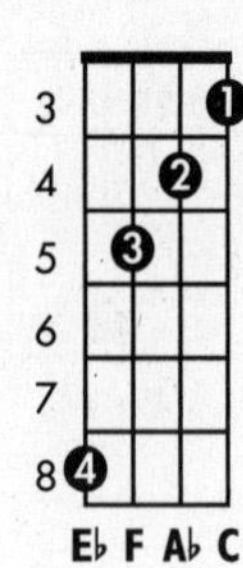

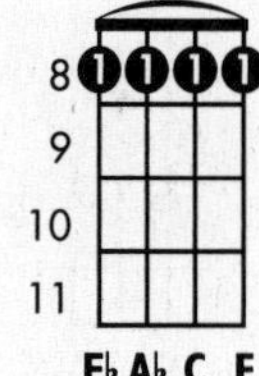

A♭m6 — A♭ Minor Sixth

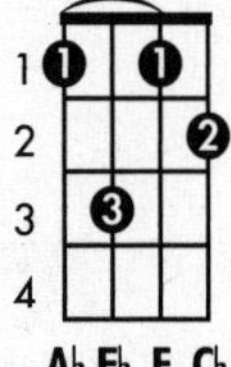

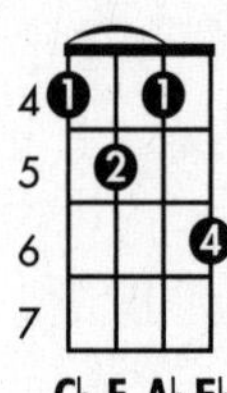

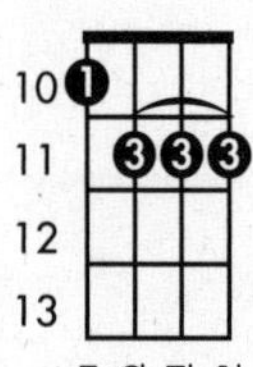

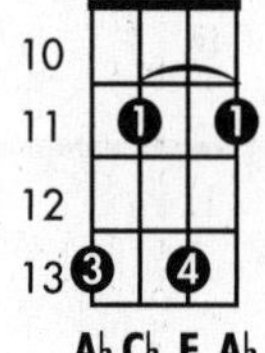

A♭maj7 — A♭ Major Seventh

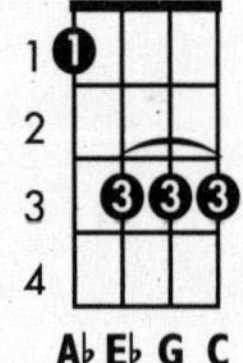

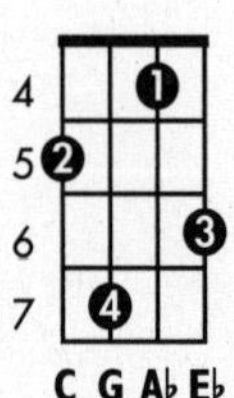

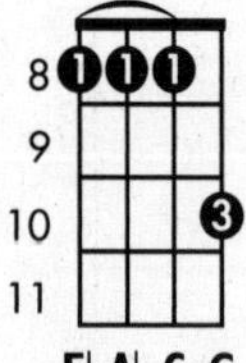

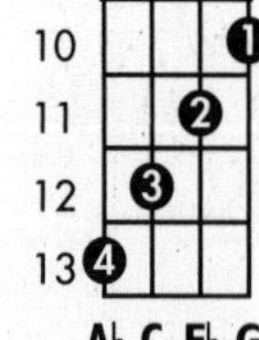

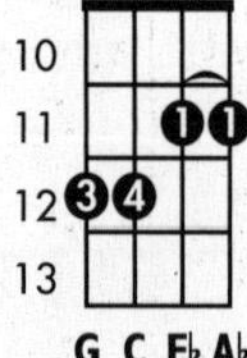

A♭7 — A♭ Seventh

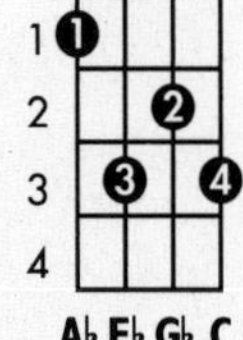

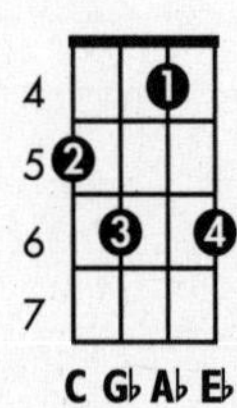

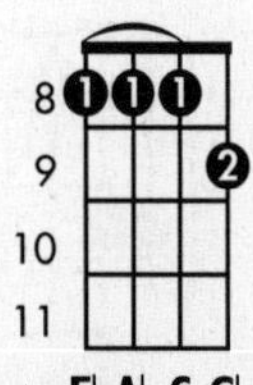

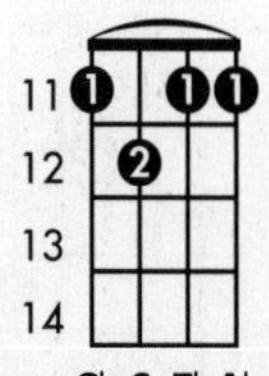

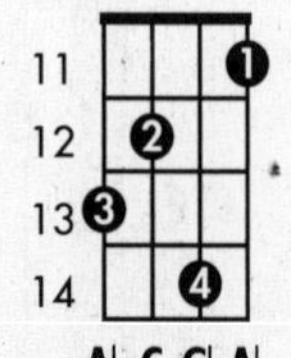

A♭ Minor Seventh

A♭m7

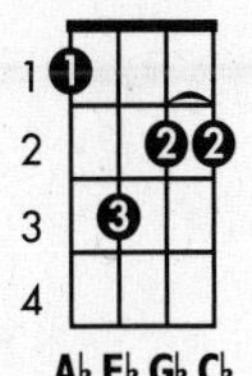
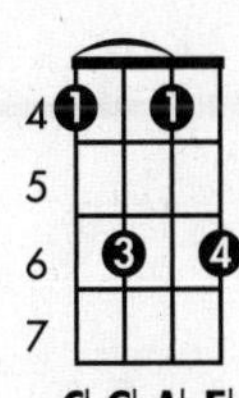
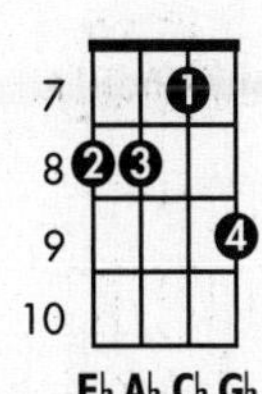
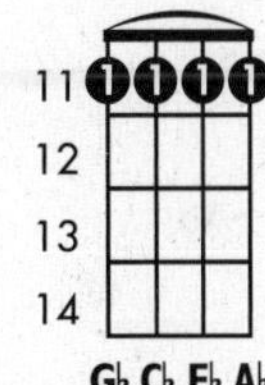
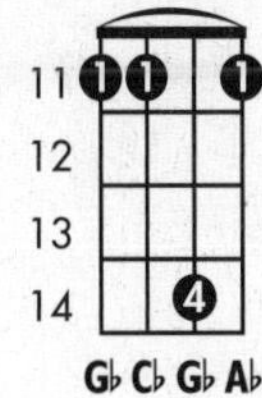

A♭ Minor Seventh Flat Fifth

A♭m7(♭5)

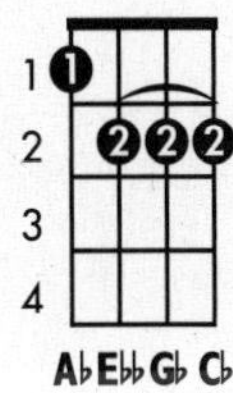
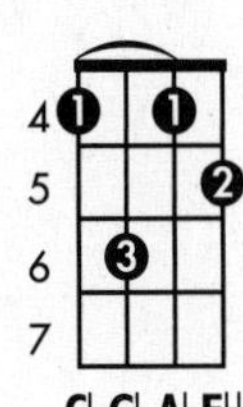
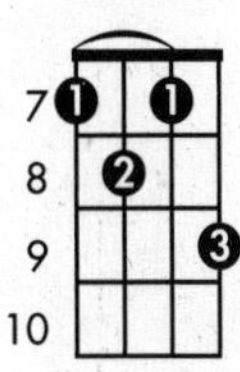
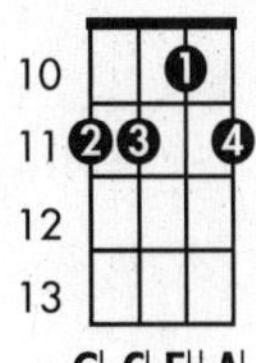

A♭ Diminished Seventh

A♭°7

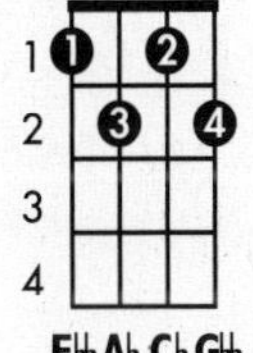
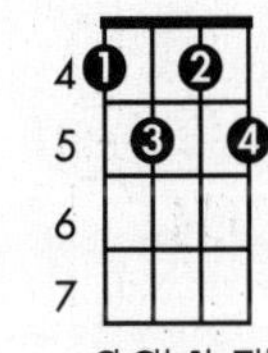
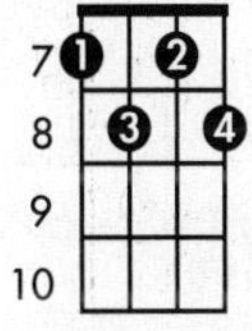
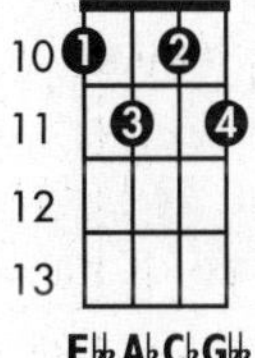

A♭ Seventh Suspended Fourth

A♭7sus

Sometimes written **A♭7sus4**

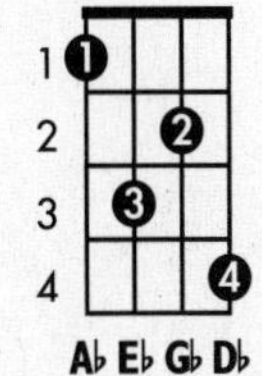
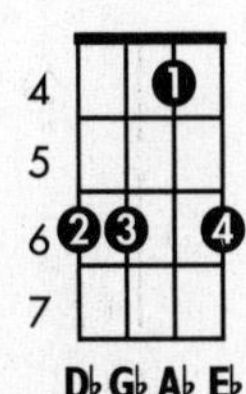
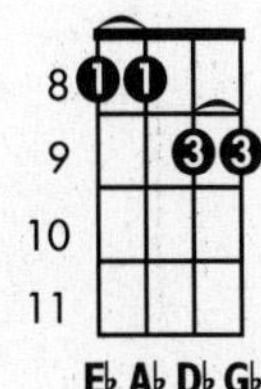
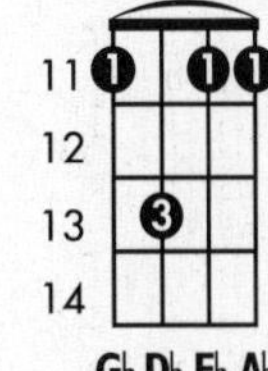

A♭(add9) — A♭ Major Add Ninth

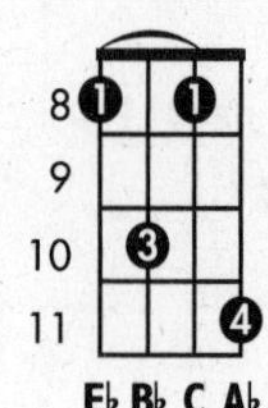
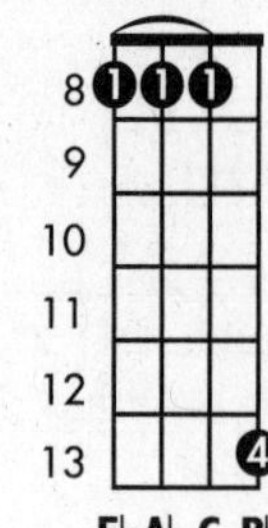
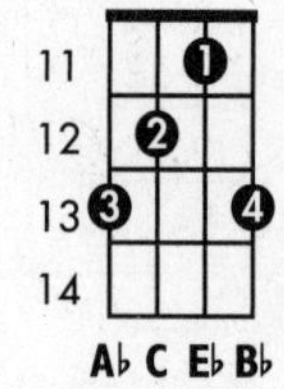

A♭maj9 — A♭ Major Ninth

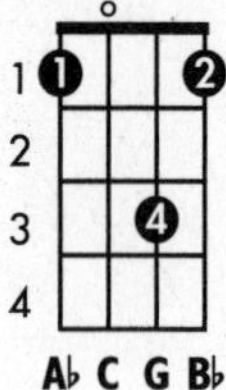
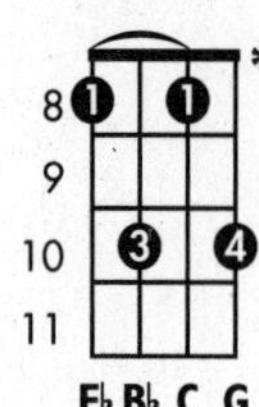
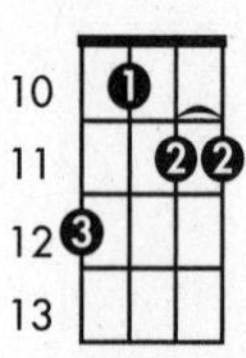
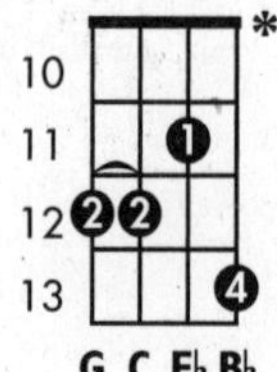

A♭9 — A♭ Ninth

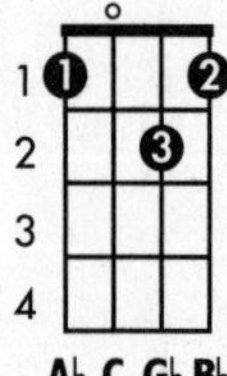
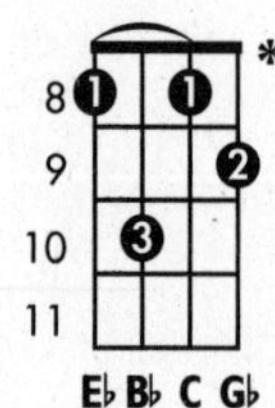
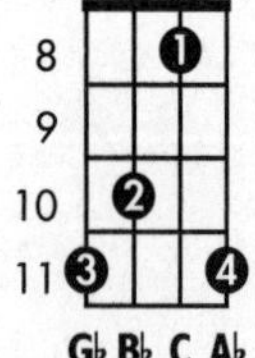
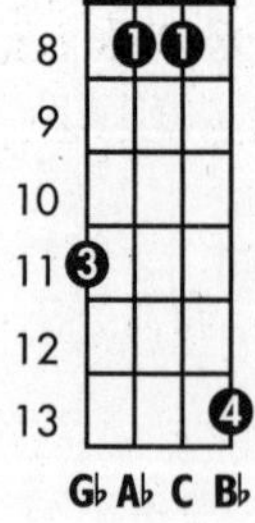

A♭m9 — A♭ Minor Ninth

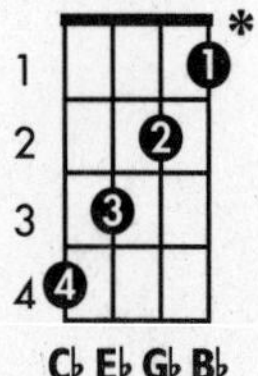
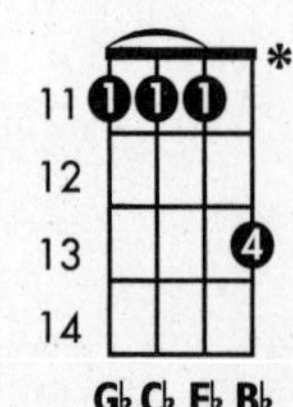
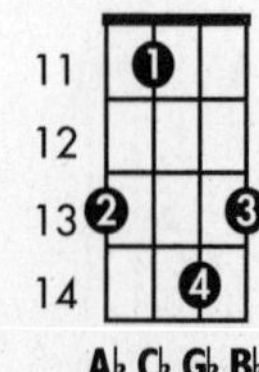

A♭ Sixth Add Ninth

A♭6/9

Sometimes written **A♭9/6**

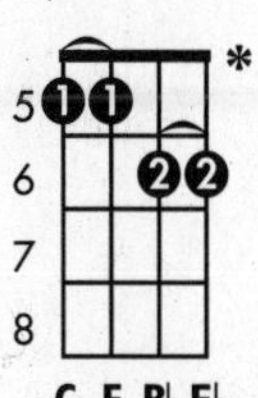

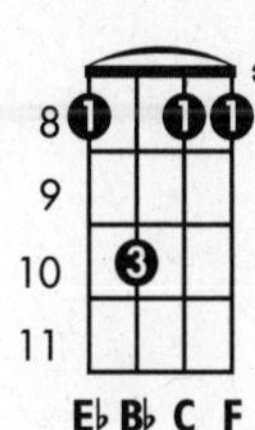

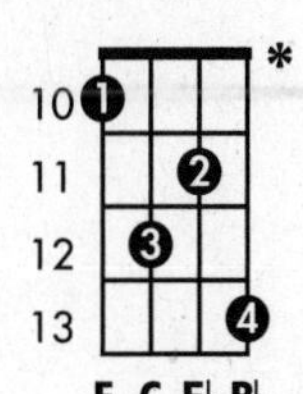

A♭ Minor Sixth Add Ninth

A♭m6/9

Sometimes written **A♭m9/6**

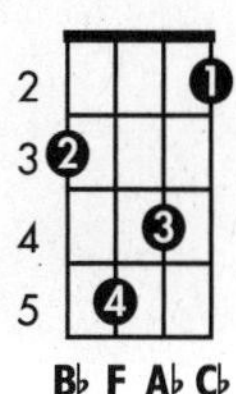

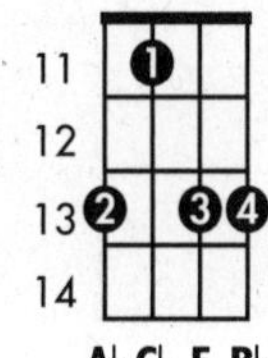

A♭ Minor Major Seventh

A♭m(maj7)

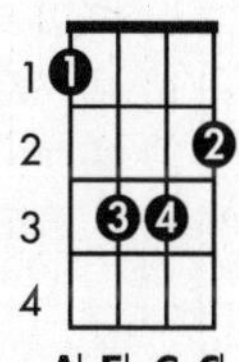

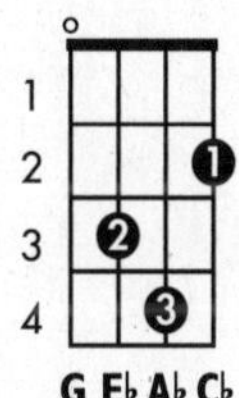

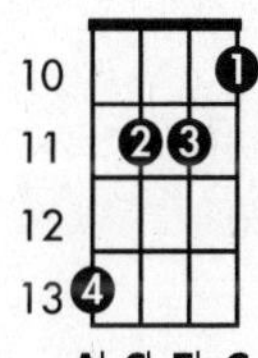

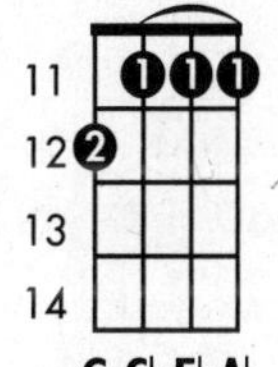

A♭ Minor Ninth Major Seventh

A♭m9(maj7)

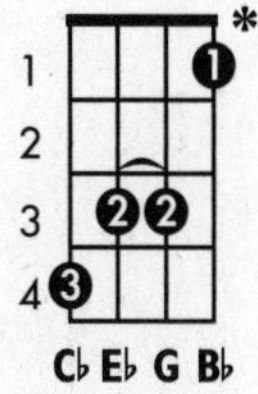

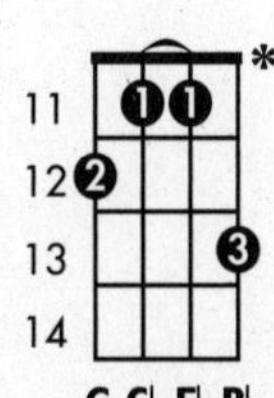

A♭11 — A♭ Eleventh

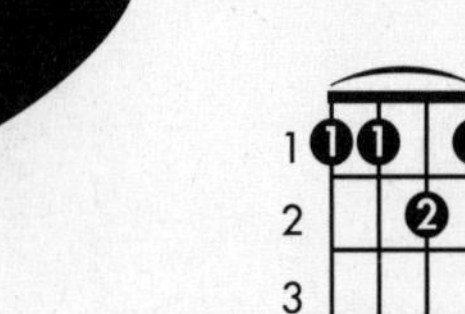

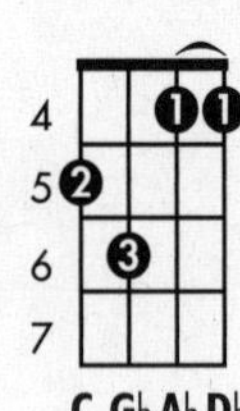

D♭ A♭ C G♭

A♭m11 — A♭ Minor Eleventh

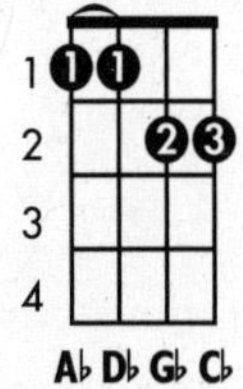

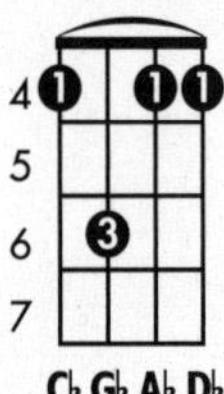

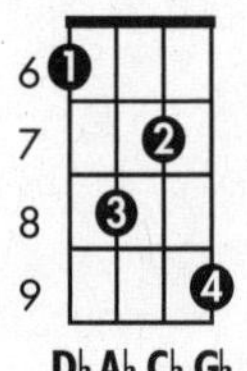

A♭13 — A♭ Thirteenth

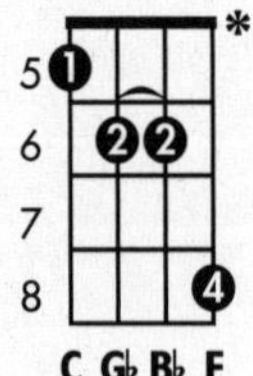

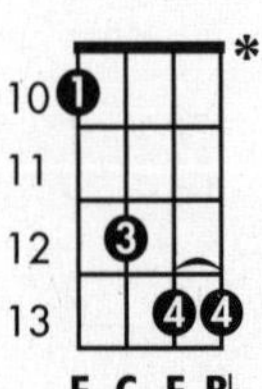

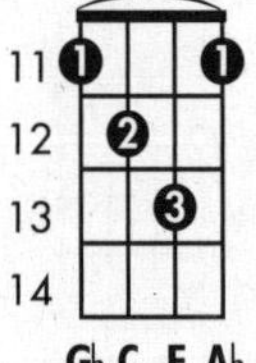

A♭(♭5) — A♭ Flat Fifth

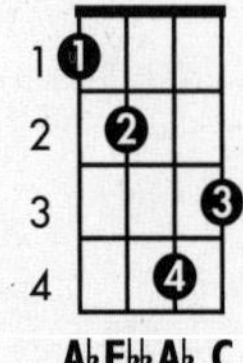

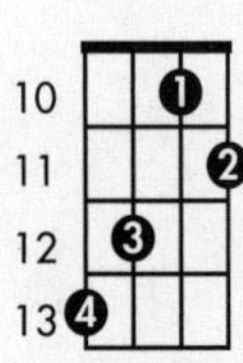

A♭ Seventh Flat Fifth — A♭7(♭5)

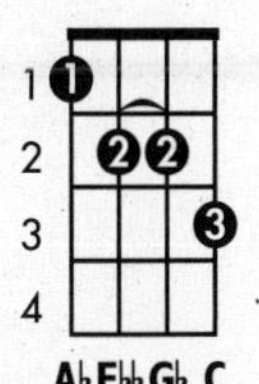

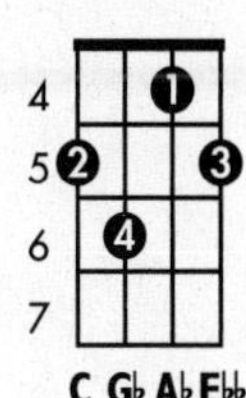

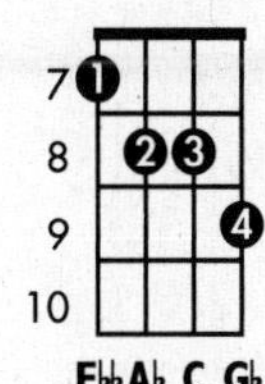

10
11
12
13
G♭ C E♭♭ A♭

A♭ Seventh Augmented Fifth — A♭7+

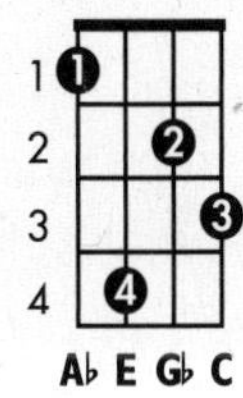

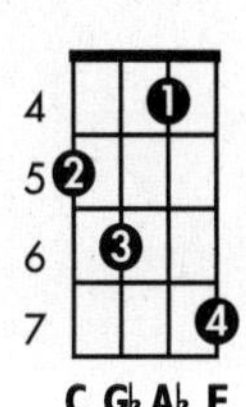

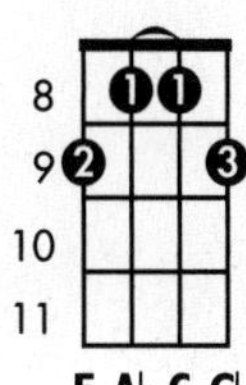

A♭ Major Seventh Flat Fifth — A♭maj7(♭5)

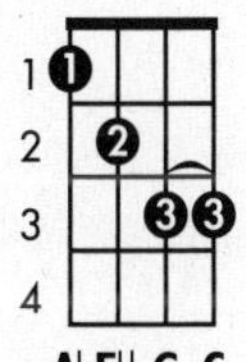

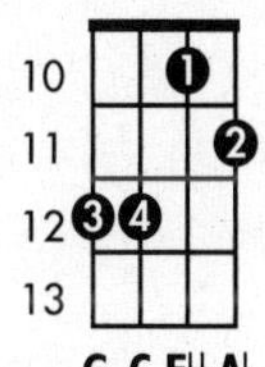

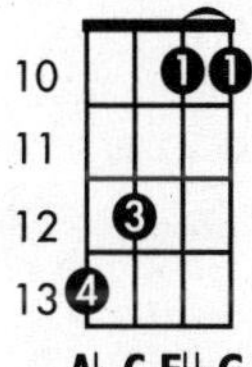

A♭ Seventh Flat Ninth — A♭7(♭9)

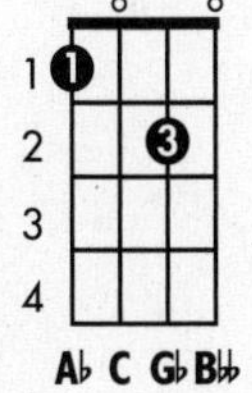

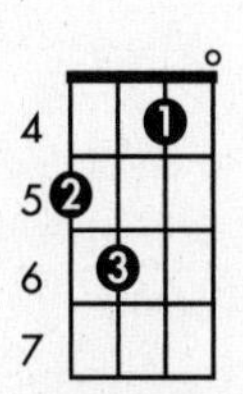

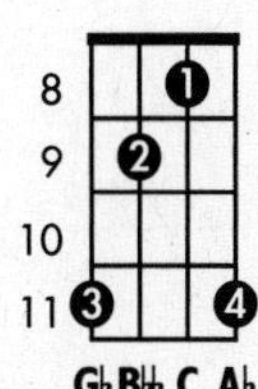

A♭7(♯9) — A♭ Seventh Sharp Ninth

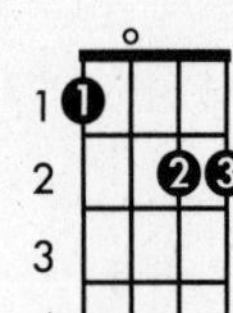

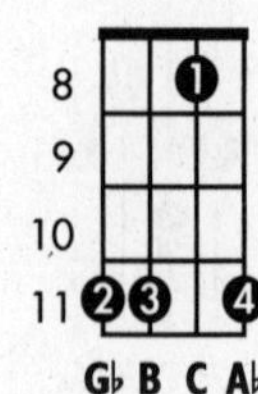
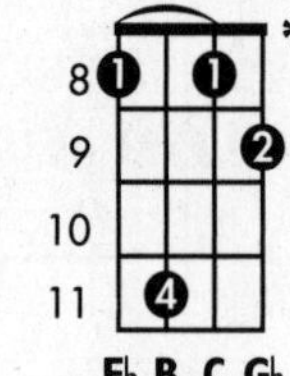

A♭7+(♭9) — A♭ Seventh Flat Ninth Augmented Fifth

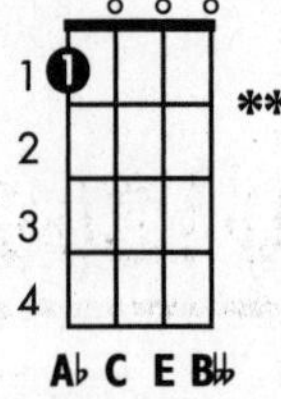
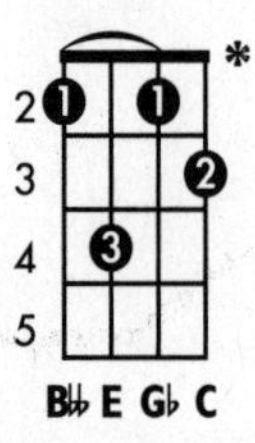
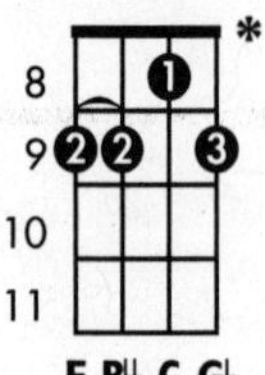

A♭9+ — A♭ Ninth Augmented Fifth

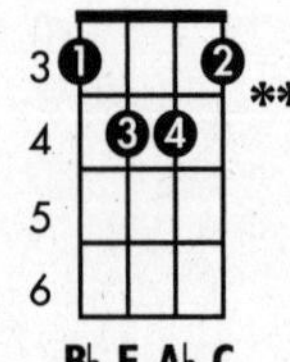
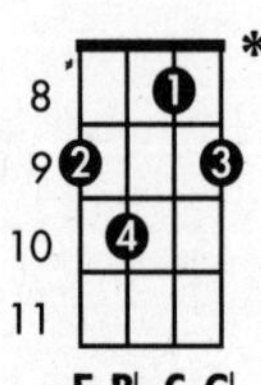

A♭9(♭5) — A♭ Ninth Flat Fifth

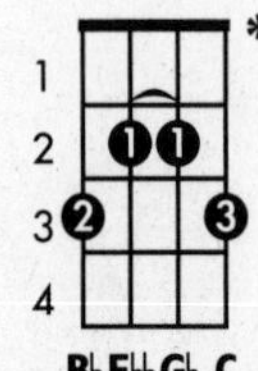
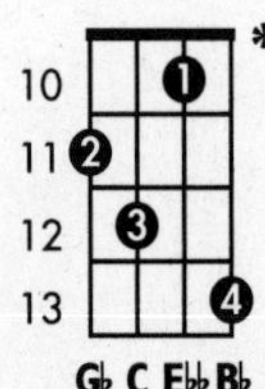

A♭ Ninth Sharp Eleventh — A♭9(#11)

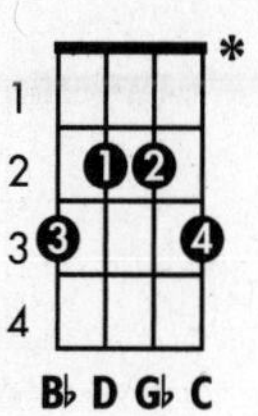

*
10
11
12
13
G♭ C D B♭

A♭ Thirteenth Flat Ninth — A♭13(♭9)

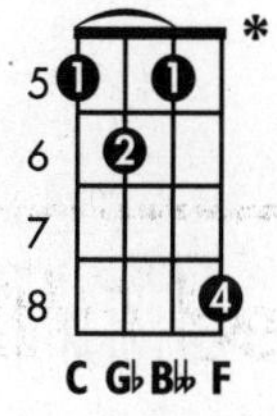

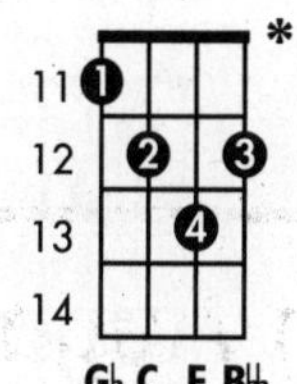

A♭ Thirteenth Flat Ninth Flat Fifth — A♭13(♭9 ♭5)

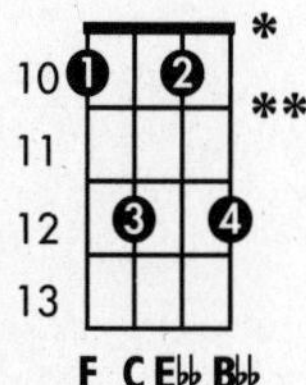

A — A Major

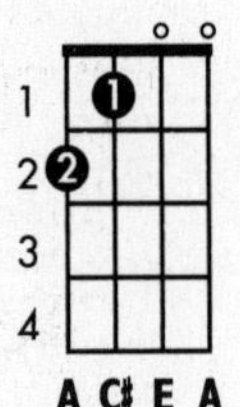

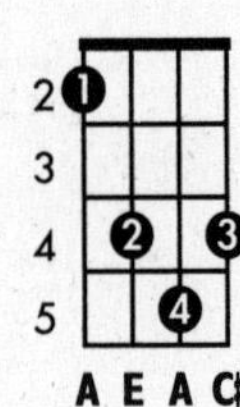

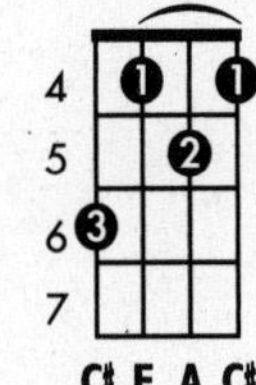

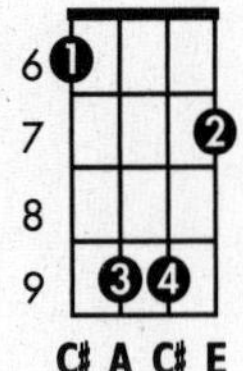

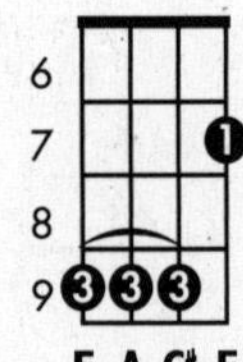

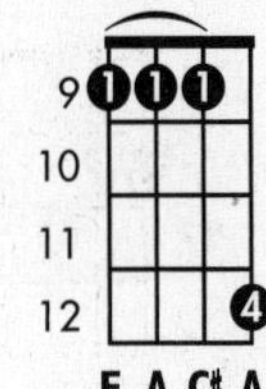

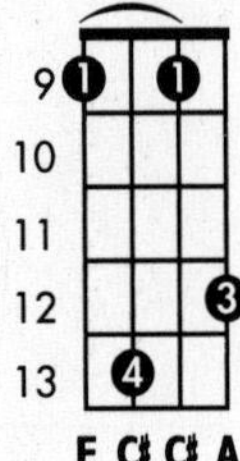

Am — A Minor

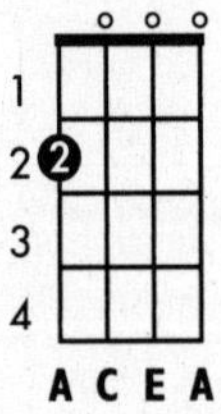

A C E A

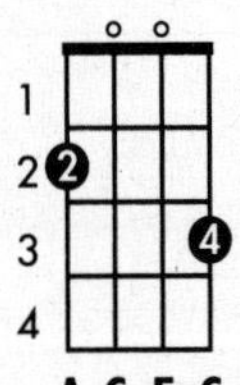

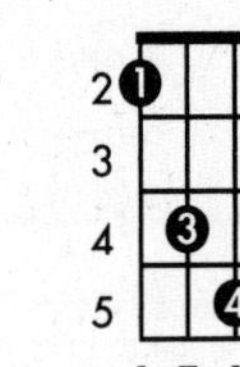

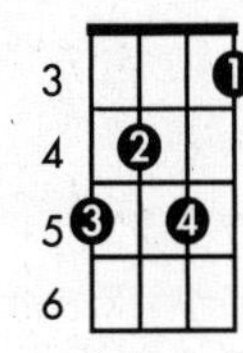

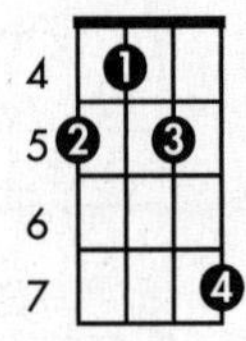

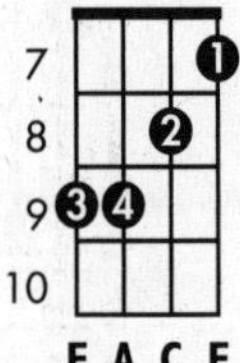

A° — A Diminished

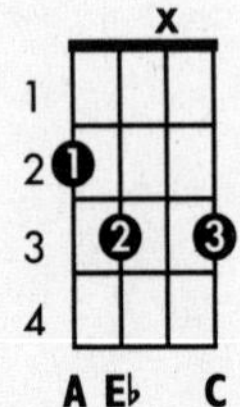

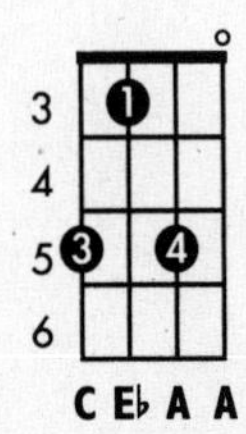

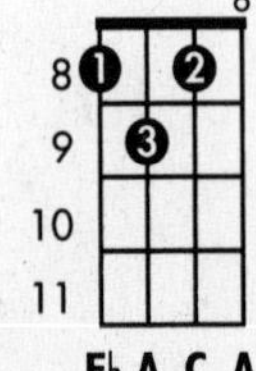

A Augmented

A+

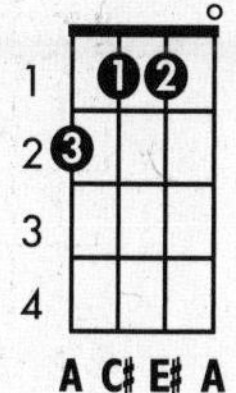

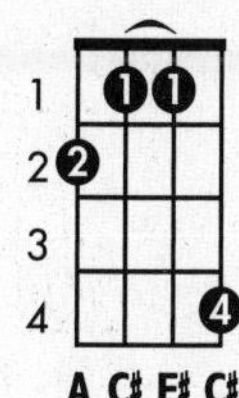

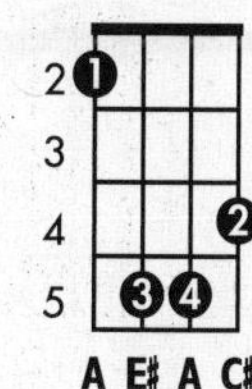

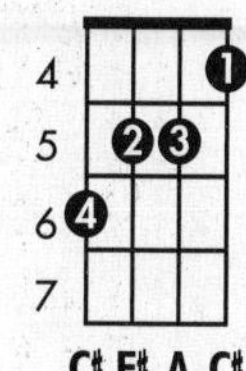

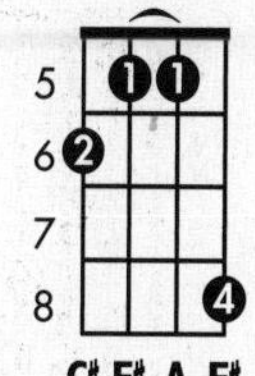

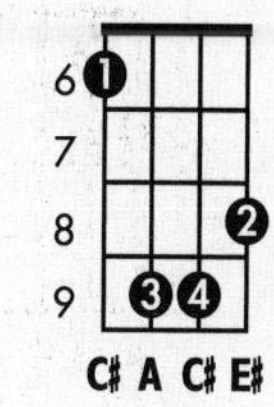

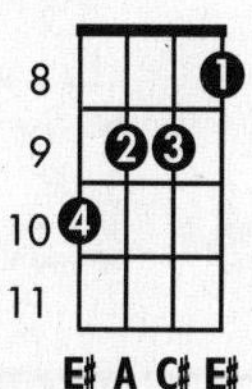

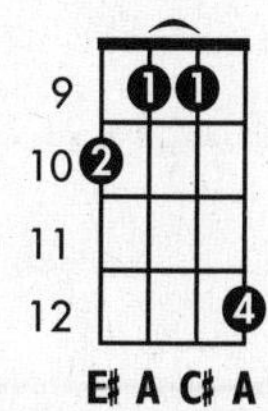

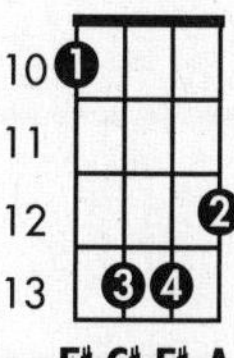

A Fifth

A5

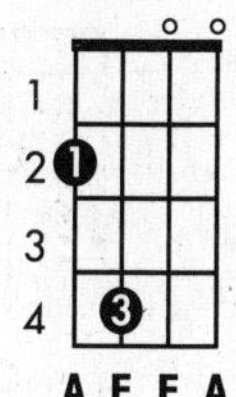

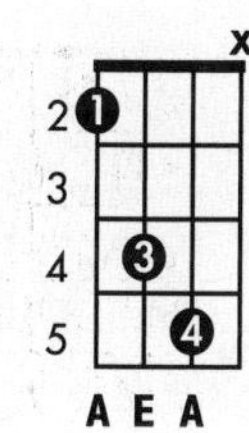

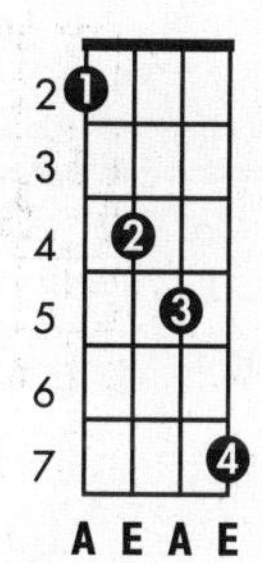

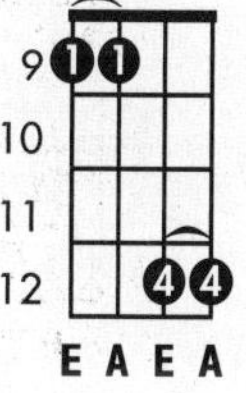

A Major Suspended Fourth

Asus

Sometimes written **Asus4**

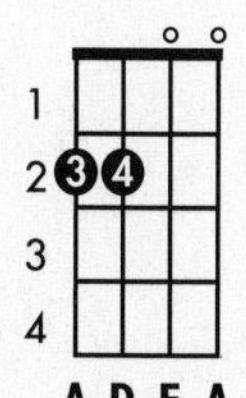

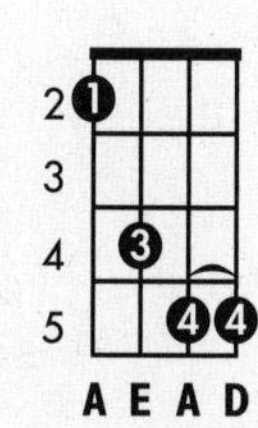

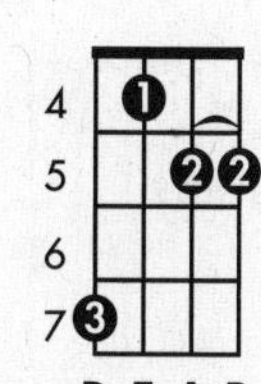

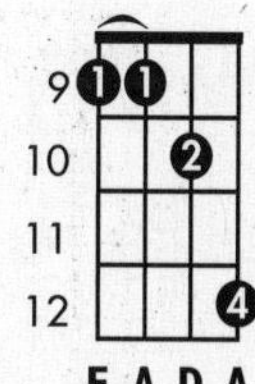

A6 — A Major 6th

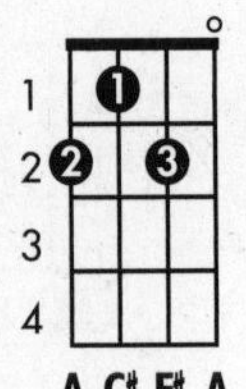

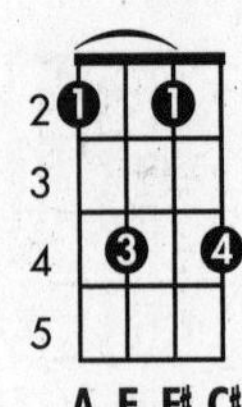

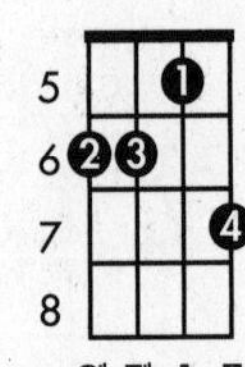

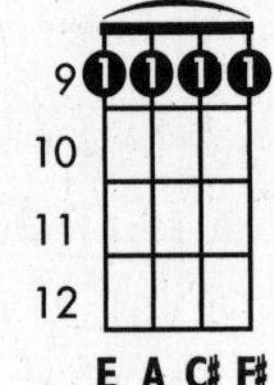

Am6 — A Minor Sixth

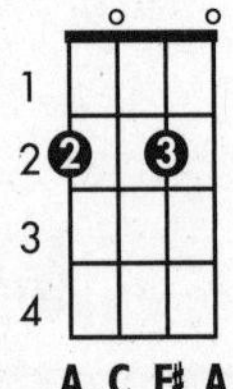

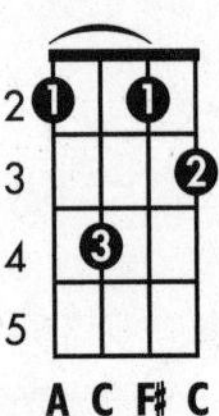

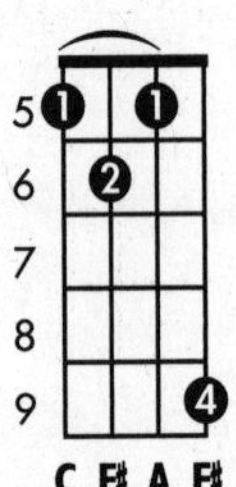

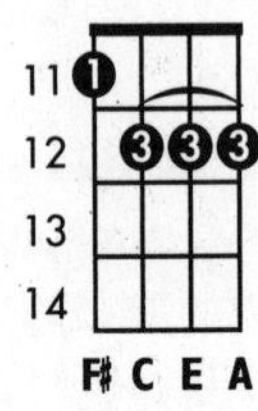

Amaj7 — A Major Seventh

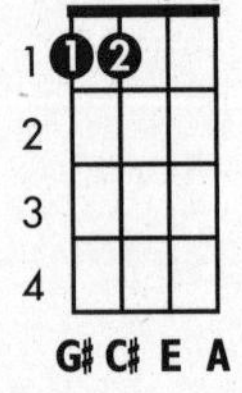

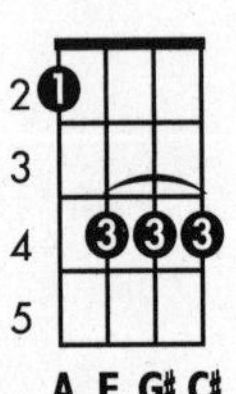

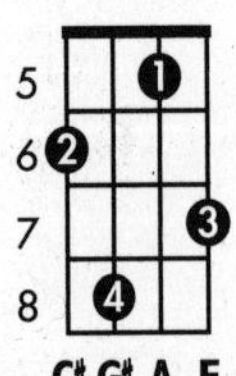

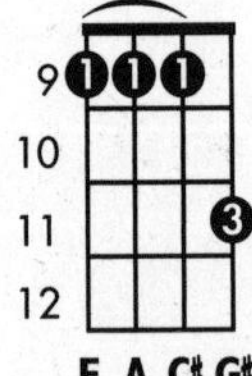

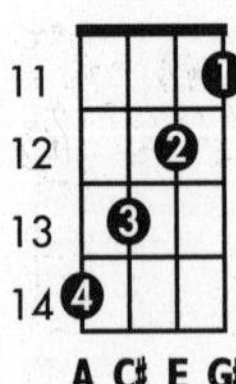

A7 — A Seventh

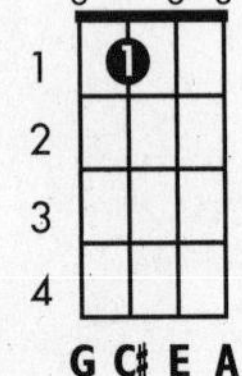

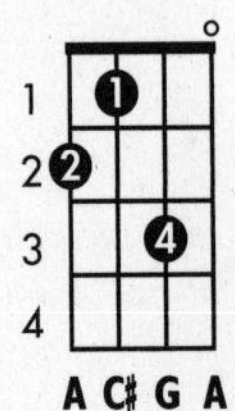

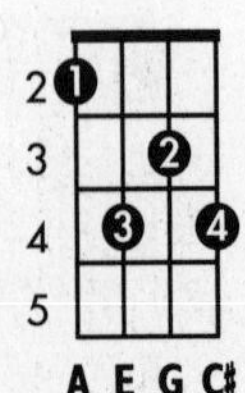

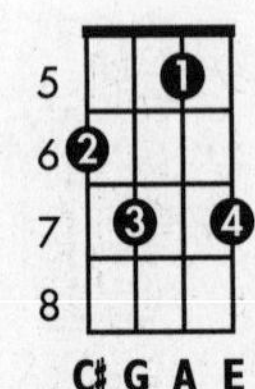

A Minor Seventh

Am7

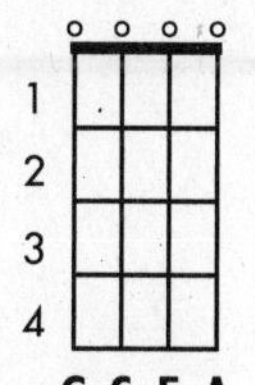
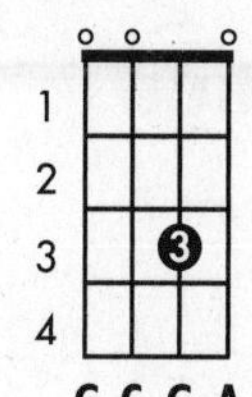
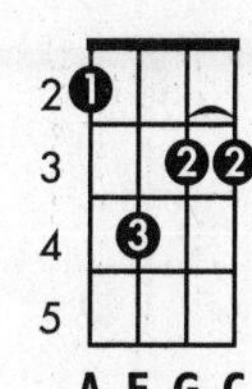
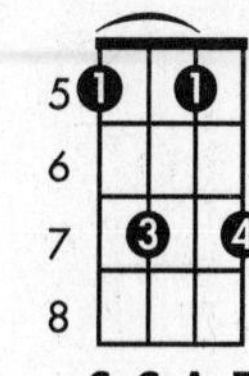
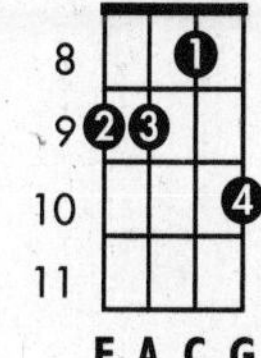

A Minor Seventh Flat Fifth

Am7(♭5)

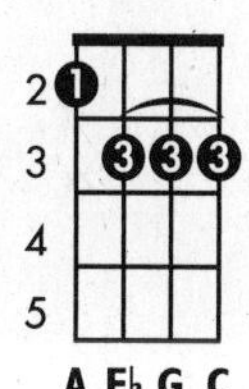
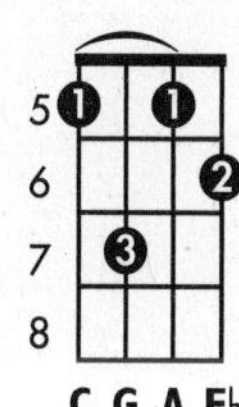
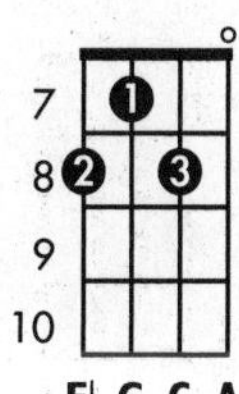

8 9 10 11

E♭ A C G

A Diminished Seventh

A°7

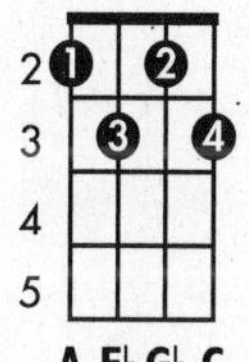
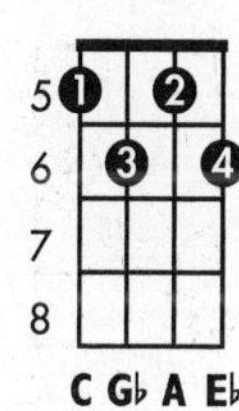

8 9 10 11

E♭ A C G♭

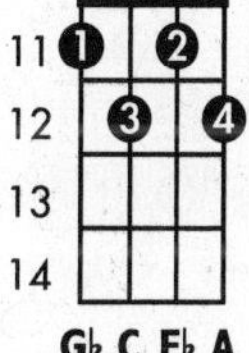

A Seventh Suspended Fourth

A7sus

Sometimes written **A7sus4**

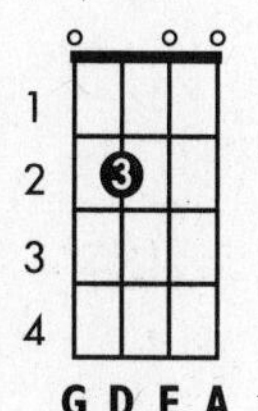
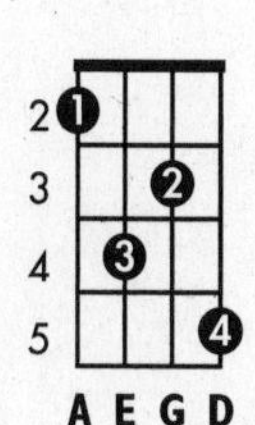
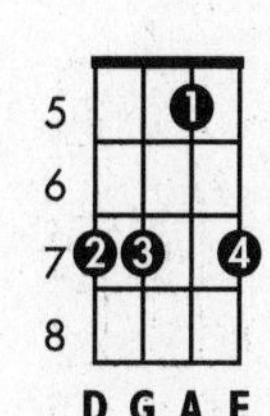
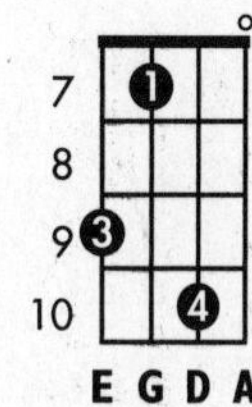

A(add9) — A Major Add Ninth

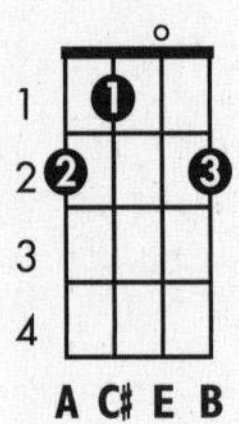

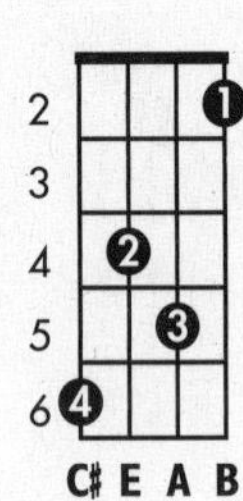

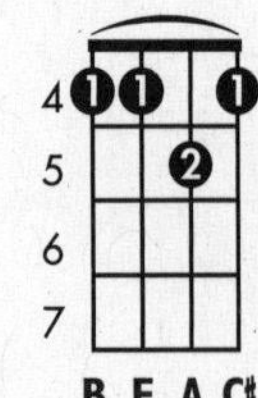

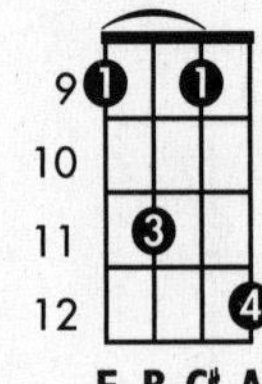

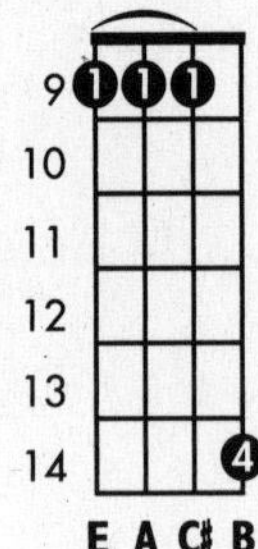

Amaj9 — A Major Ninth

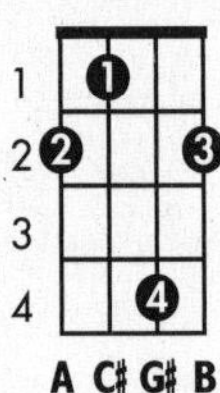

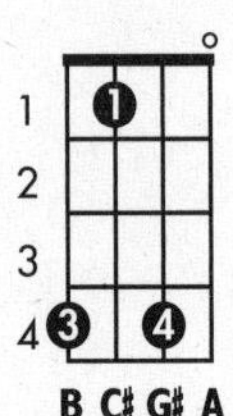

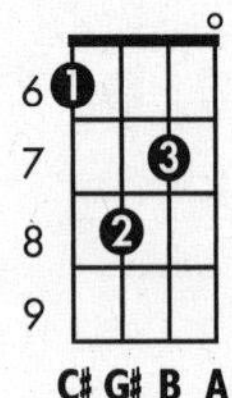

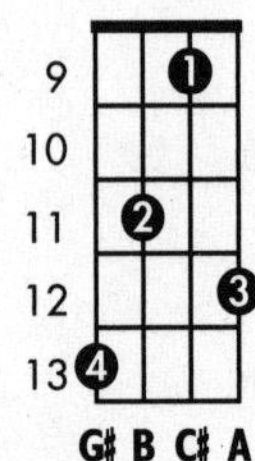

A9 — A Ninth

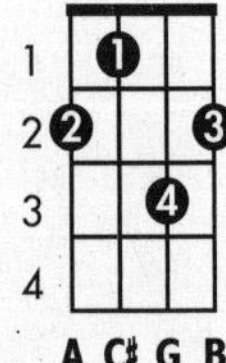

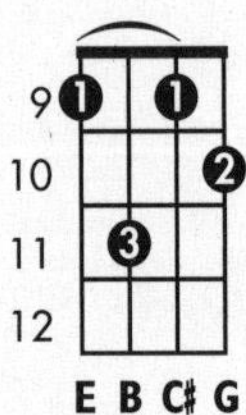

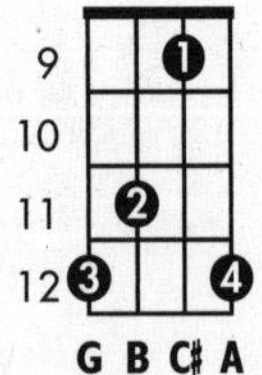

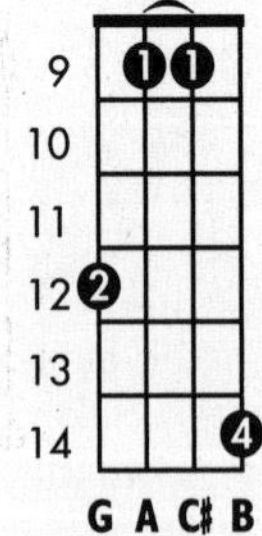

Am9 — A Minor Ninth

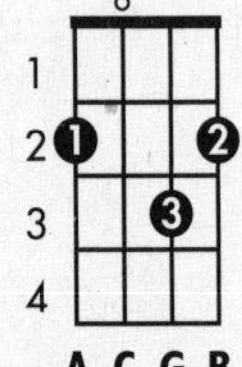

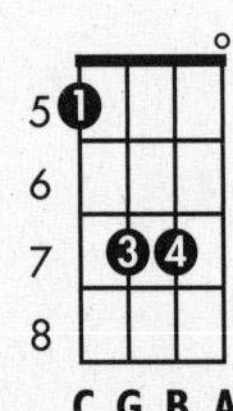

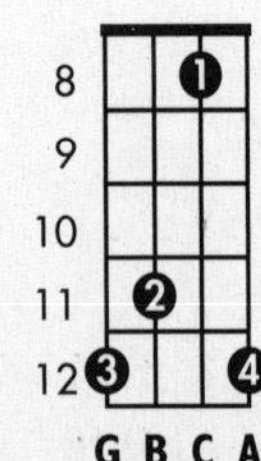

A Sixth Add Ninth

A6/9

Sometimes written $\mathbf{A^{9/6}}$

A Minor Sixth Add Ninth

Am6/9

Sometimes written $\mathbf{Am^{9/6}}$

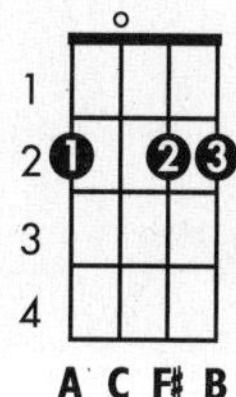

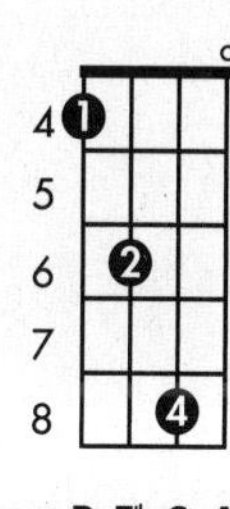

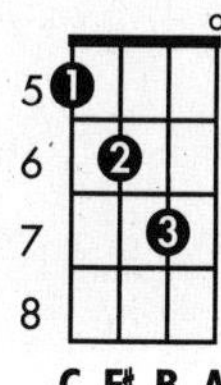

A Minor Major Seventh

Am(maj7)

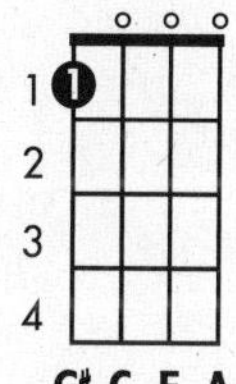

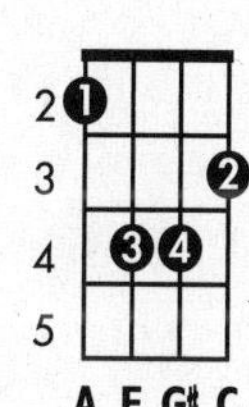

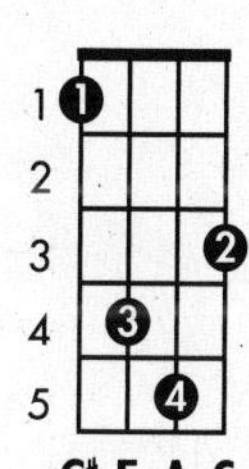

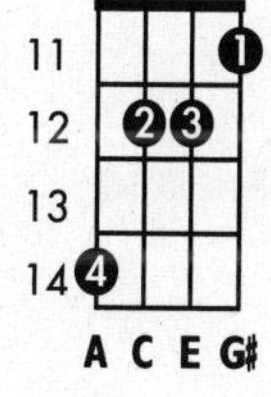

A Minor Ninth Major Seventh

Am9(maj7)

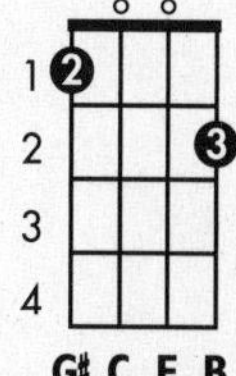

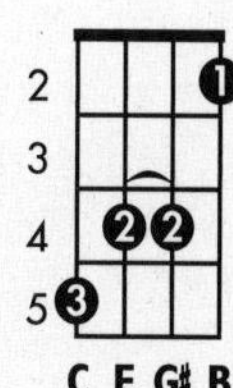

A11 — A Eleventh

1 2 3 4

A D G B

Am11 — A Minor Eleventh

1 2 3 4

A D G C

5 6 7 8

C G A D

7 8 9 10

D G C A

A13 — A Thirteenth

1 2 3 4

G C♯ F♯ A

3 4 5 6

C♯ F♯ G A

9 10 11 12

G A C♯ F♯

A(♭5) — A Flat Fifth

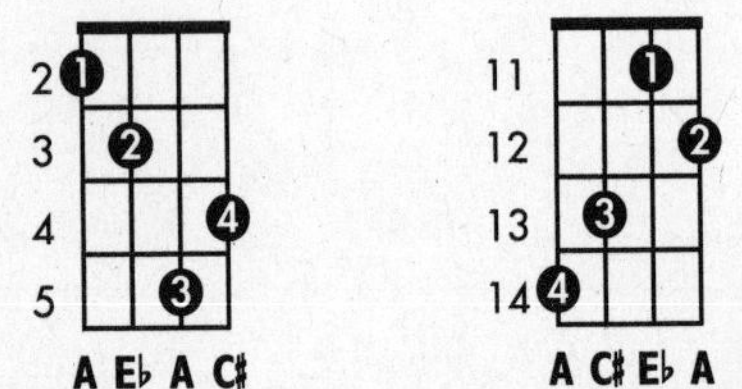

11 12 13 14

A C♯ E♭ A

A Seventh Flat Fifth

A7(♭5)

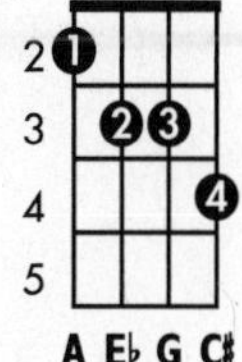

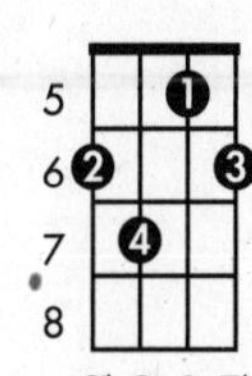

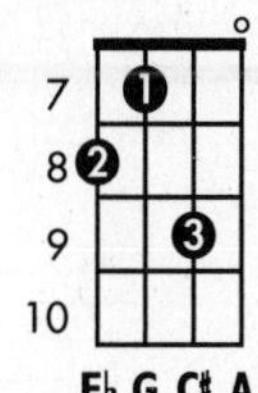

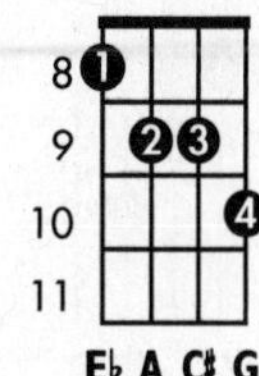

A

A Seventh Augmented Fifth

A7+

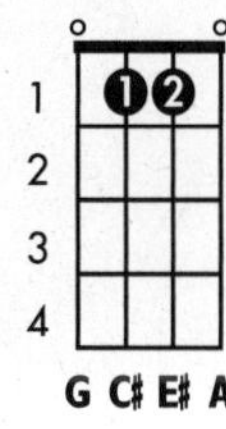

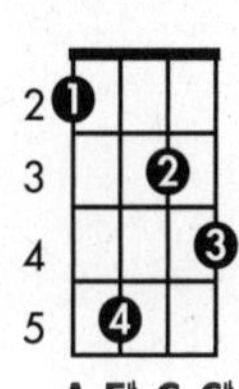

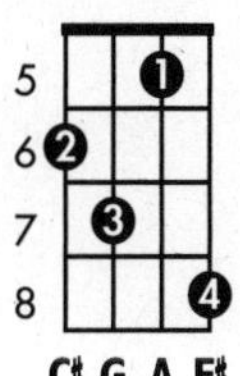

A Major Seventh Flat Fifth

Amaj7(♭5)

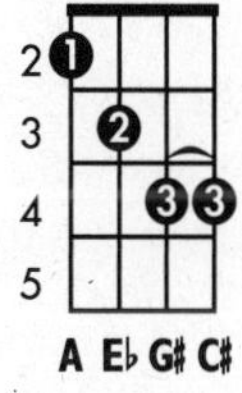

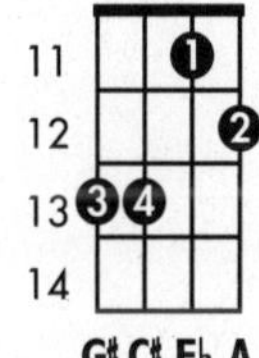

A Seventh Flat Ninth

A7(♭9)

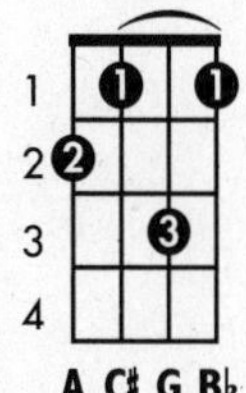

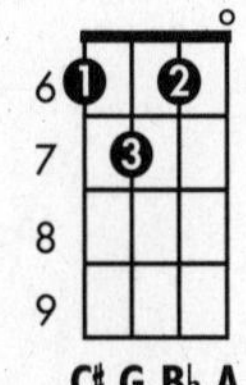

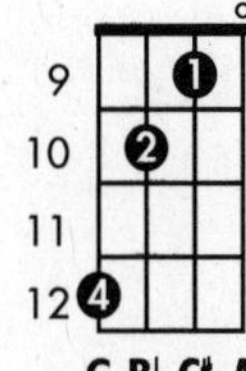

A7(♯9) — A Seventh Sharp Ninth

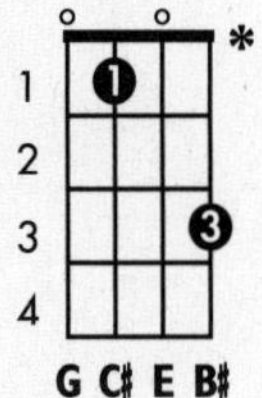

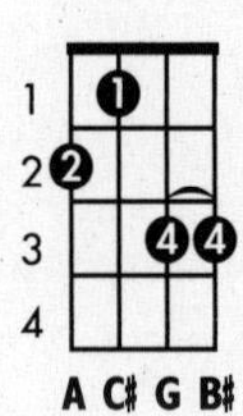

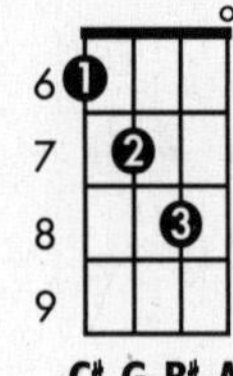

A7+(♭9) — A Seventh Flat Ninth Augmented Fifth

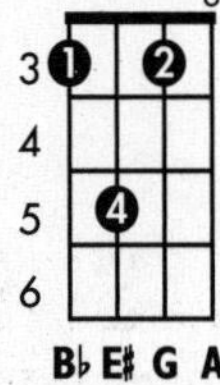

A9+ — A Ninth Augmented Fifth

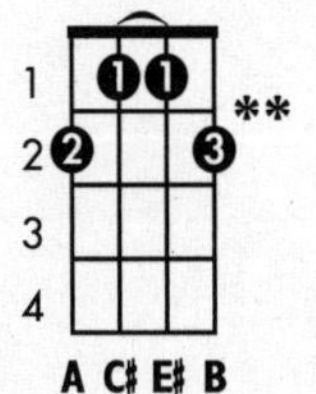

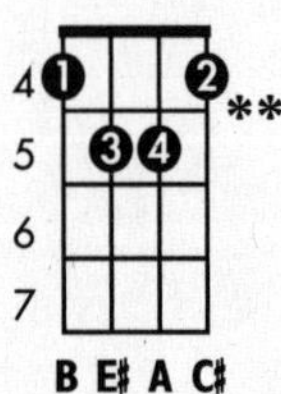

A9(♭5) — A Ninth Flat Fifth

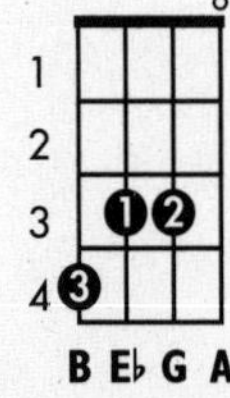

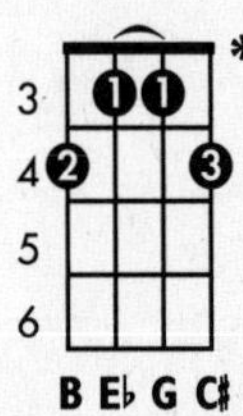

A Ninth Sharp Eleventh

A9(♯11)

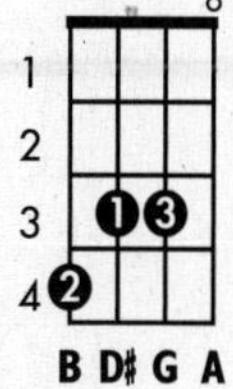

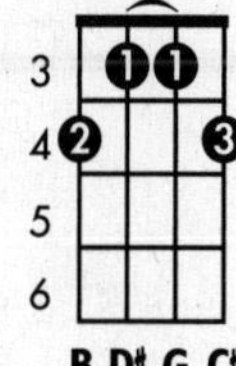

A Thirteenth Flat Ninth

A13(♭9)

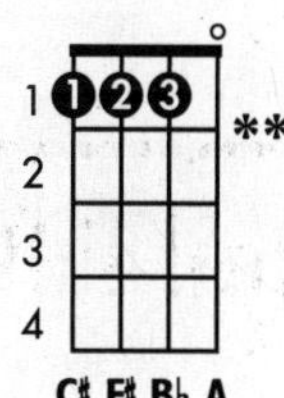

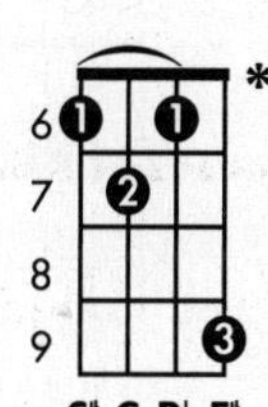

A Thirteenth Flat Ninth Flat Fifth

A13(♭9 ♭5)

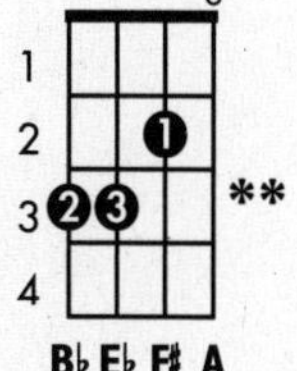

Bb

B♭

B♭ Major

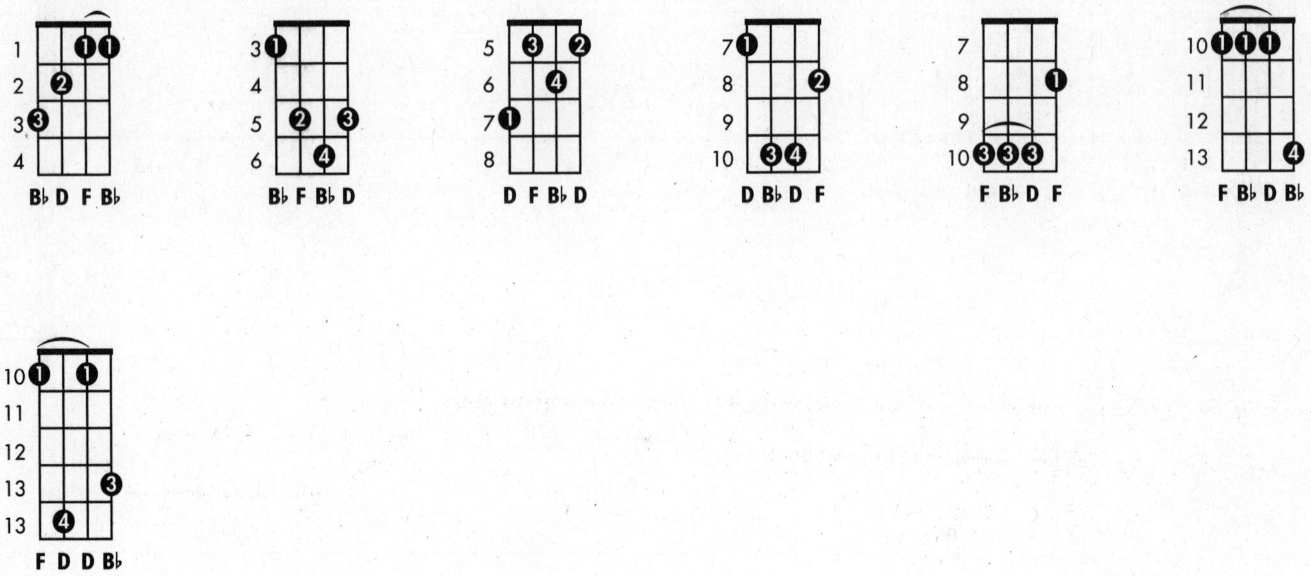

B♭ D F B♭
B♭ F B♭ D
D F B♭ D
D B♭ D F
F B♭ D F
F B♭ D B♭
F D D B♭

B♭m

B♭ Minor

B♭ D♭ F B♭
B♭ D♭ F D♭
B♭ F B♭ D♭
D♭ F B♭ D♭
D♭ F B♭ F
F B♭ D♭ F
F D♭ F B♭

B♭°

B♭ Diminished

B♭ D♭ F♭ B♭
B♭ F♭ F♭ D♭
D♭ F♭ B♭ F♭

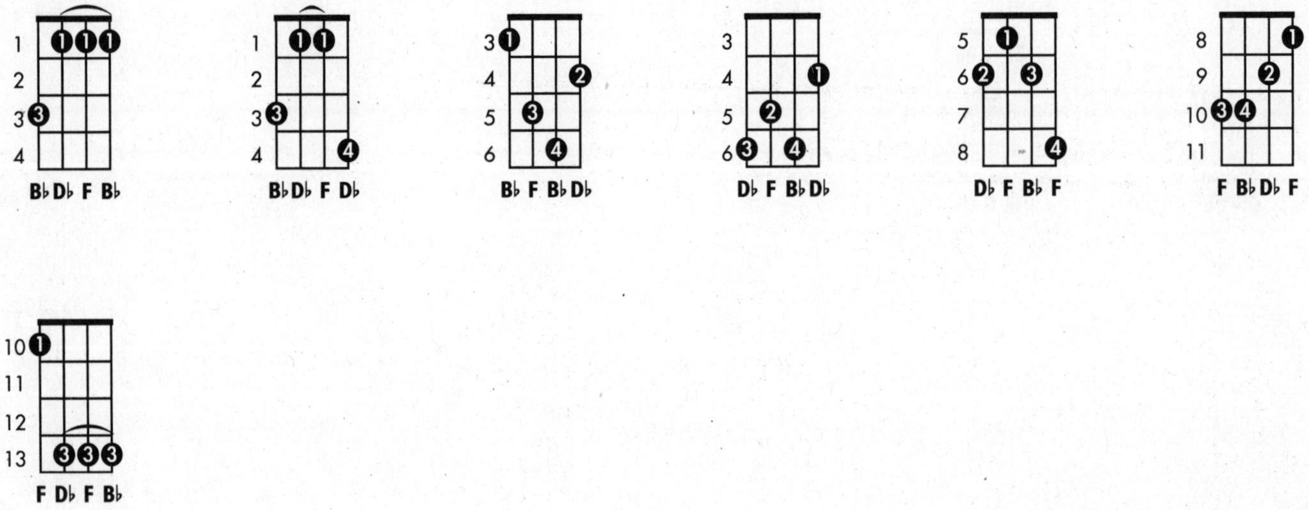

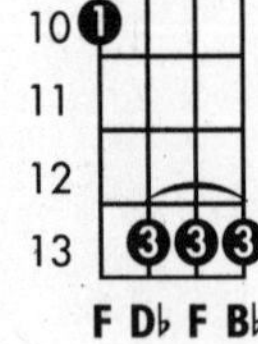

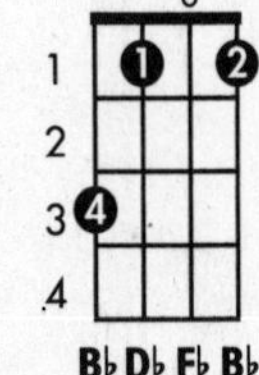

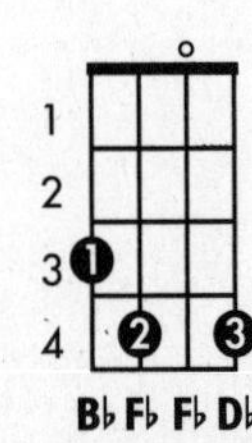

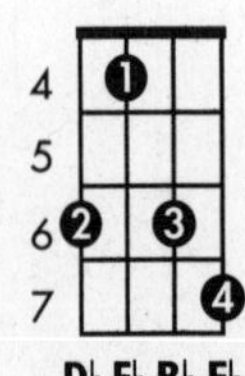

B♭ Augmented

B♭+

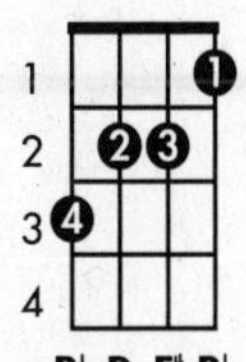
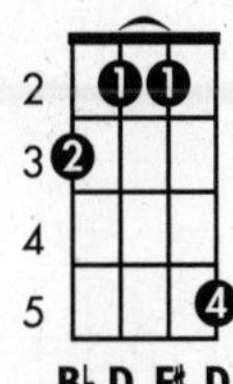
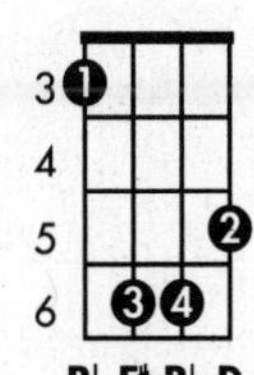
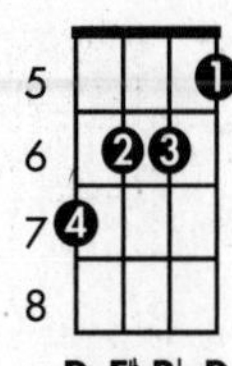
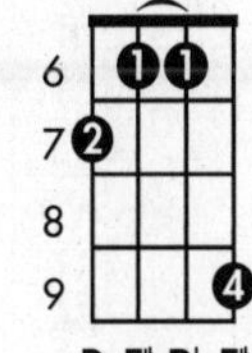
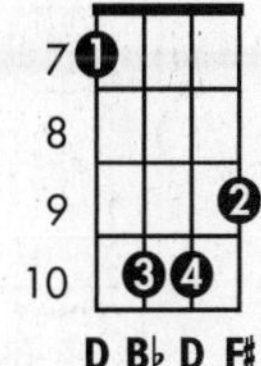
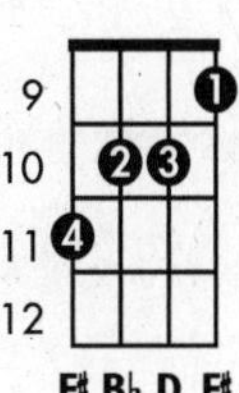
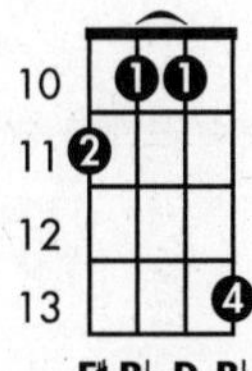

B♭ Fifth

B♭5

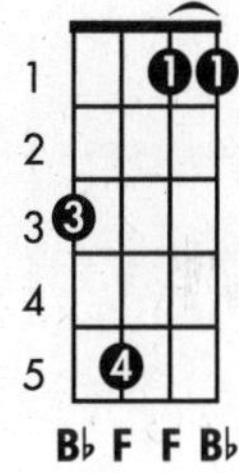
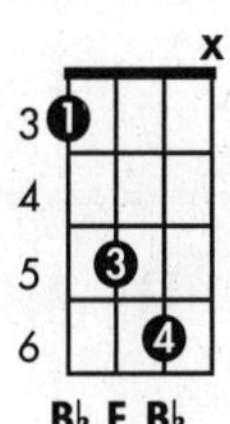
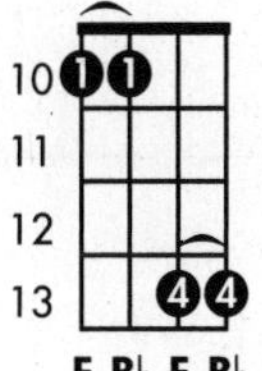

B♭ Major Suspended Fourth

B♭sus4

Sometimes written **B♭sus4**

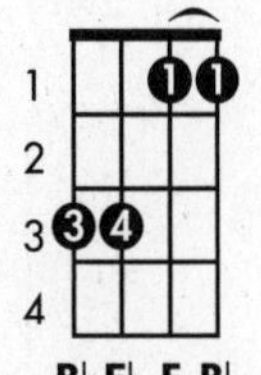
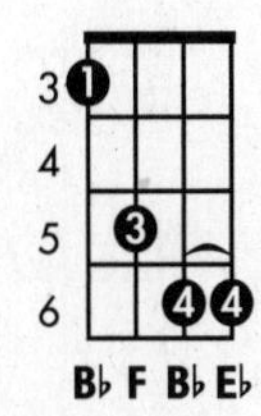
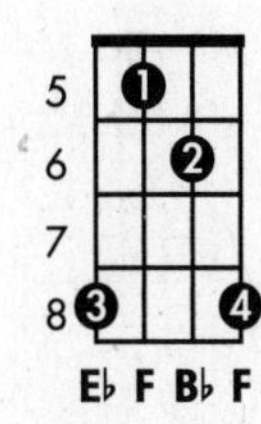
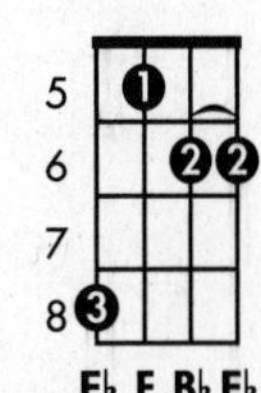
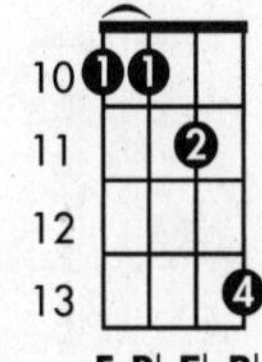

B♭6 — B♭ Major 6th

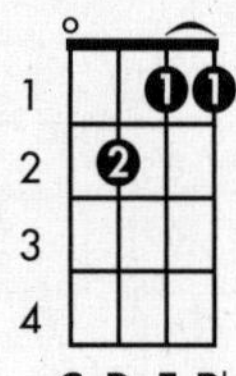

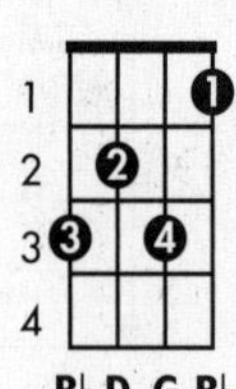

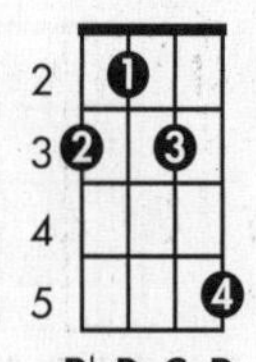

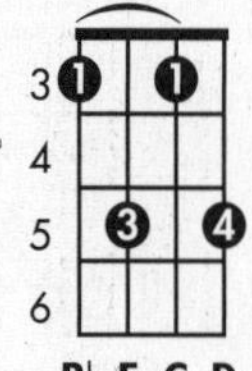

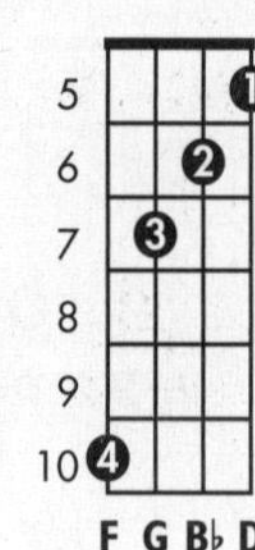

B♭m6 — B♭ Minor Sixth

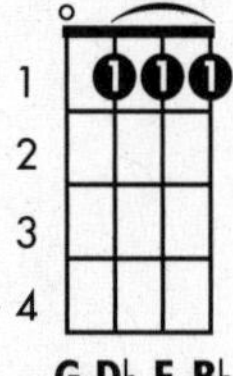

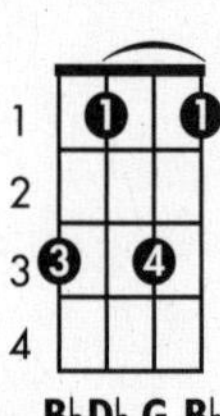

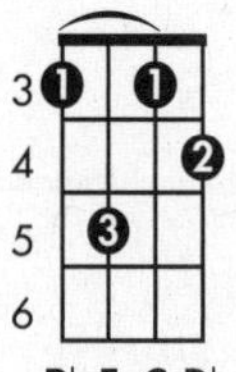

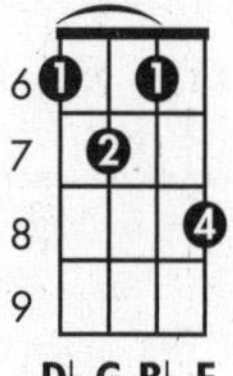

B♭maj7 — B♭ Major Seventh

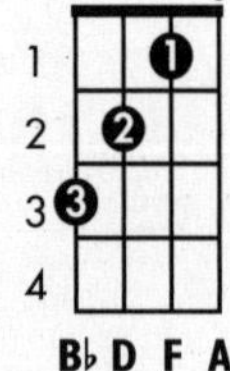

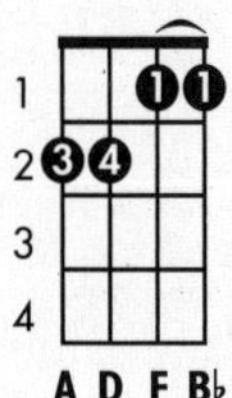

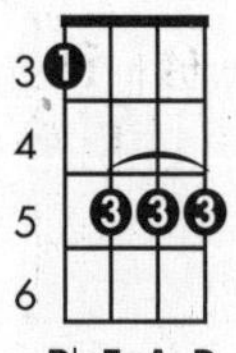

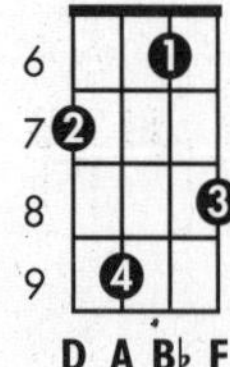

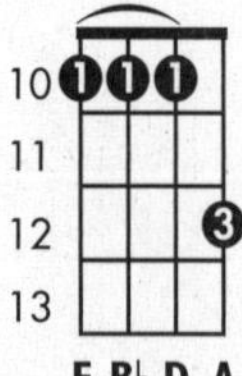

B♭7 — B♭ Seventh

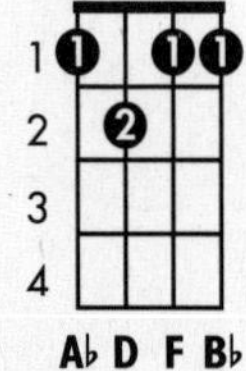

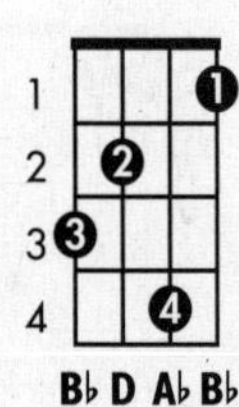

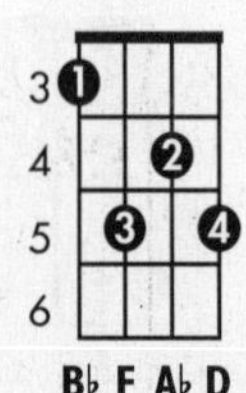

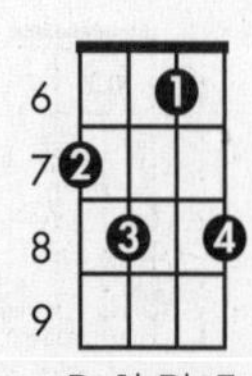

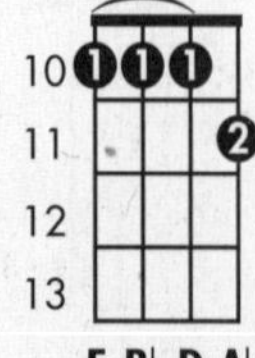

B♭ Minor Seventh

B♭m7

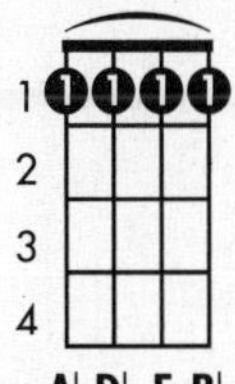

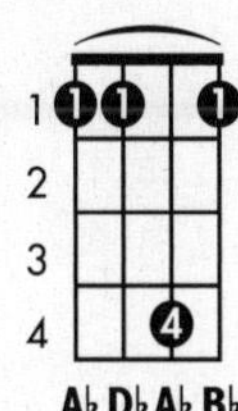

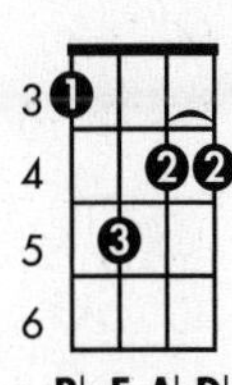

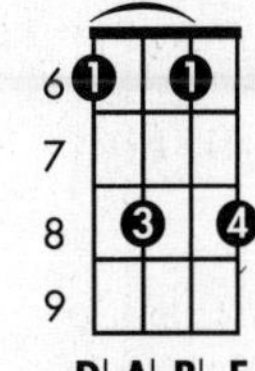

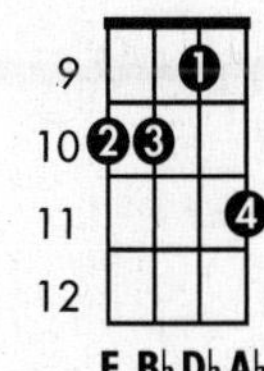

B♭ Minor Seventh Flat Fifth

B♭m7(♭5)

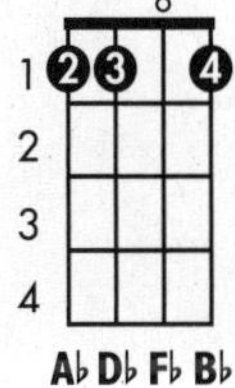

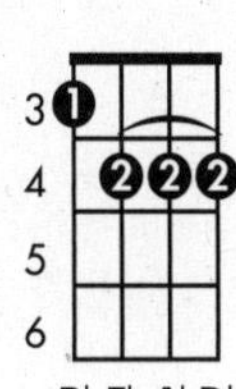

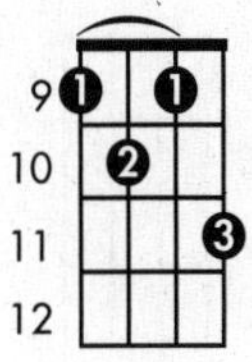

B♭ Diminished Seventh

B♭°7

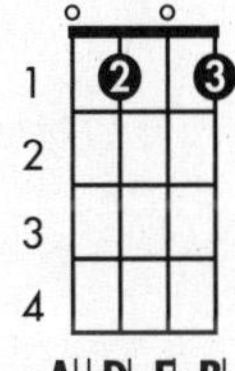

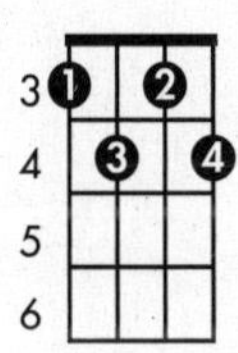

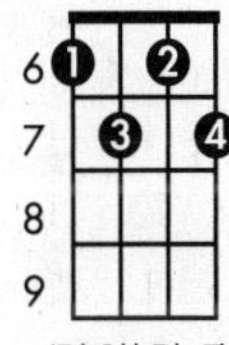

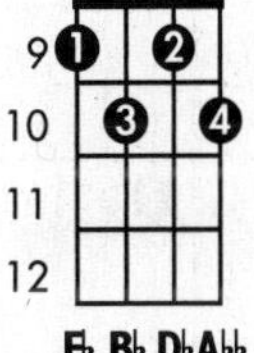

B♭ Seventh Suspended Fourth

B♭7sus

Sometimes written **B♭7sus4**

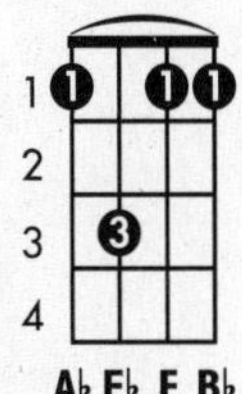

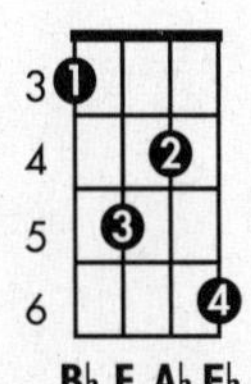

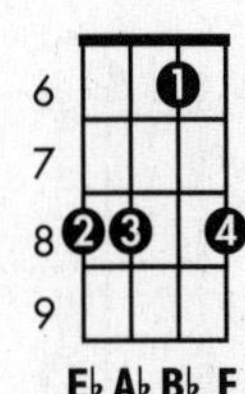

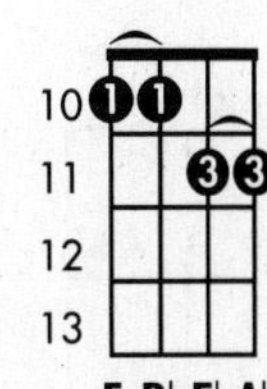

B♭(add9) — B♭ Major Add Ninth

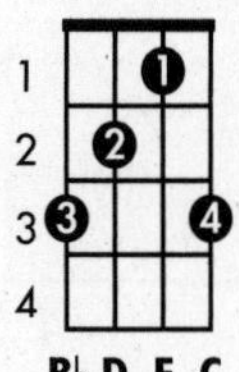

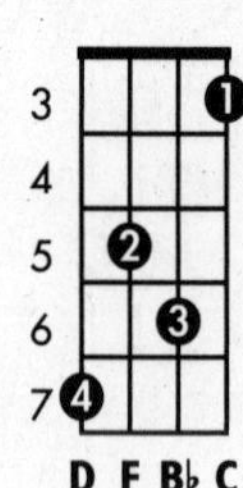

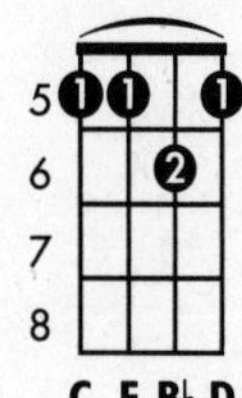

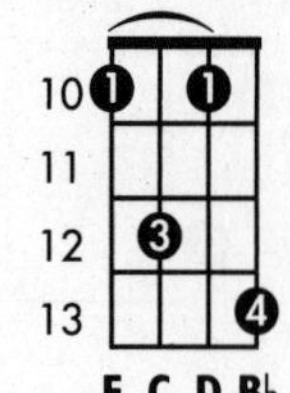

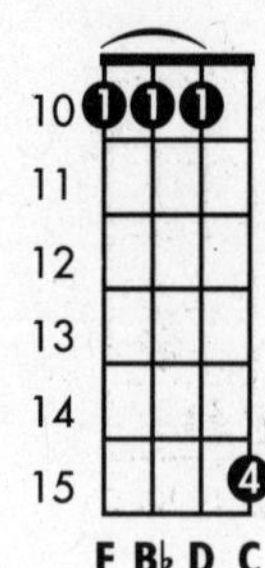

B♭maj9 — B♭ Major Ninth

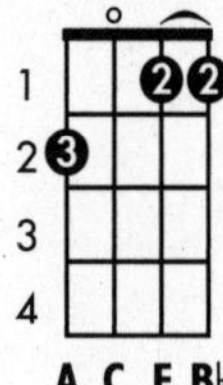

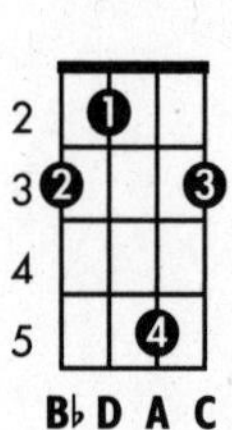

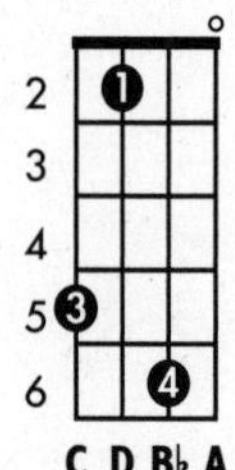

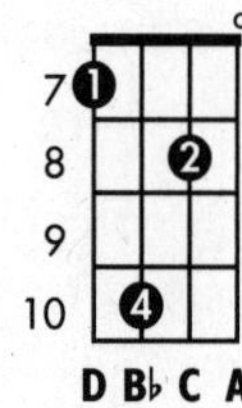

B♭9 — B♭ Ninth

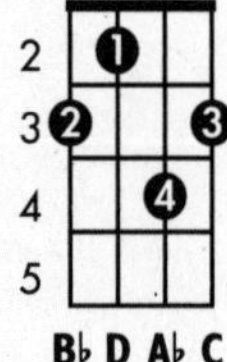

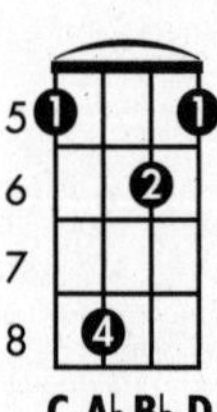

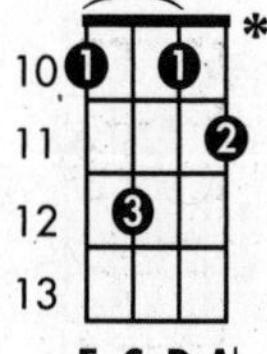

10
11
12
13
A♭ C D B♭

B♭m9 — B♭ Minor Ninth

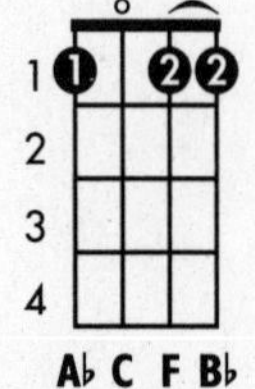

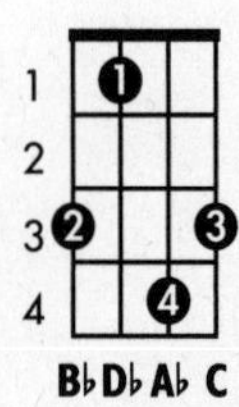

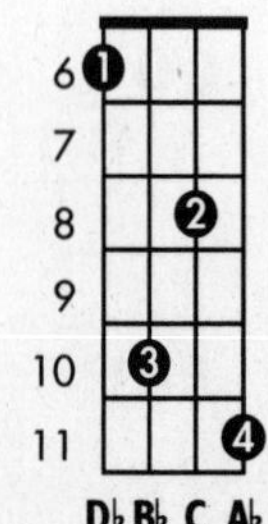

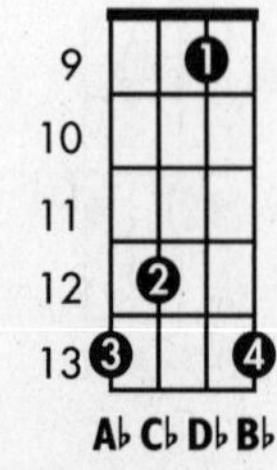

B♭ Sixth Add Ninth

B♭6/9

Sometimes written B♭9/6

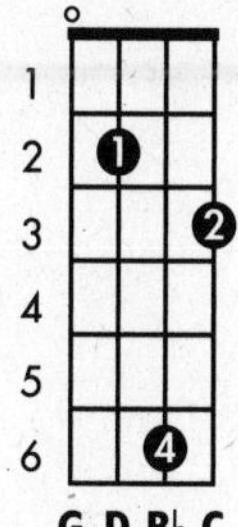

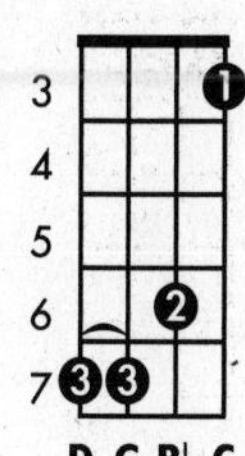

B♭ Minor Sixth Add Ninth

B♭m6/9

Sometimes written B♭m9/6

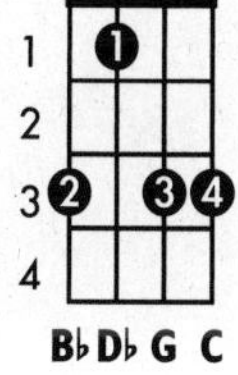

B♭ Minor Major Seventh

B♭m(maj7)

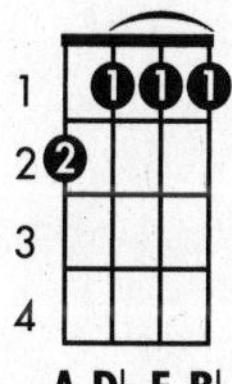

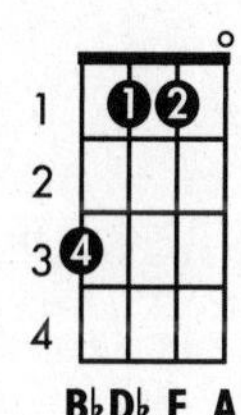

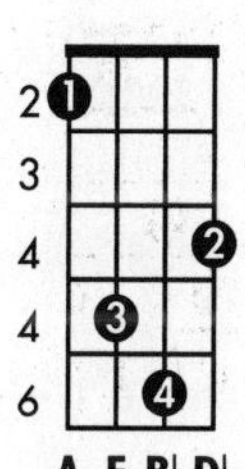

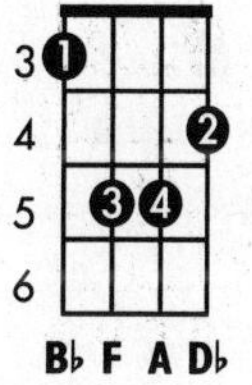

B♭ Minor Ninth Major Seventh

B♭m9(maj7)

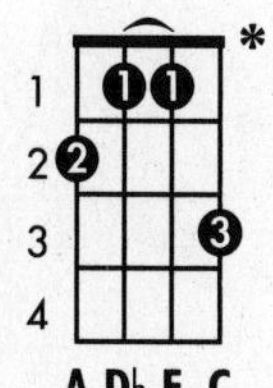

B♭11 — B♭ Eleventh

B♭ E♭ A♭ C

E♭ A♭ B♭ F

A♭ D E♭ B♭

B♭

B♭m11 — B♭ Minor Eleventh

B♭ E♭ A♭ D♭

D♭ A♭ B♭ E♭

E♭ B♭ D♭ A♭

B♭13 — B♭ Thirteenth

A♭ D G B♭

G D A♭ B♭

D A♭ C G *

A♭ B♭ D G

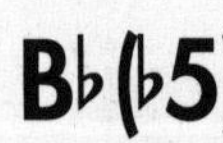

B♭(♭5) — B♭ Flat Fifth

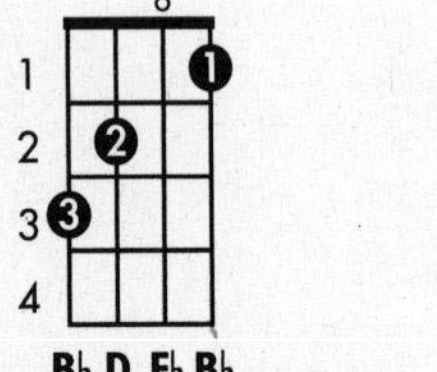

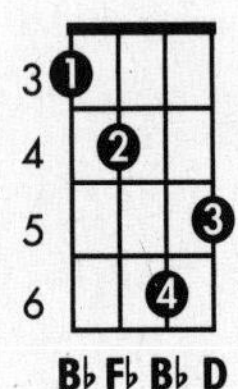

B♭ Seventh Flat Fifth

B♭7(♭5)

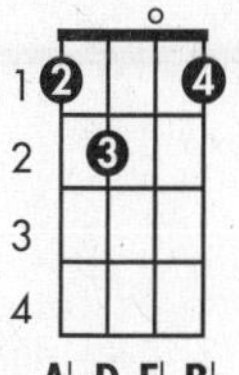

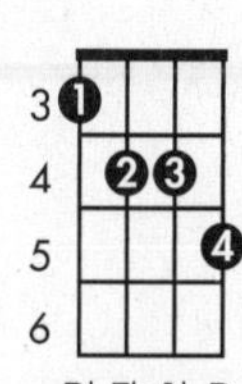

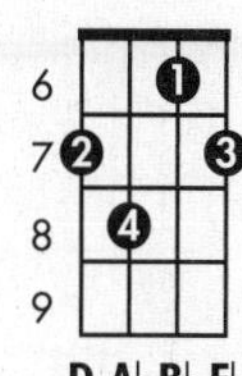

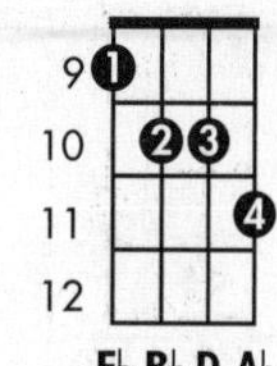

B♭ Seventh Augmented Fifth

B♭7+

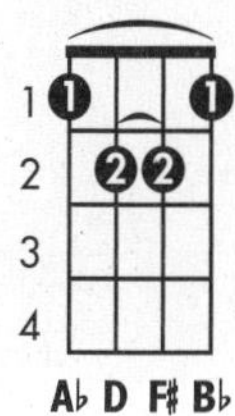

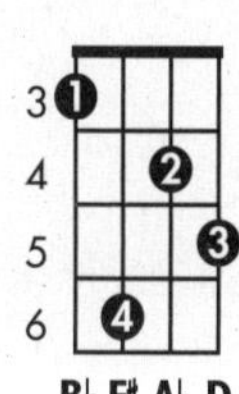

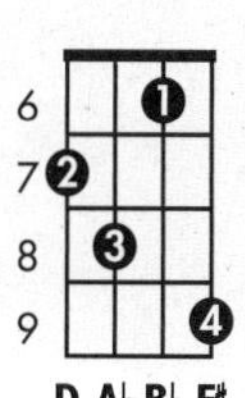

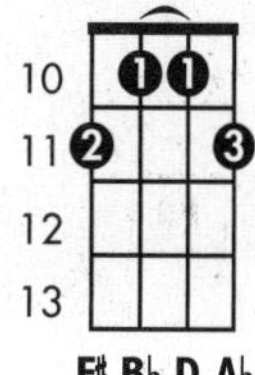

B♭ Major Seventh Flat Fifth

B♭maj7(♭5)

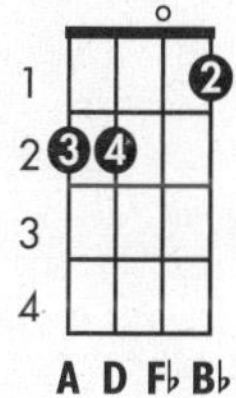

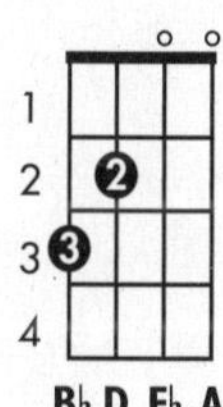

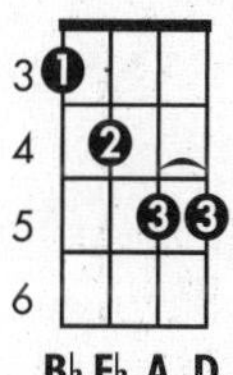

B♭ Seventh Flat Ninth

B♭7(♭9)

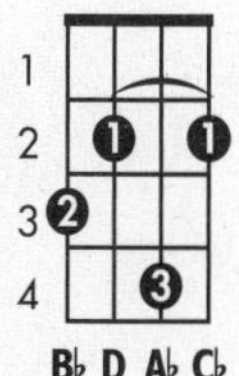

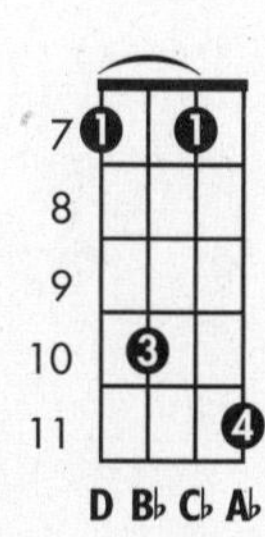

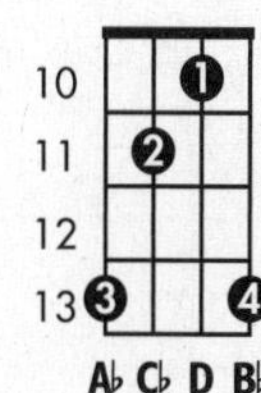

B♭7(♯9)

B♭ Seventh Sharp Ninth

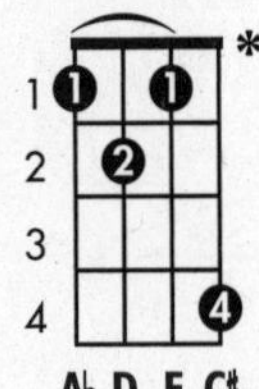

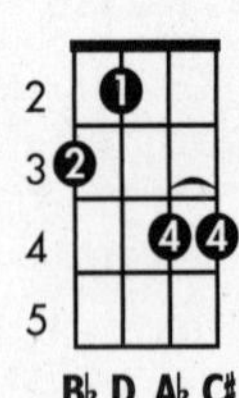

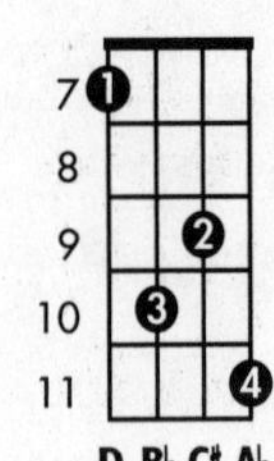

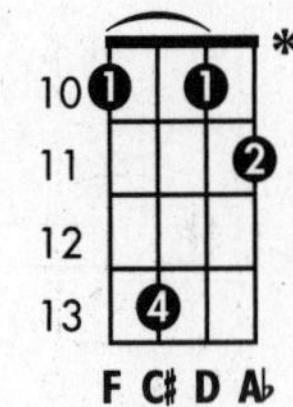

B♭

B♭7+(♭9)

B♭ Seventh Flat Ninth Augmented Fifth

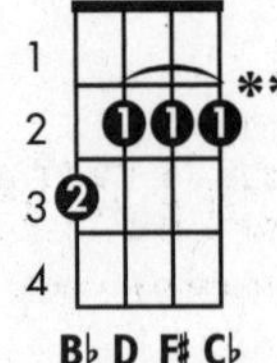

B♭9+

B♭ Ninth Augmented Fifth

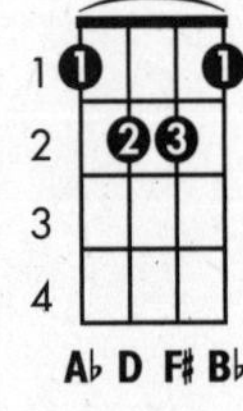

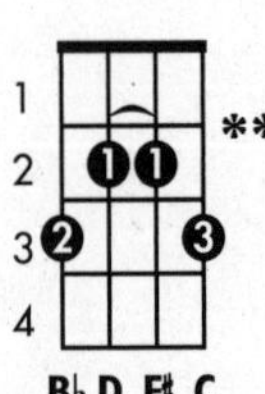

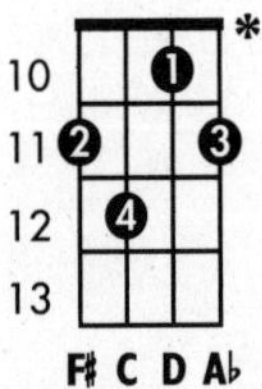

B♭9(♭5)

B♭ Ninth Flat Fifth

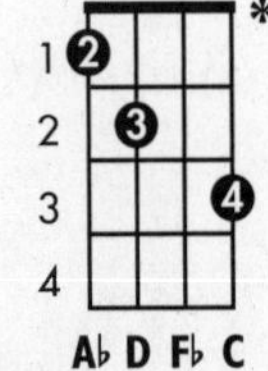

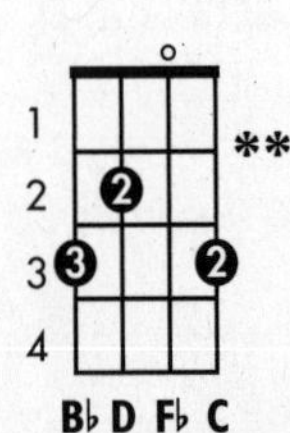

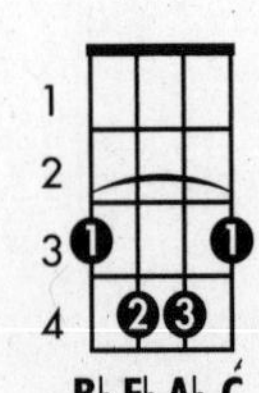

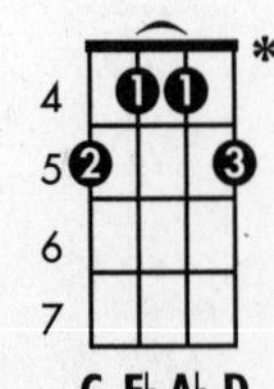

B♭ Ninth Sharp Eleventh

B♭9(♯11)

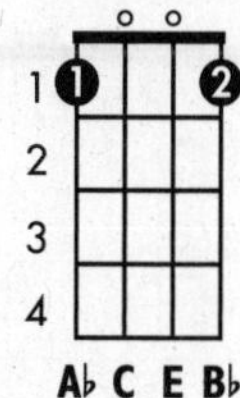

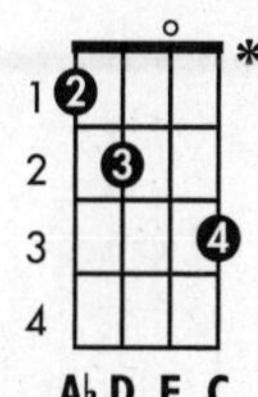

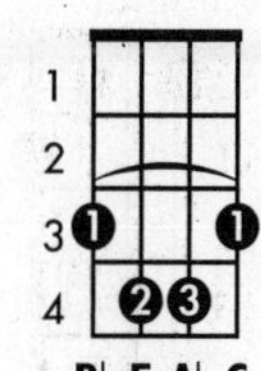

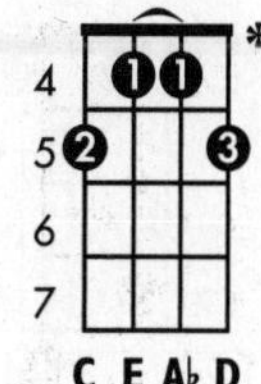

B♭ Thirteenth Flat Ninth

B♭13(♭9)

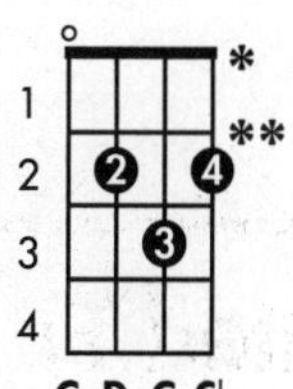

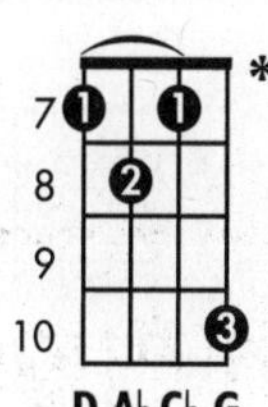

B♭ Thirteenth Flat Ninth Flat Fifth

B♭13(♭9 ♭5)

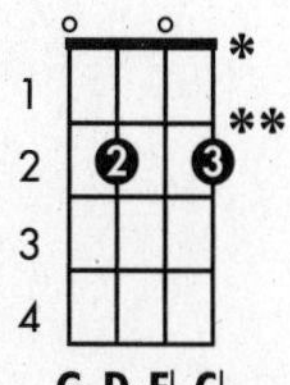

B — B Major

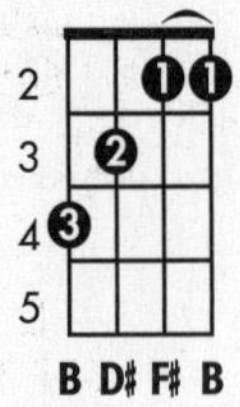

B D♯ F♯ B

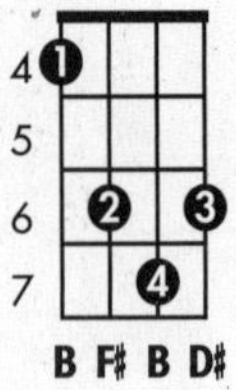

B F♯ B D♯

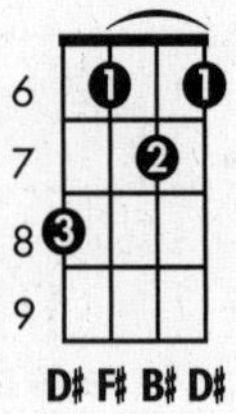

D♯ F♯ B♯ D♯

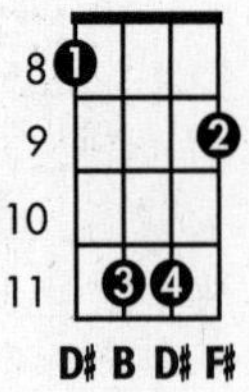

D♯ B D♯ F♯

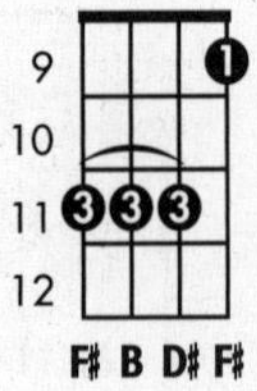

F♯ B D♯ F♯

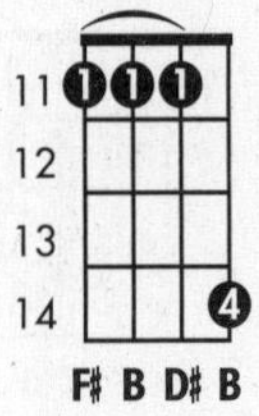

F♯ B D♯ B

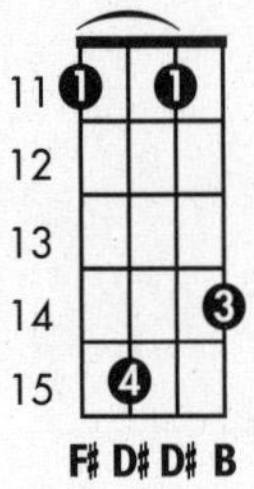

F♯ D♯ D♯ B

B

Bm — B Minor

F♯ D F♯ B

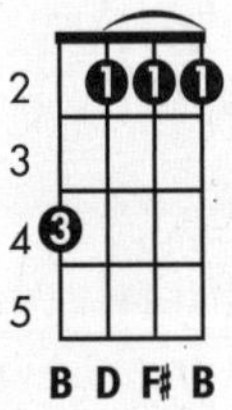

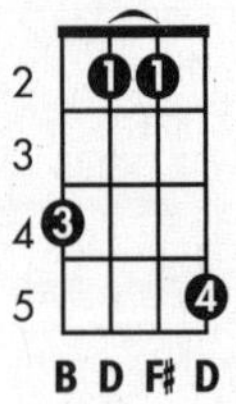

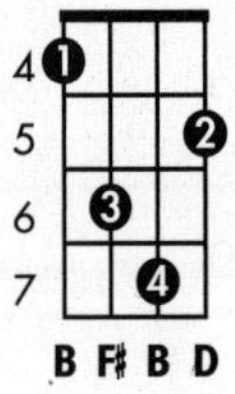

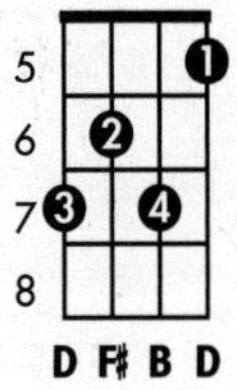

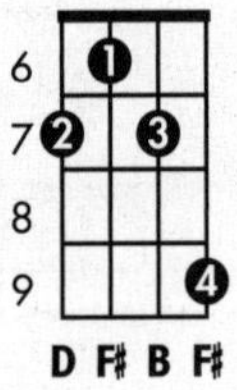

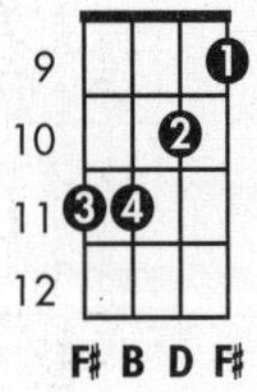

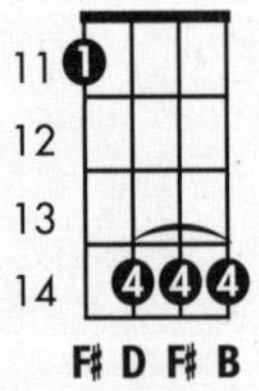

B° — B Diminished

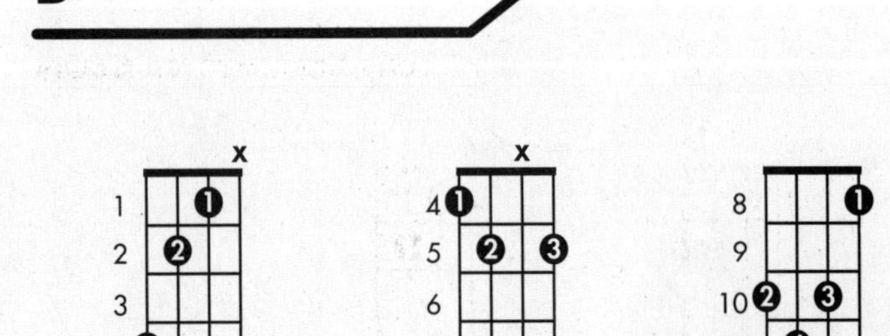

B Augmented

B+

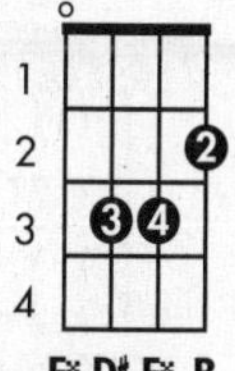

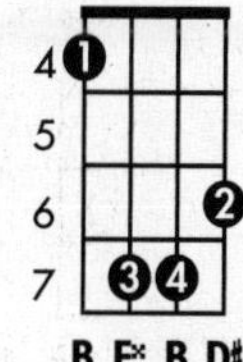
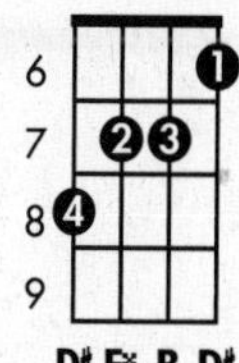
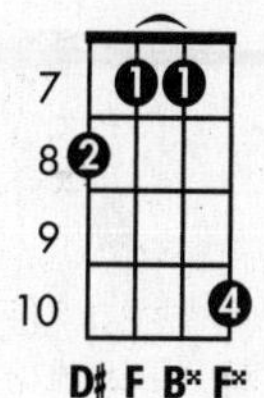
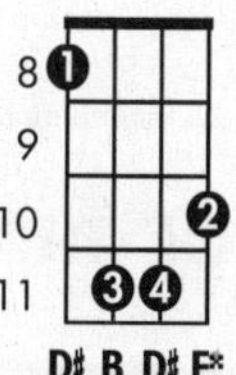
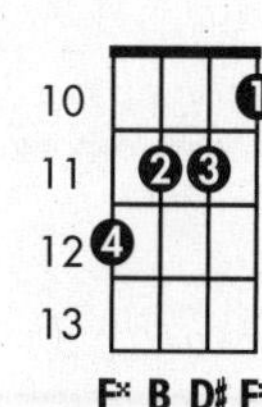
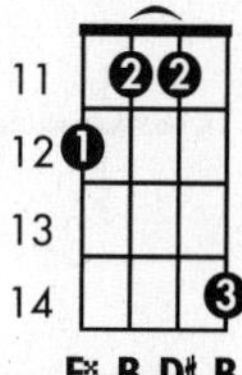

B Fifth

B5

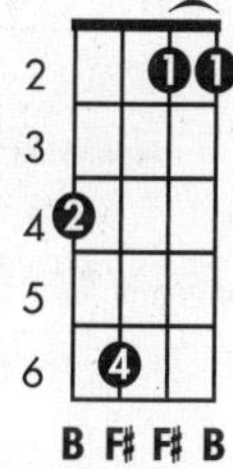
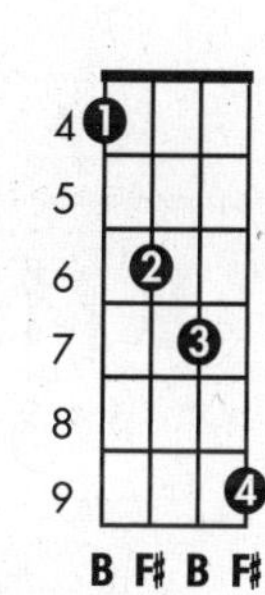
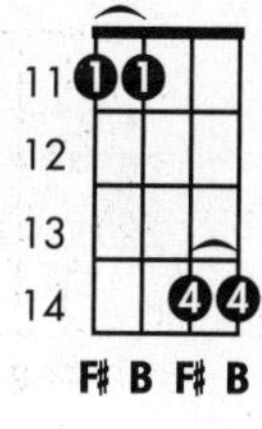

B Major Suspended Fourth

Bsus

Sometimes written **Bsus4**

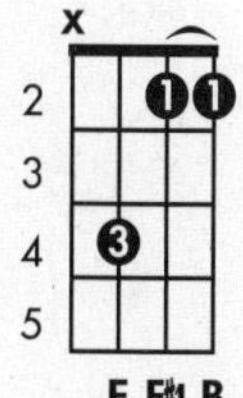
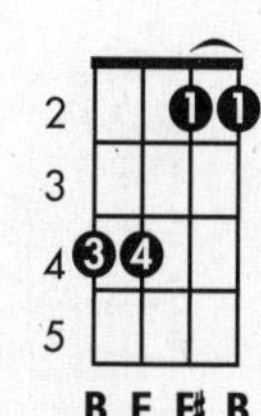
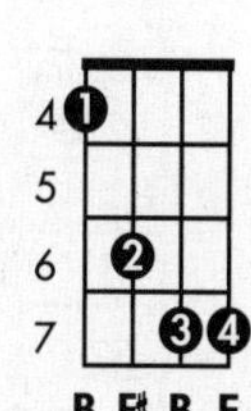

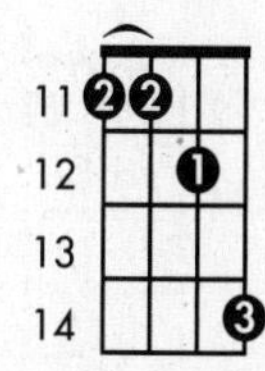

B6 — B Major 6th

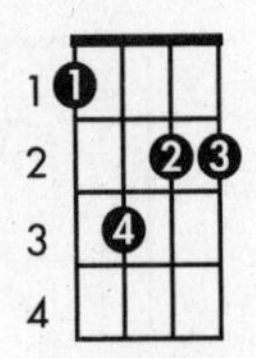

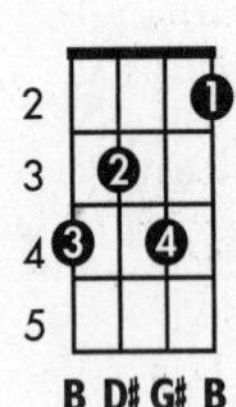

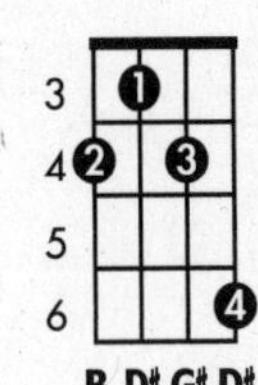

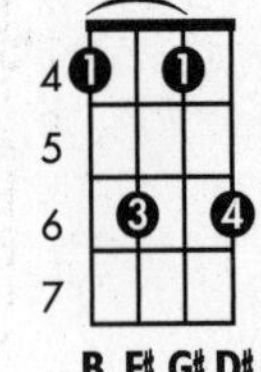

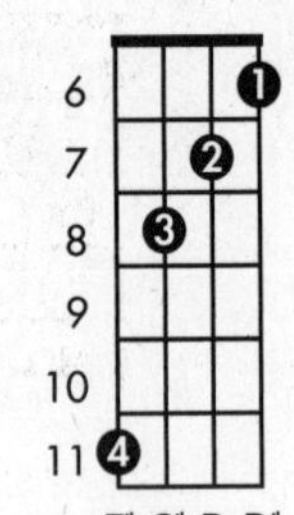

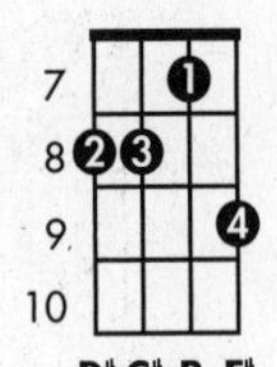

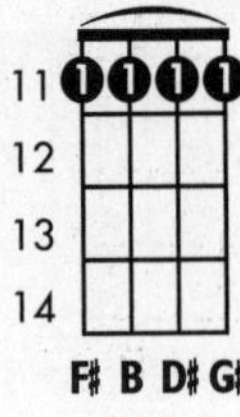

B

Bm6 — B Minor Sixth

G♯ D F♯ B

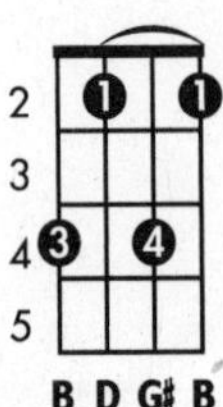

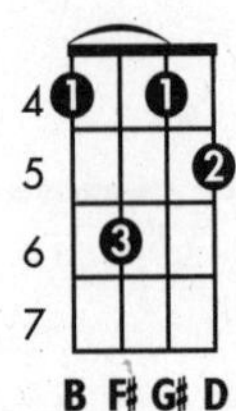

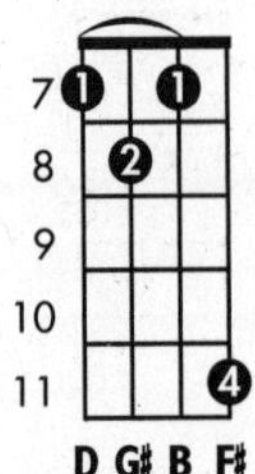

Bmaj7 — B Major Seventh

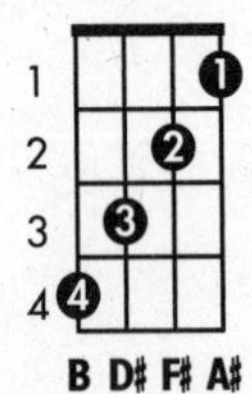

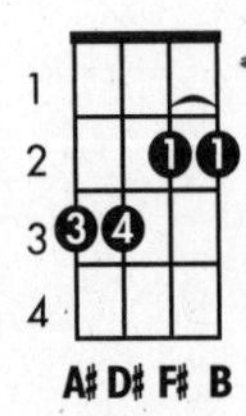

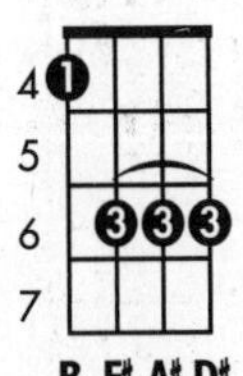

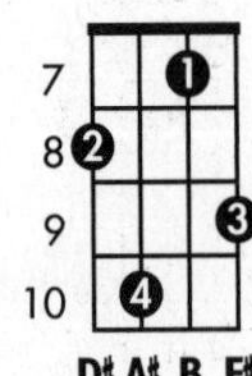

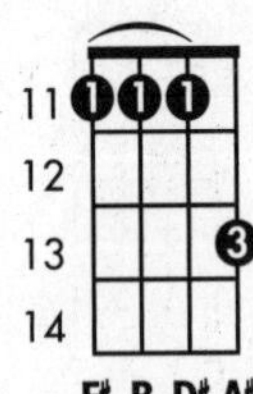

B7 — B Seventh

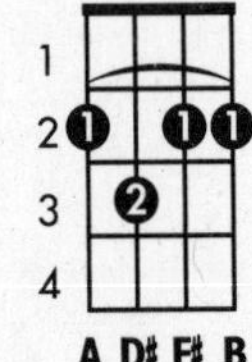

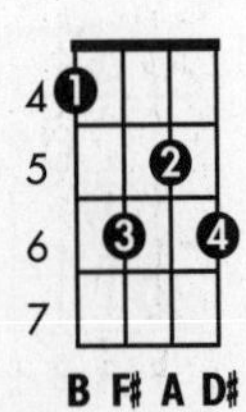

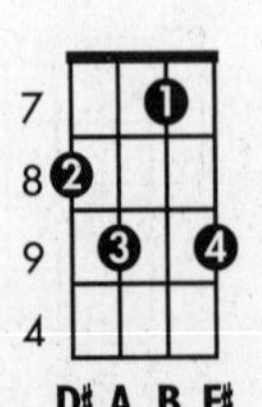

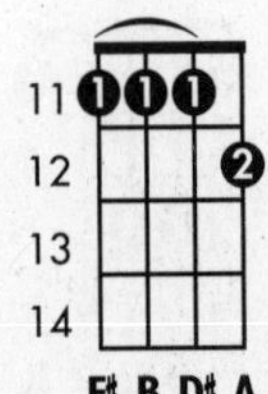

B Minor Seventh

Bm7

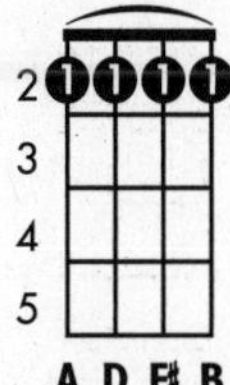

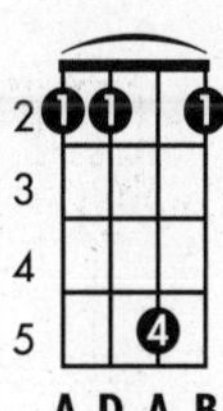

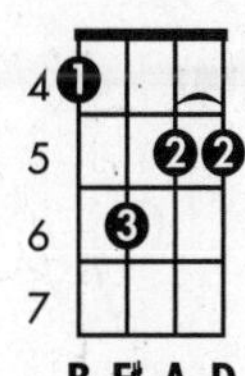

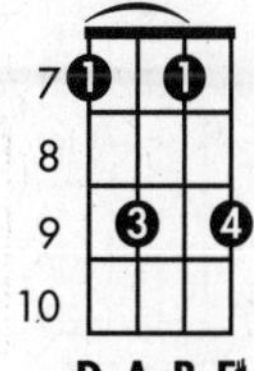

F♯ B D A

B Minor Seventh Flat Fifth

Bm7(♭5)

B

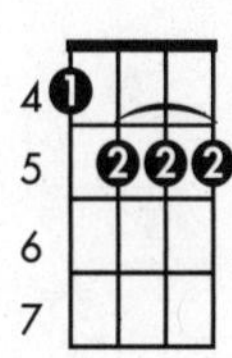

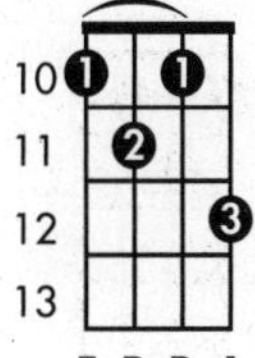

B Diminished Seventh

B°7

Sometimes written **B♭9/6**

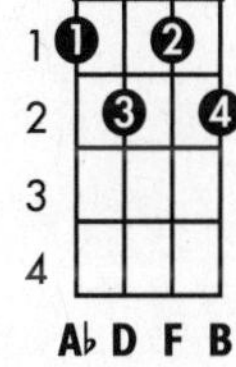

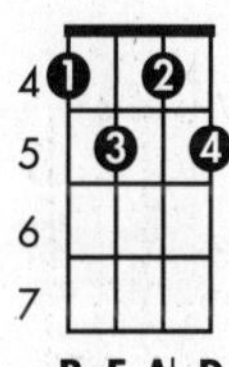

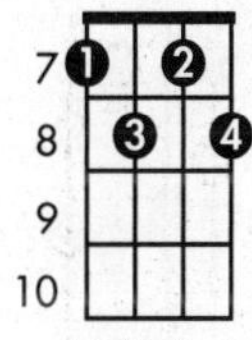

F B D A♭

B Seventh Suspended Fourth

B7sus

Sometimes written **B7sus4**

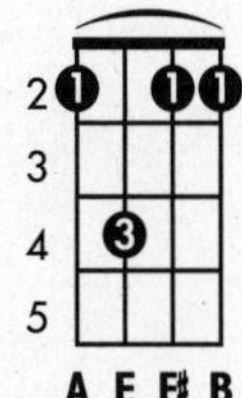

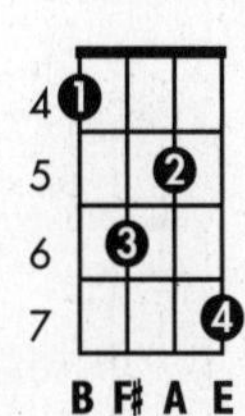

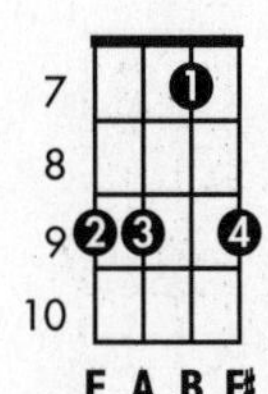

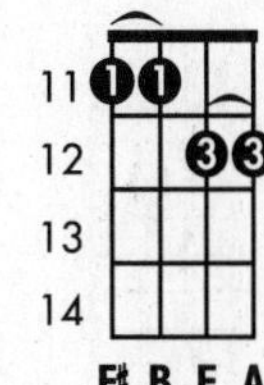

B(add9) — B Major Add Ninth

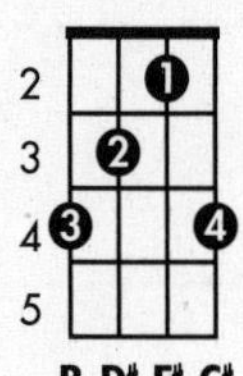

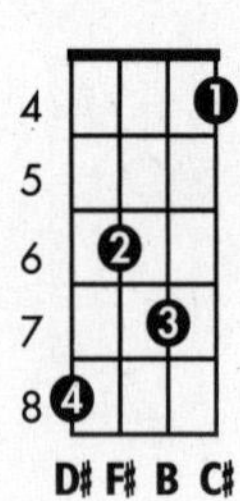

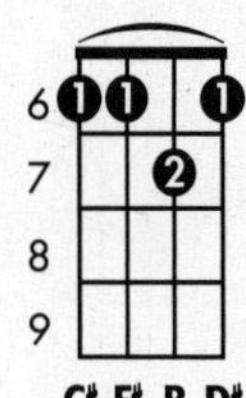

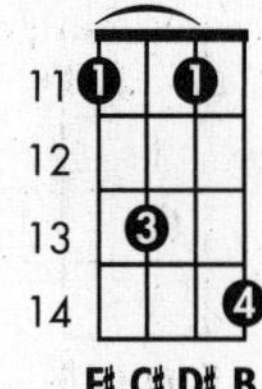

Bmaj9 — B Major Ninth

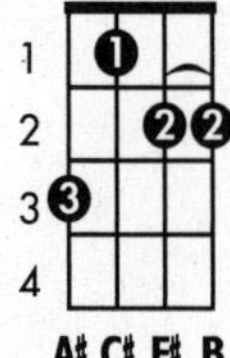

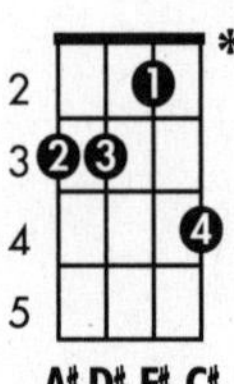

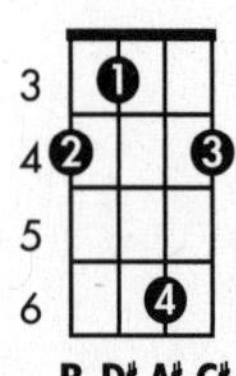

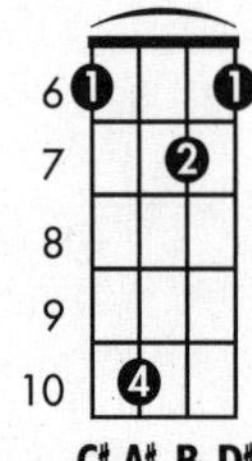

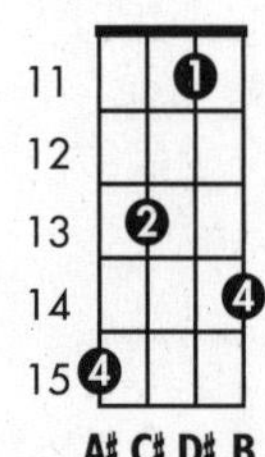

B9 — B Ninth

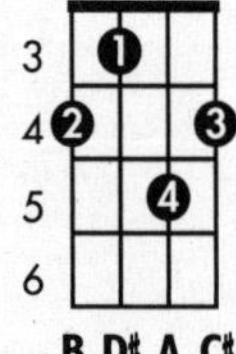

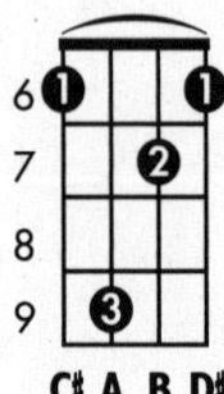

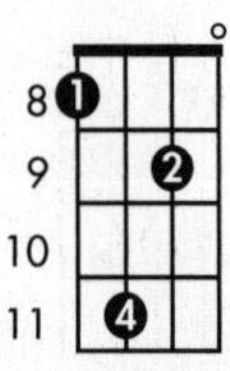

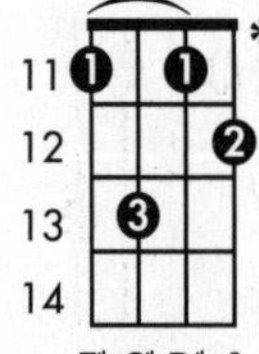

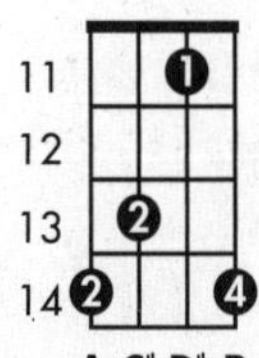

Bm9 — B Minor Ninth

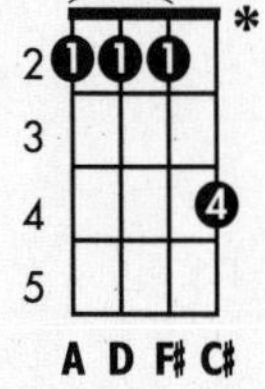

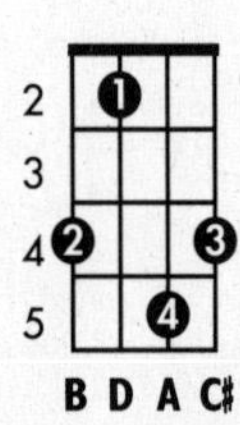

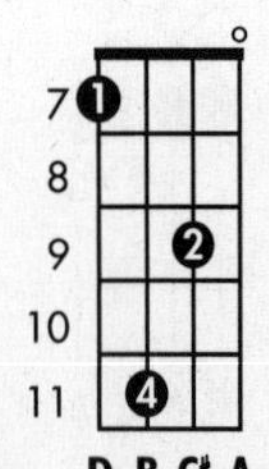

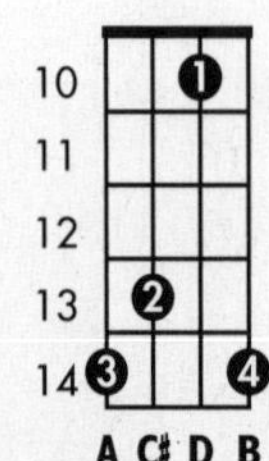

B Sixth Add Ninth

B6/9

Sometimes written $\mathbf{B}^{9/6}$

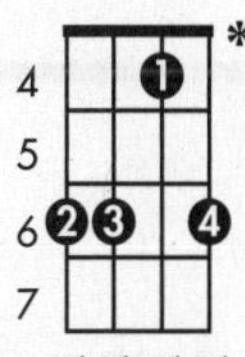

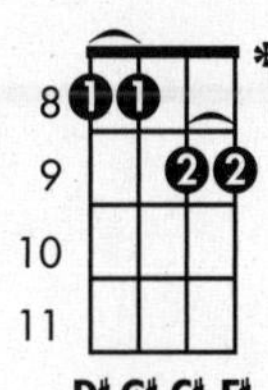

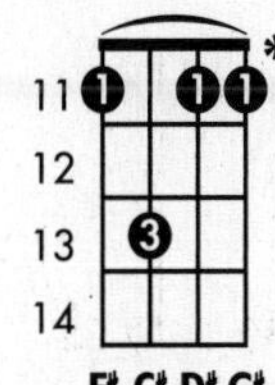

B Minor Sixth Add Ninth

Bm6/9

Sometimes written $\mathbf{Bm}^{9/6}$

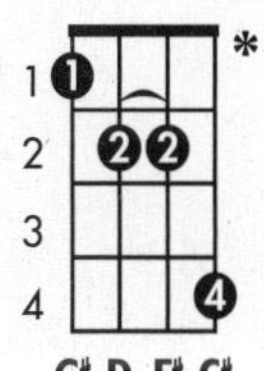

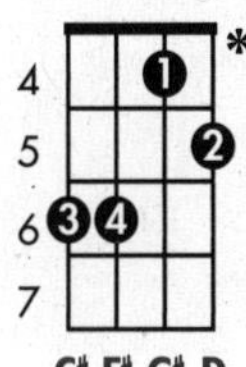

B Minor Major Seventh

Bm(maj7)

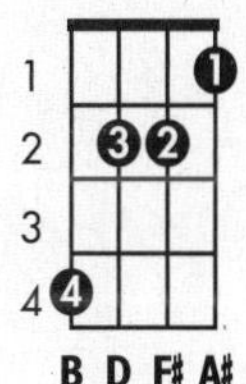

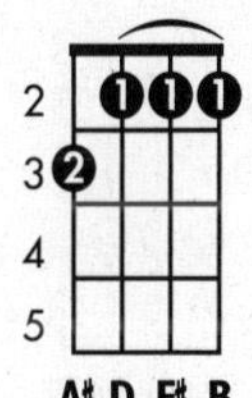

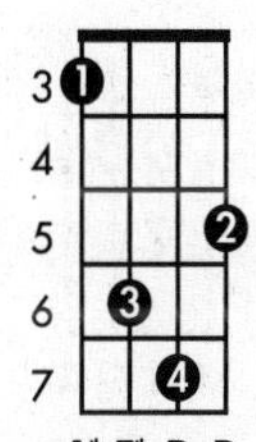

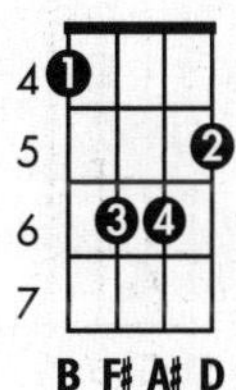

B Minor Ninth Major Seventh

Bm9(maj7)

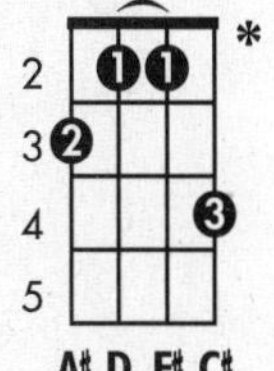

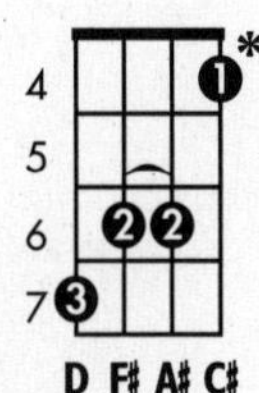

B11

B Eleventh

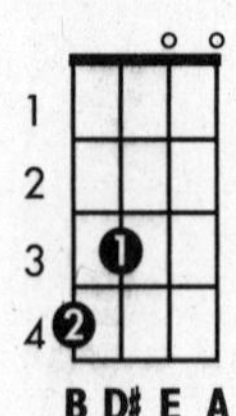
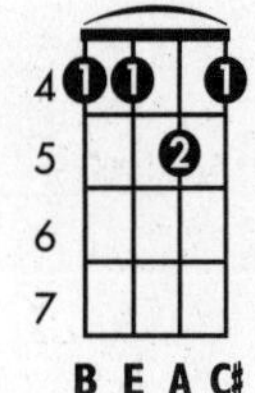

Bm11

B Minor Eleventh

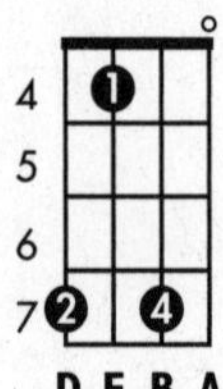
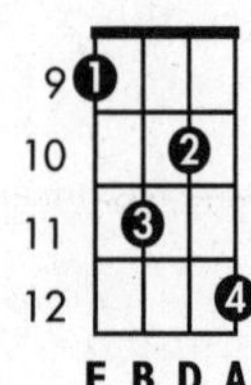

B13

B Thirteenth

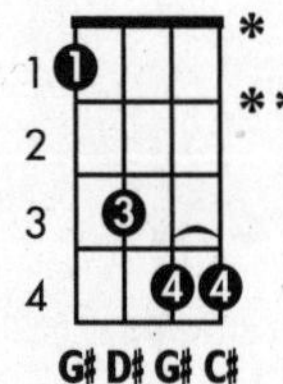
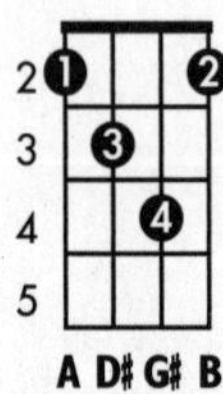
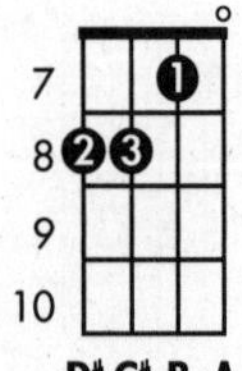
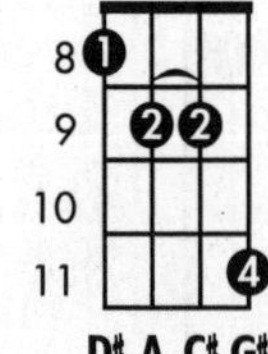
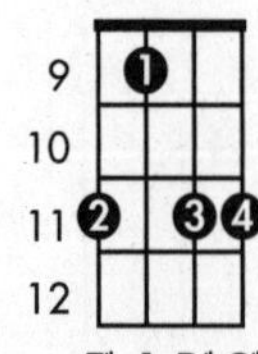

B(♭5)

B Flat Fifth

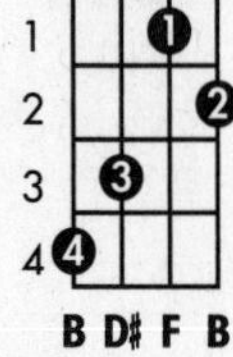
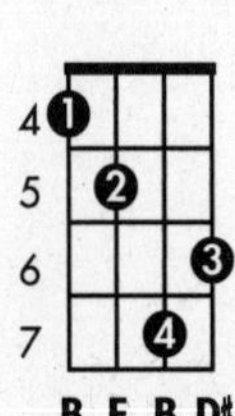

B Seventh Flat Fifth

B7(♭5)

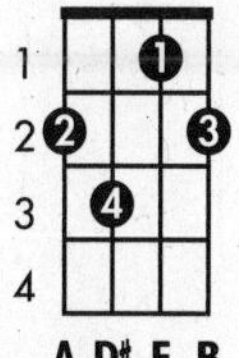

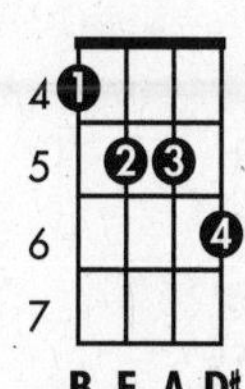

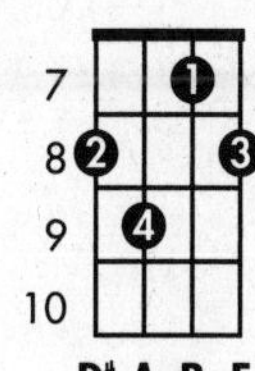

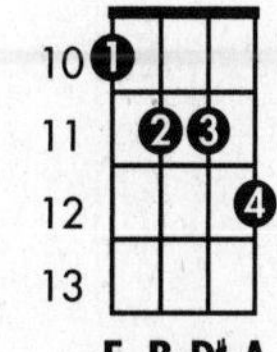

B Seventh Augmented Fifth

B7+

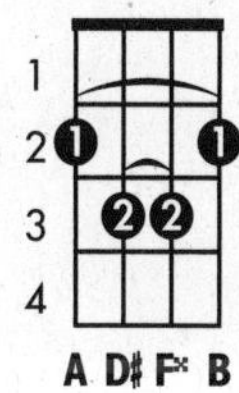

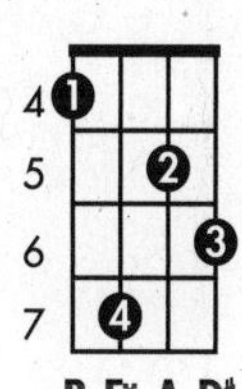

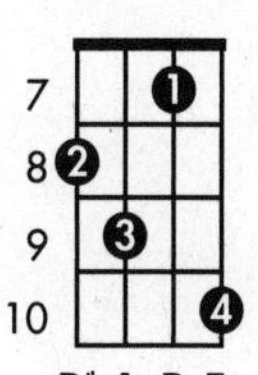

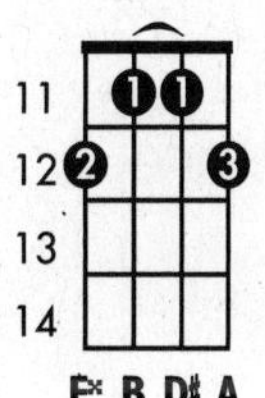

B Major Seventh Flat Fifth

Bmaj7(♭5)

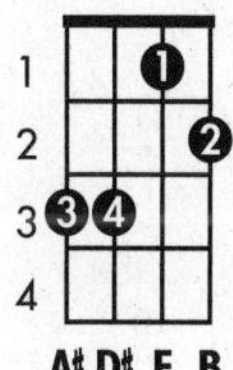

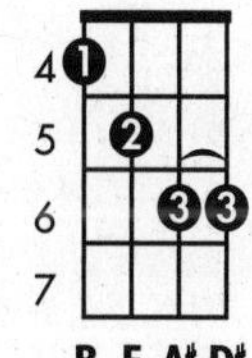

B Seventh Flat Ninth

B7(♭9)

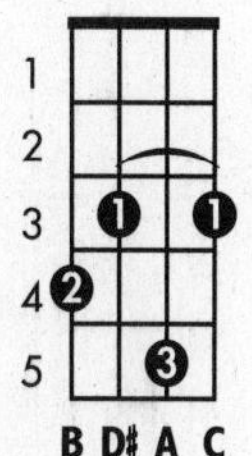

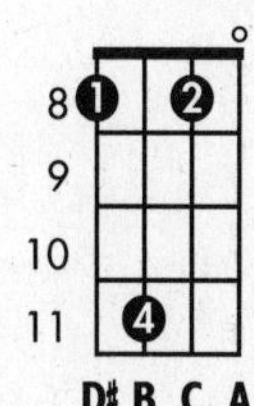

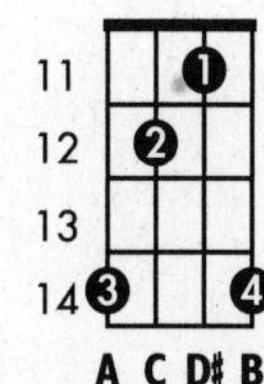

B7(♯9) — B Seventh Sharp Ninth

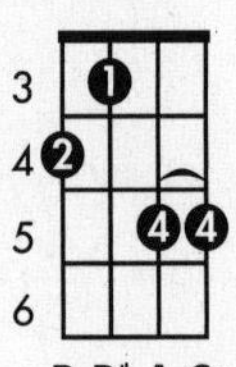

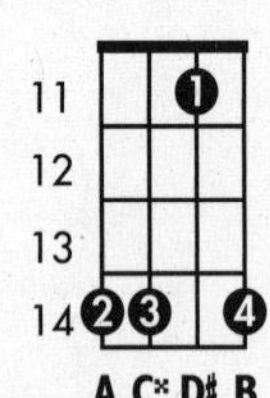

11 12 13 14
F♯ C× D♯ A

B

B7+(♭9) — B Seventh Flat Ninth Augmented Fifth

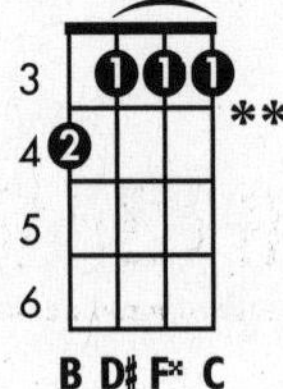

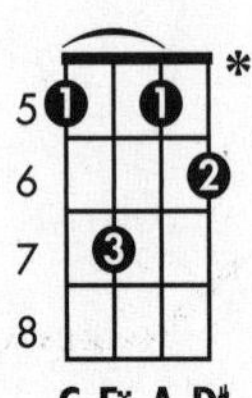

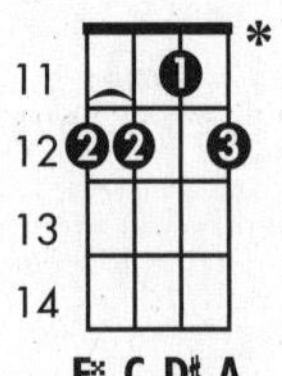

B9+ — B Ninth Augmented Fifth

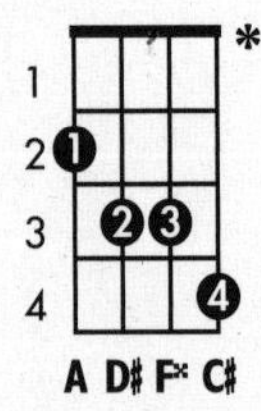

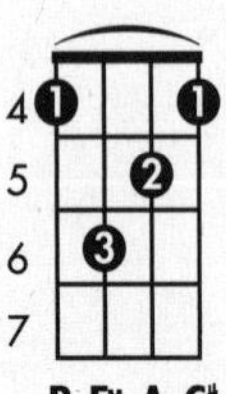

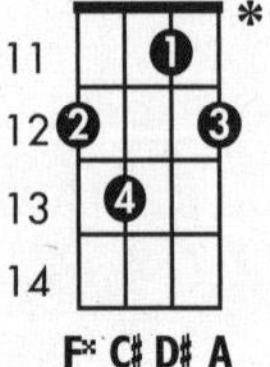

B9(♭5) — B Ninth Flat Fifth

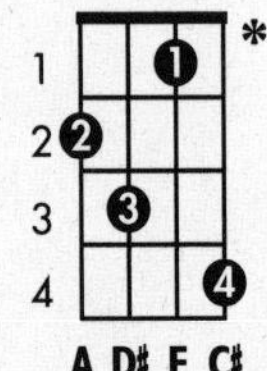

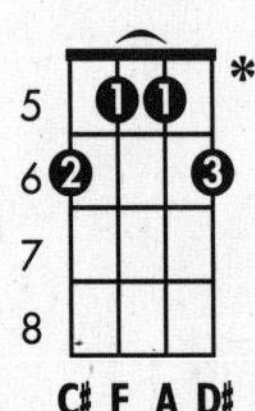

B Ninth Sharp Eleventh

B9(#11)

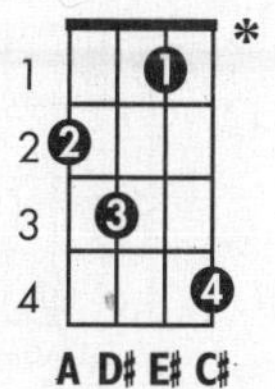

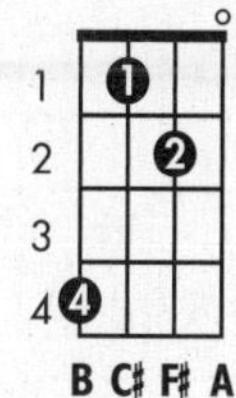

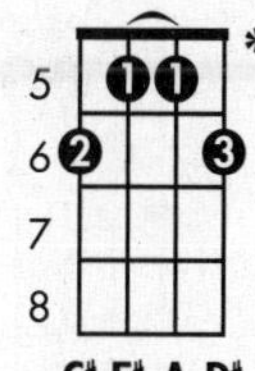

B Thirteenth Flat Ninth

B13(♭9)

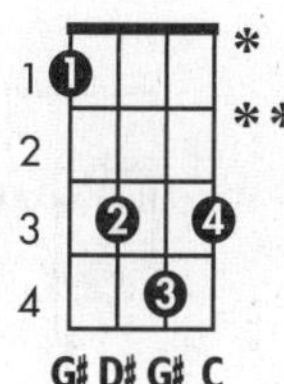

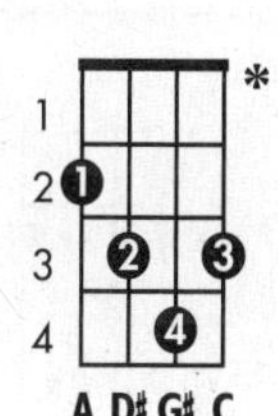

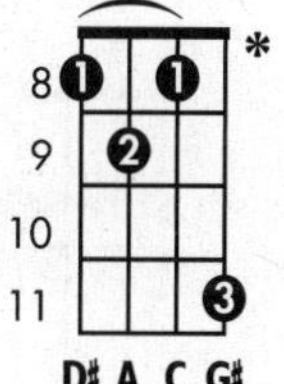

B Thirteenth Flat Ninth Flat Fifth

B13(♭9 ♭5)

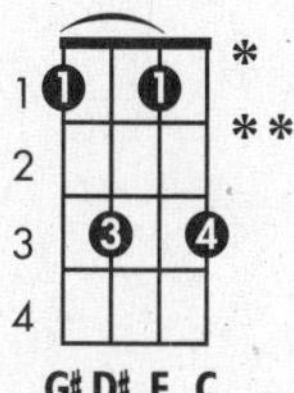

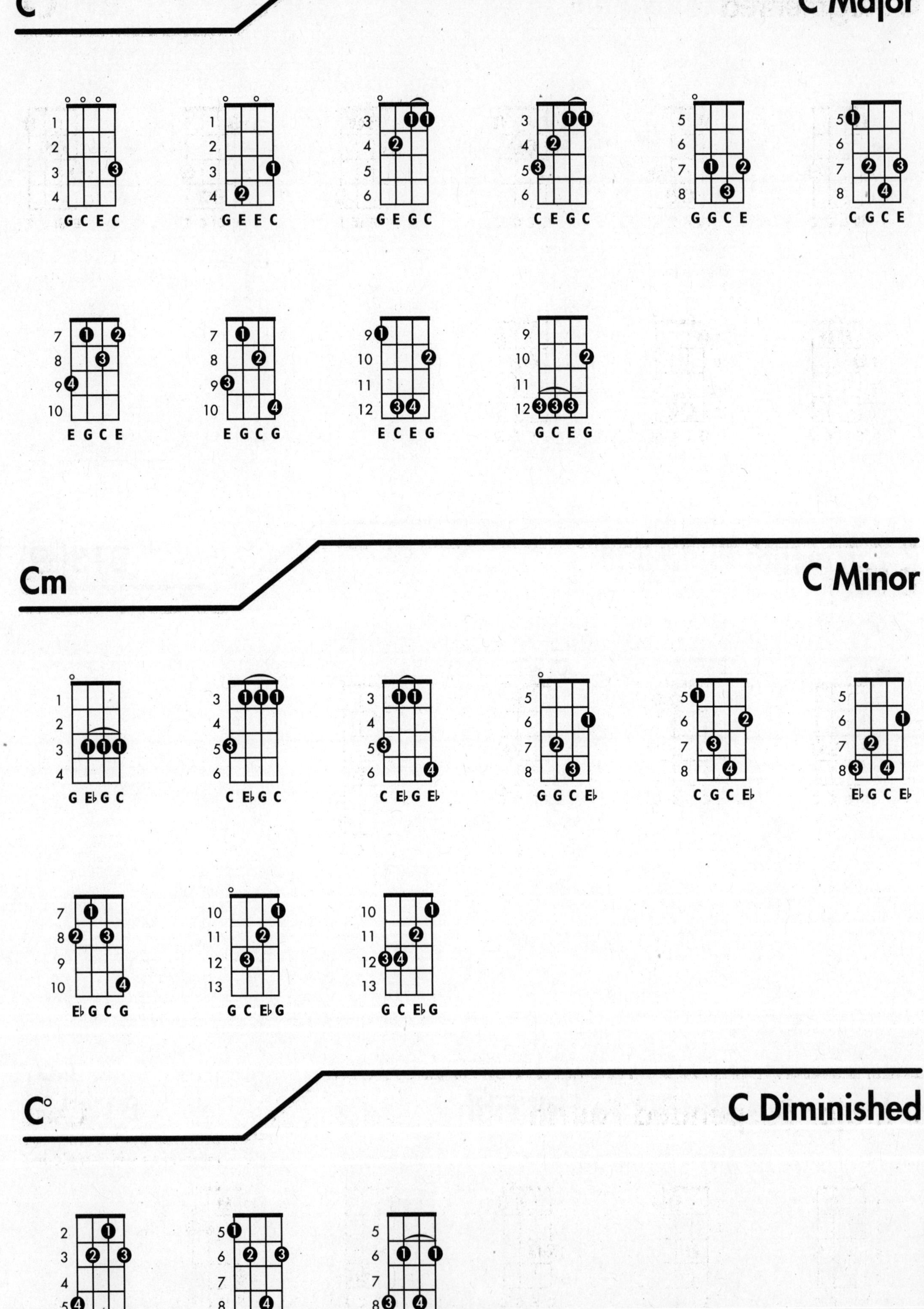
C
C Major
G C E C
G E E C
G E G C
C E G C
G G C E
C G C E
E G C E
E G C G
E C E G
G C E G
C
Cm
C Minor
G E♭ G C
C E♭ G C
C E♭ G E♭
G G C E♭
C G C E♭
E♭ G C E♭
E♭ G C G
G C E♭ G
G C E♭ G
C°
C Diminished
C E♭ G♭ C
C G♭ C E♭
E♭ G♭ C E♭

C Augmented

C+

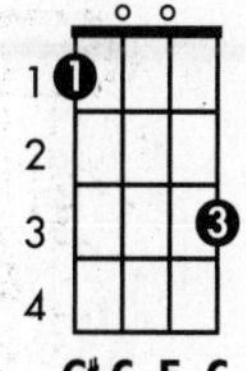

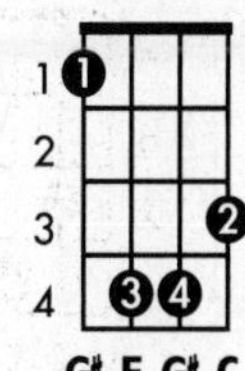

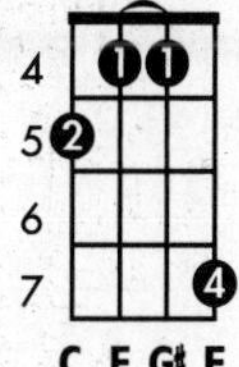

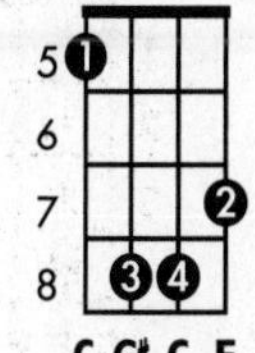

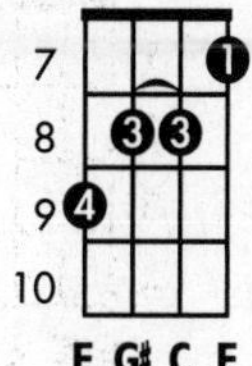

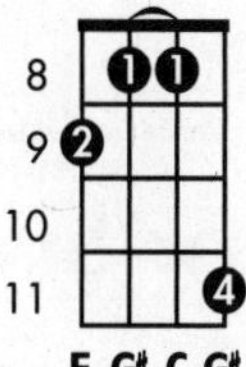

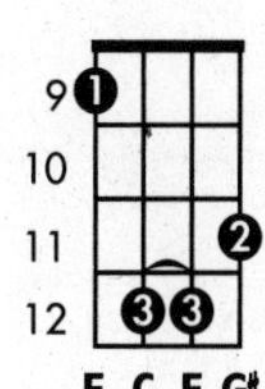

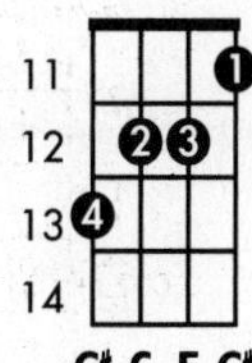

C

C Fifth

C5

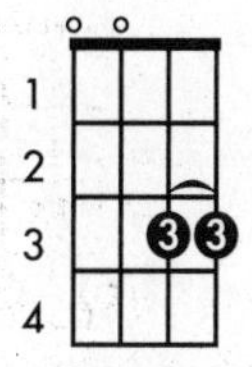

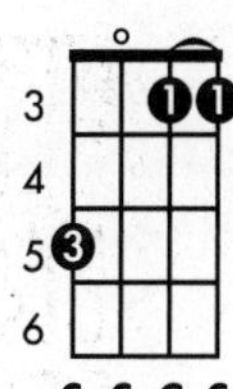

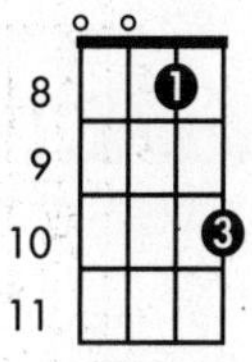

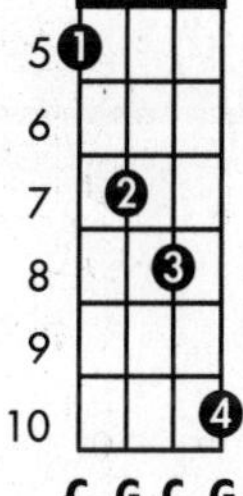

C Major Suspended Fourth

Csus

Sometimes written **Csus4**

1 2 3 4
G C F C

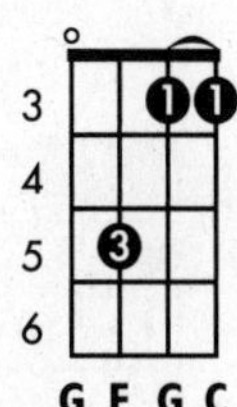

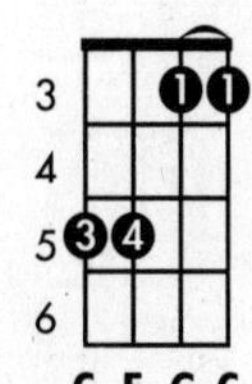

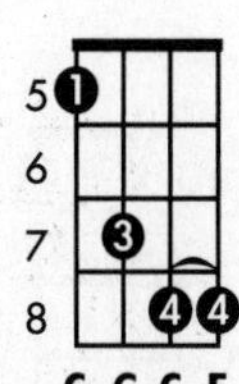

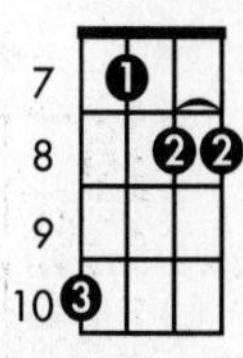

C6 — C Major 6th

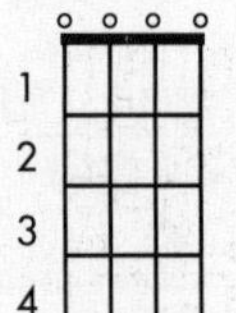

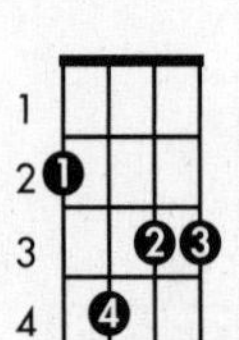

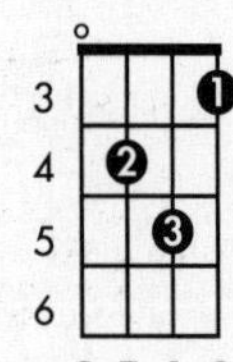

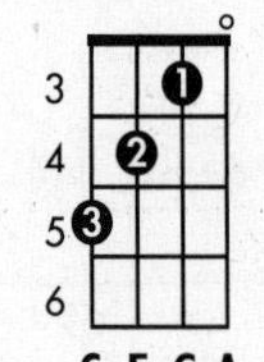

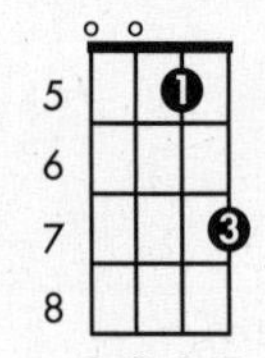

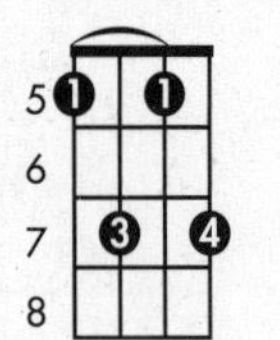

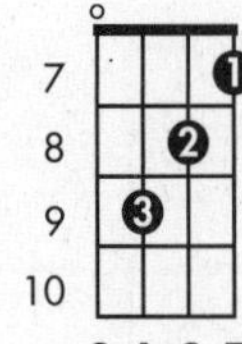

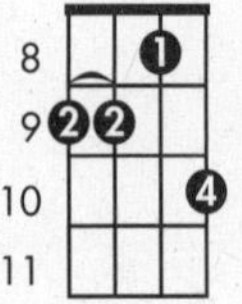

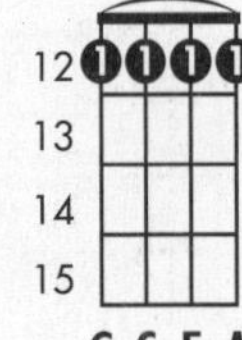

Cm6 — C Minor Sixth

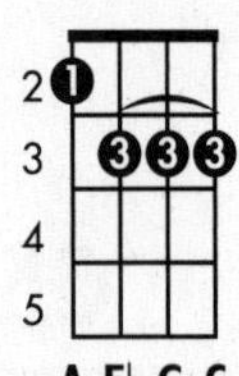

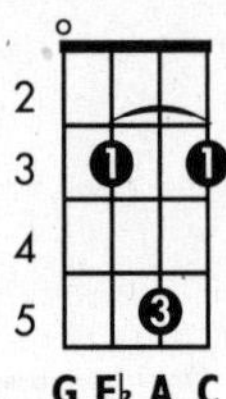

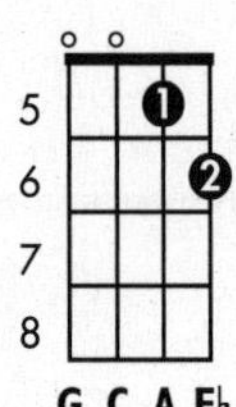

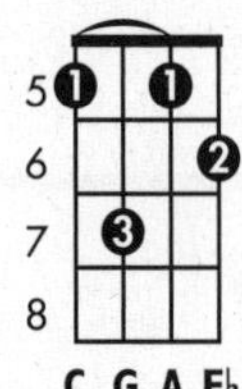

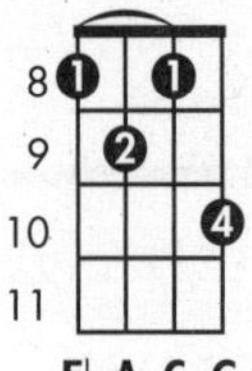

Cmaj7 — C Major Seventh

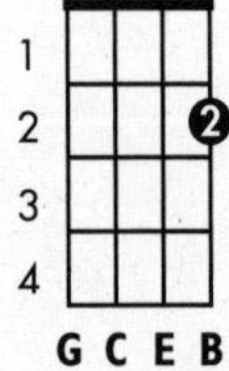

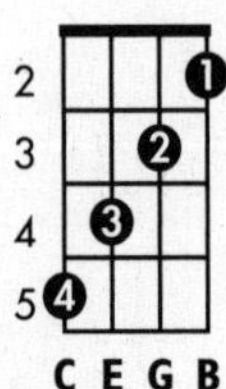

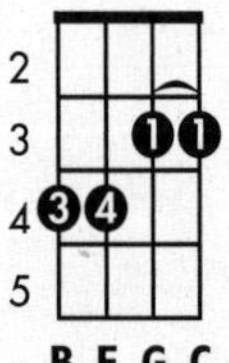

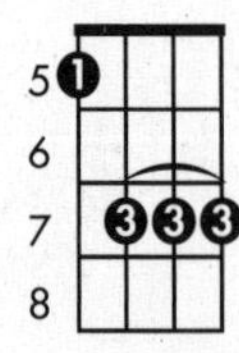

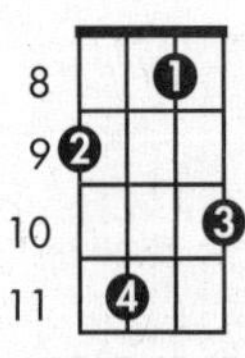

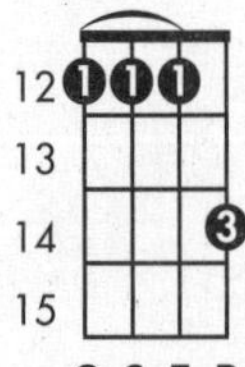

C7 — C Seventh

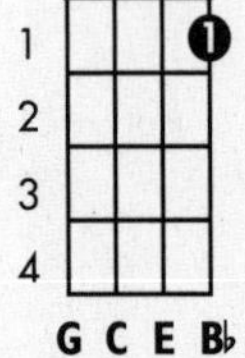

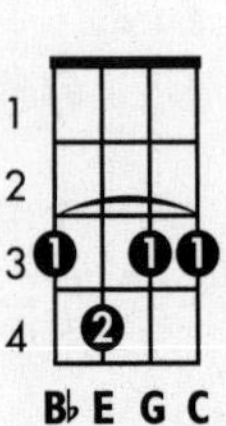

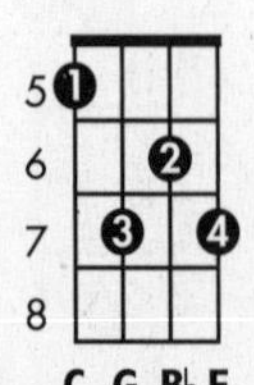

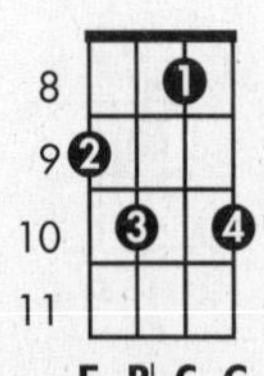

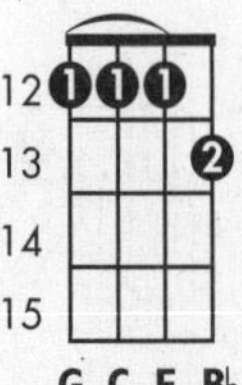

C Minor Seventh

Cm7

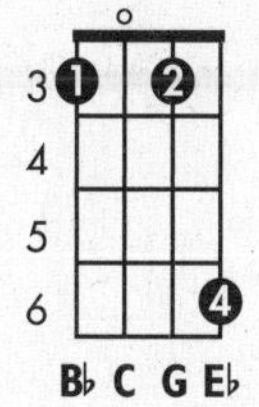

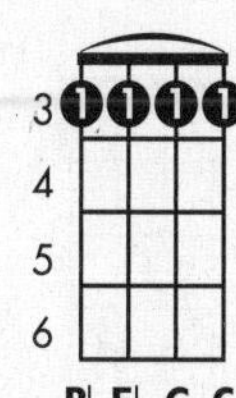

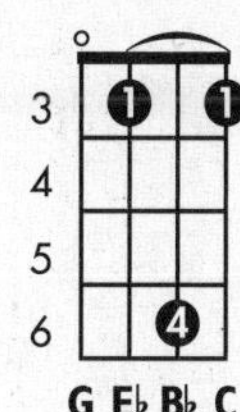

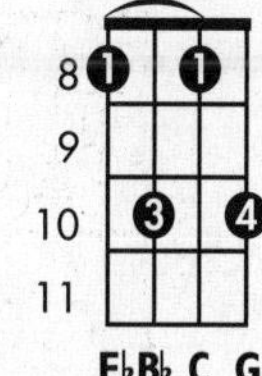

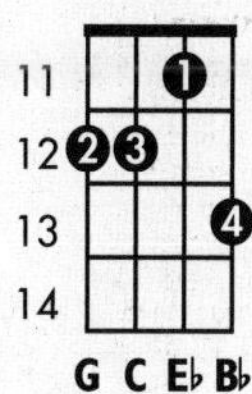

C Minor Seventh Flat Fifth

Cm7(♭5)

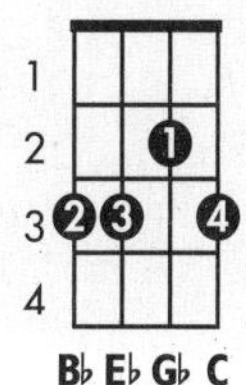

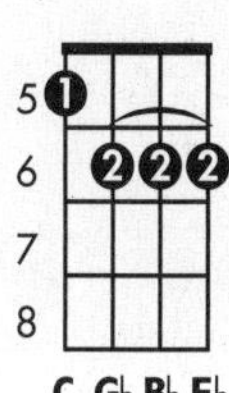

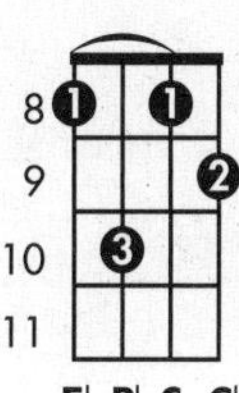

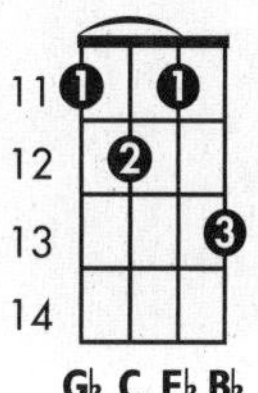

C

C Diminished Seventh

C°7

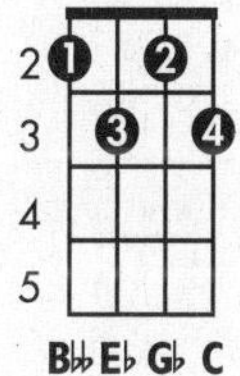

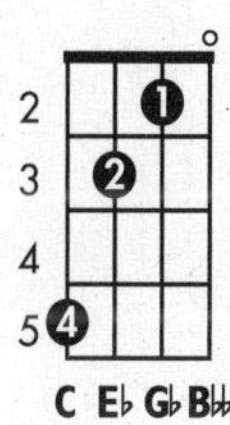

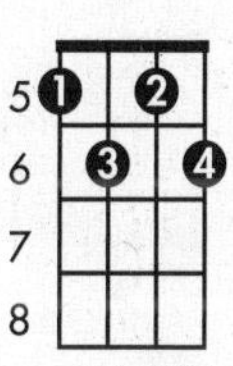

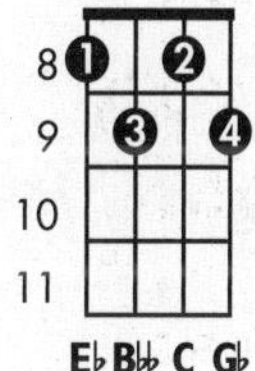

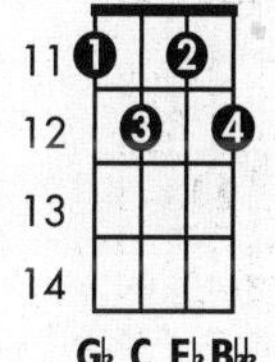

C Seventh Suspended Fourth

C7sus

Sometimes written **C7sus4**

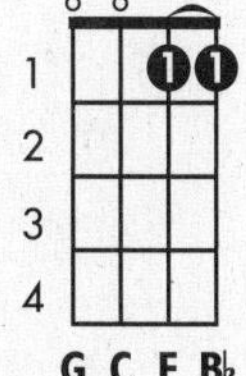

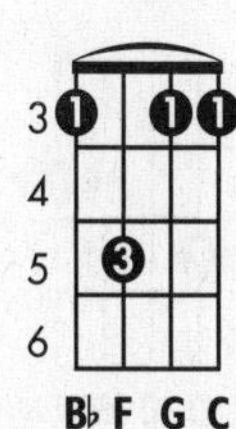

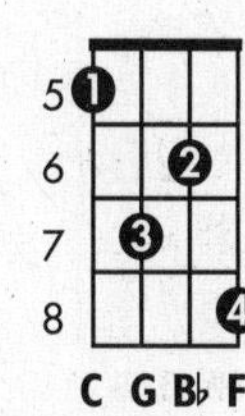

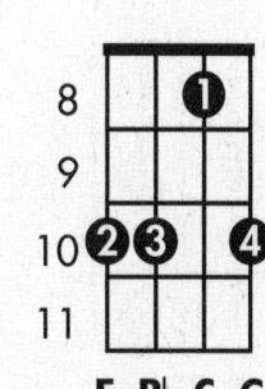

C(add9) — C Major Add Ninth

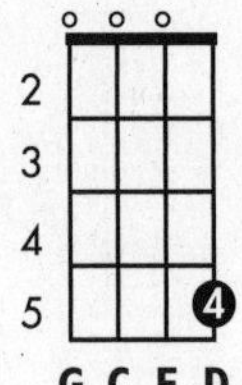

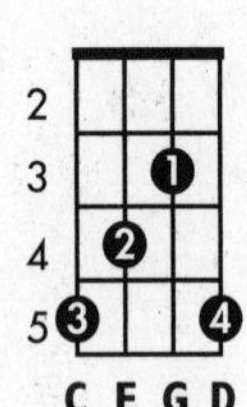

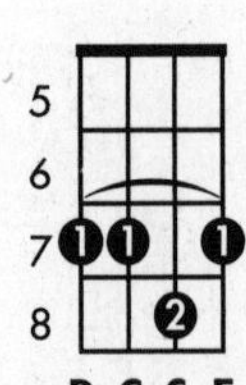

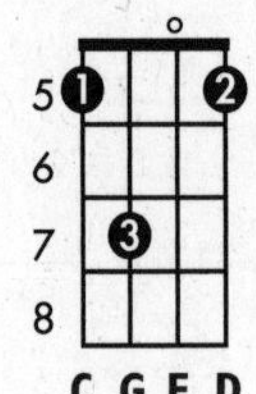

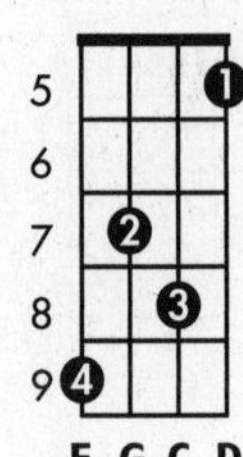

Cmaj9 — C Major Ninth

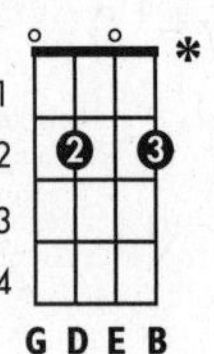

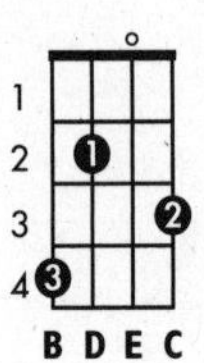

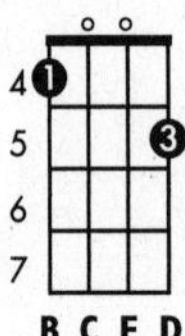

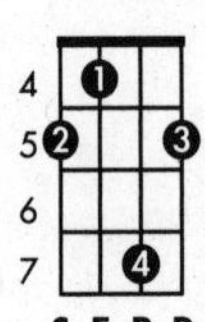

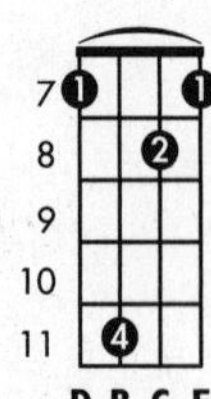

C9 — C Ninth

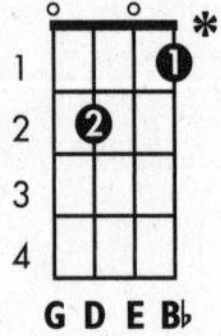

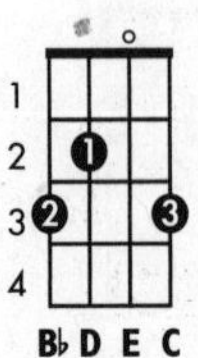

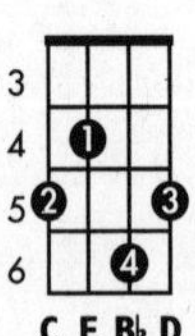

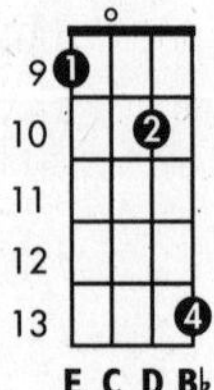

Cm9 — C Minor Ninth

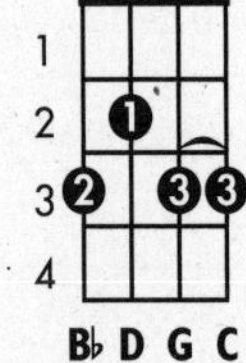

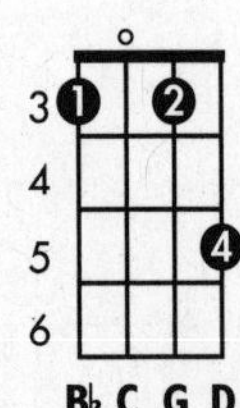

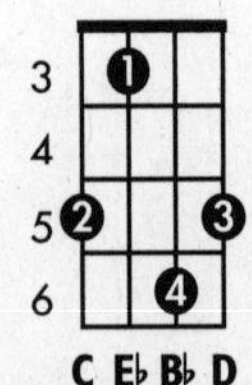

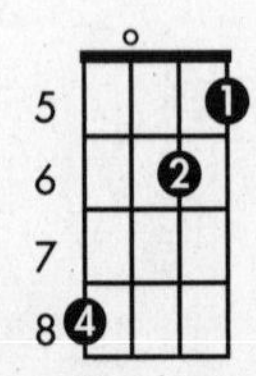

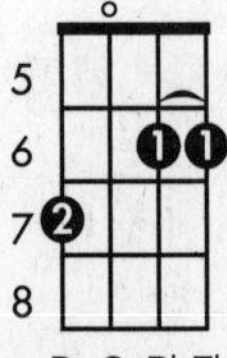

C Sixth Add Ninth

C6/9

Sometimes written $C^{9/6}$

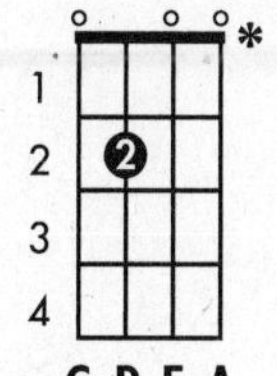

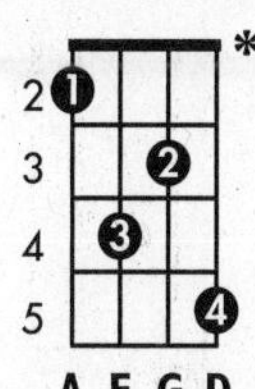

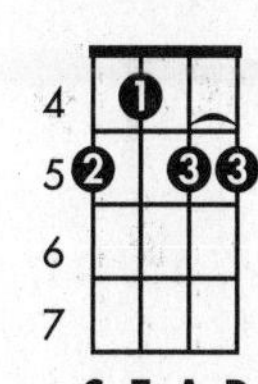

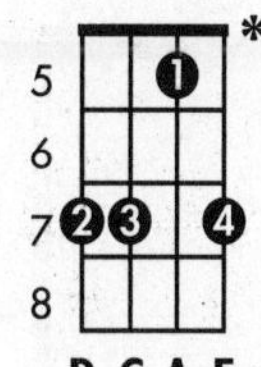

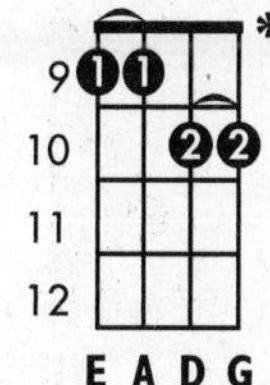

C Minor Sixth Add Ninth

Cm6/9

Sometimes written $Cm^{9/6}$

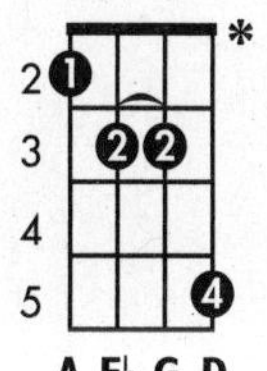

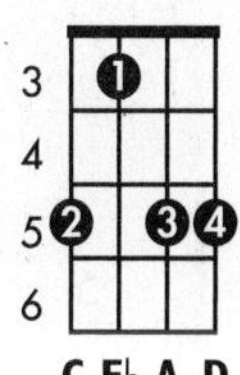

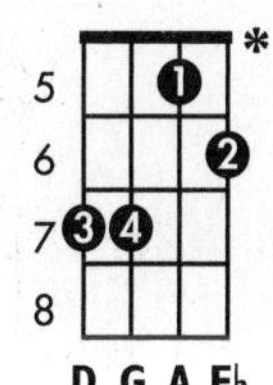

C

C Minor Major Seventh

Cm(maj7)

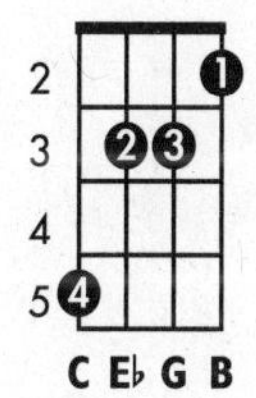

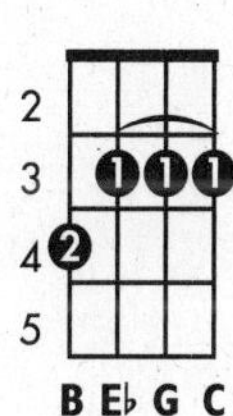

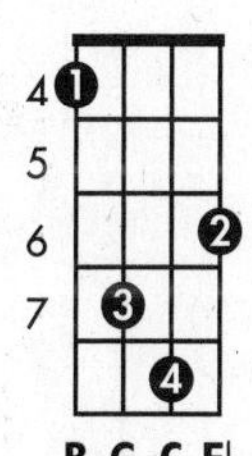

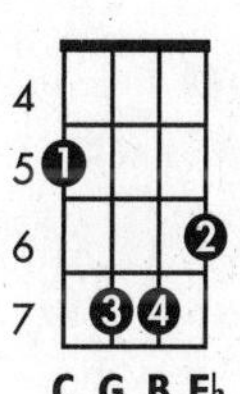

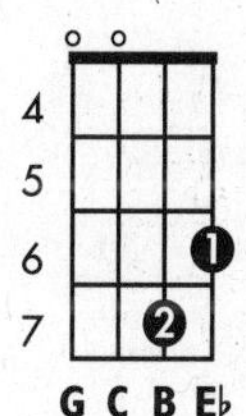

C Minor Ninth Major Seventh

Cm9(maj7)

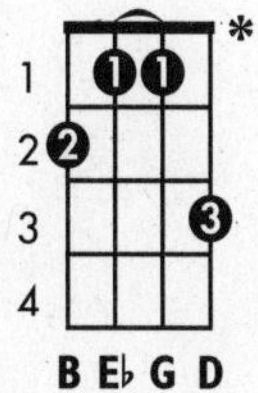

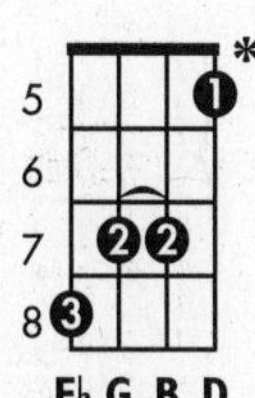

C11 — C Eleventh

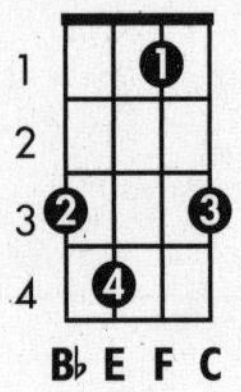

1 2 3 4

B♭ E F C

Cm11 — C Minor Eleventh

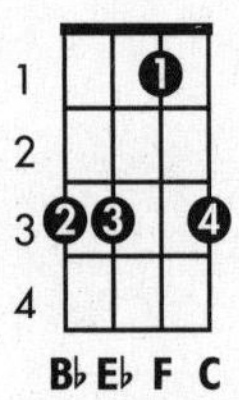

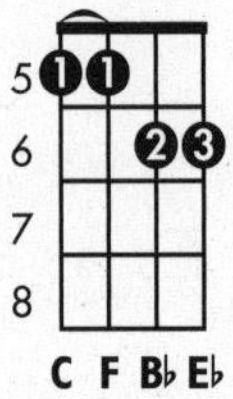

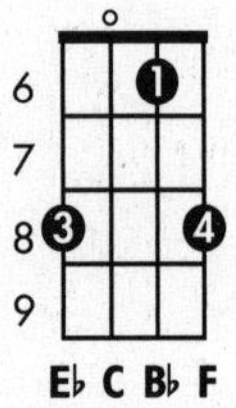

1 2 3 4

B♭ E♭ F C

5 6 7 8

C F B♭ E♭

6 7 8 9

E♭ C B♭ F

C13 — C Thirteenth

3 4 5 6 *

B♭ E A D

3 4 5 6

B♭ E A C

9 10 11 12 *

E B♭ D A

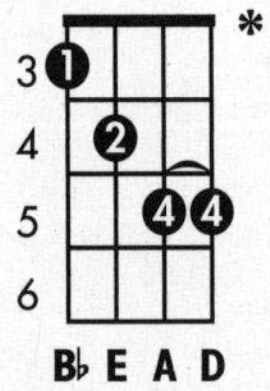

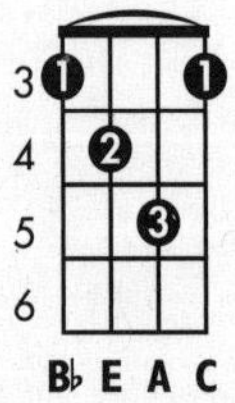

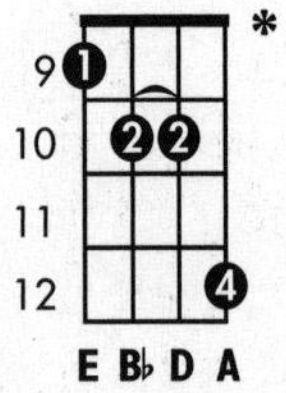

C(♭5) — C Flat Fifth

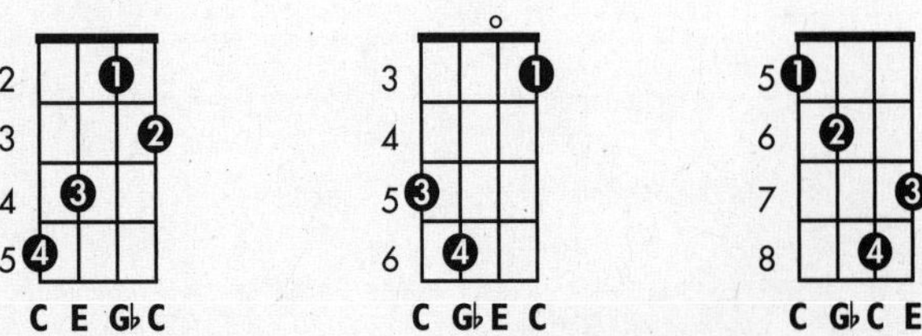

C Seventh Flat Fifth

C7(♭5)

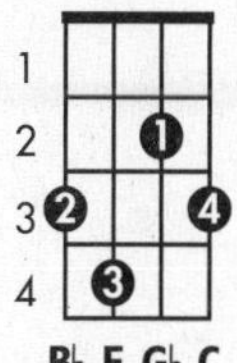

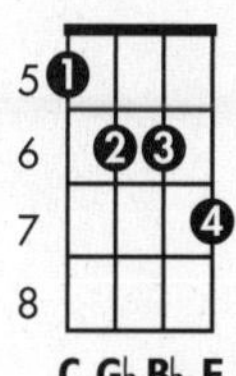

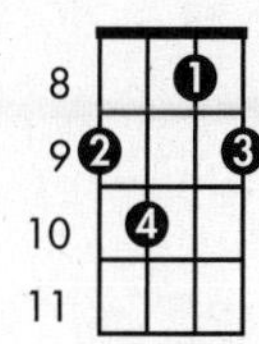

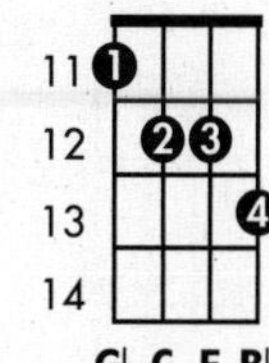

C Seventh Augmented Fifth

C7+

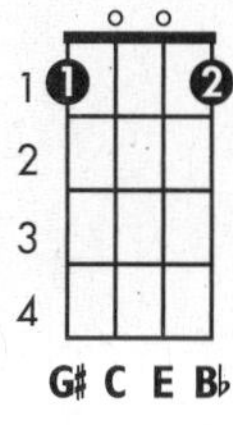

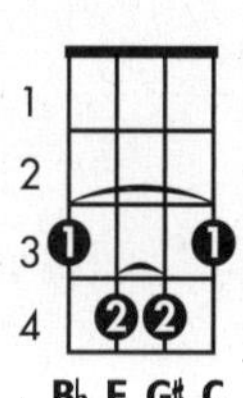

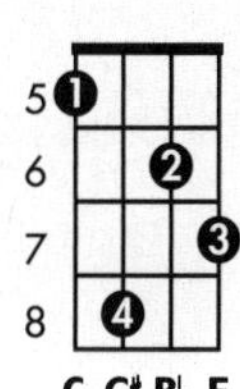

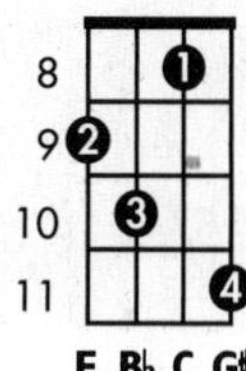

C

C Major Seventh Flat Fifth

Cmaj7(♭5)

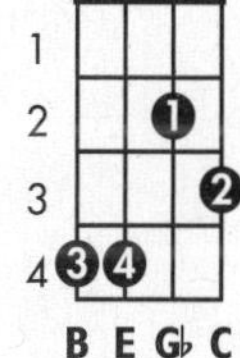

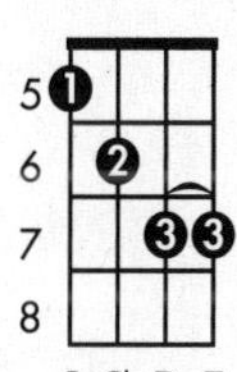

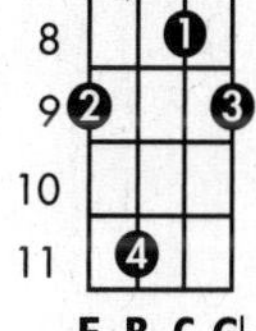

C Seventh Flat Ninth

C7(♭9)

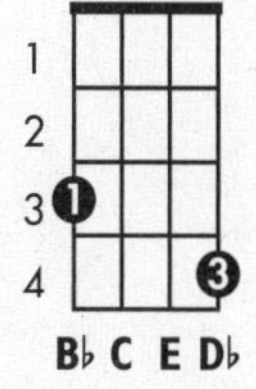

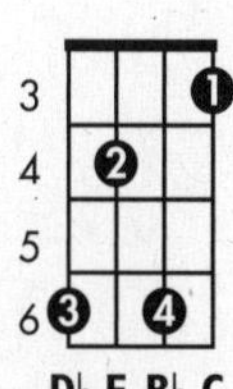

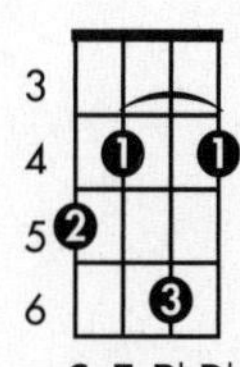

C7(♯9) — C Seventh Sharp Ninth

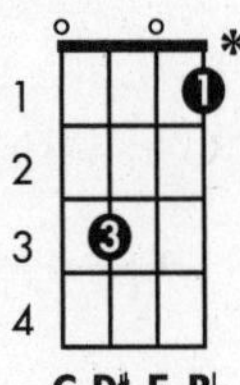

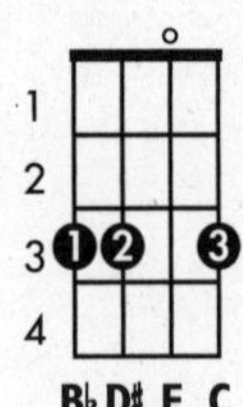

C E B♭ D♯

C7+(♭9) — C Seventh Flat Ninth Augmented Fifth

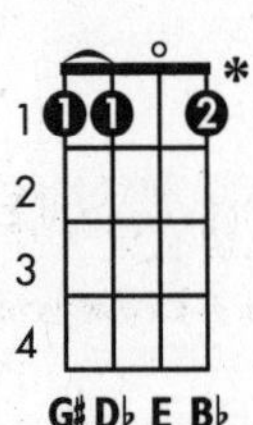

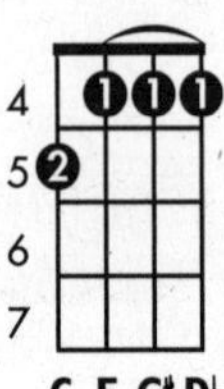

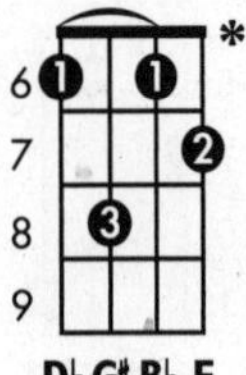

C9+ — C Ninth Augmented Fifth

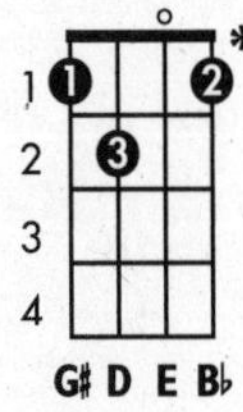

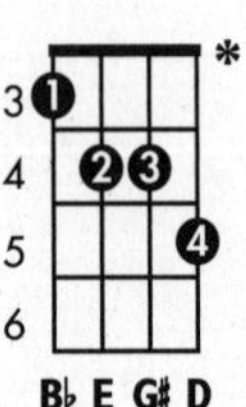

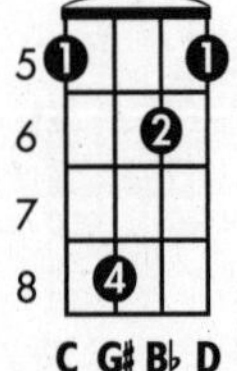

C9(♭5) — C Ninth Flat Fifth

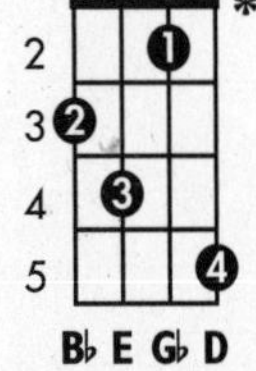

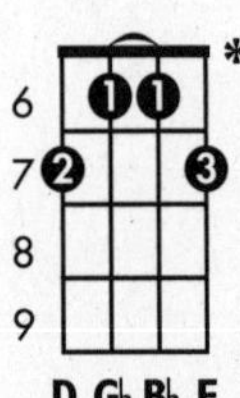

C Ninth Sharp Eleventh

C9(♯11)

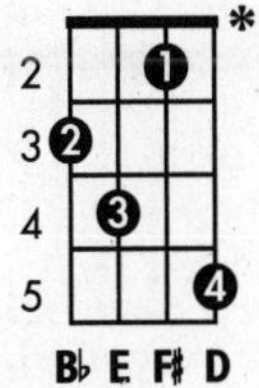

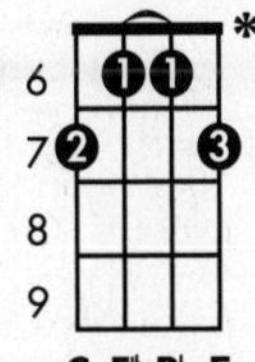

C Thirteenth Flat Ninth

C13(♭9)

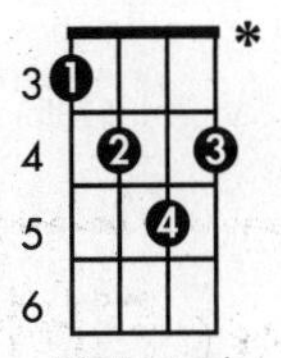

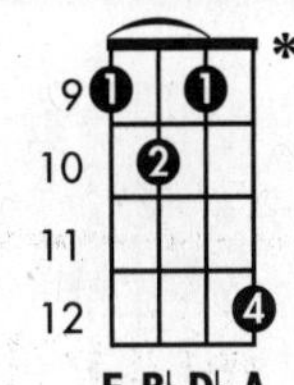

C Thirteenth Flat Ninth Flat Fifth

C13(♭9 ♭5)

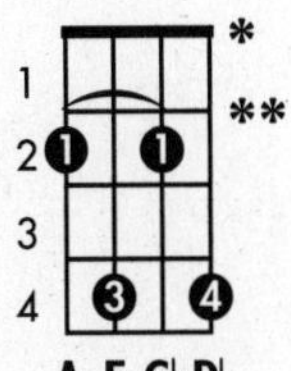

C♯

C♯ Major

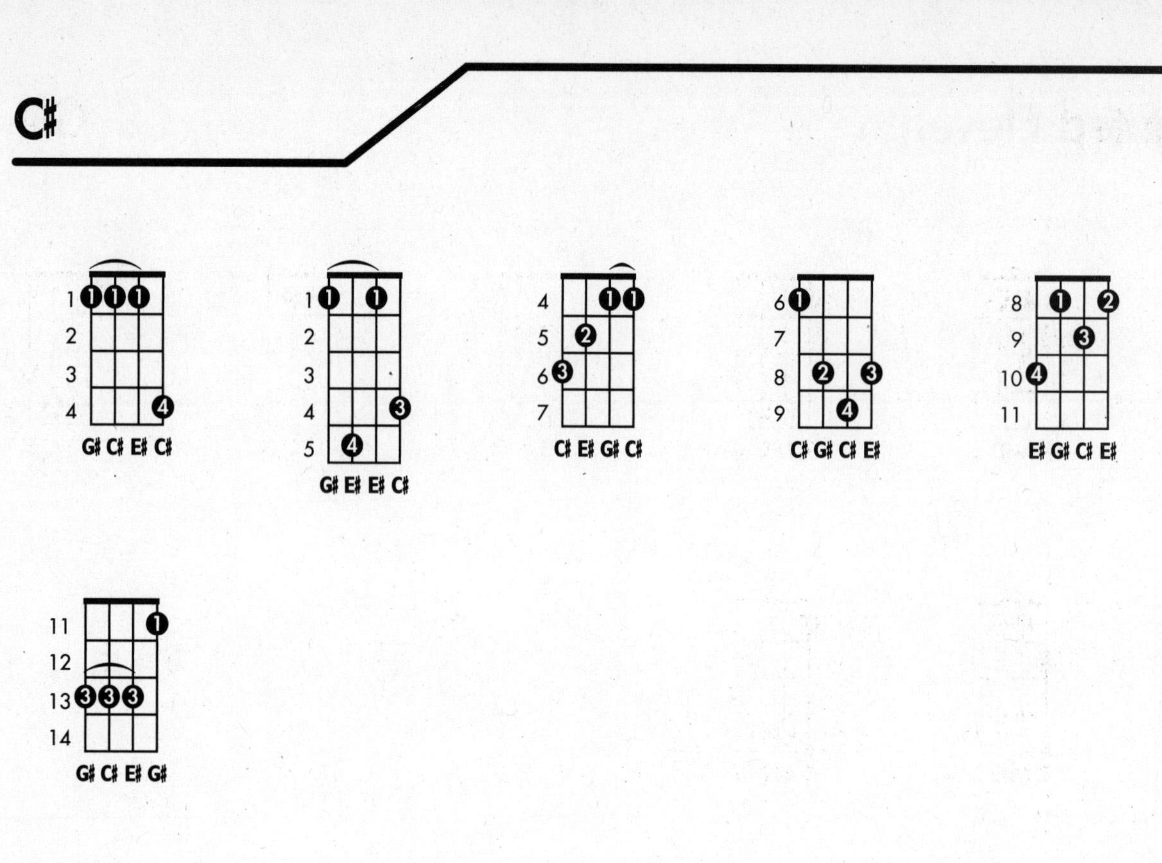

C♯m

C♯ Minor

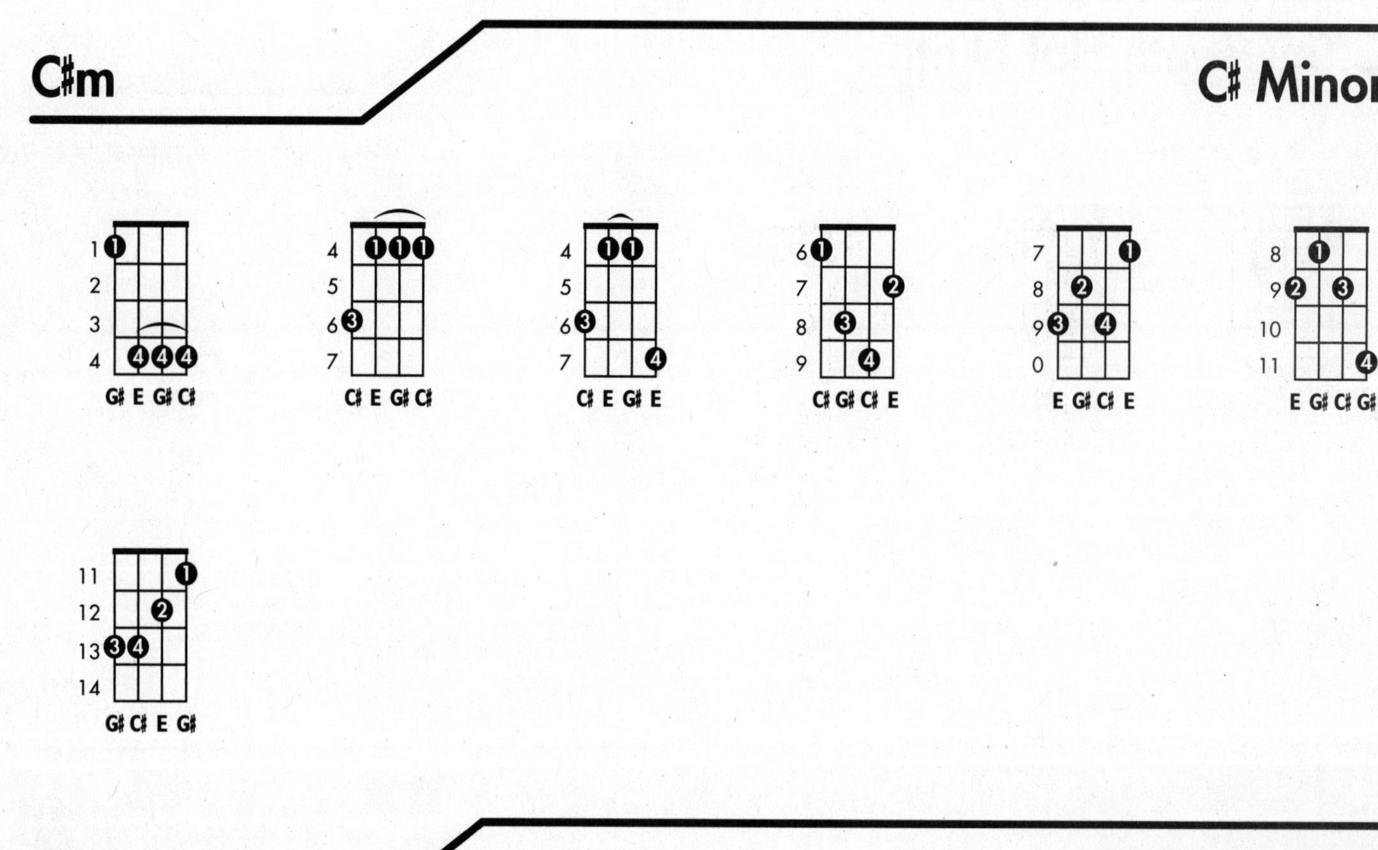

C♯°

C♯ Diminished

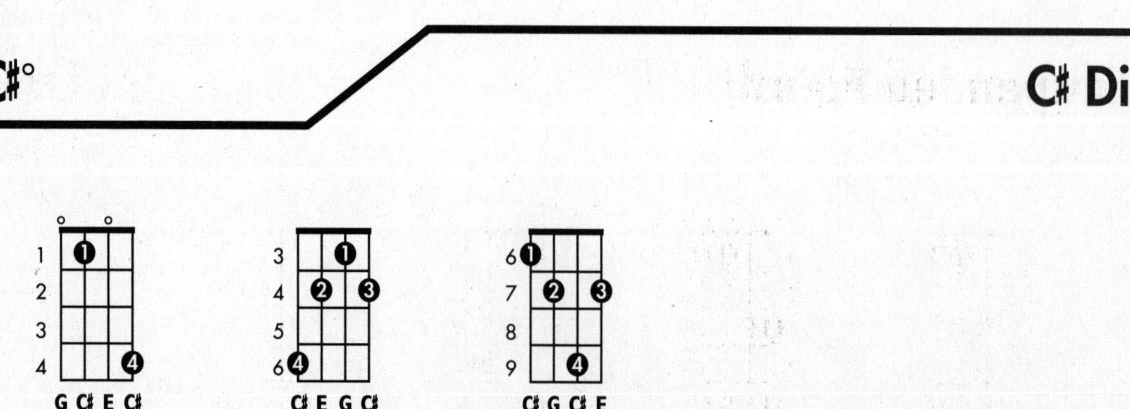

C♯ Augmented

C♯+

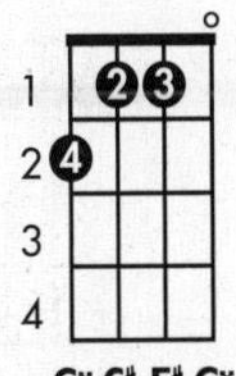

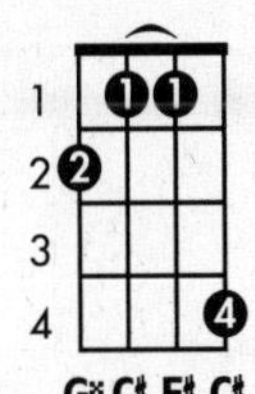

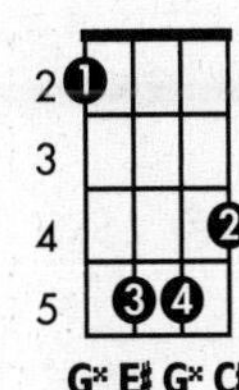

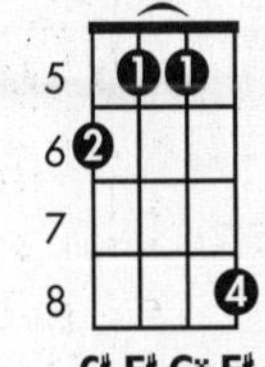

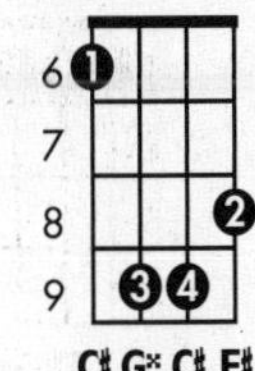

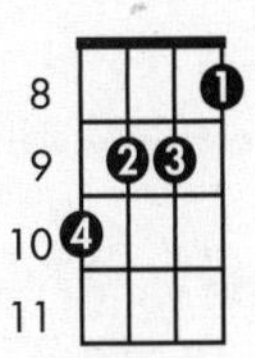

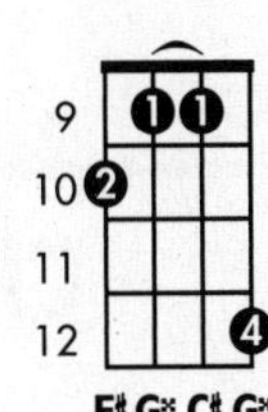

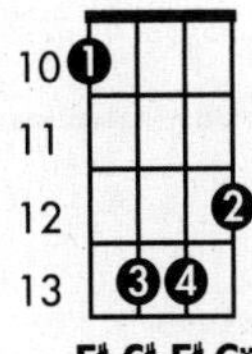

C♯ Fifth

C♯5

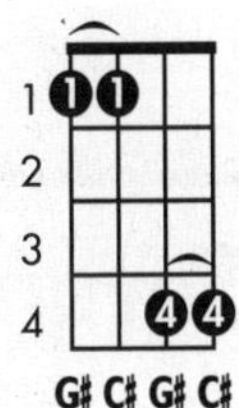

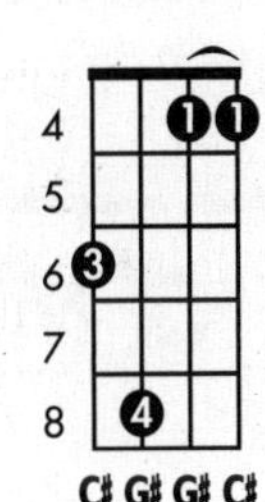

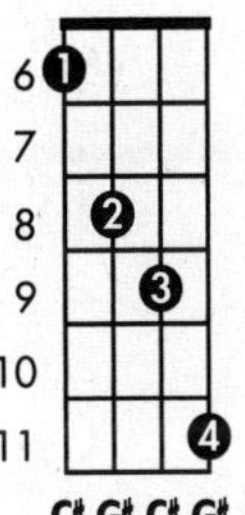

C♯ Major Suspended Fourth

C♯sus

Sometimes written **C♯sus4**

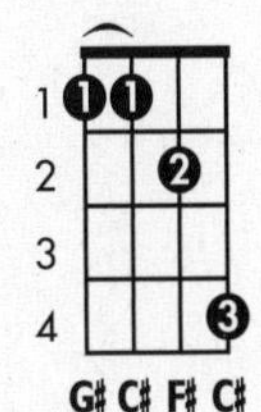

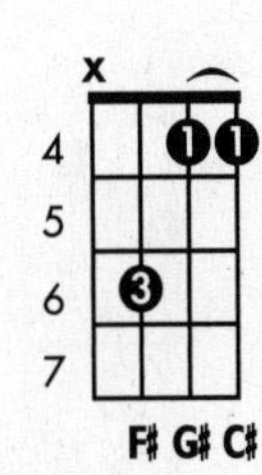

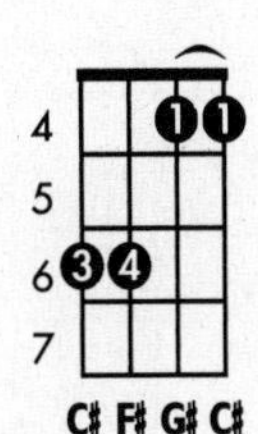

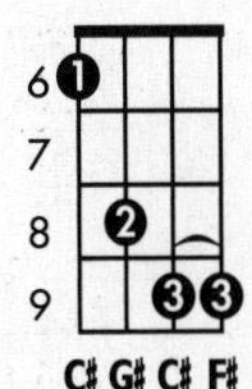

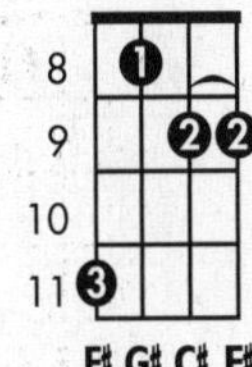

C♯6

C♯ Major 6th

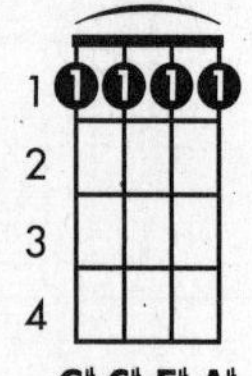

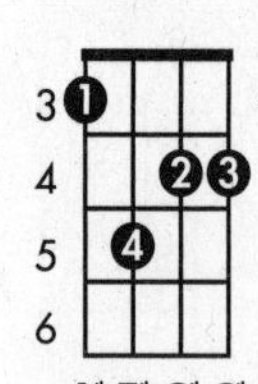

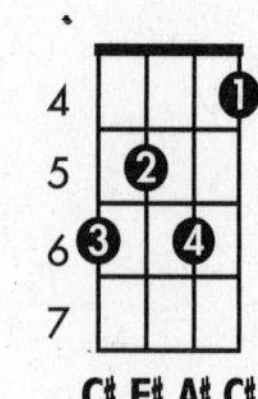

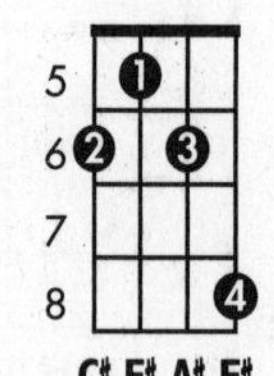

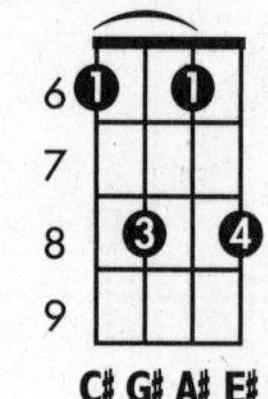

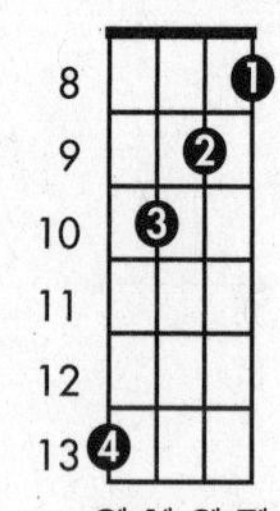

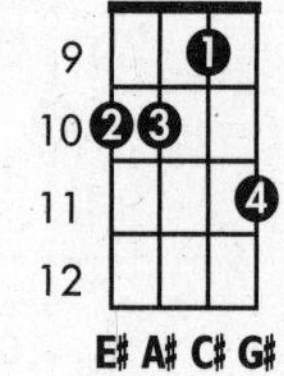

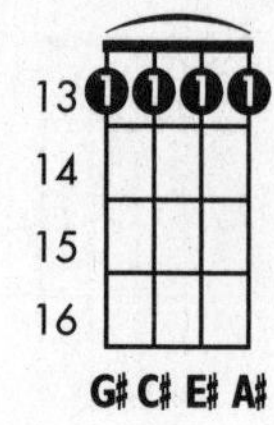

C♯m6

C♯ Minor Sixth

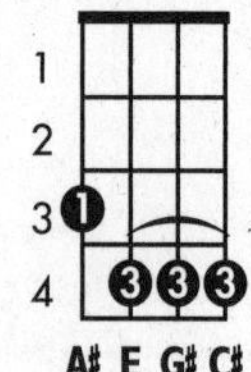

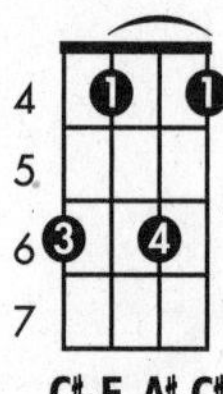

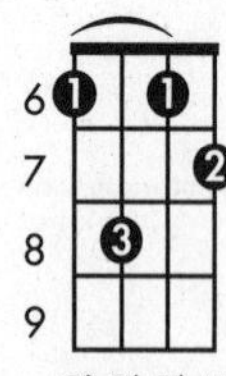

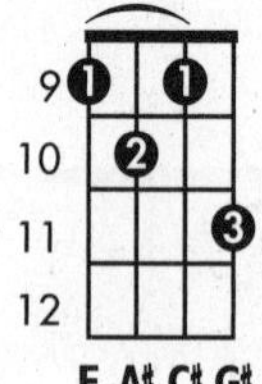

C♯

C♯maj7

C♯ Major Seventh

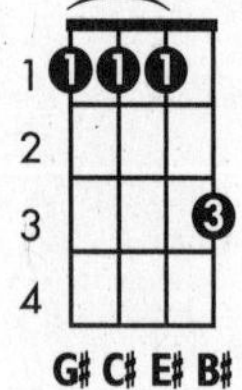

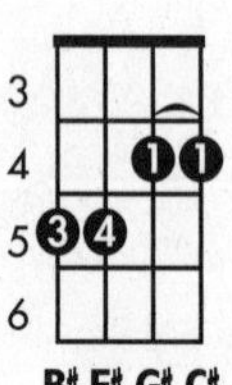

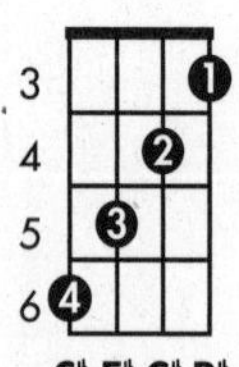

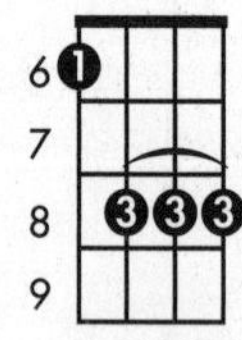

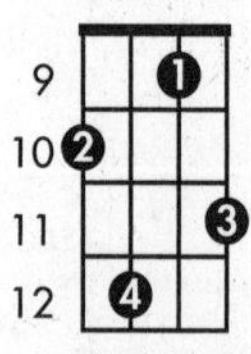

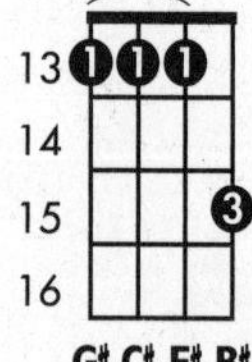

C♯7

C♯ Seventh

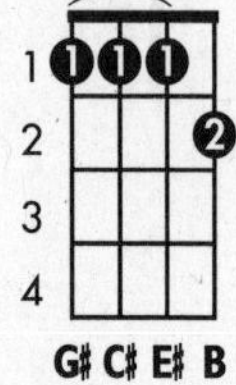

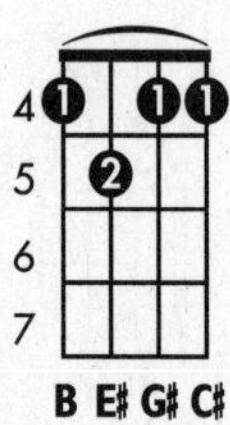

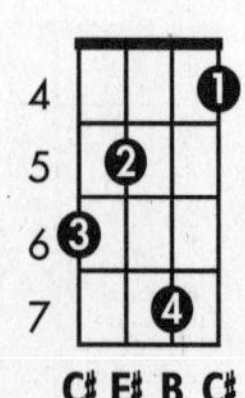

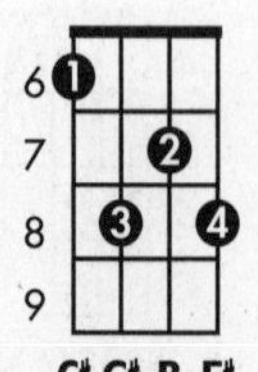

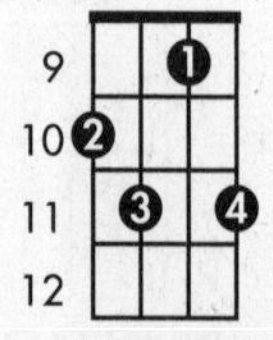

C♯ Minor Seventh

C♯m7

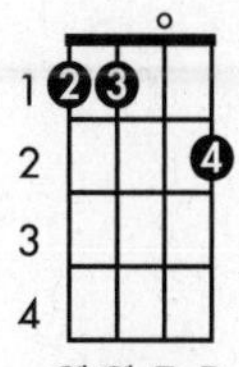
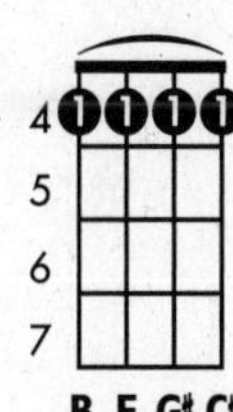

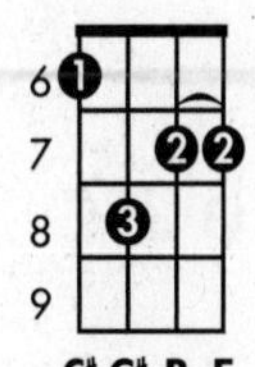
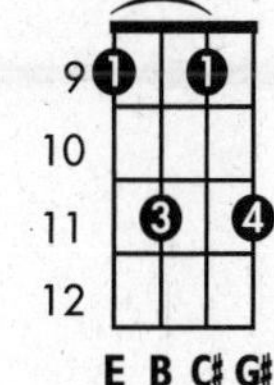

C♯ Minor Seventh Flat Fifth

C♯m7(♭5)

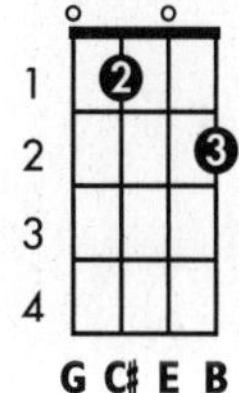
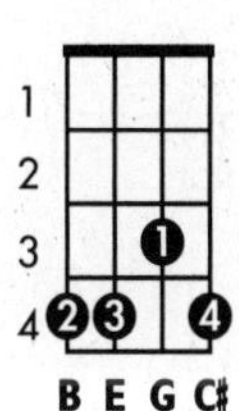
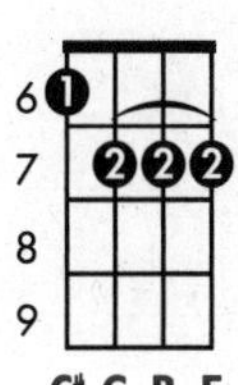
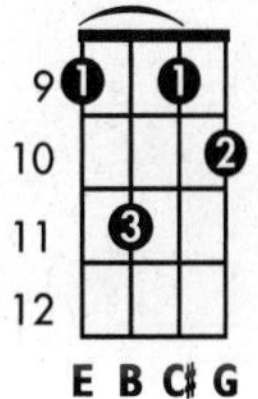

C♯ Diminished Seventh

C♯°7

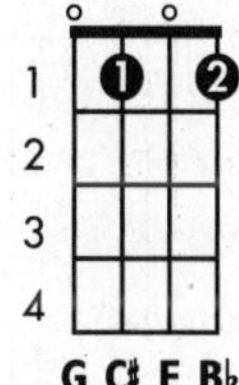
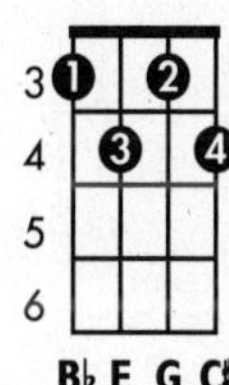
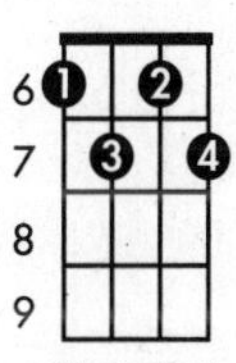
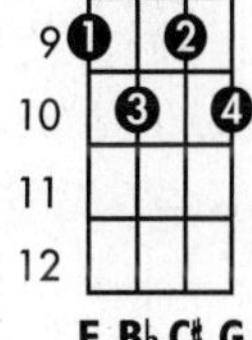
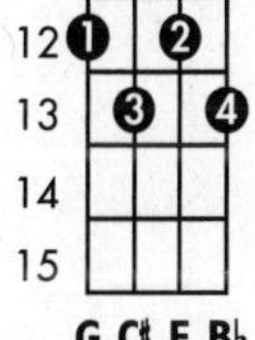

C♯ Seventh Suspended Fourth

C♯7sus

Sometimes written **C♯7sus4**

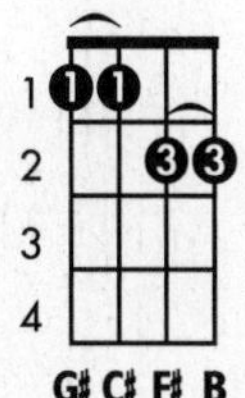

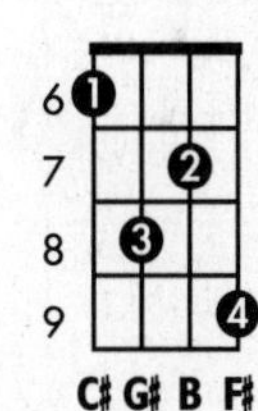
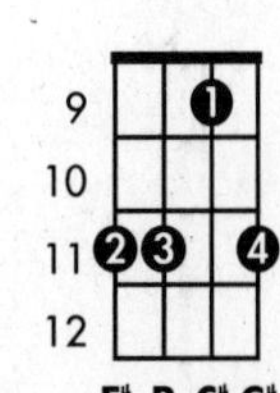

C♯(add9) C♯ Major Add Ninth

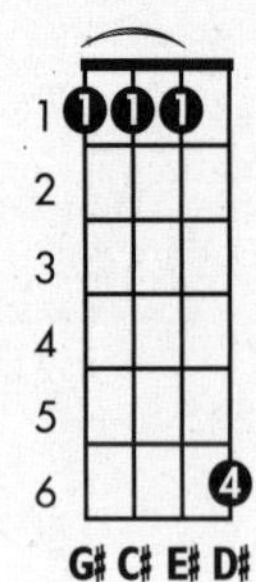
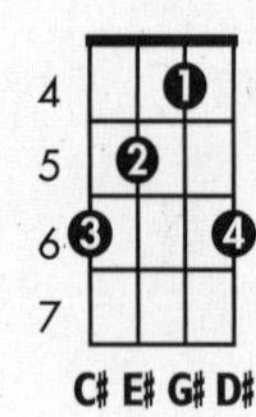
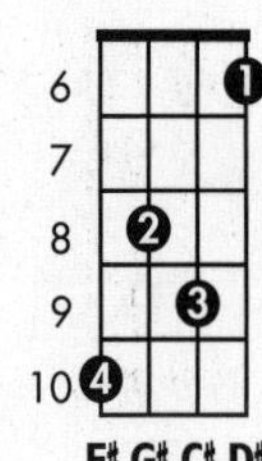
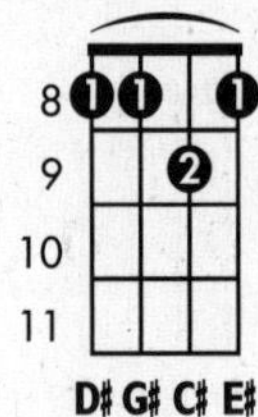

C♯maj9 C♯ Major Ninth

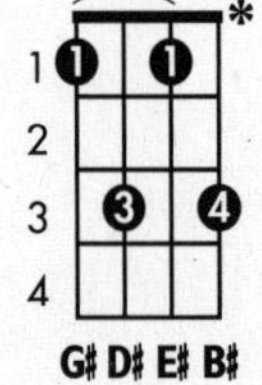
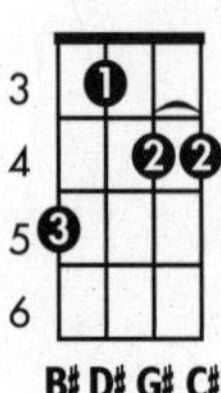
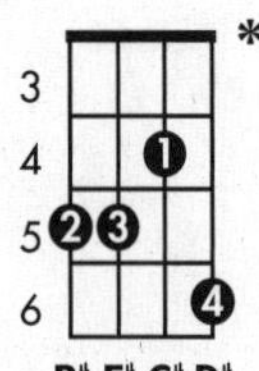
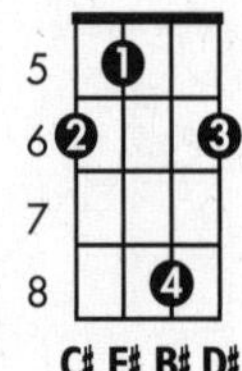

C♯

C♯9 C♯ Ninth

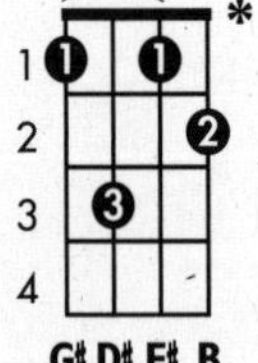
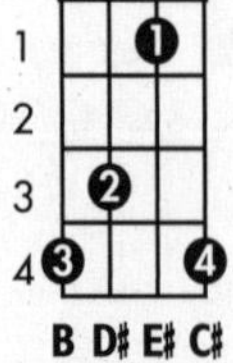
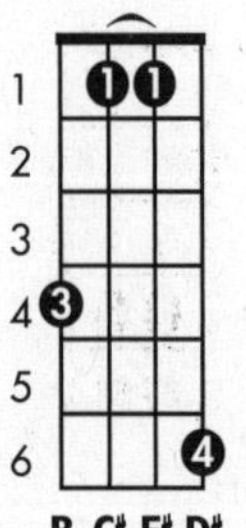
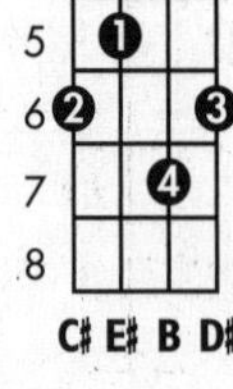

C♯m9 C♯ Minor Ninth

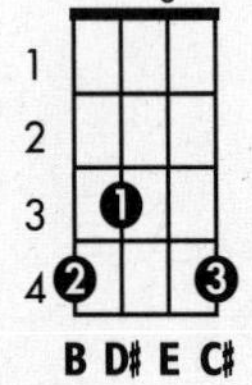
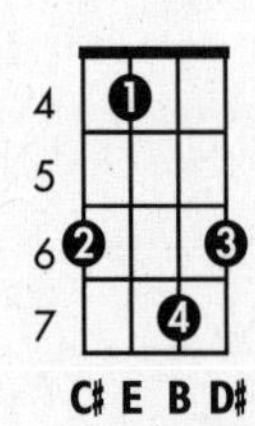
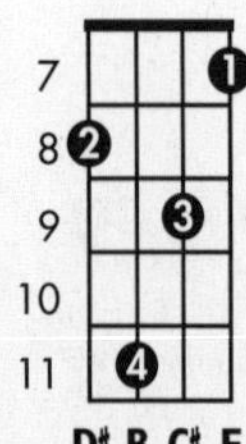

C♯ Sixth Add Ninth

C♯6/9

Sometimes written C♯9/6

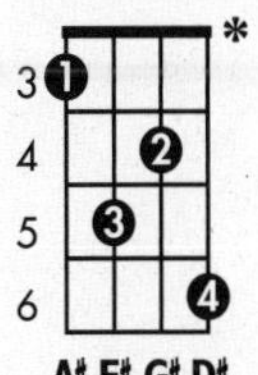

A♯ E♯ G♯ D♯

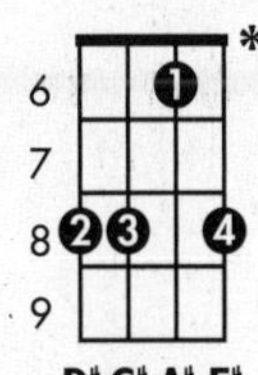

D♯ G♯ A♯ E♯

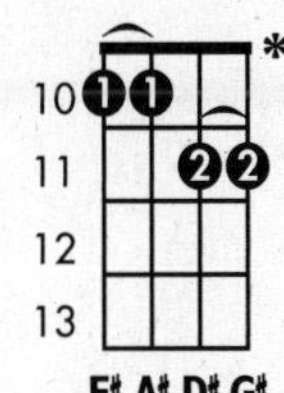

E♯ A♯ D♯ G♯

C♯ Minor Sixth Add Ninth

C♯m6/9

Sometimes written C♯m9/6

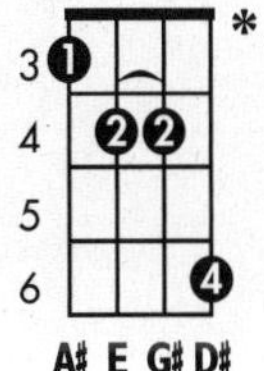

A♯ E G♯ D♯

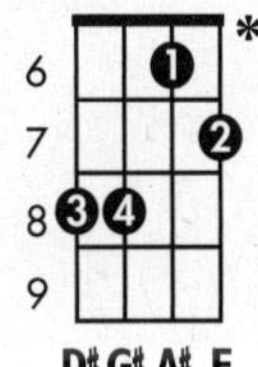

D♯ G♯ A♯ E

C♯ Minor Major Seventh

C♯m(maj7)

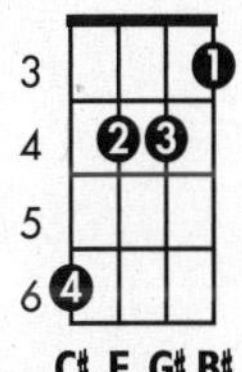

C♯ E G♯ B♯

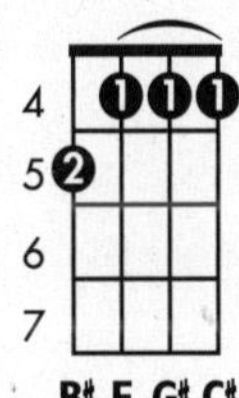

B♯ E G♯ C♯

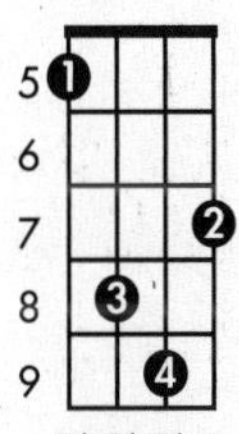

B♯ G♯ C♯ E

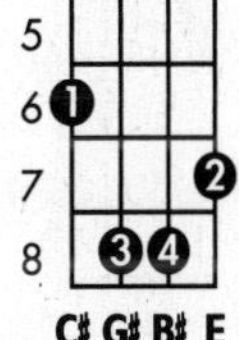

C♯ G♯ B♯ E

C♯ Minor Ninth Major Seventh

C♯m9(maj7)

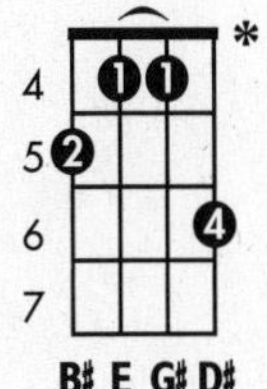

B♯ E G♯ D♯

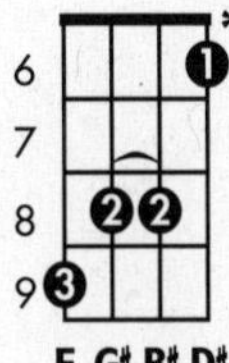

E G♯ B♯ D♯

C♯11 — C♯ Eleventh

C♯m11 — C♯ Minor Eleventh

C♯13 — C♯ Thirteenth

C♯(♭5) — C♯ Flat Fifth

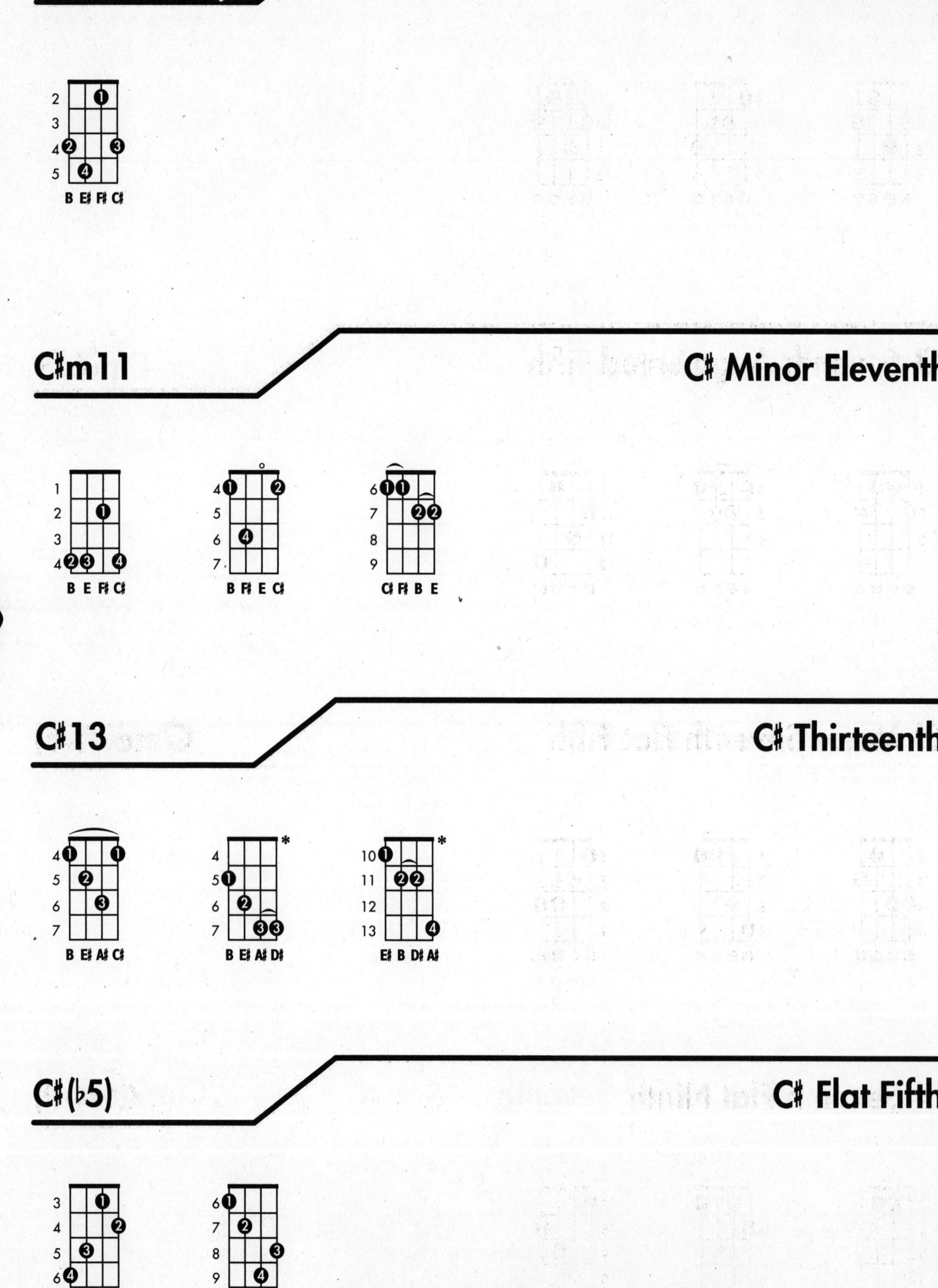

C♯ Seventh Flat Fifth

C♯7(♭5)

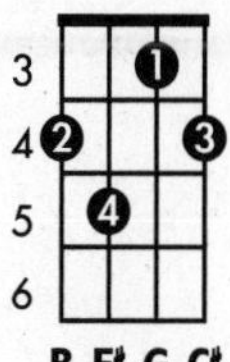

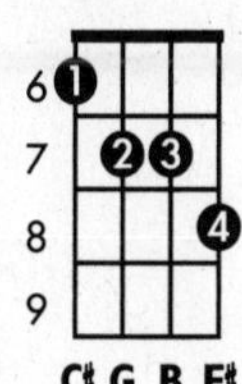

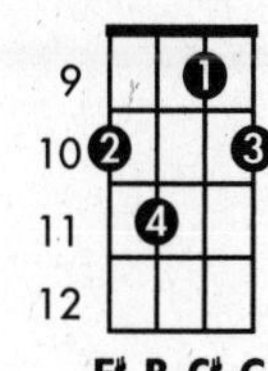

C♯ Seventh Augmented Fifth

C♯7+

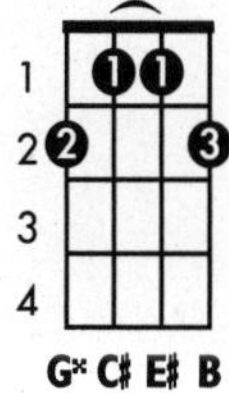

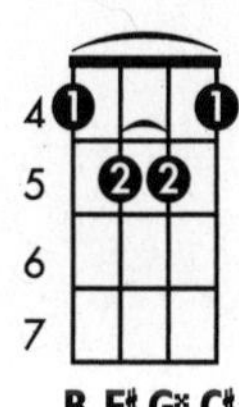

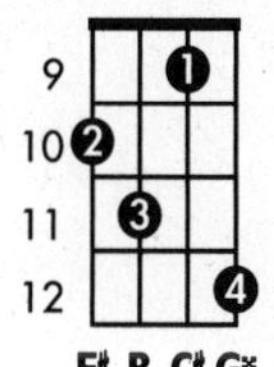

C♯ Major Seventh Flat Fifth

C♯maj7(♭5)

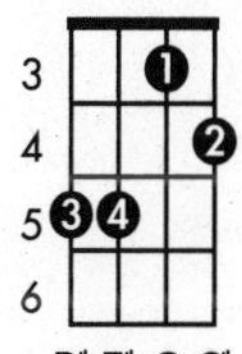

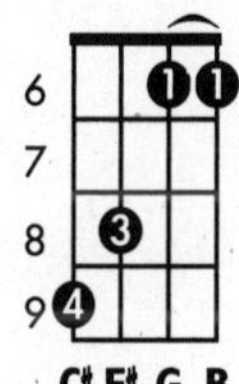

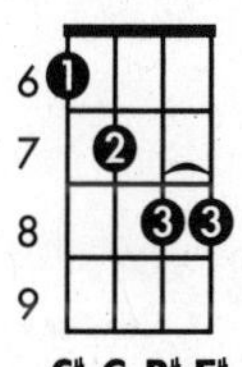

C♯ Seventh Flat Ninth

C♯7(♭9)

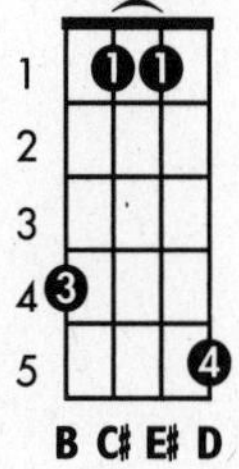

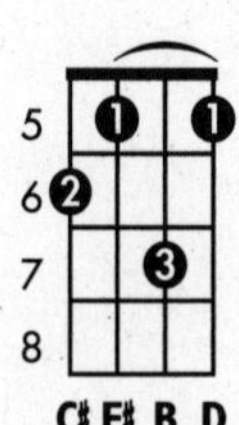

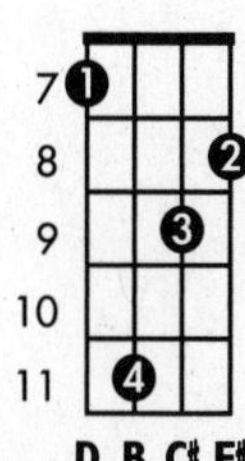

C♯7(♯9) — C♯ Seventh Sharp Ninth

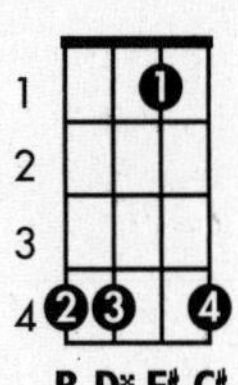

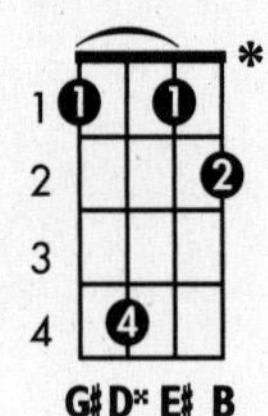

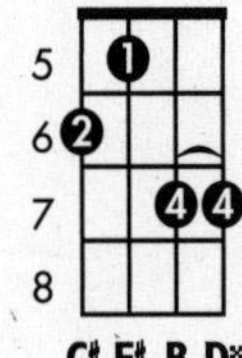

C♯7+(♭9) — C♯ Seventh Flat Ninth Augmented Fifth

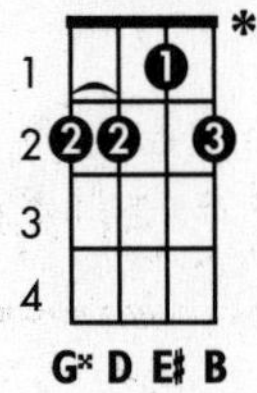

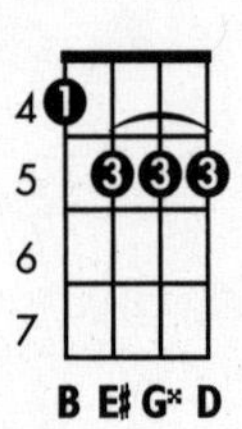

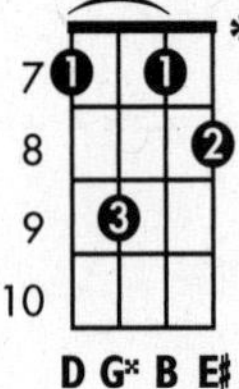

C♯9+ — C♯ Ninth Augmented Fifth

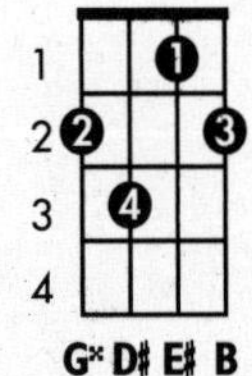

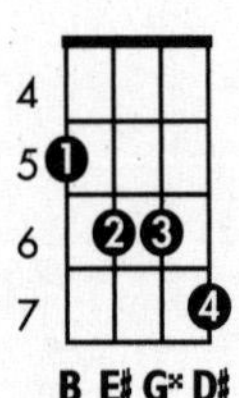

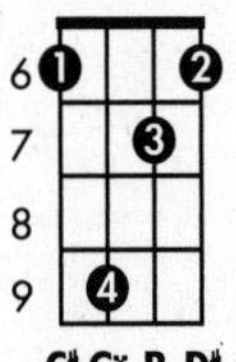

C♯9(♭5) — C♯ Ninth Flat Fifth

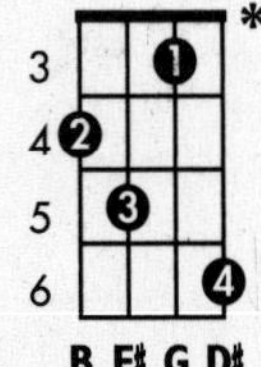

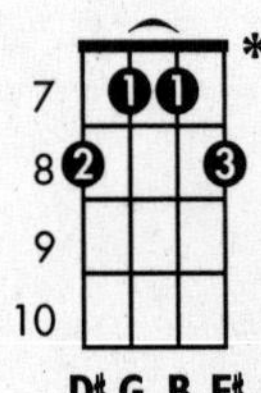

C♯ Ninth Augmented Eleventh

C♯9(♯11)

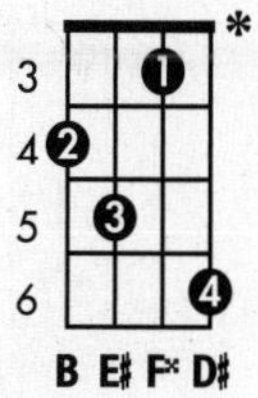
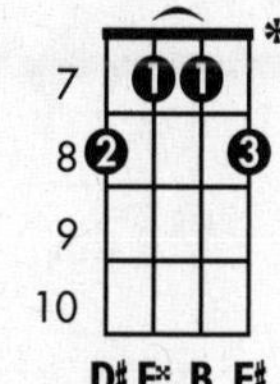

C♯ Thirteenth Flat Ninth

C♯13(♭9)

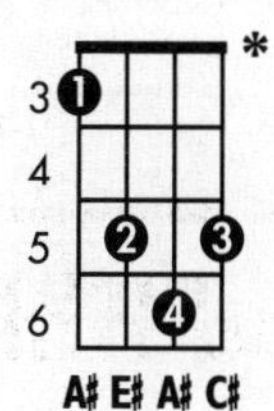
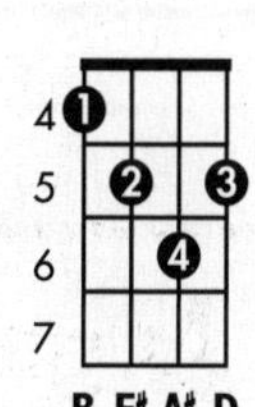
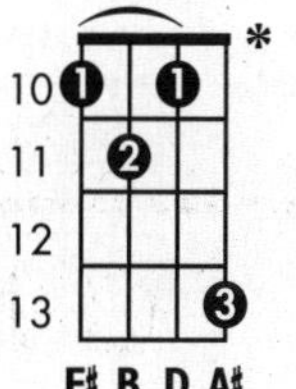

C♯ Thirteenth Flat Ninth Flat Fifth

C♯13(♭9/♭5)

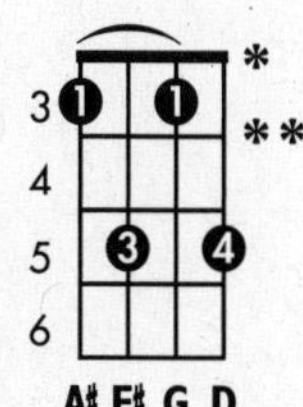

D — D Major

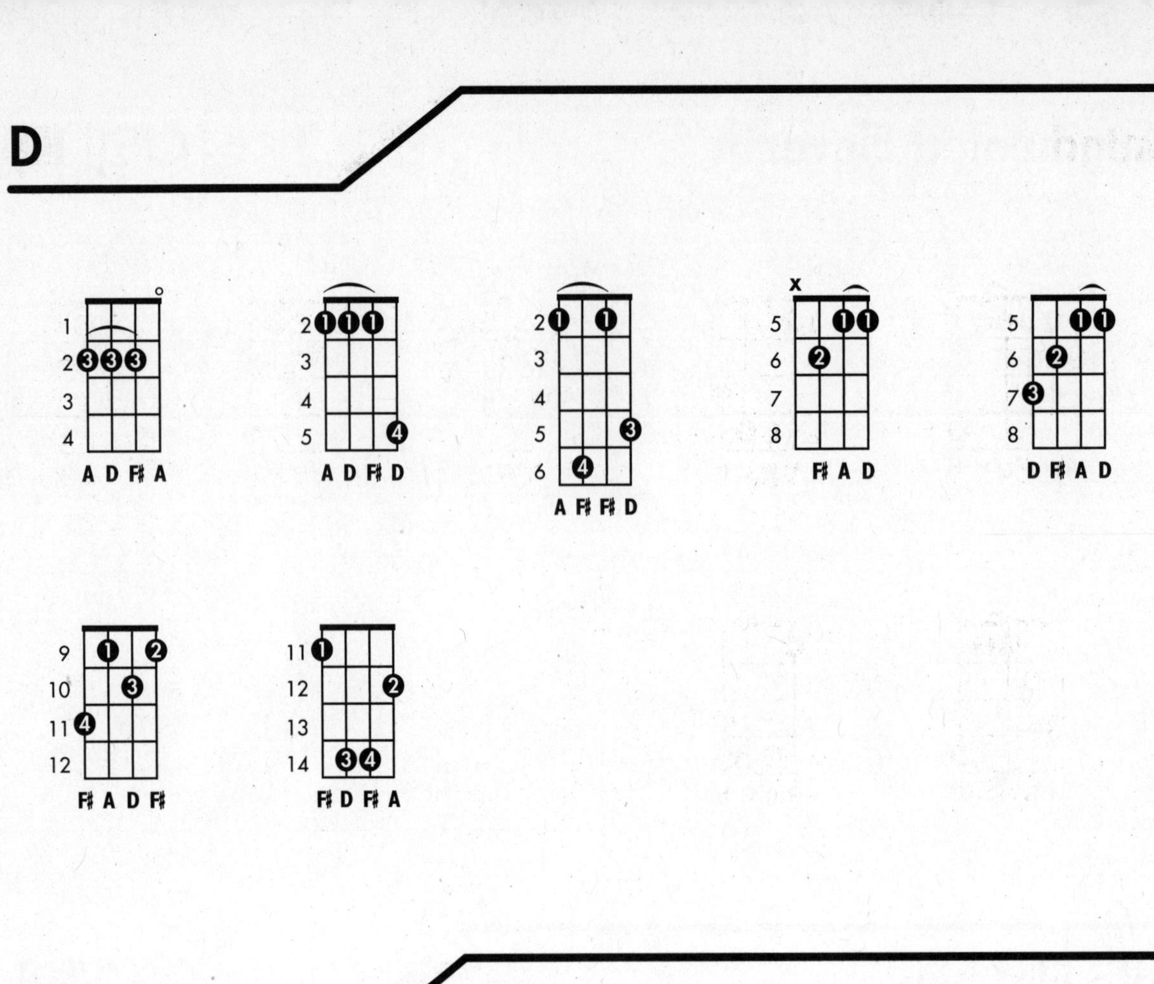

Dm — D Minor

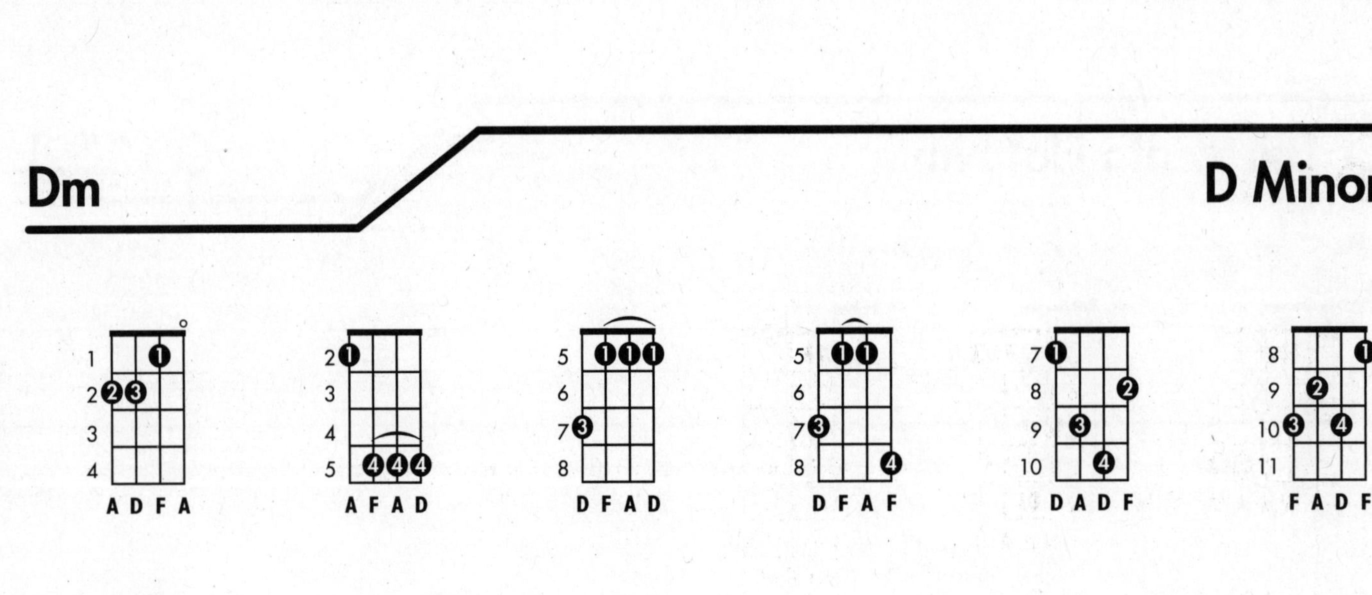

D° — D Diminished

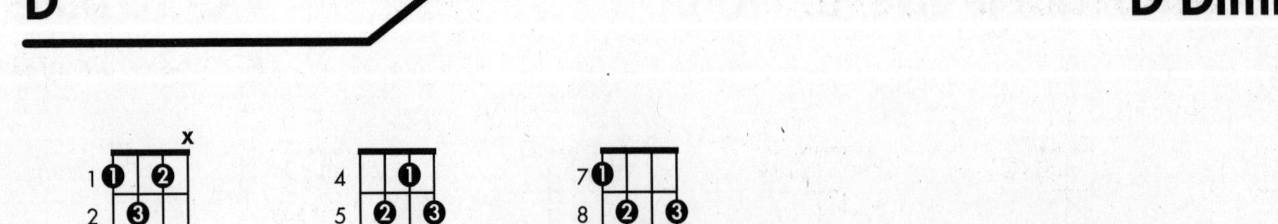

D

D Augmented

D+

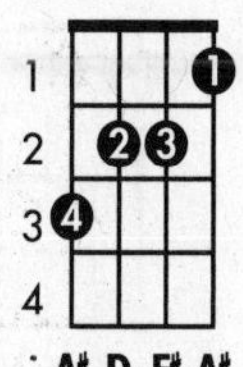
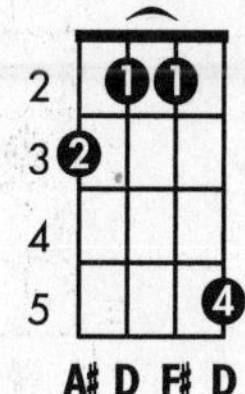
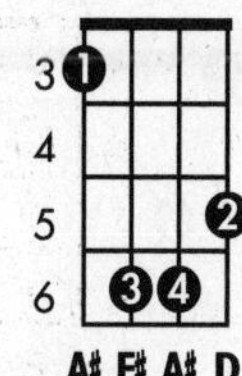
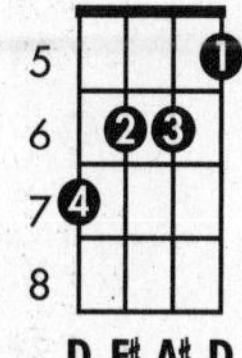
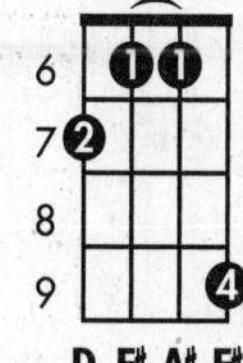
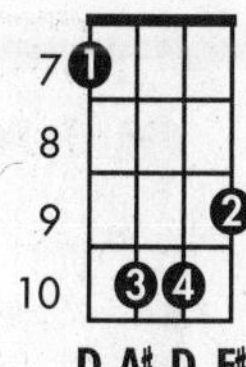
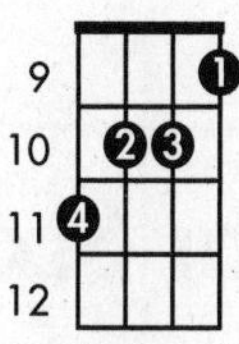
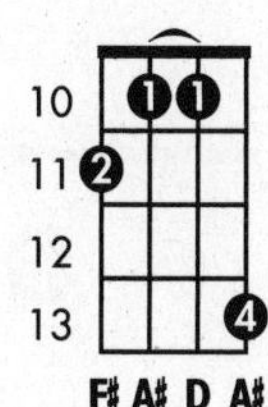
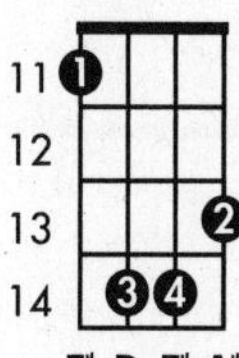

D Fifth

D5

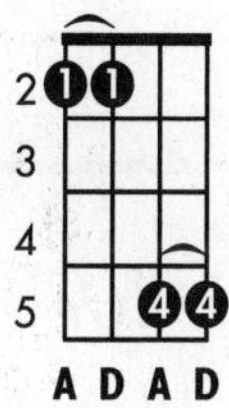
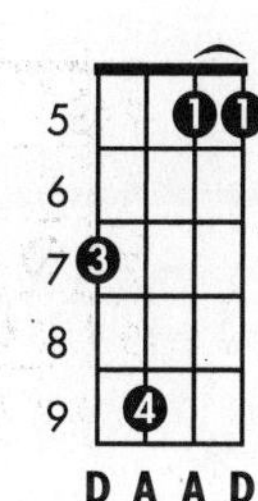
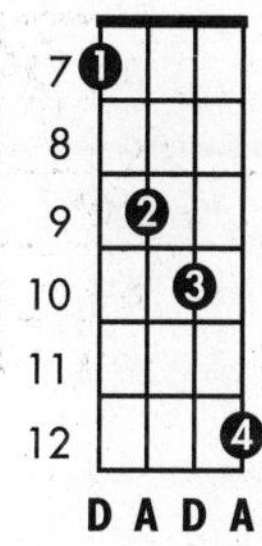

D Major Suspended Fourth

Dsus

Sometimes written **Dsus4**

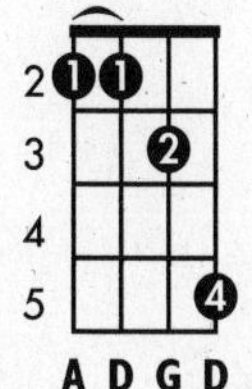
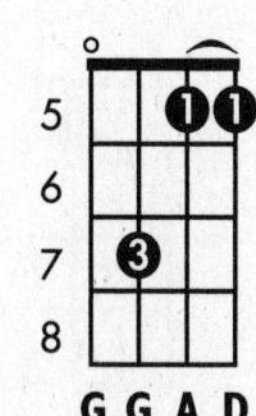
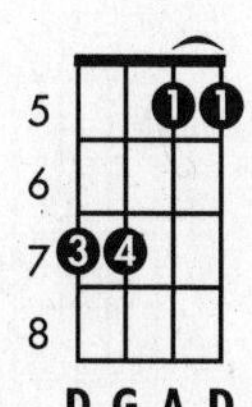

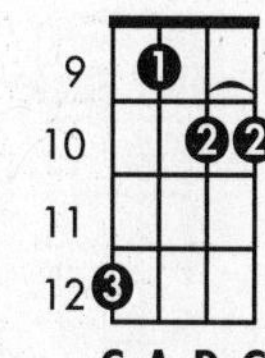

D6

D Major 6th

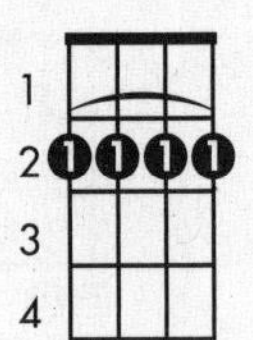
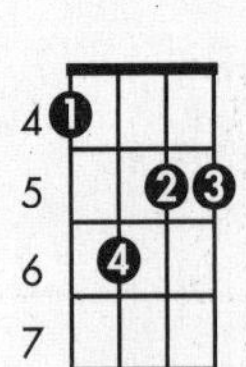
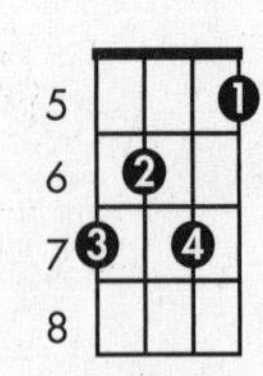
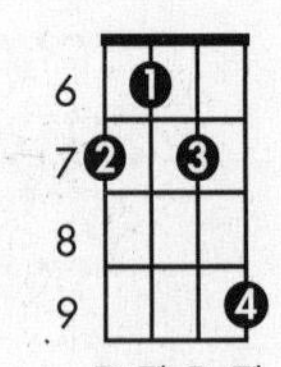
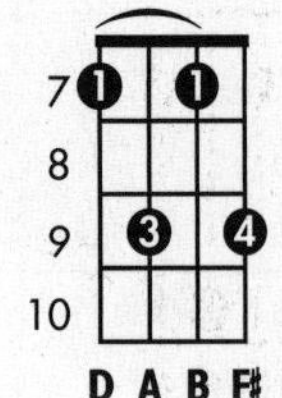
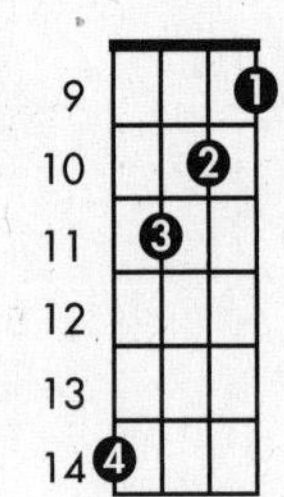
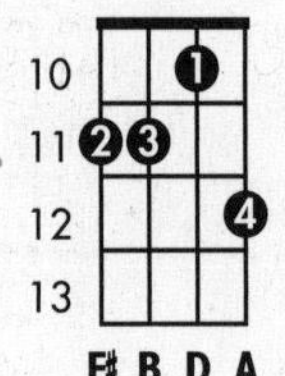
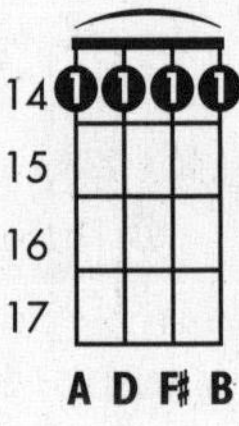

Dm6

D Minor Sixth

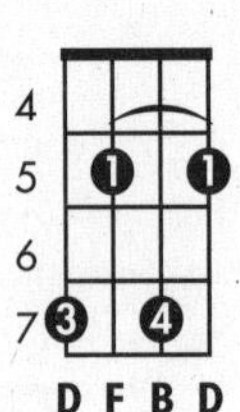
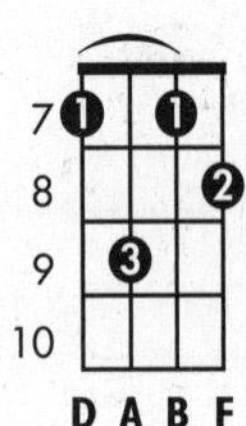
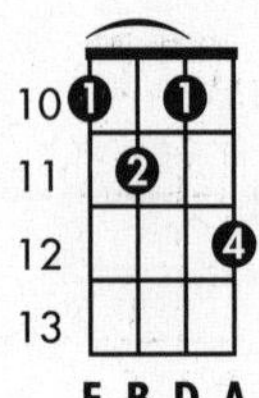

Dmaj7

D Major Seventh

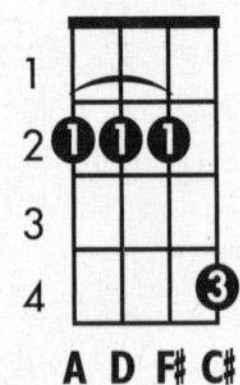
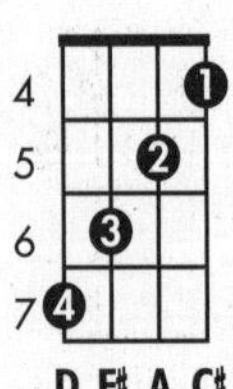
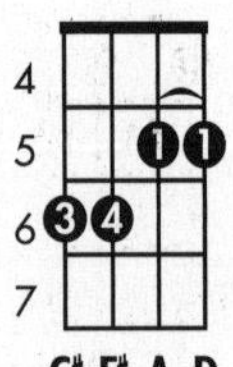
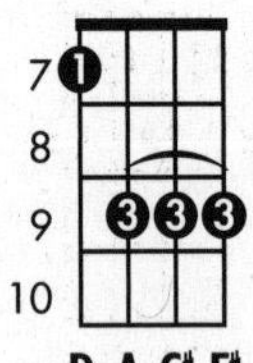
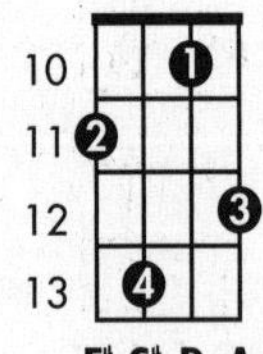
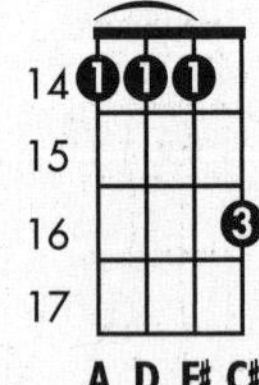

D7

D Seventh

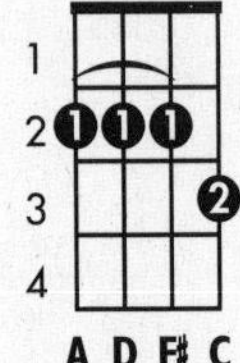
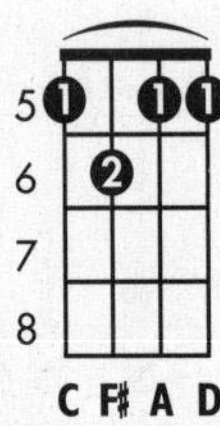
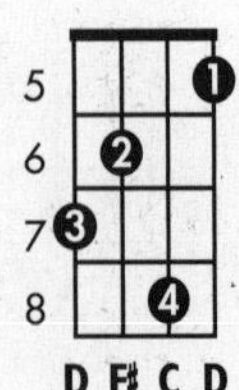
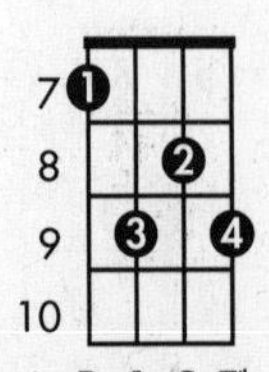
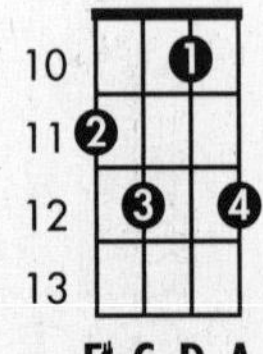

D Minor Seventh

Dm7

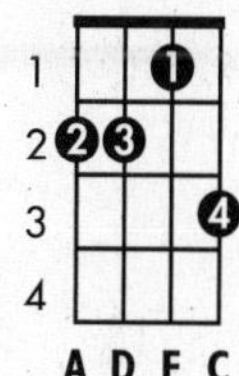

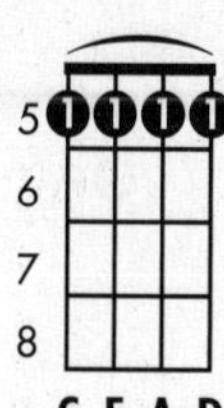

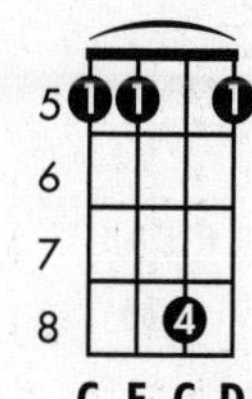

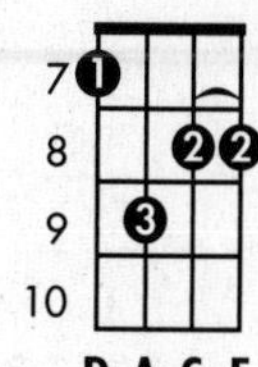

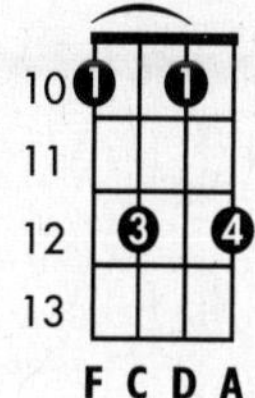

D Minor Seventh Flat Fifth

Dm7(♭5)

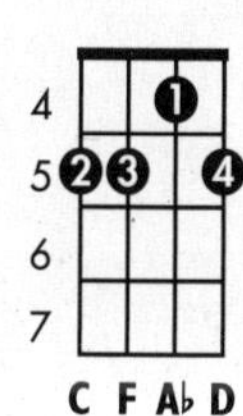

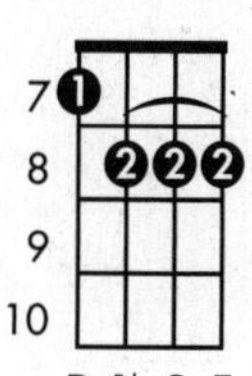

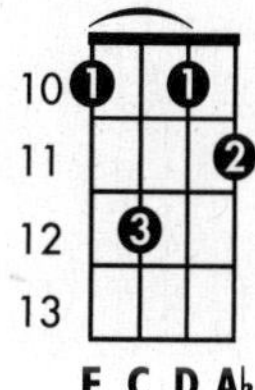

D Diminished Seventh

D°7

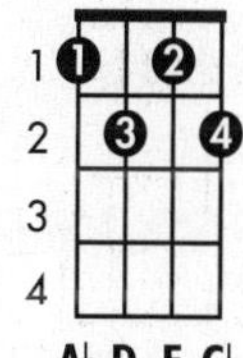

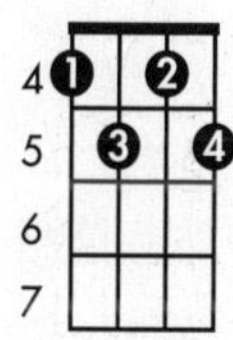

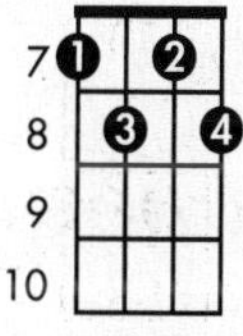

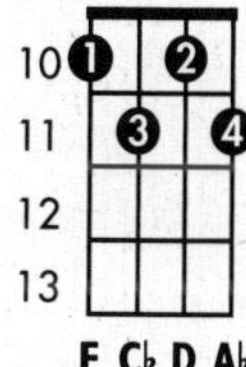

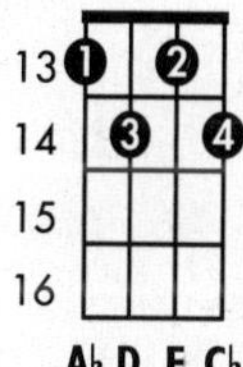

D Seventh Suspended Fourth

D7sus

Sometimes written **D7sus4**

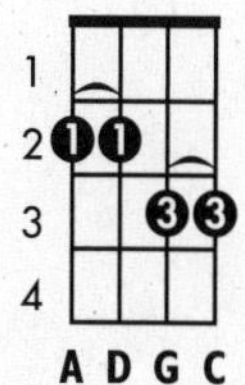

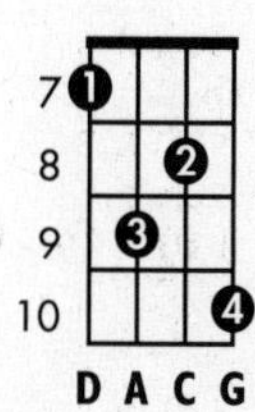

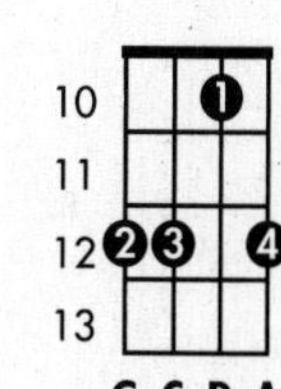

D(add9)

D Major Add Ninth

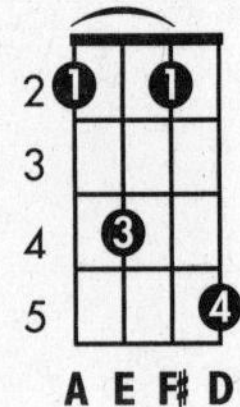

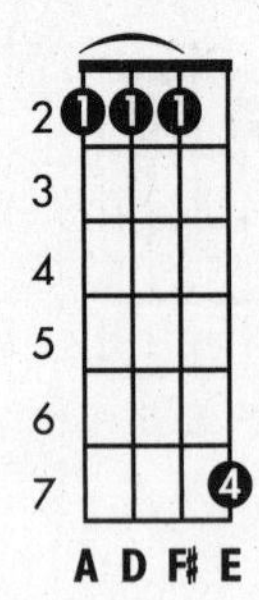

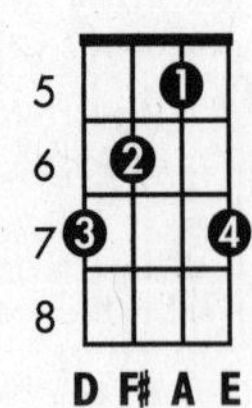

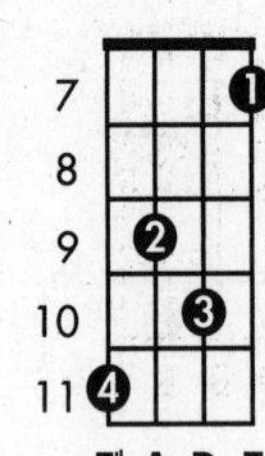

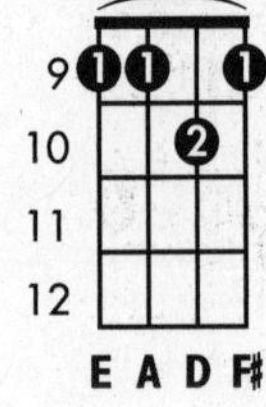

Dmaj9

D Major Ninth

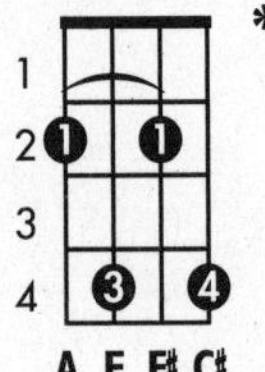

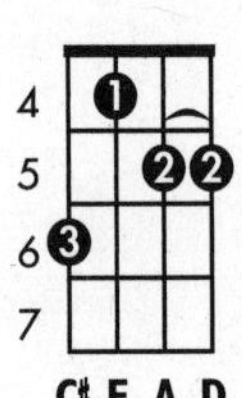

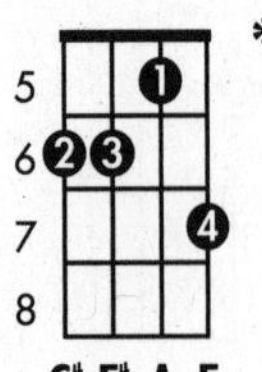

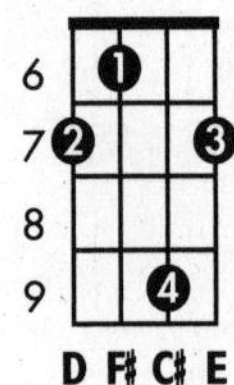

D

D9

D Ninth

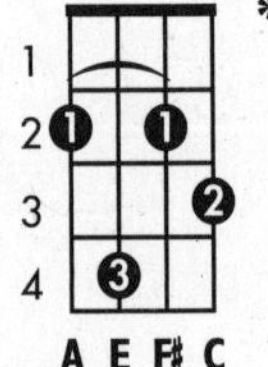

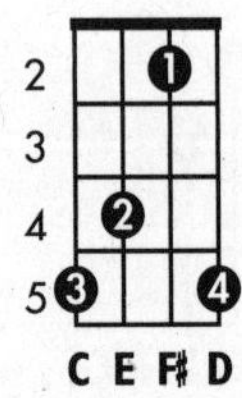

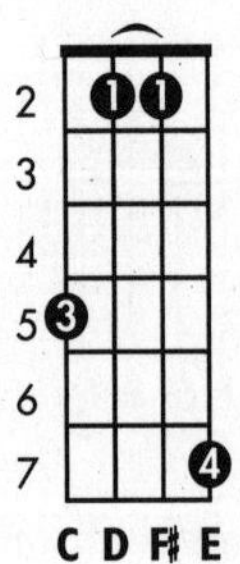

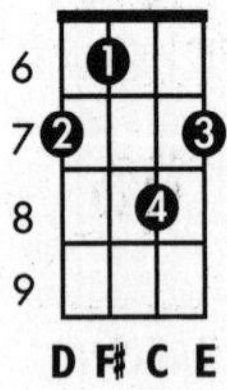

Dm9

D Minor Ninth

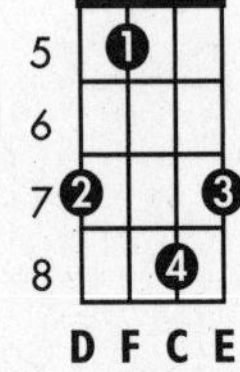

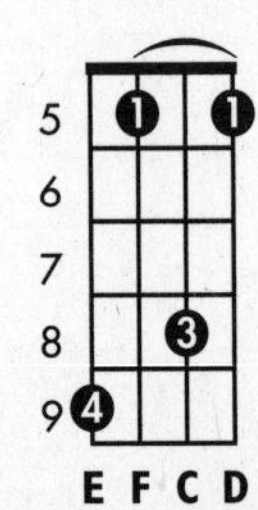

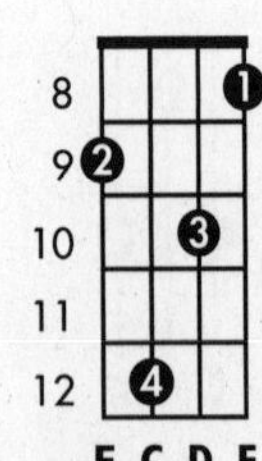

D Sixth Add Ninth

D6/9

Sometimes written **D$^{9/6}$**

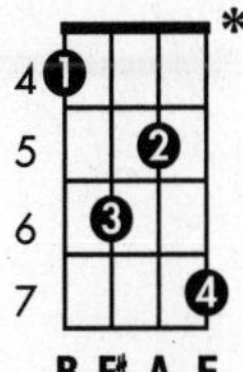
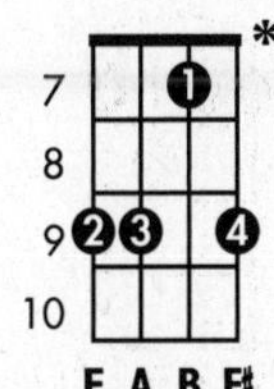
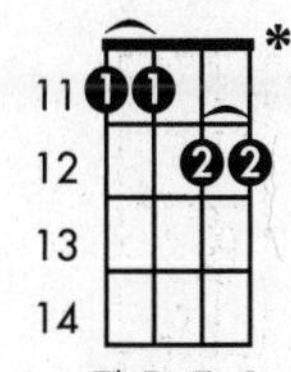

D Minor Sixth Add Ninth

Dm6/9

Sometimes written **Dm$^{9/6}$**

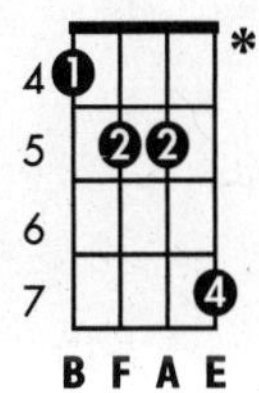
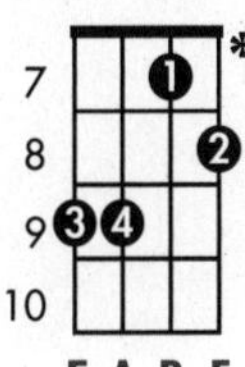

D Minor Major Seventh

Dm(maj7)

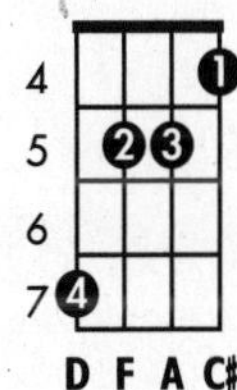
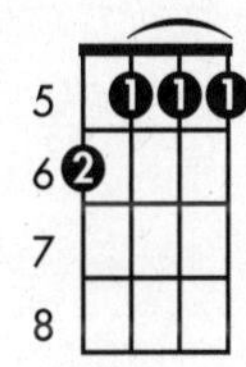
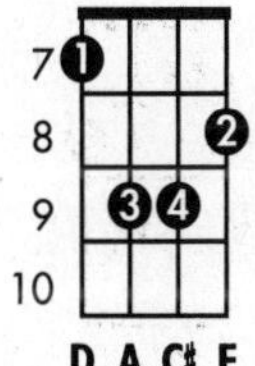

D Minor Ninth Major Seventh

Dm9(maj7)

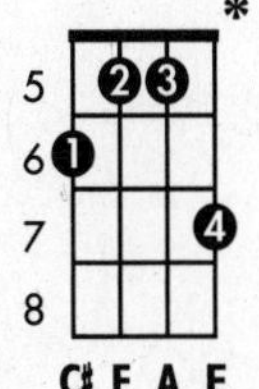
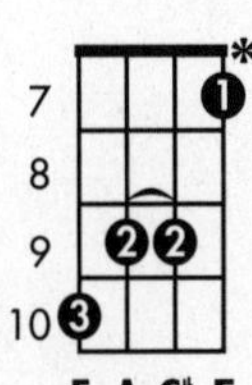

D11 — D Eleventh

Dm11 — D Minor Eleventh

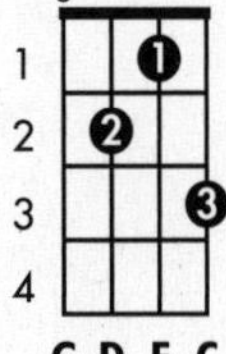
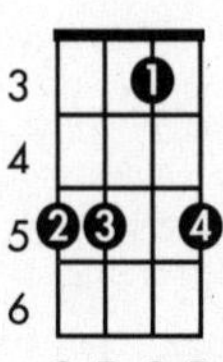
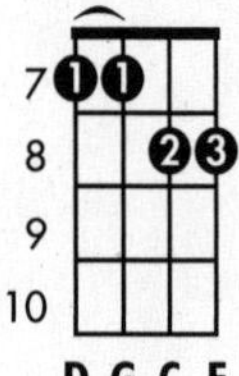

D

D13 — D Thirteenth

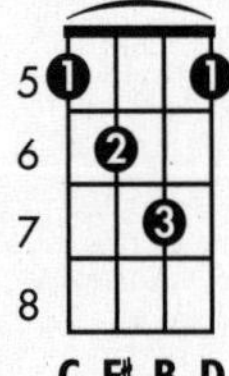
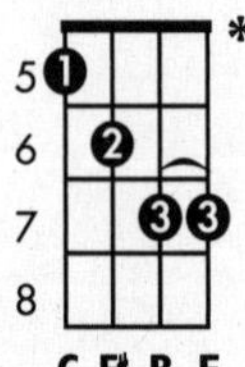
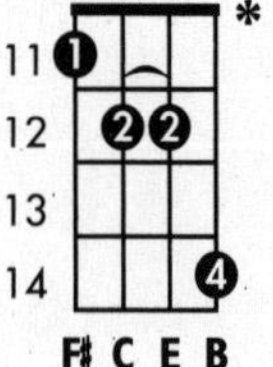

D(♭5) — D Flat Fifth

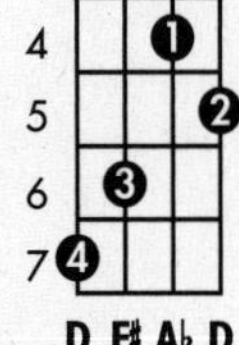
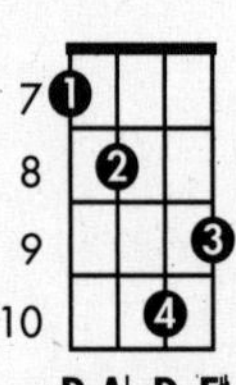

D Seventh Flat Fifth

D7(♭5)

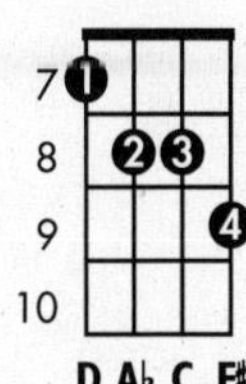

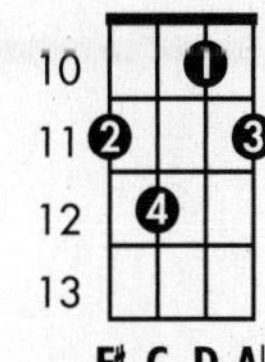

D Seventh Augmented Fifth

D7+

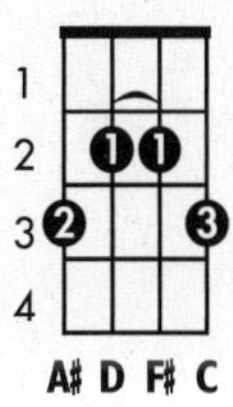

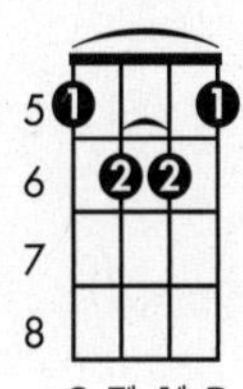

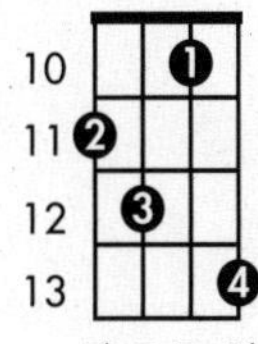

D Major Seventh Flat Fifth

Dmaj7(♭5)

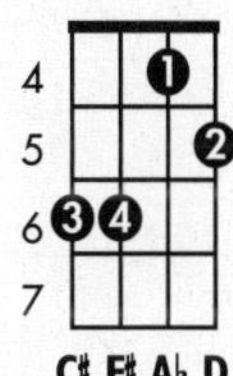

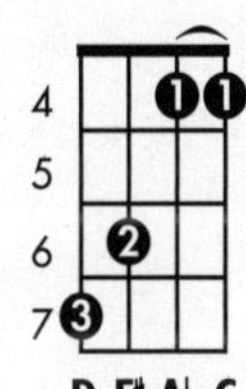

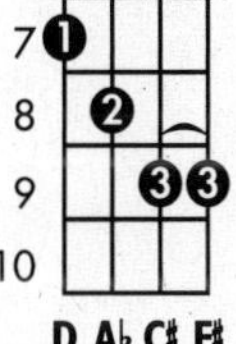

D Seventh Flat Ninth

D7(♭9)

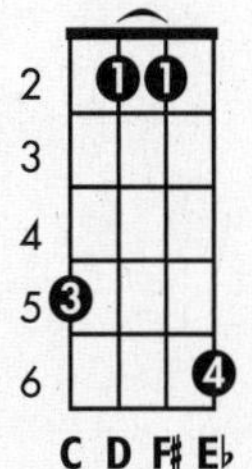

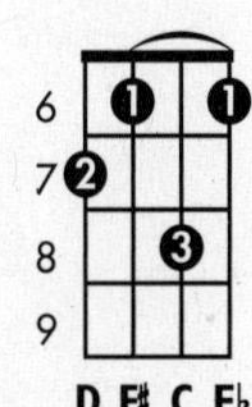

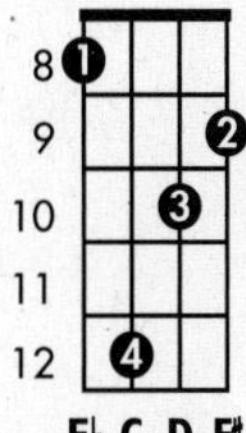

D7(♯9) D Seventh Sharp Ninth

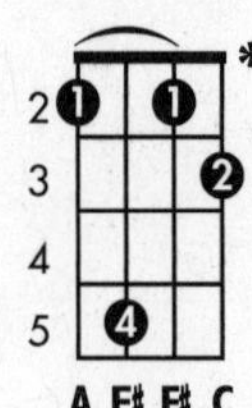

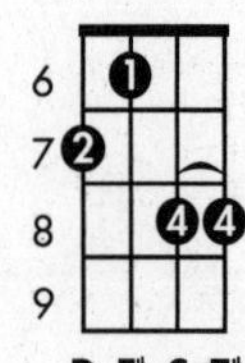

D7+(♭9) D Seventh Flat Ninth Augmented Fifth

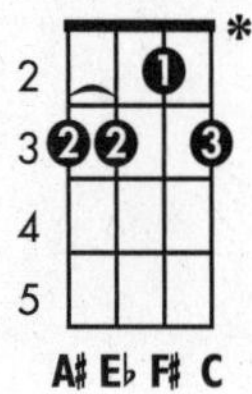

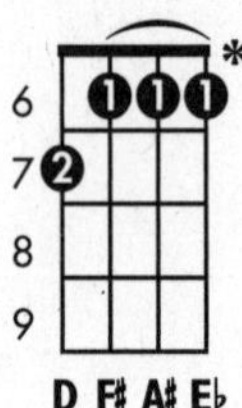

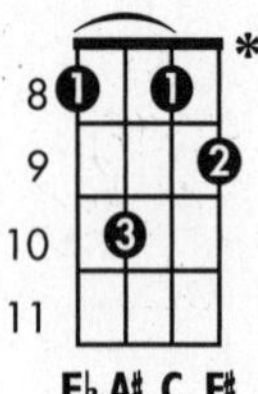

D9+ D Ninth Augmented Fifth

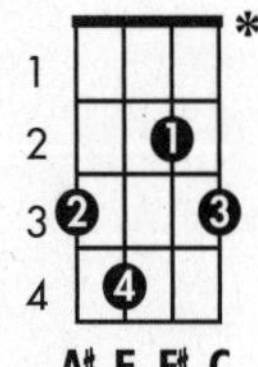

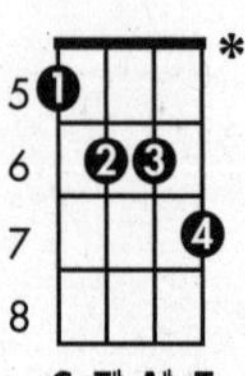

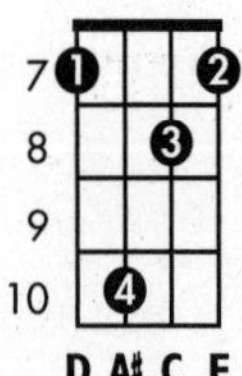

D9(♭5) D Ninth Flat Fifth

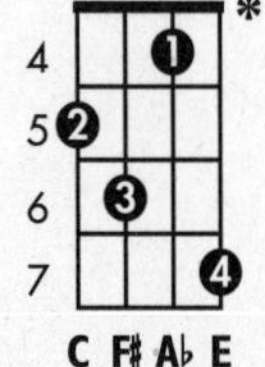

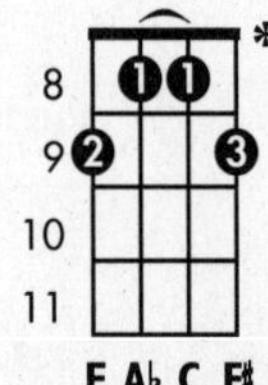

D Ninth Sharp Eleventh

D9(♯11)

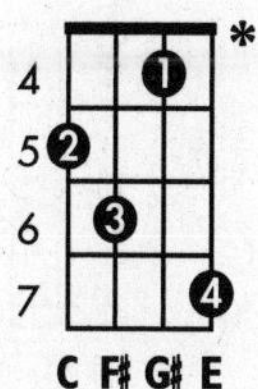

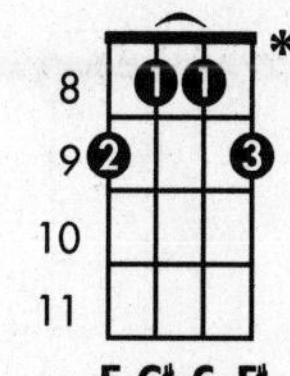

D Thirteenth Flat Ninth

D13(♭9)

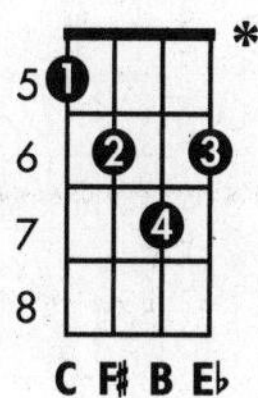

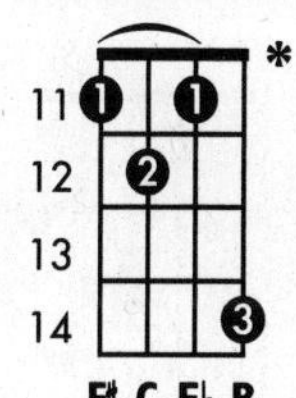

D Thirteenth Flat Ninth Flat Fifth

D13(♭9 ♭5)

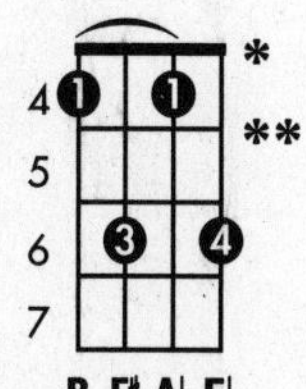

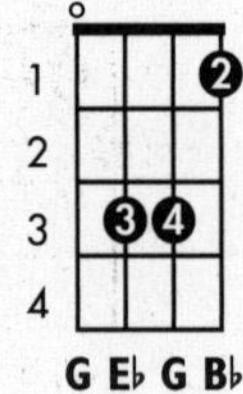

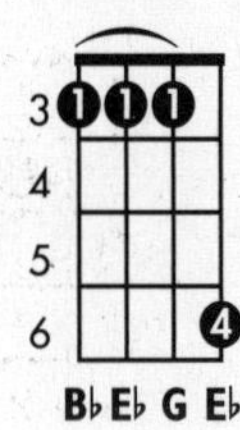

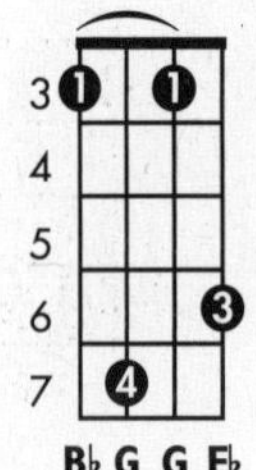

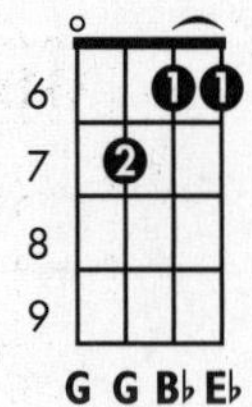

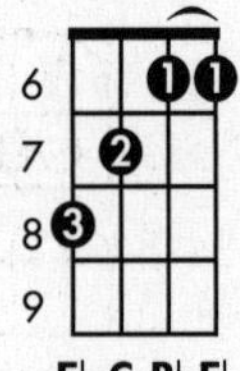

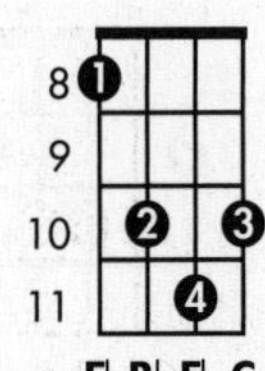

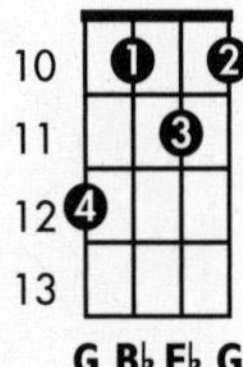

E♭m

E♭ Minor

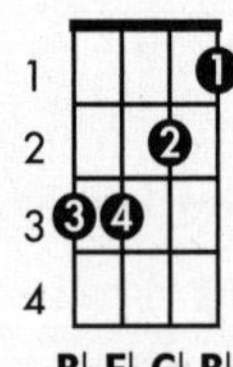

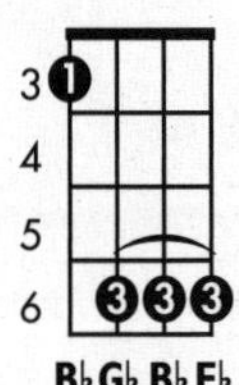

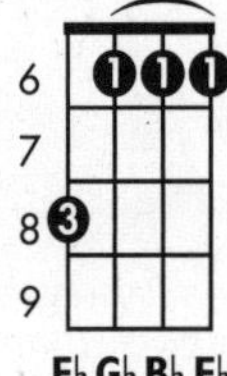

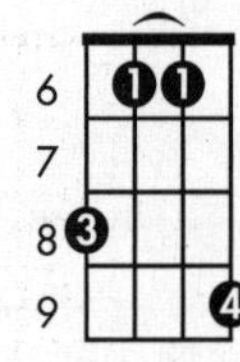

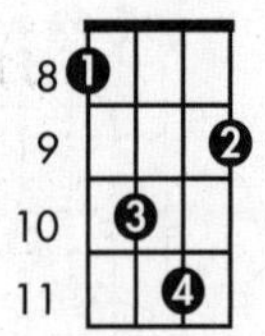

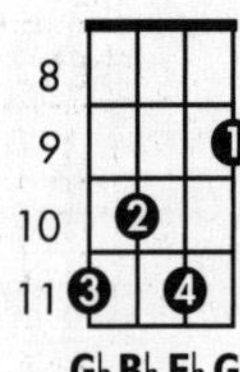

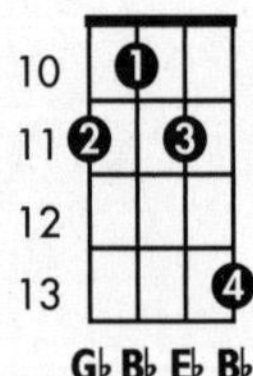

E♭°

E♭ Diminished

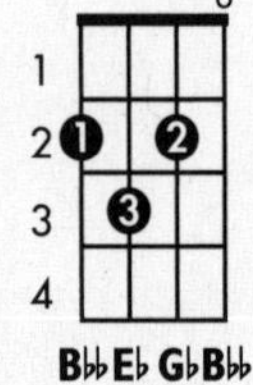

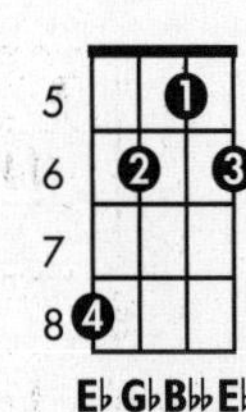

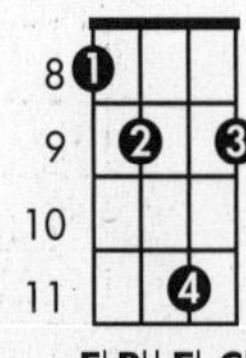

E♭ Augmented

E♭+

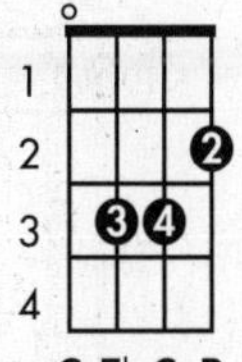
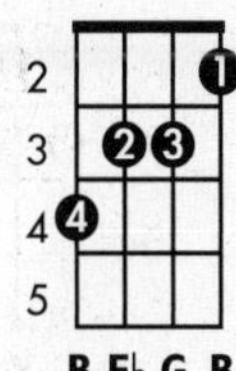
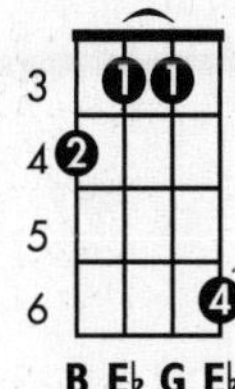
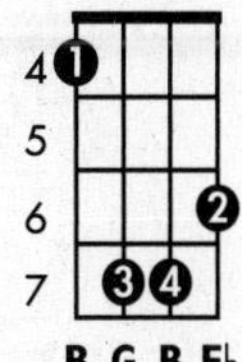
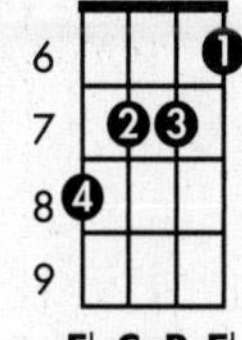
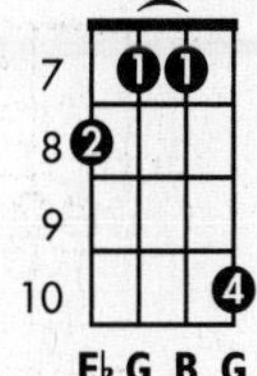
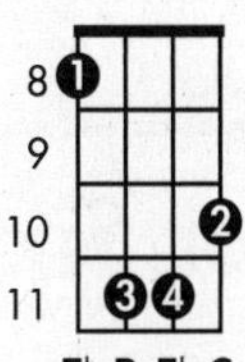
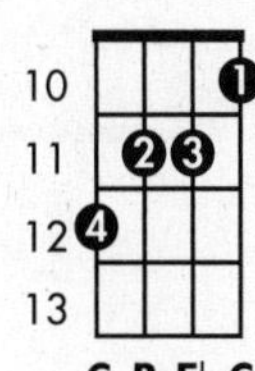
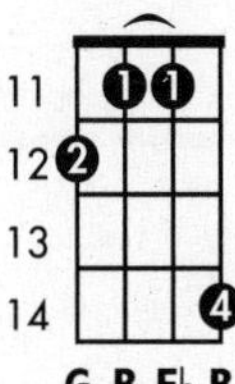

E♭ Fifth

E♭5

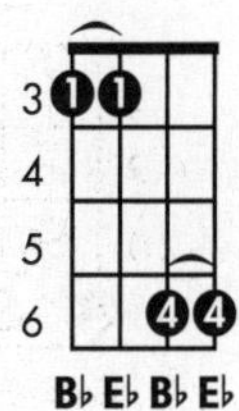
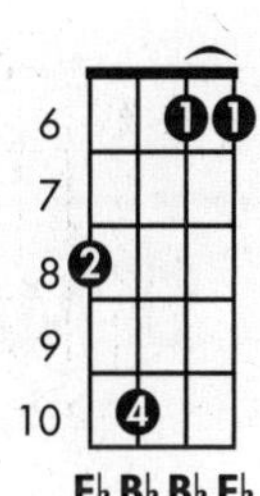
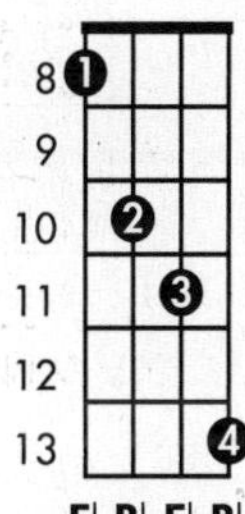

E♭ Major Suspended Fourth

E♭sus

Sometimes written **E♭sus4**

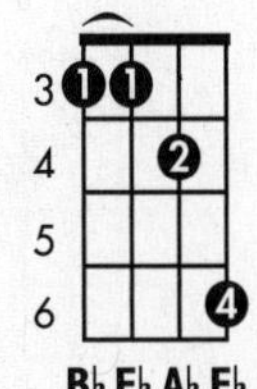
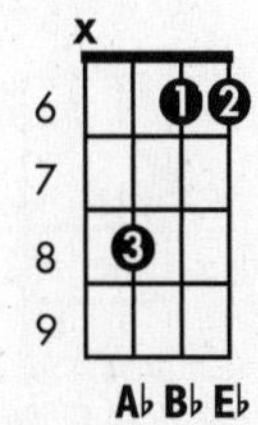
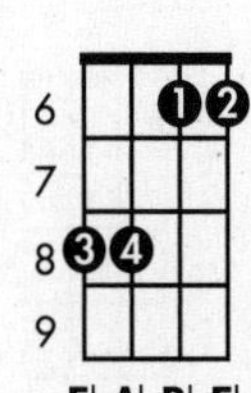
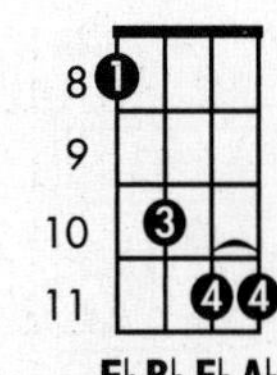
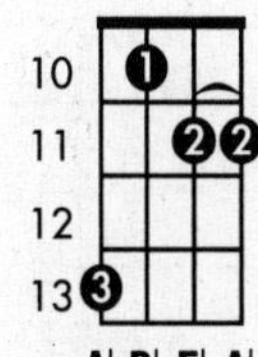

E♭6 — E♭ Major 6th

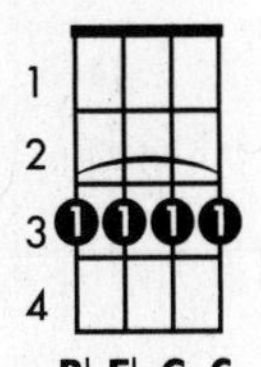

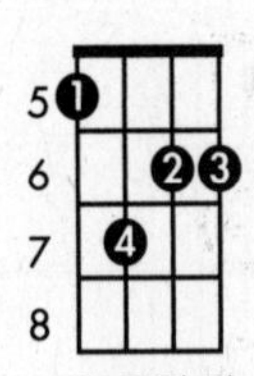

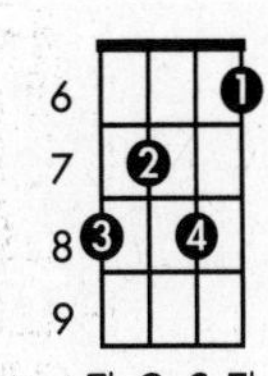

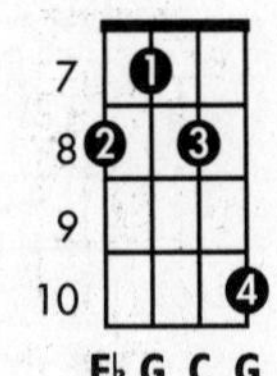

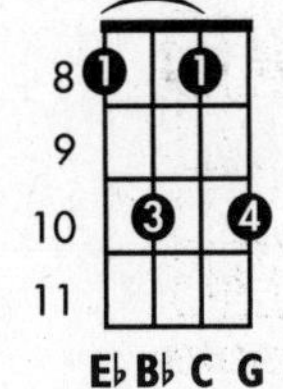

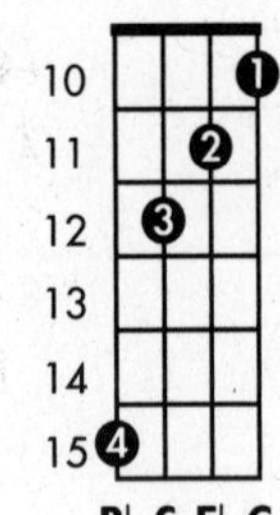

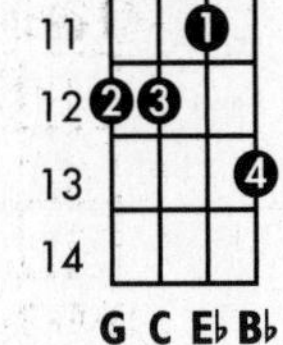

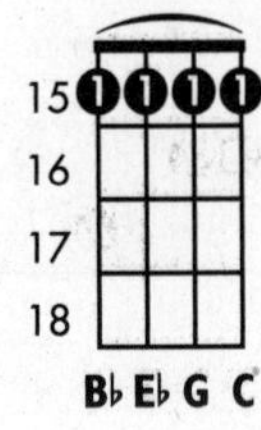

E♭m6 — E♭ Minor Sixth

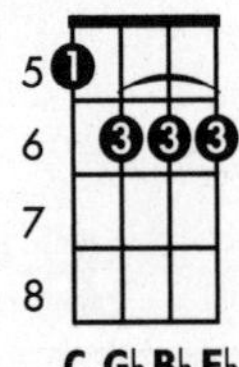

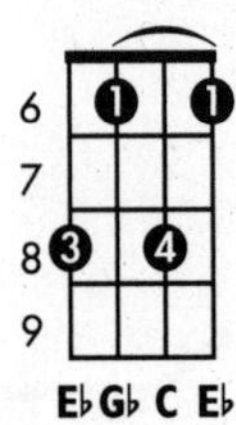

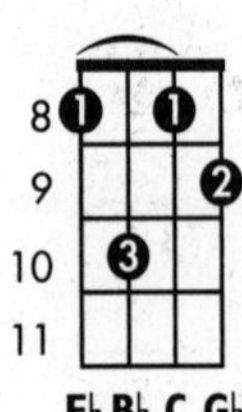

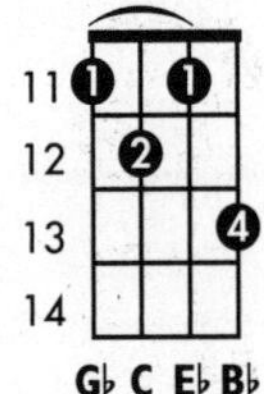

E♭maj7 — E♭ Major Seventh

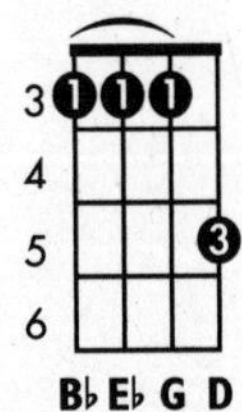

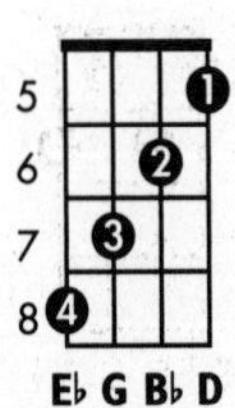

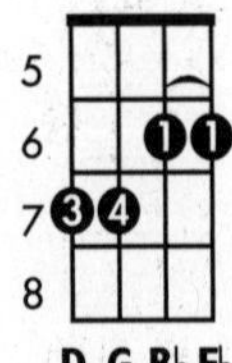

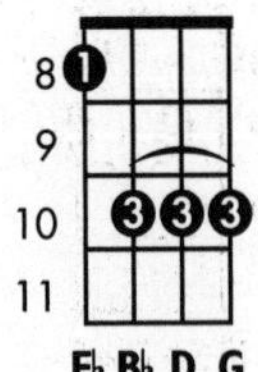

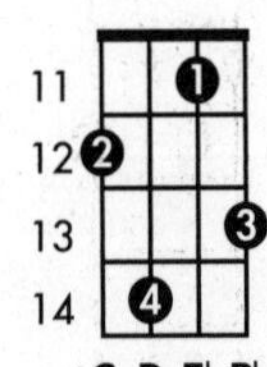

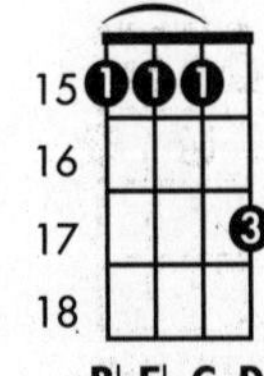

E♭

E♭7 — E♭ Seventh

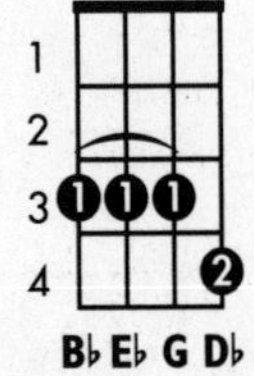

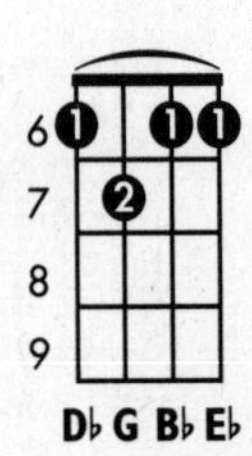

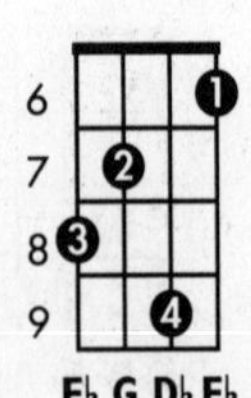

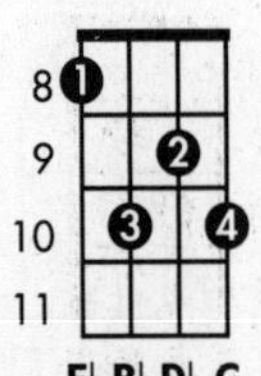

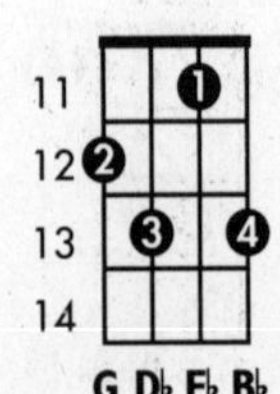

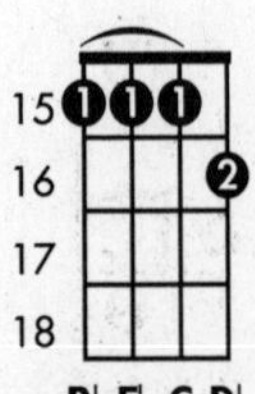

E♭ Minor Seventh

E♭m7

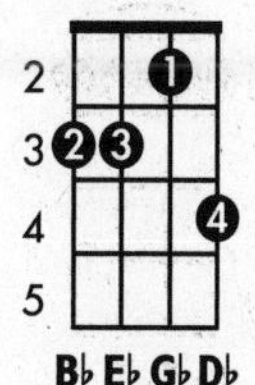

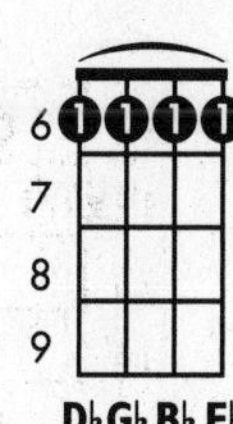

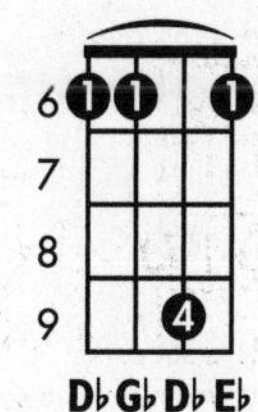

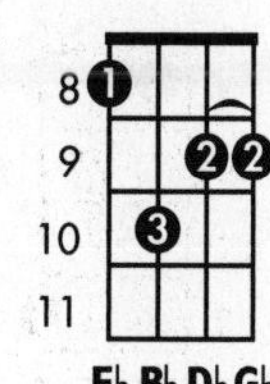

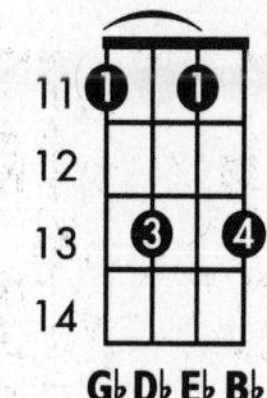

E♭ Minor Seventh Flat Fifth

E♭m7(♭5)

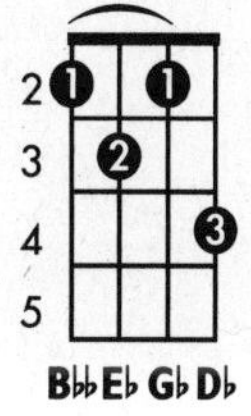

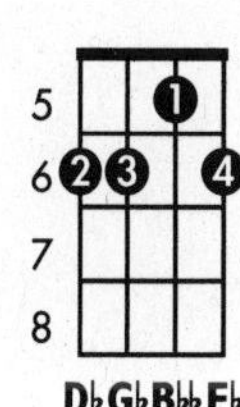

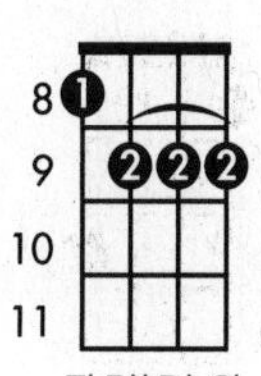

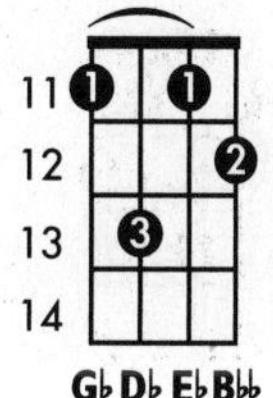

E♭ Diminished Seventh

E♭°7

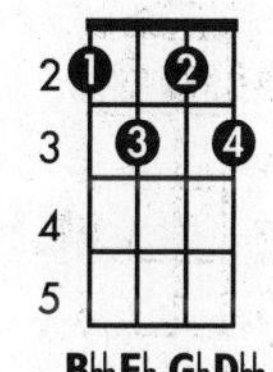

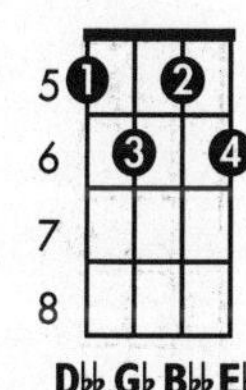

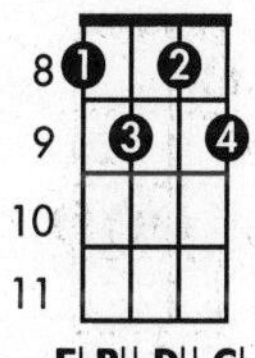

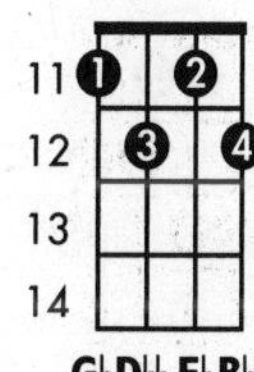

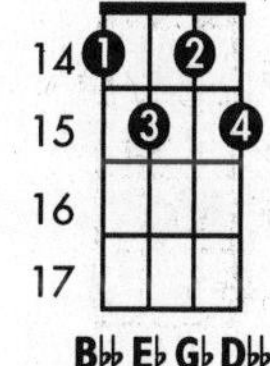

E♭ Seventh Suspended Fourth

E♭7sus

Sometimes written **E♭7sus4**

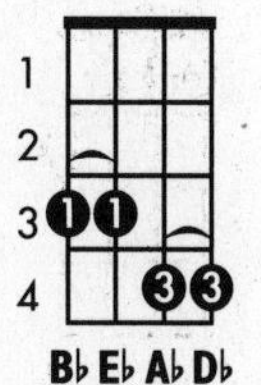

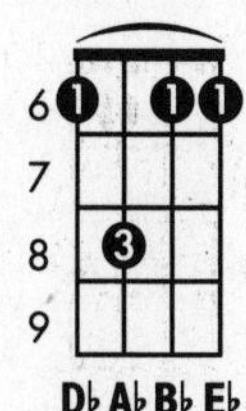

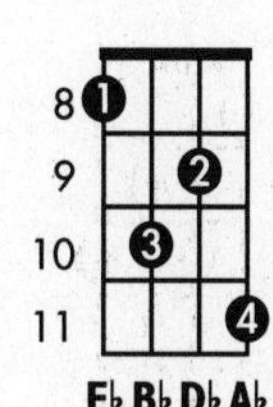

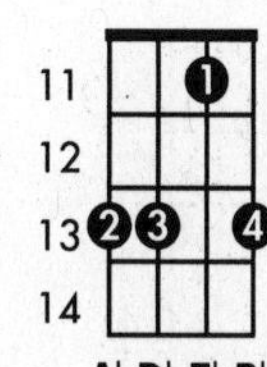

E♭

E♭(add9) — E♭ Major Add Ninth

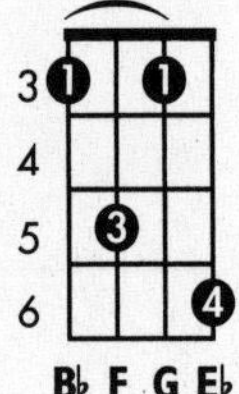
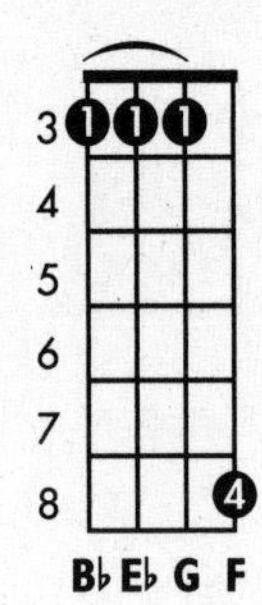
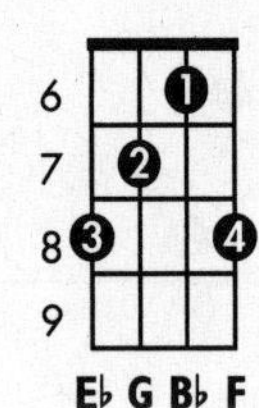
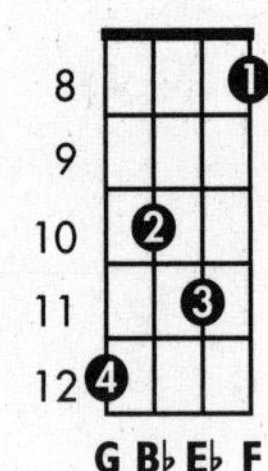
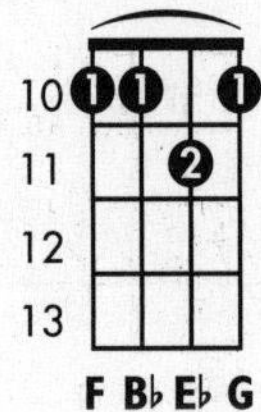

E♭maj9 — E♭ Major Ninth

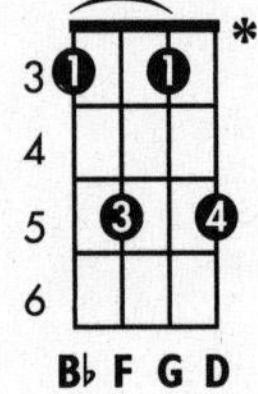
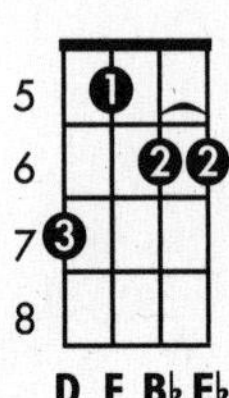
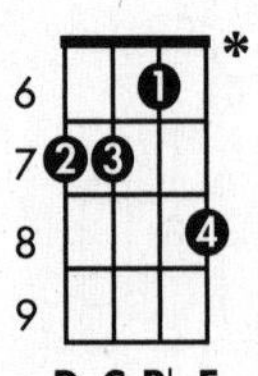
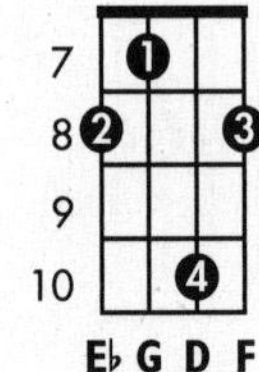

E♭9 — E♭ Ninth

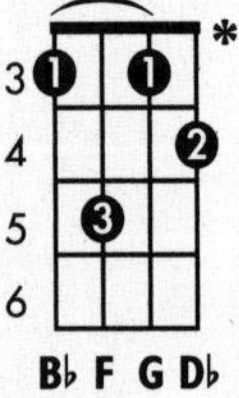
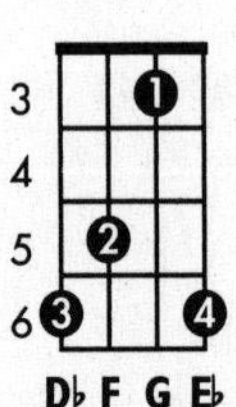
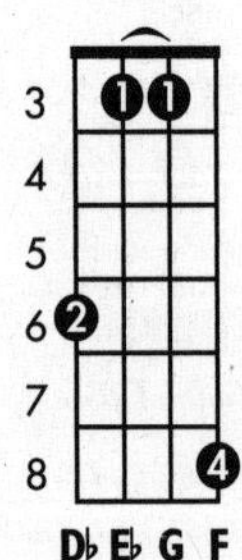
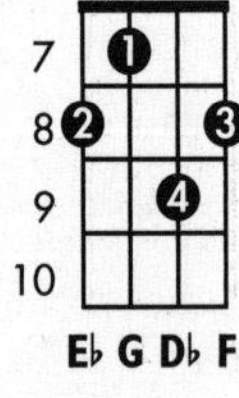

E♭m9 — E♭ Minor Ninth

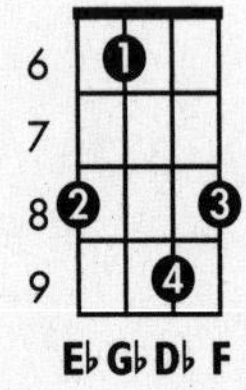
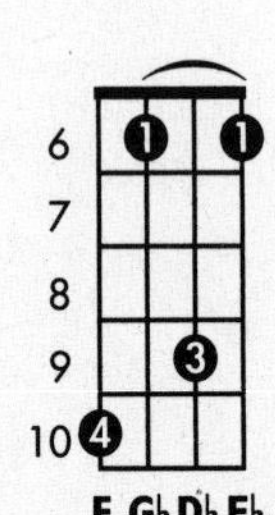
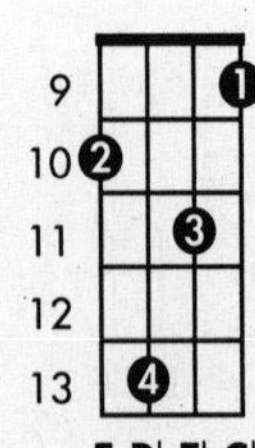

E♭ Sixth Add Ninth

E♭6/9

Sometimes written E♭9/6

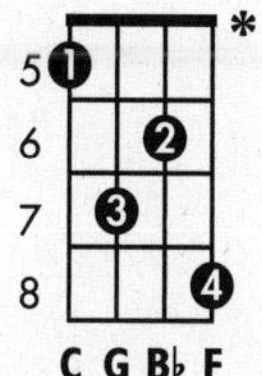
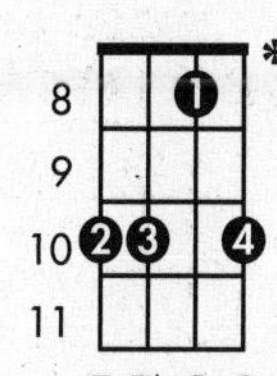
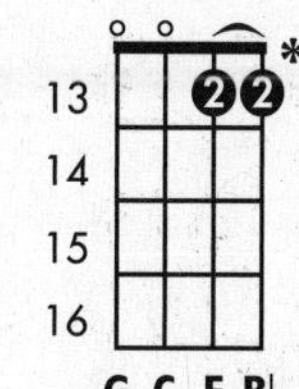

E♭ Minor Sixth Add Ninth

E♭m6/9

Sometimes written E♭m9/6

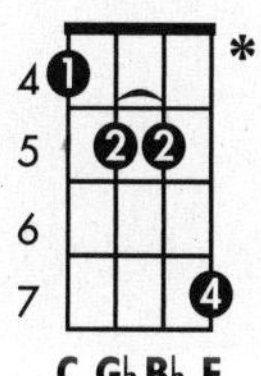
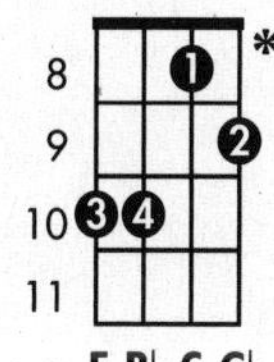

E♭ Minor Major Seventh

E♭m(maj7)

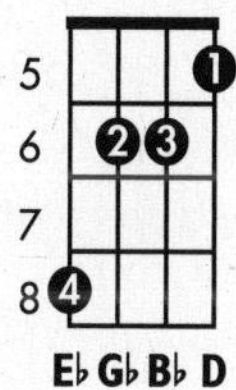
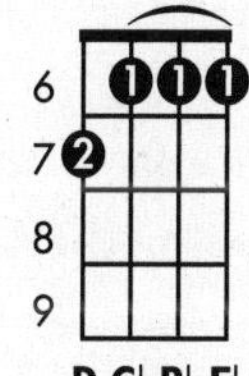
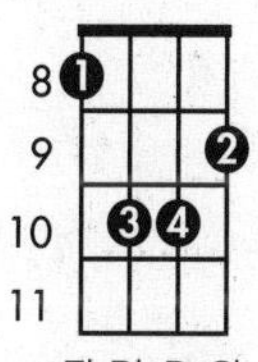
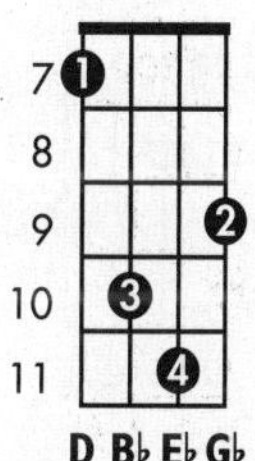

E♭ Minor Ninth Major Seventh

E♭m9(maj7)

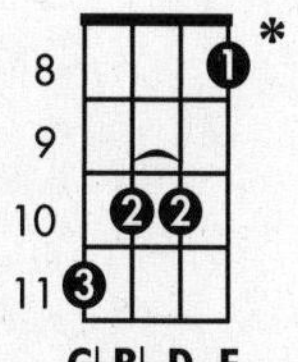
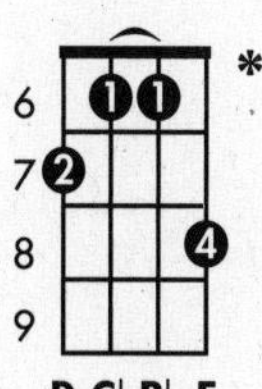

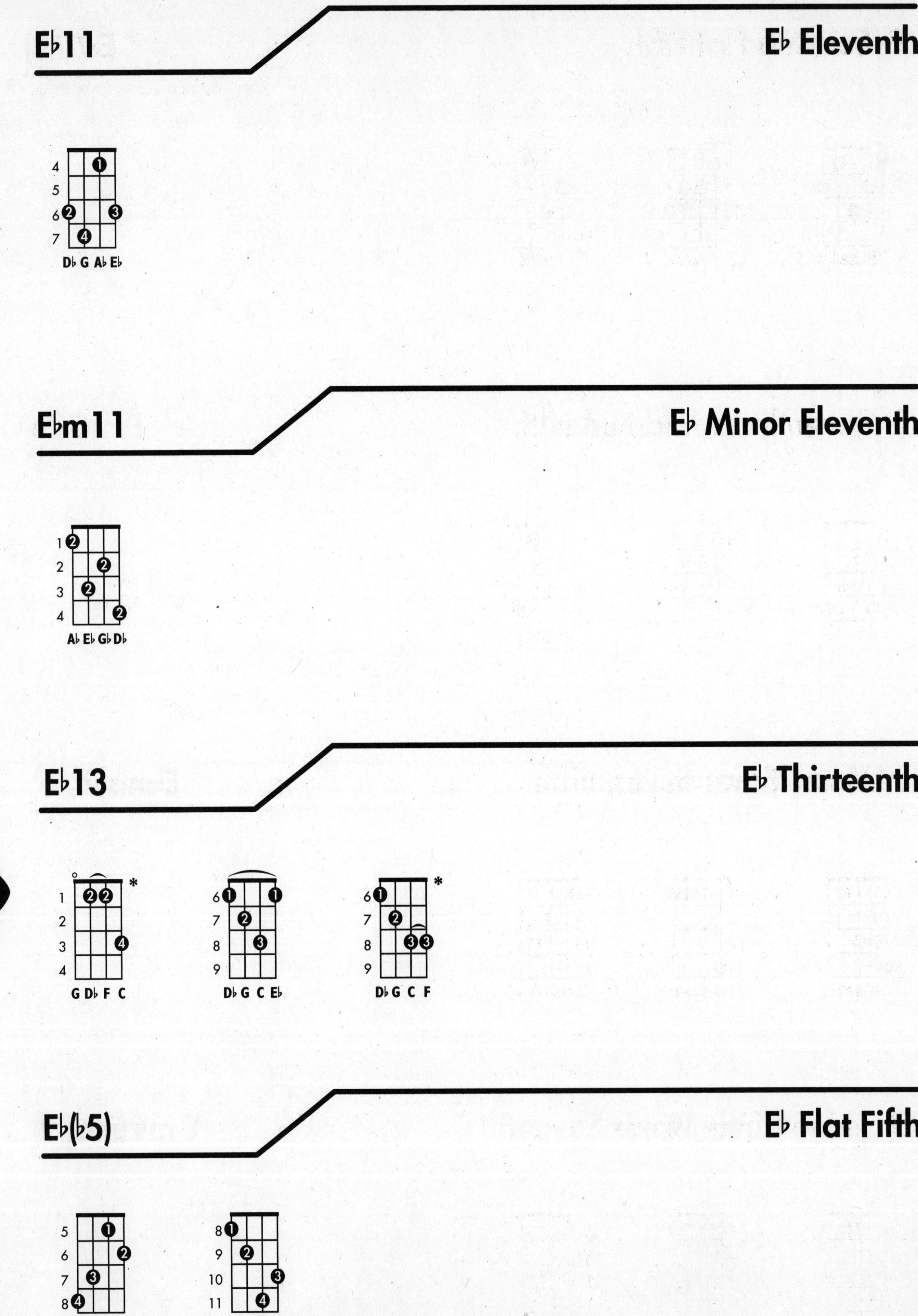
E♭11
E♭ Eleventh
4
5
6
7
D♭ G A♭ E♭
E♭m11
E♭ Minor Eleventh
1
2
3
4
A♭ E♭ G♭ D♭
E♭13
E♭ Thirteenth
1
2
3
4
G D♭ F C
6
7
8
9
D♭ G C E♭
6
7
8
9
D♭ G C F
E♭(♭5)
E♭ Flat Fifth
5
6
7
8
E♭ G B♭♭ E♭
8
9
10
11
E♭ B♭♭ E♭ G
E♭

E♭ Seventh Flat Fifth

E♭7(♭5)

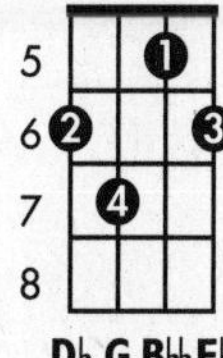

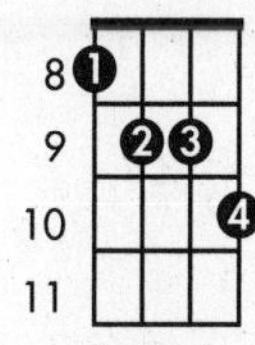

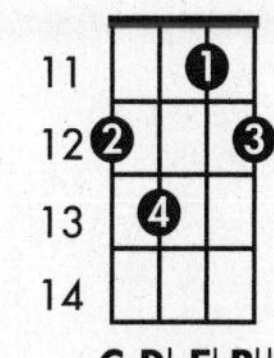

E♭ Seventh Augmented Fifth

E♭7+

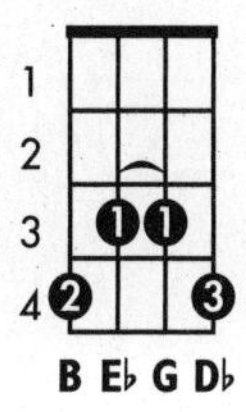

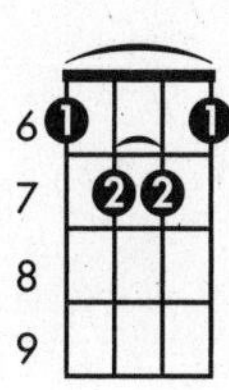

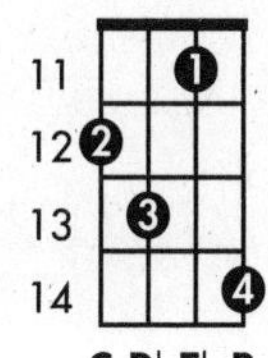

E♭ Major Seventh Flat Fifth

E♭maj7(♭5)

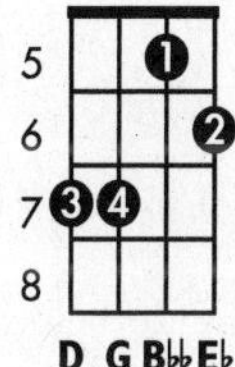

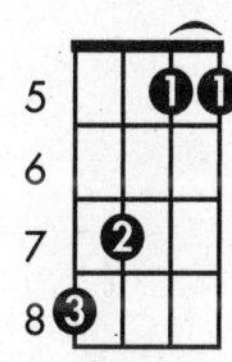

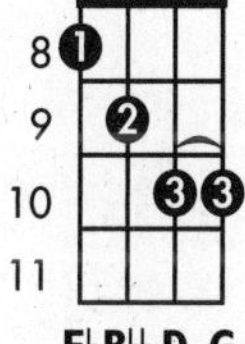

E♭ Seventh Flat Ninth

E♭7(♭9)

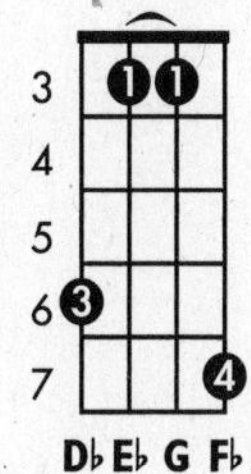

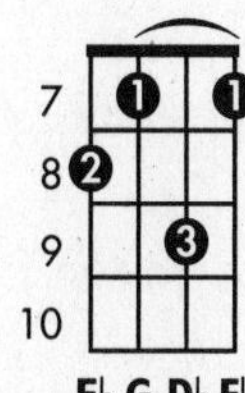

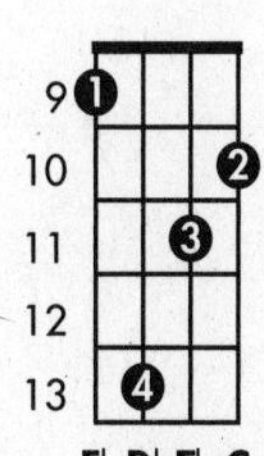

E♭7(♯9) — E♭ Seventh Sharp Ninth

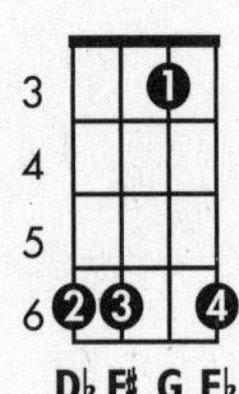

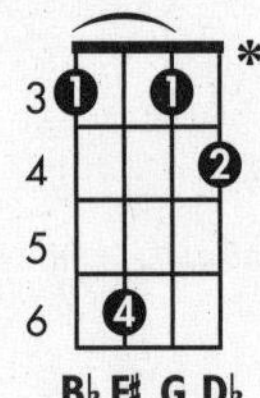

E♭ G D♭ F♯

E♭7+(♭9) — E♭ Seventh Flat Ninth Augmented Fifth

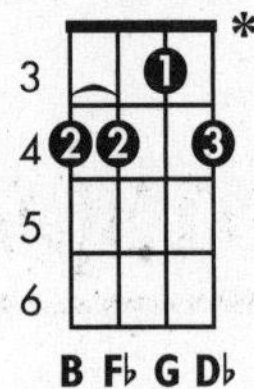

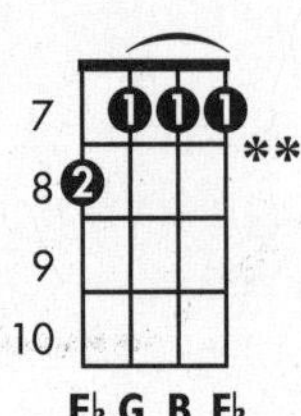

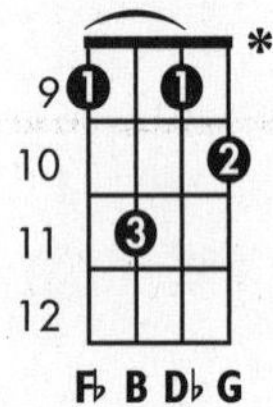

E♭9+ — E♭ Ninth Augmented Fifth

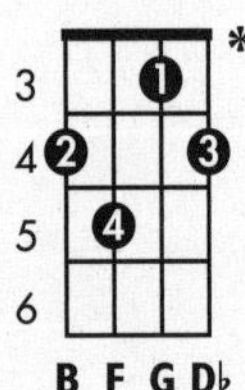

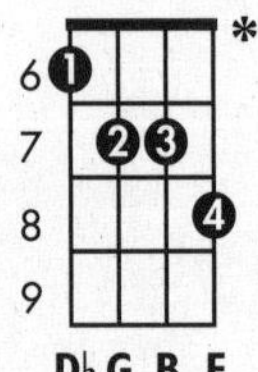

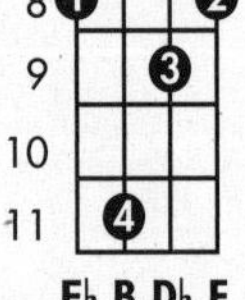

E♭9(♭5) — E♭ Ninth Flat Fifth

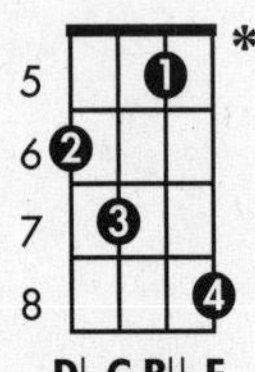

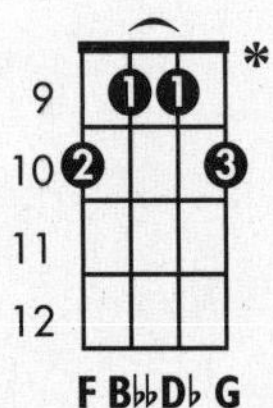

E♭ Ninth Sharp Eleventh

E♭9(♯11)

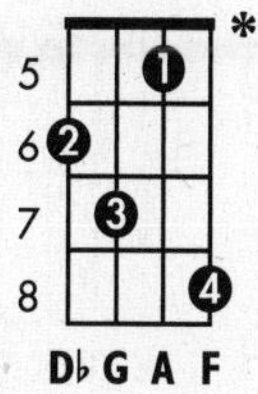
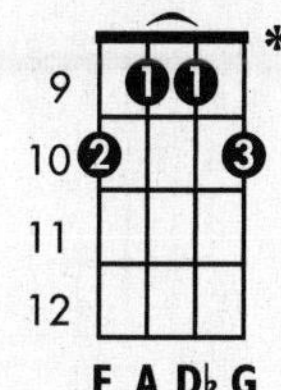

E♭ Thirteenth Flat Ninth

E♭13(♭9)

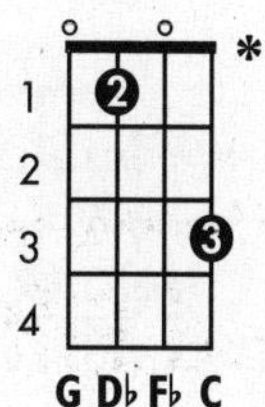
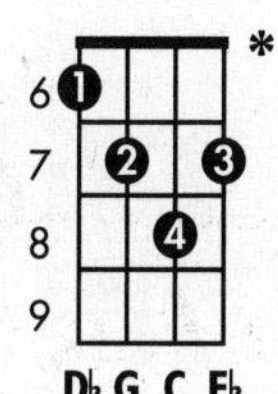

E♭ Thirteenth Flat Ninth Flat Fifth

E♭13(♭9 ♭5)

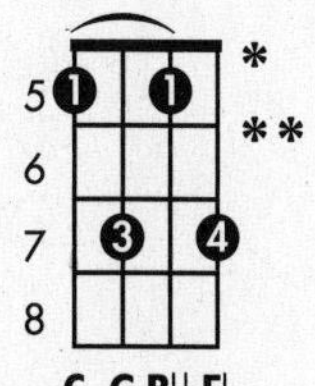

E — E Major

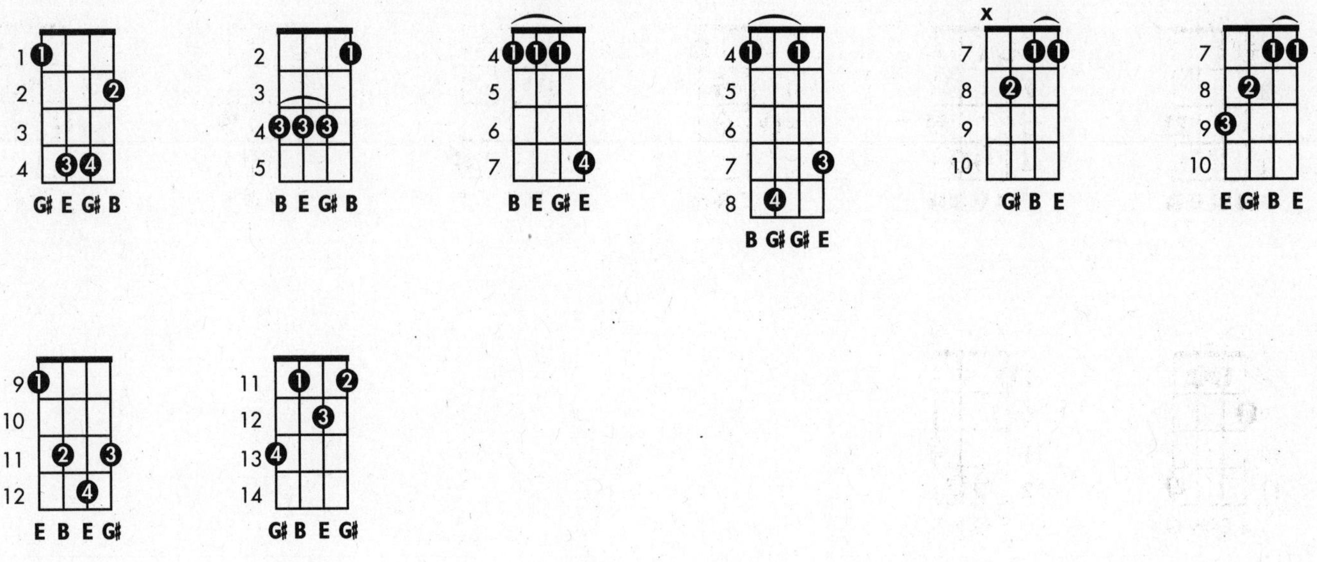

G♯ E G♯ B

B E G♯ B

B E G♯ E

B G♯ G♯ E

G♯ B E

E G♯ B E

E B E G♯

G♯ B E G♯

Em — E Minor

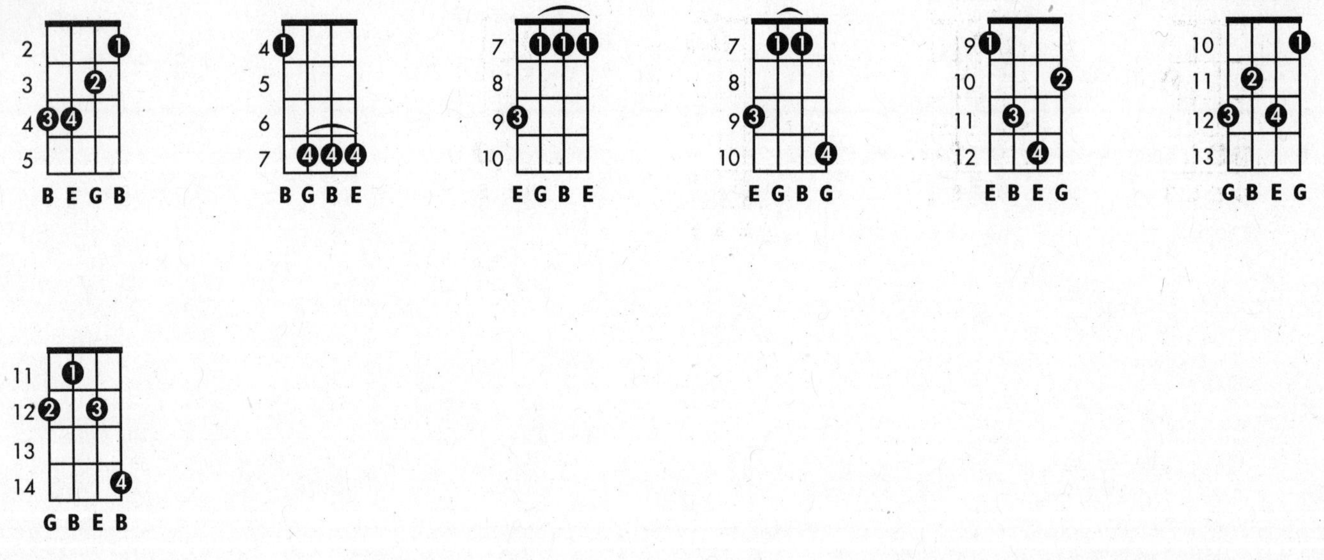

B E G B

B G B E

E G B E

E G B G

E B E G

G B E G

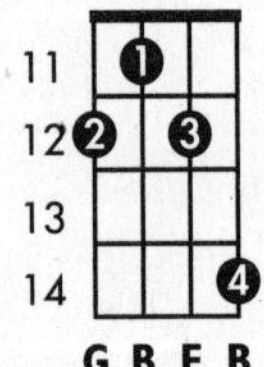

G B E B

E° — E Diminished

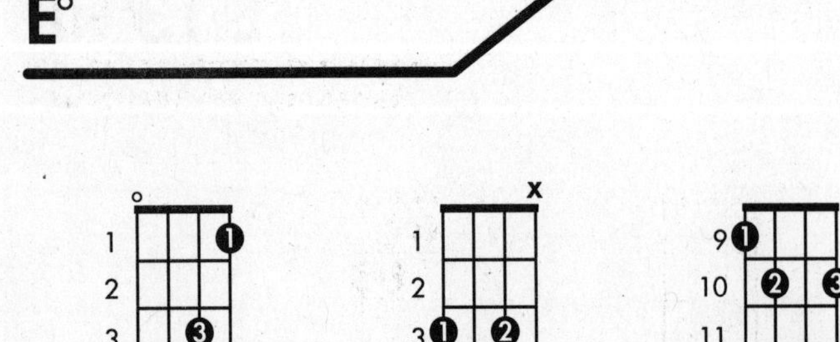

G E G B♭

B♭ E G

E B♭ E G

E

E Augmented

E+

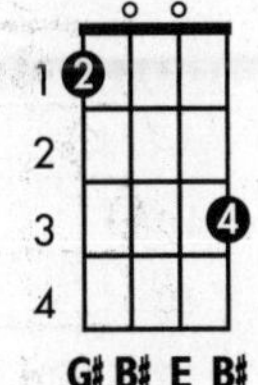

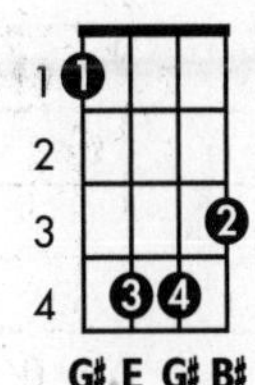

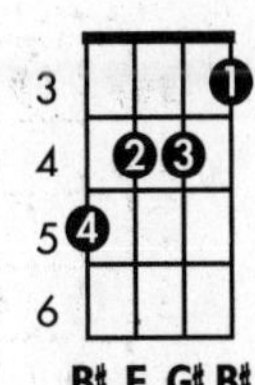

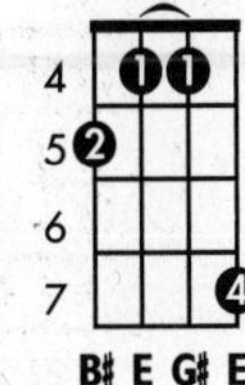

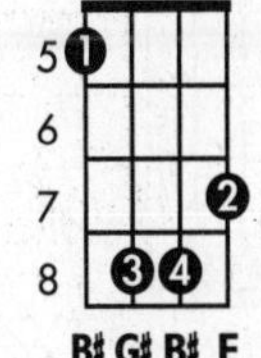

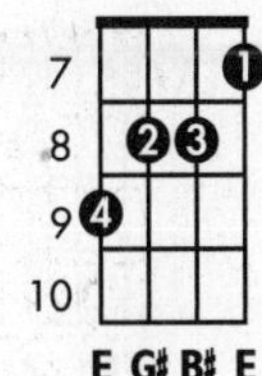

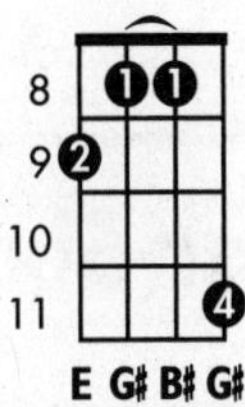

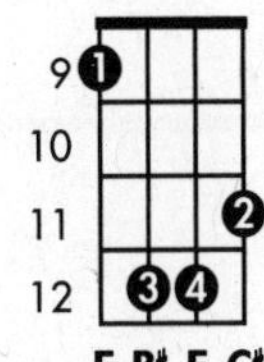

E Fifth

E5

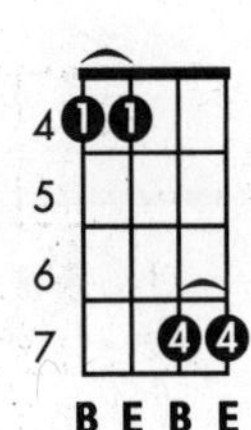

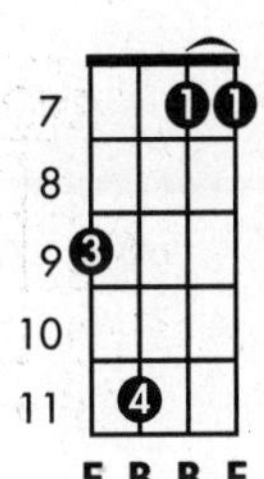

E B E

E Major Suspended Fourth

Esus

Sometimes written **Esus4**

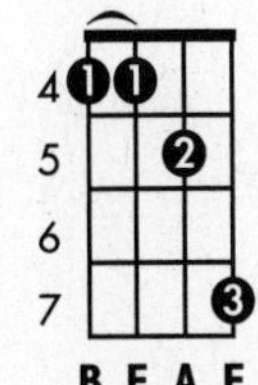

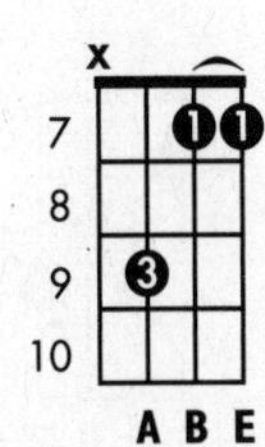

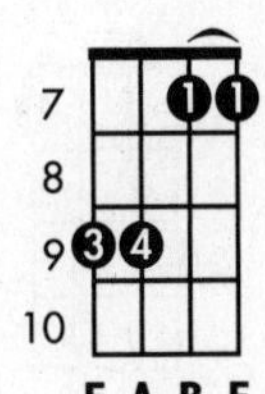

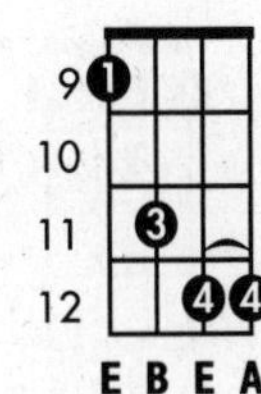

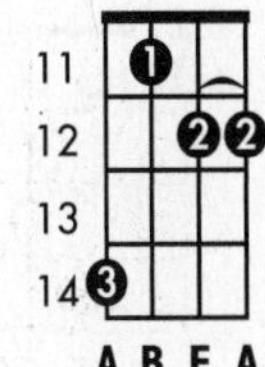

E

E6 — E Major 6th

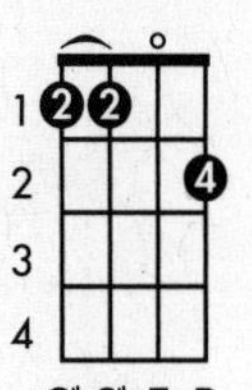
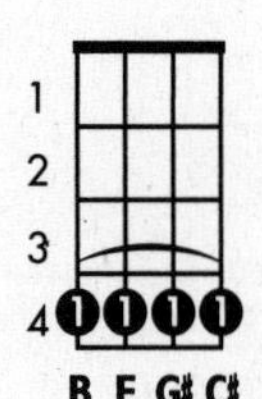
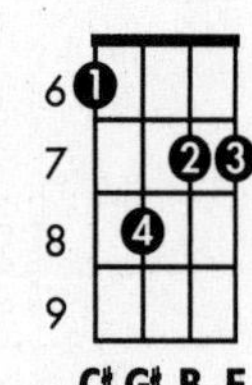
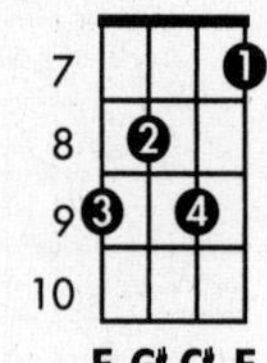
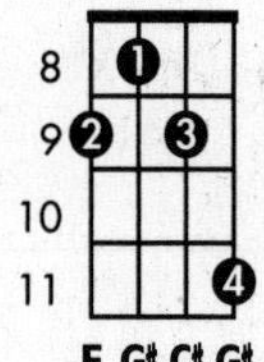
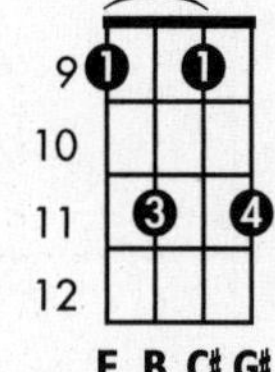
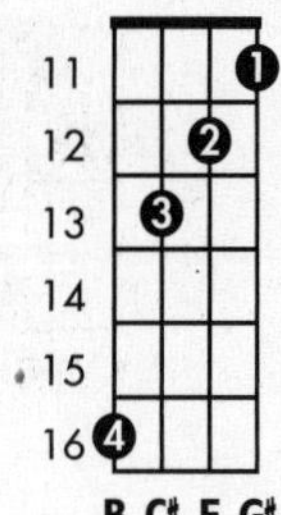
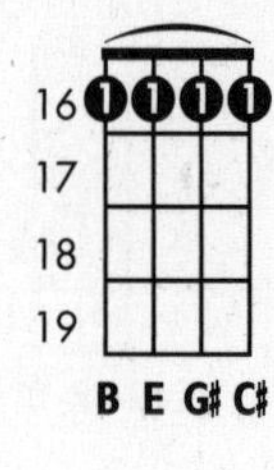

Em6 — E Minor Sixth

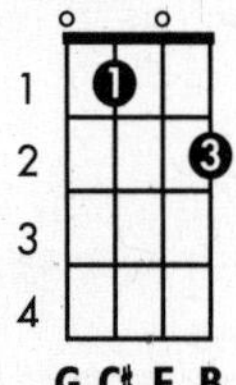
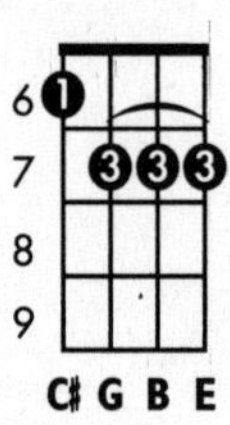
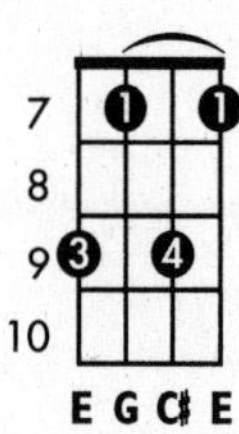
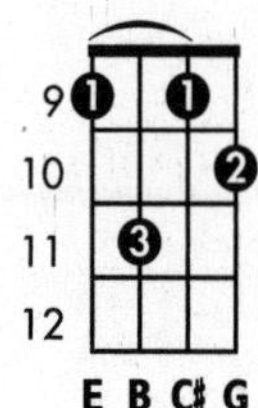

Emaj7 — E Major Seventh

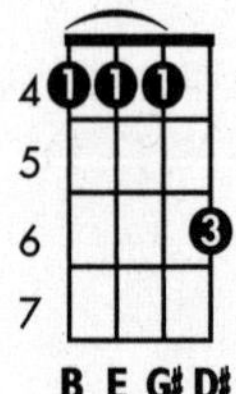
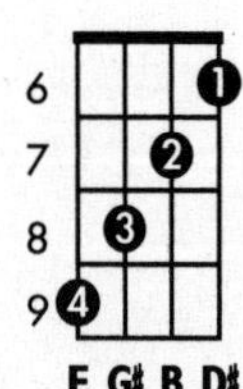
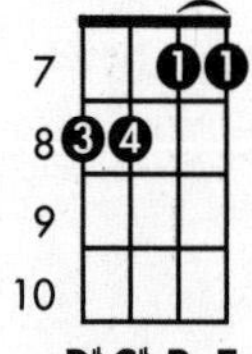
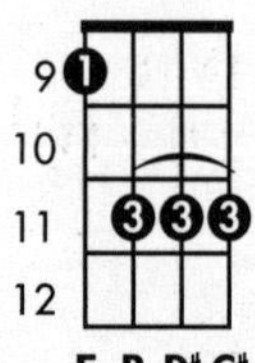
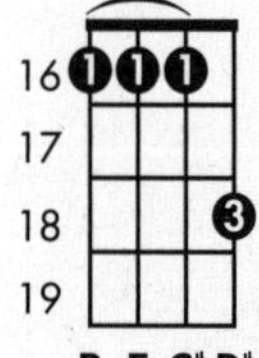

E7 — E Seventh

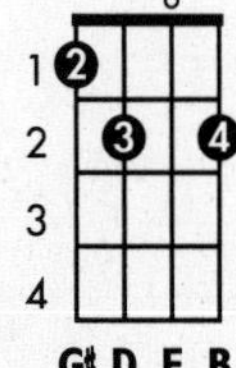
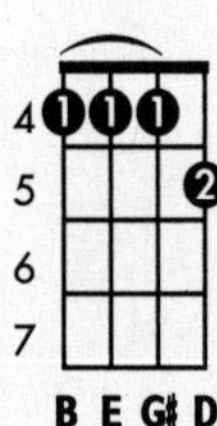
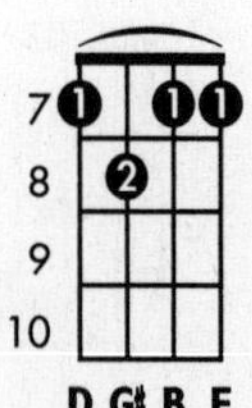
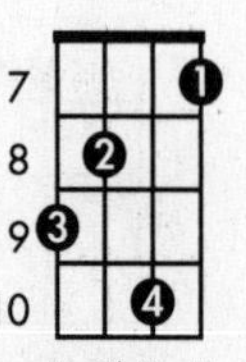
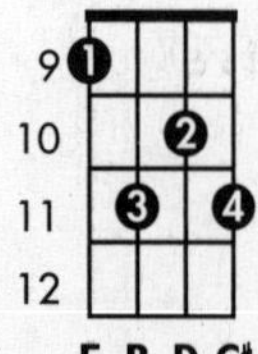

E Minor Seventh

Em7

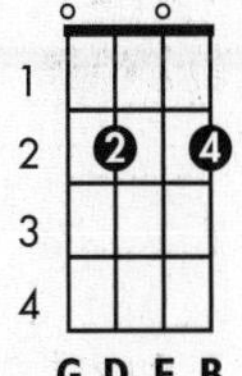

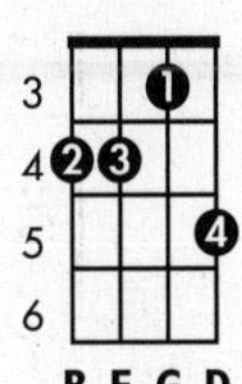

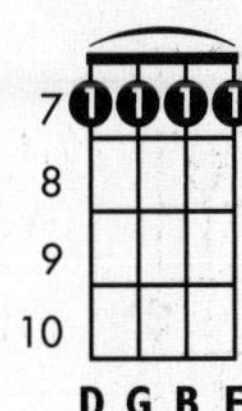

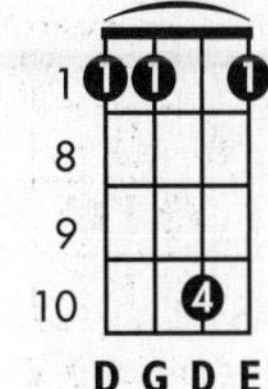

E Minor Seventh Flat Fifth

Em7(♭5)

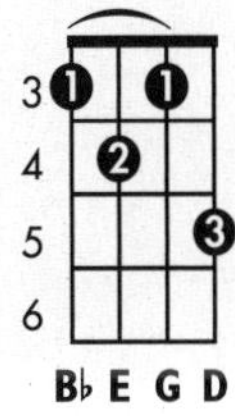

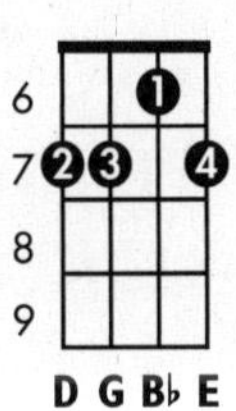

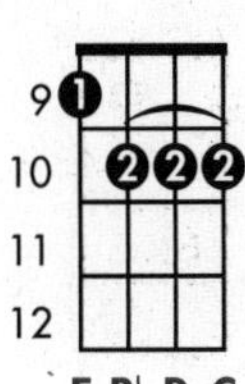

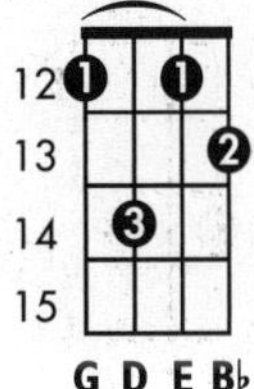

E Diminished Seventh

E°7

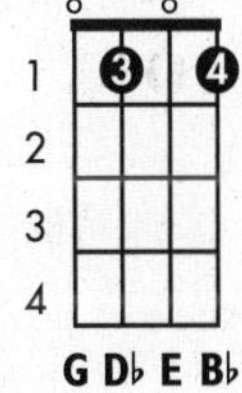

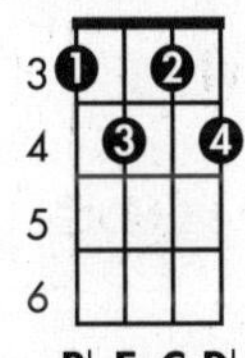

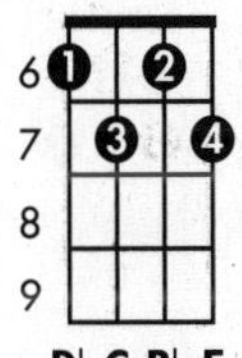

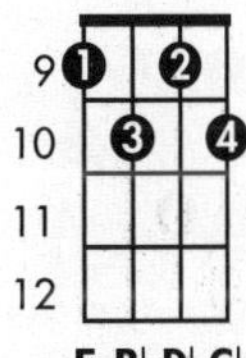

12 13 14 15

B♭ E G D♭

E

E Seventh Suspended Fourth

E7sus

Sometimes written **E7sus4**

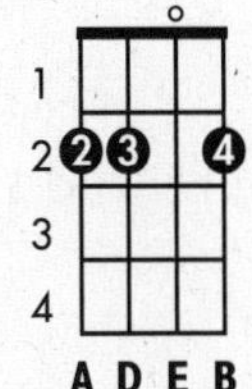

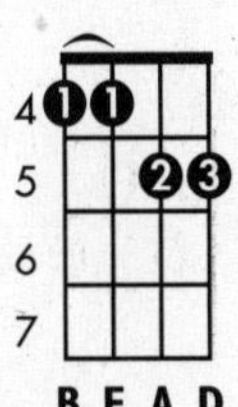

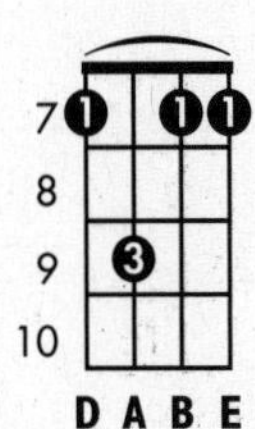

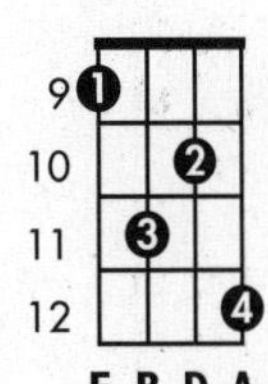

E(add9) — E Major Add Ninth

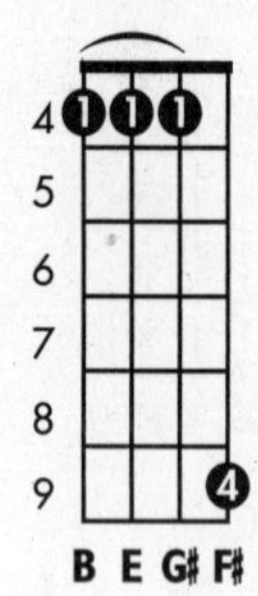

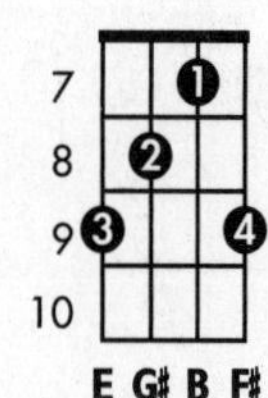

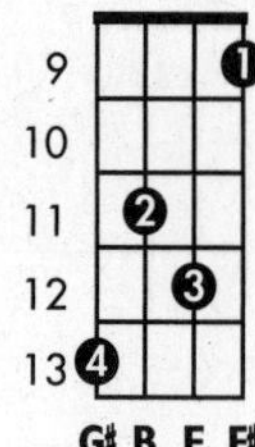

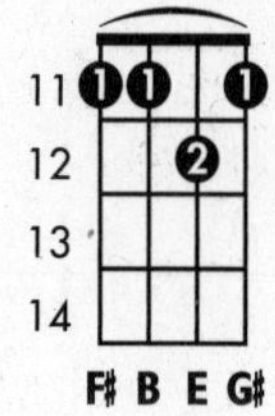

E Major Ninth — Emaj9

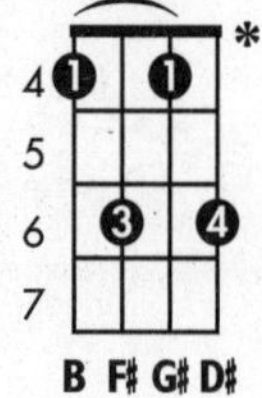

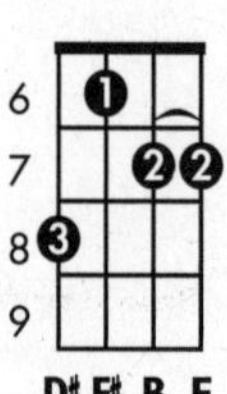

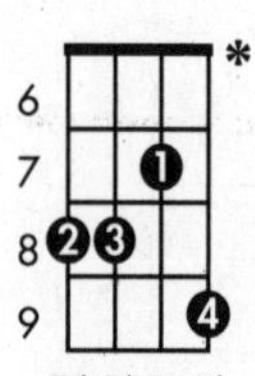

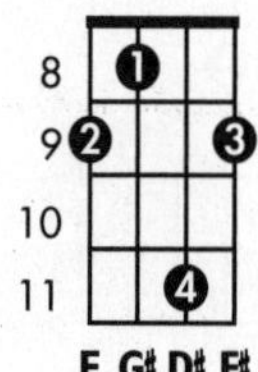

E9 — E Ninth

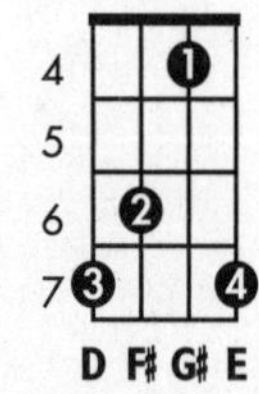

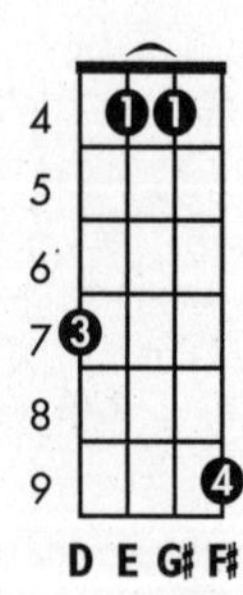

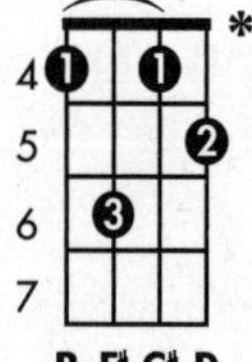

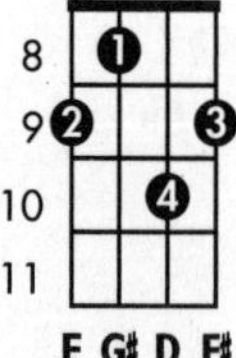

Em9 — E Minor Ninth

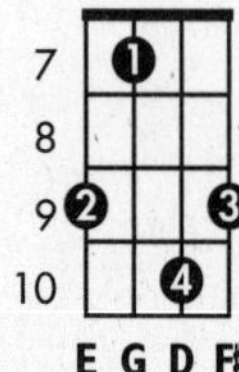

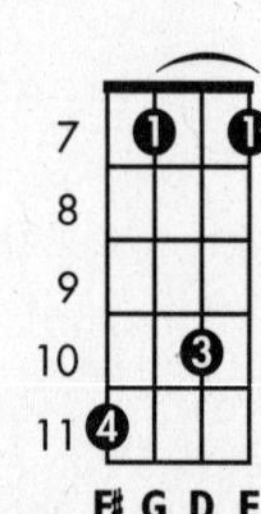

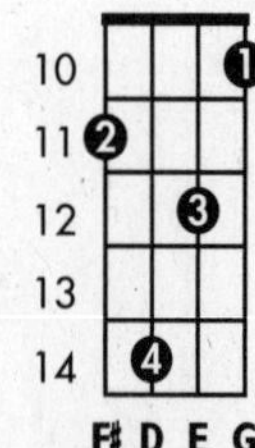

E

E Sixth Add Ninth

E6/9

Sometimes written **E9/6**

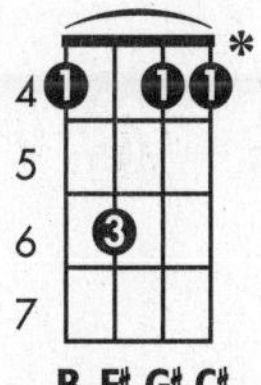

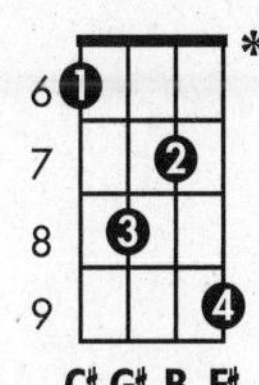

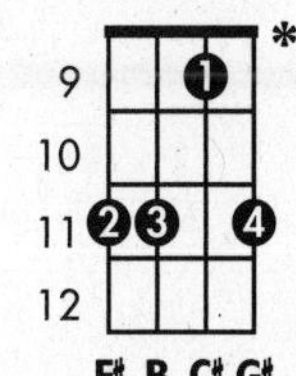

E Minor Sixth Add Ninth

Em6/9

Sometimes written **Em9/6**

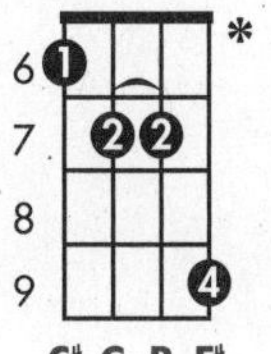

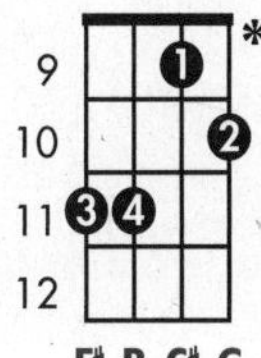

E Minor Major Seventh

Em(maj7)

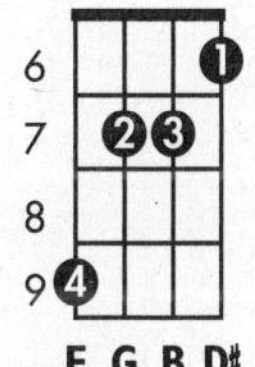

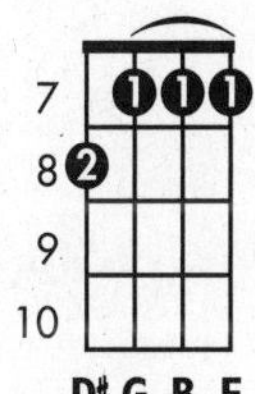

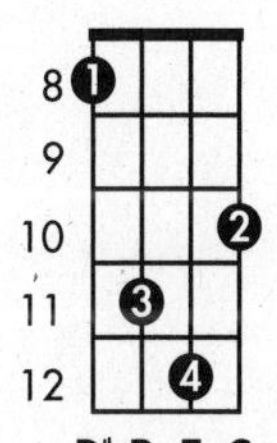

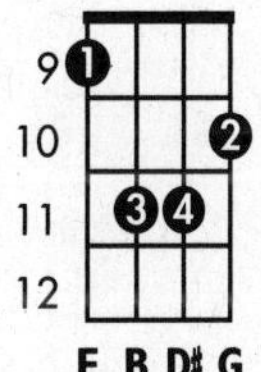

E

E Minor Ninth Major Seventh

Em9(maj7)

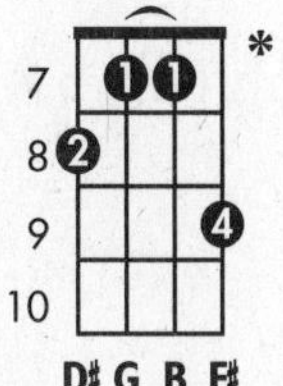

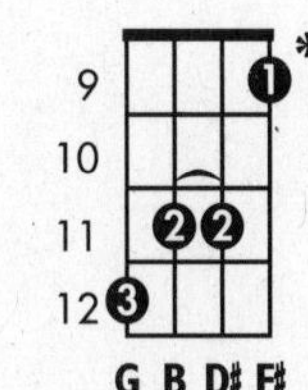

E11 — E Eleventh

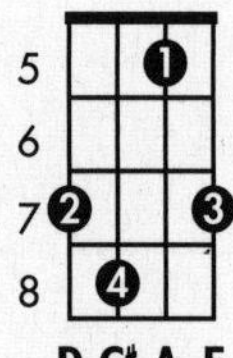

Em11 — E Minor Eleventh

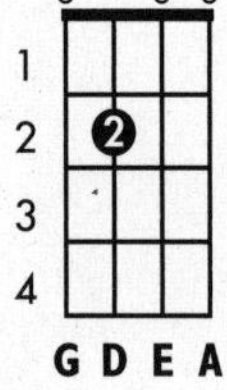

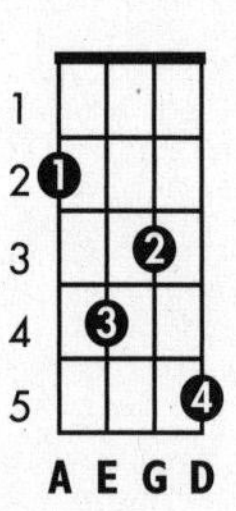

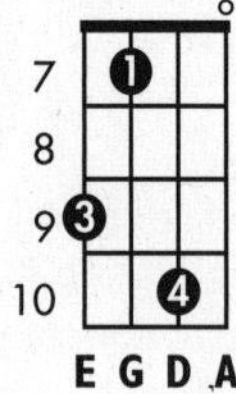

E13 — E Thirteenth

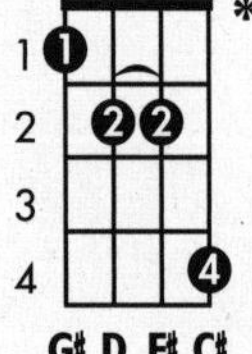

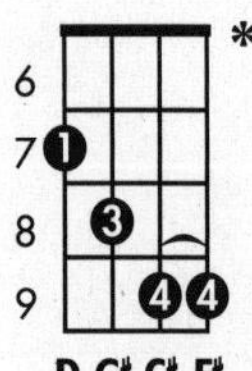

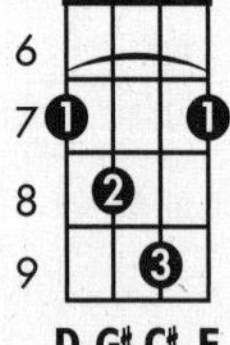

E(♭5) — E Flat Fifth

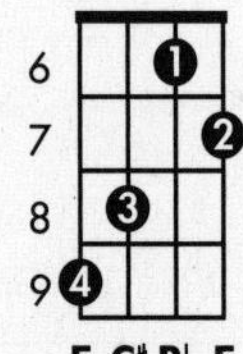

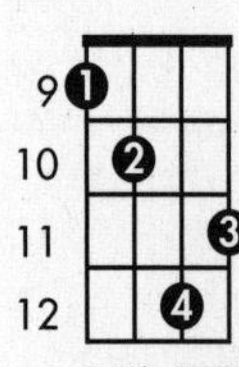

E Seventh Flat Fifth

E7(♭5)

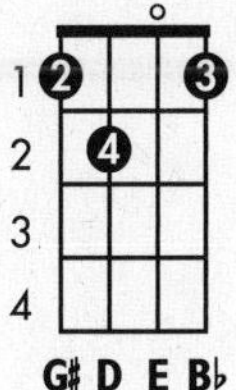

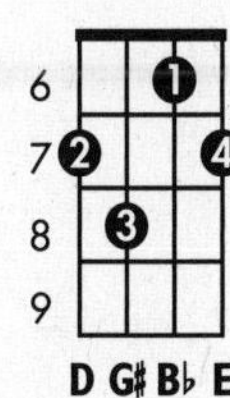

E Seventh Augmented Fifth

E7+

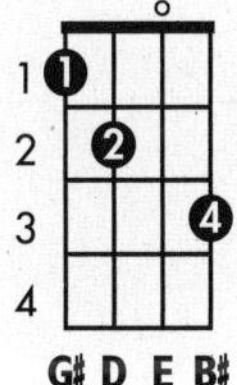

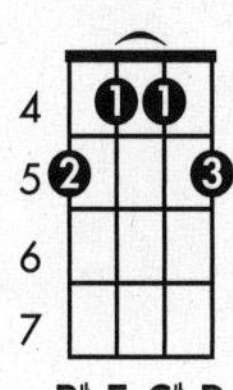

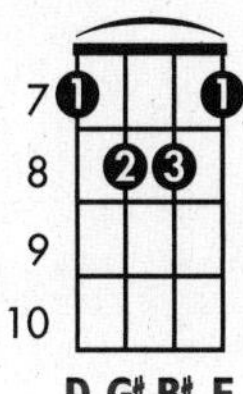

E Major Seventh Flat Fifth

Emaj7(♭5)

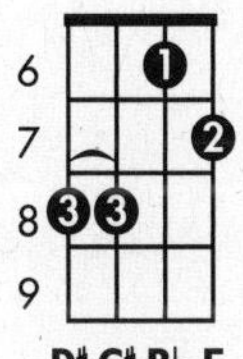

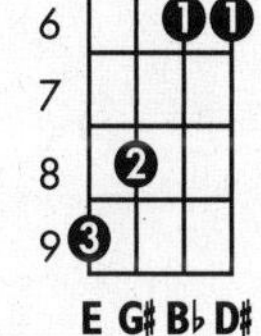

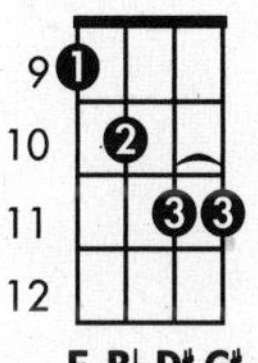

E

E Seventh Flat Ninth

E7(♭9)

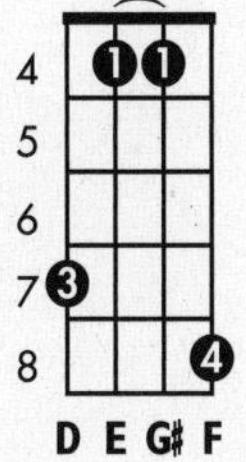

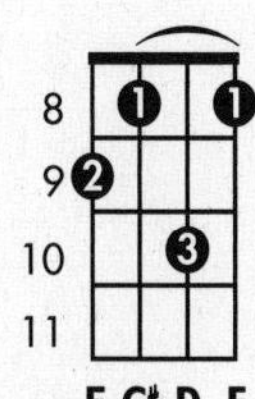

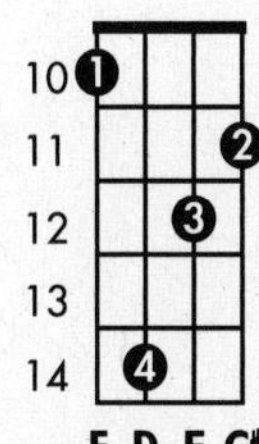

E7(♯9) — E Seventh Sharp Ninth

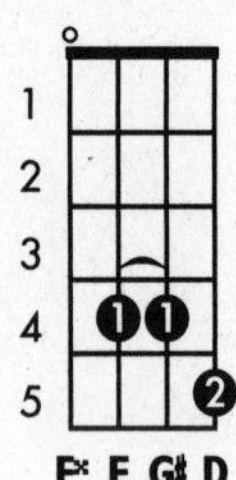

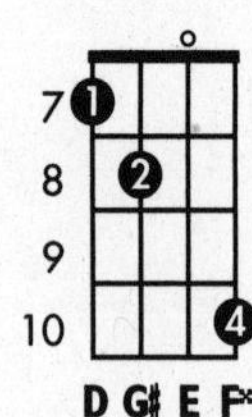

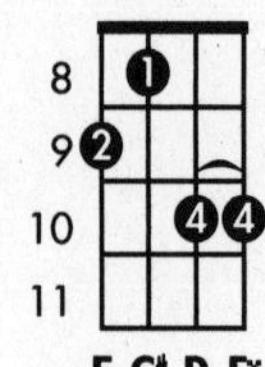

E7+(♭9) — E Seventh Flat Ninth Augmented Fifth

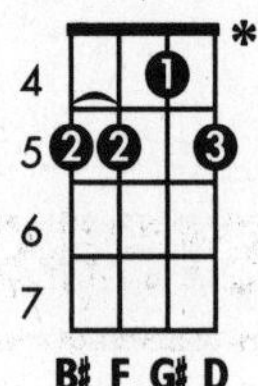

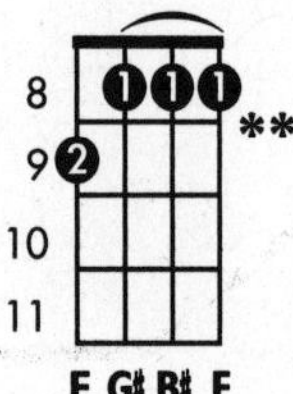

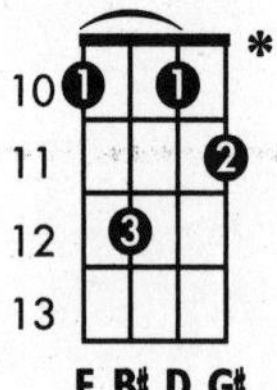

E9+ — E Ninth Augmented Fifth

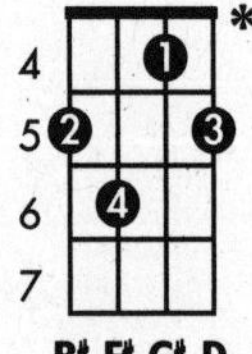

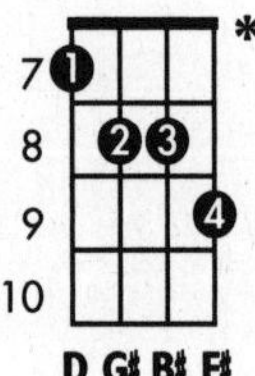

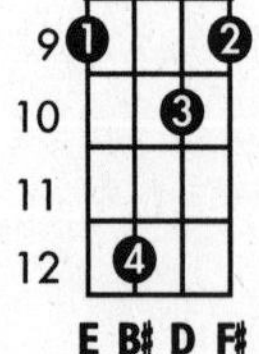

E9(♭5) — E Ninth Flat Fifth

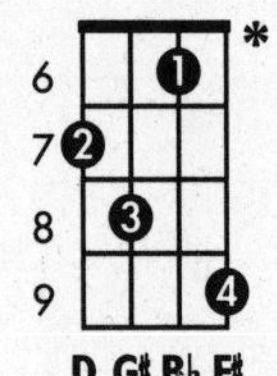

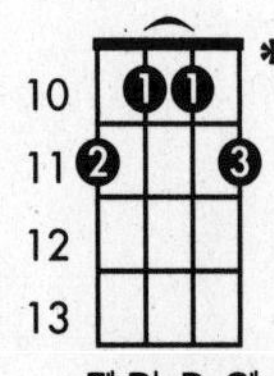

E Ninth Sharp Eleventh

E9(♯11)

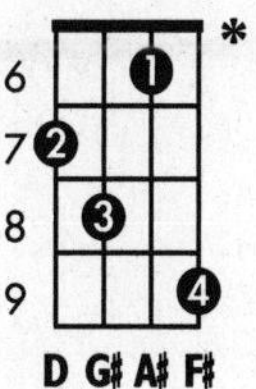

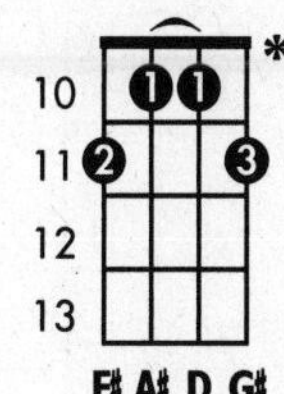

E Thirteenth Flat Ninth

E13(♭9)

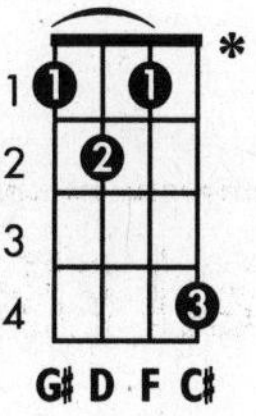

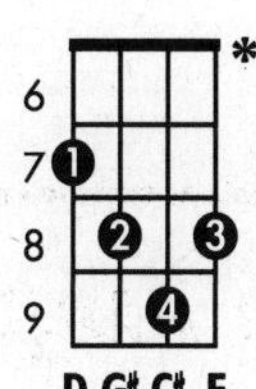

E Thirteenth Flat Ninth Flat Fifth

E13(♭9 ♭5)

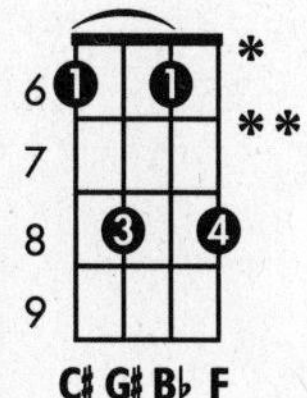

F — F Major

Fm — F Minor

F° — F Diminished

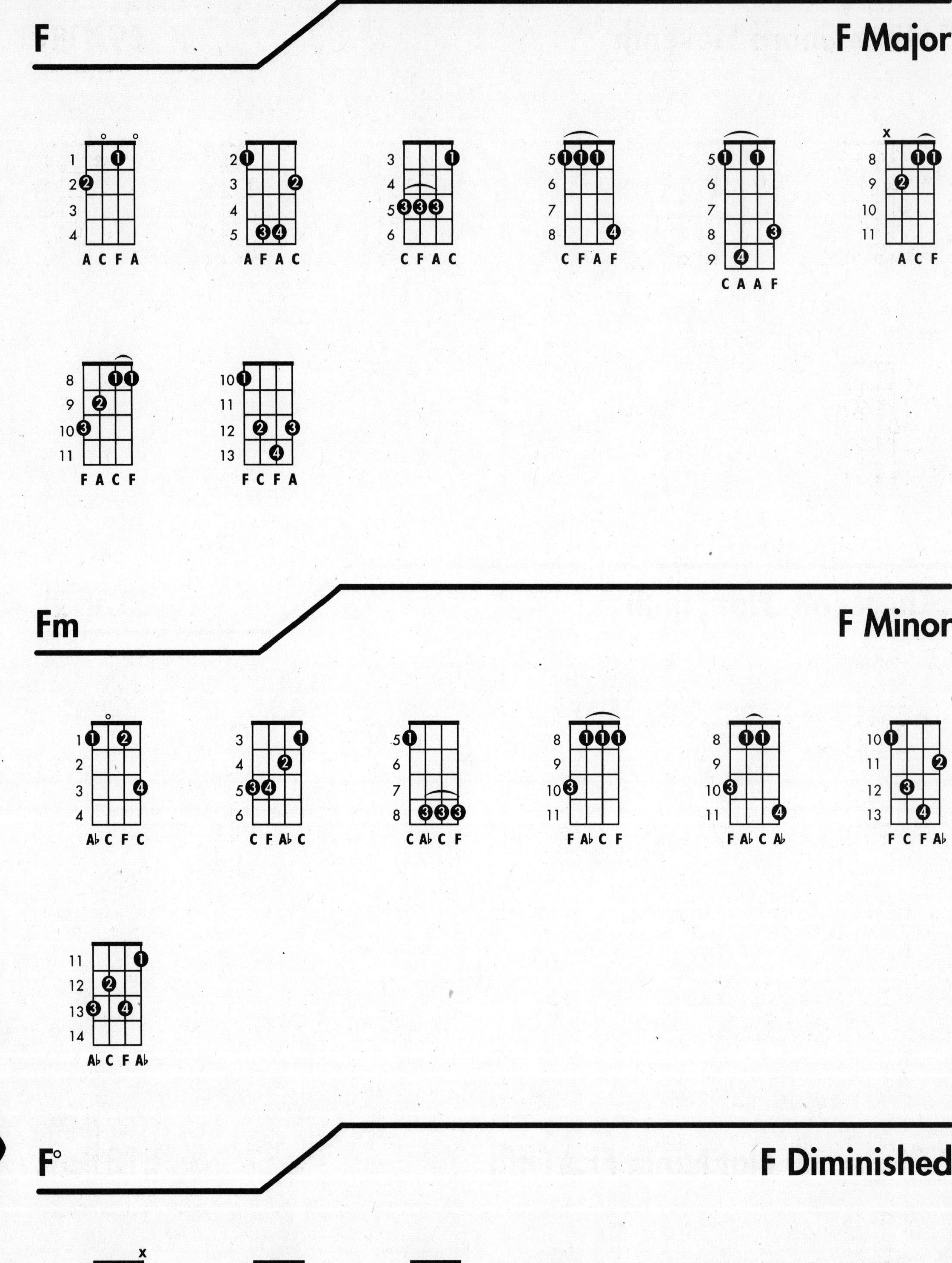

F

F Augmented

F+

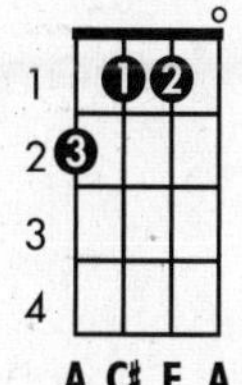

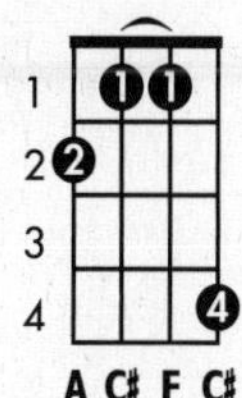

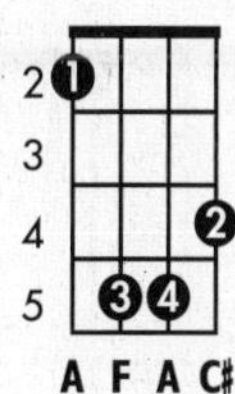

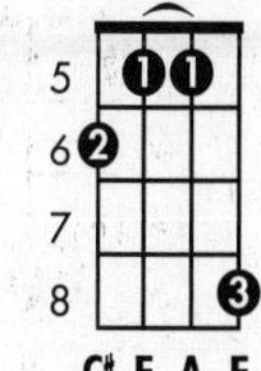

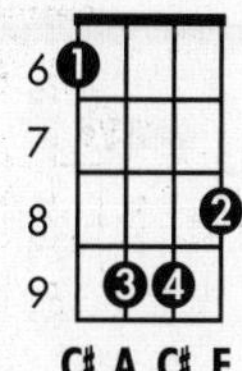

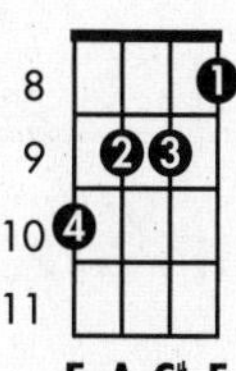

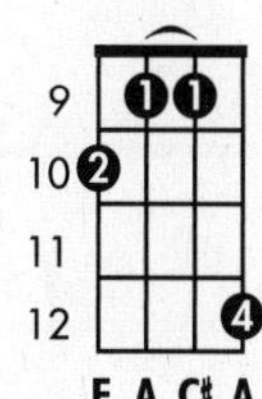

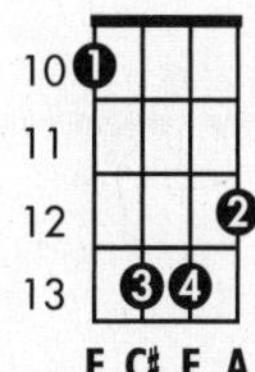

F Fifth

F5

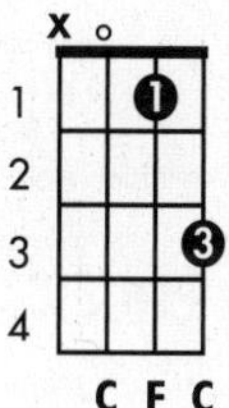

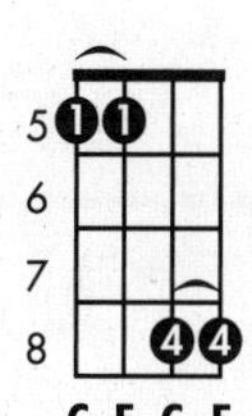

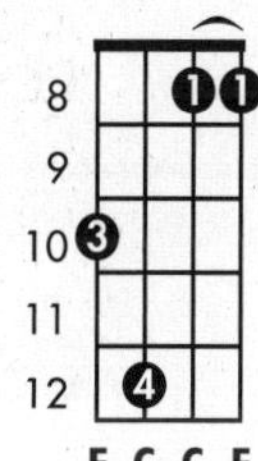

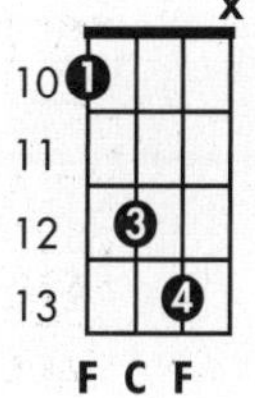

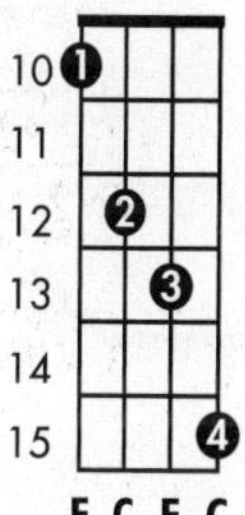

F Major Suspended Fourth

Fsus

Sometimes written **Fsus4**

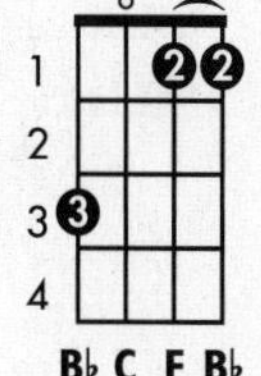

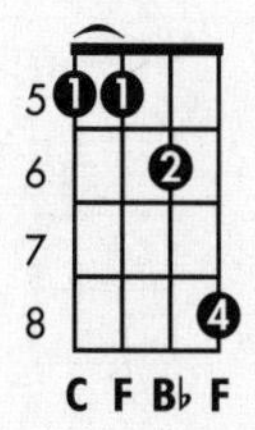

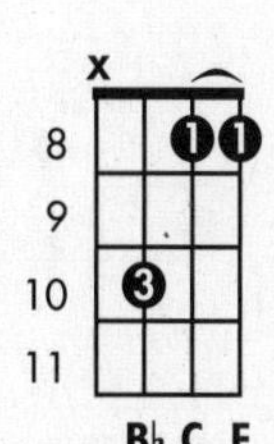

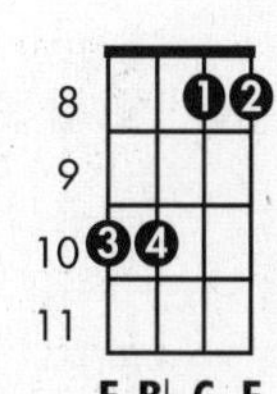

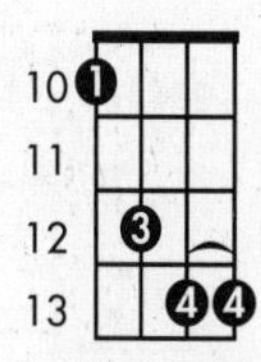

F

F6 — F Major 6th

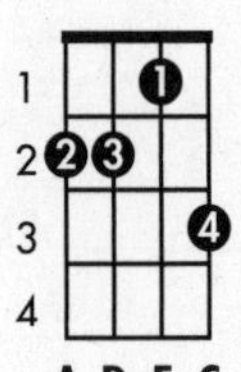
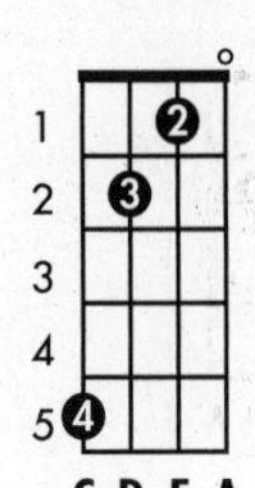
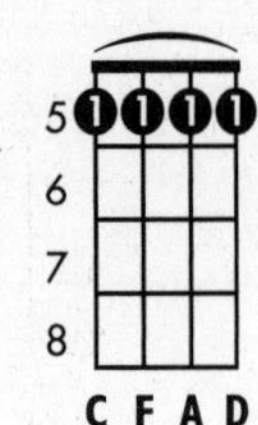
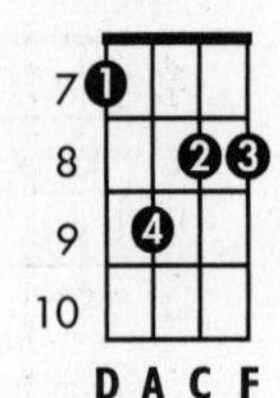
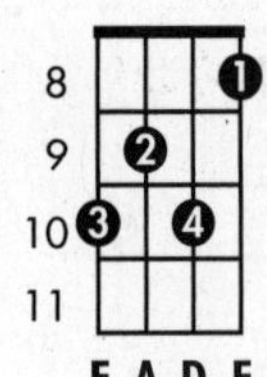
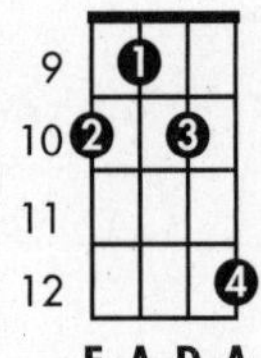
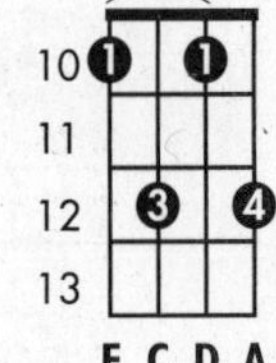
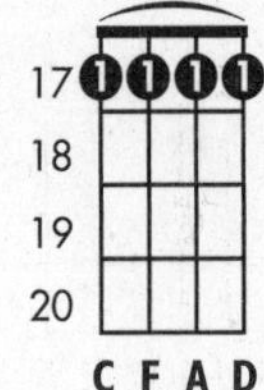

Fm6 — F Minor Sixth

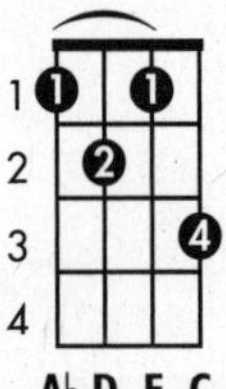
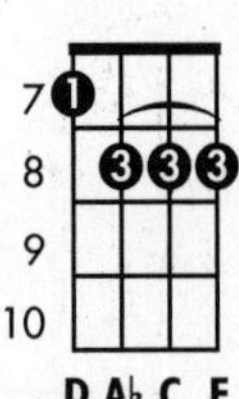
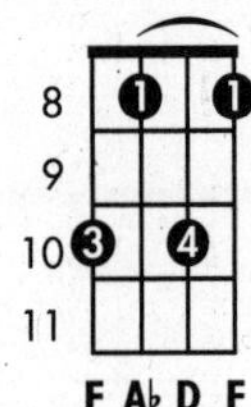
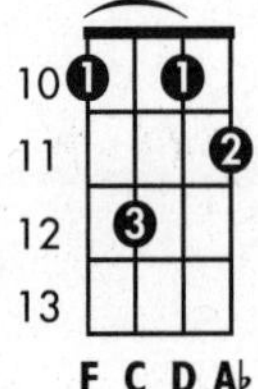

Fmaj7 — F Major Seventh

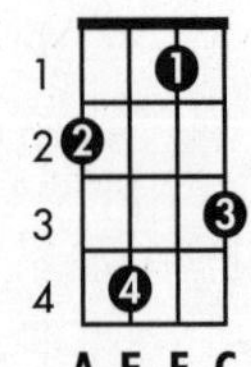
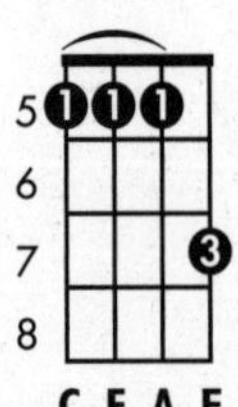
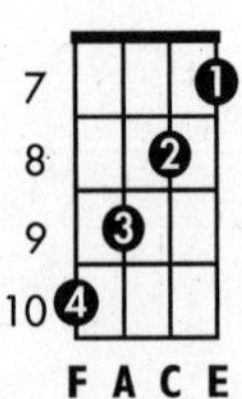
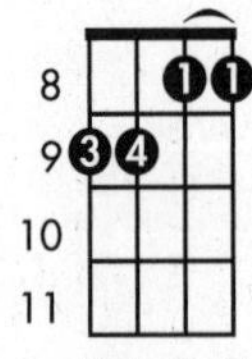
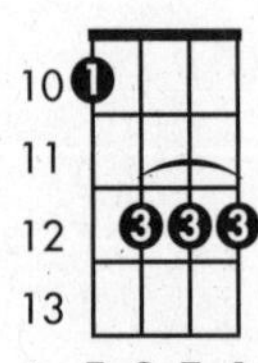
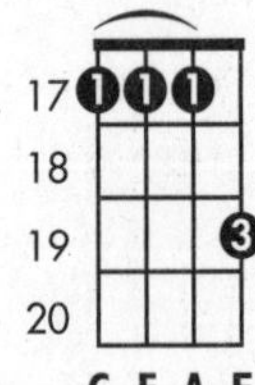

F7 — F Seventh

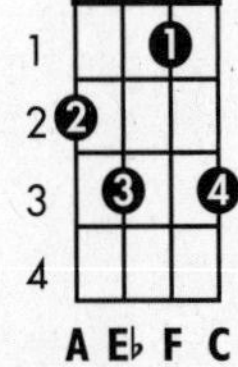
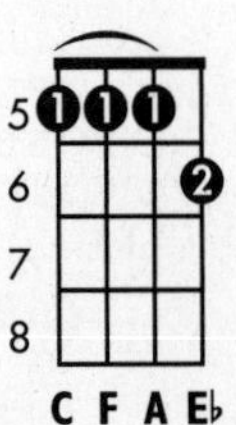
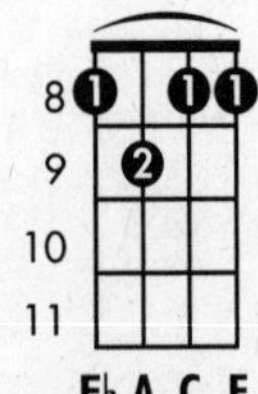
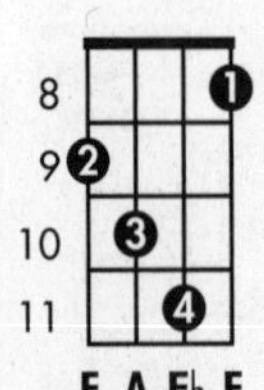
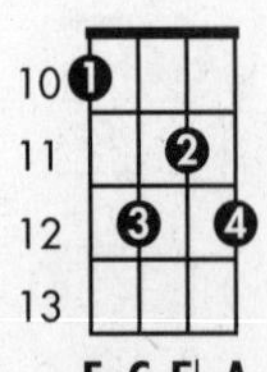
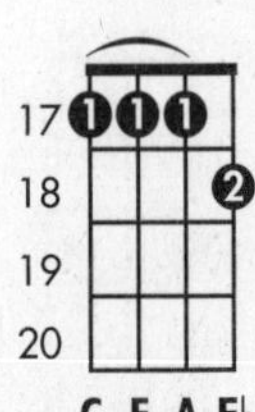

F Minor Seventh

Fm7

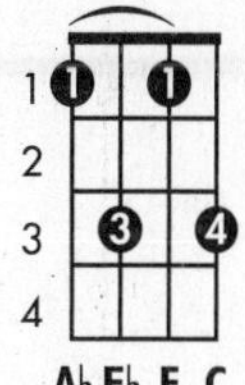

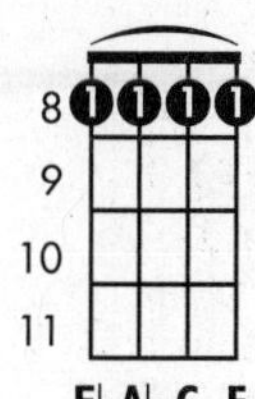

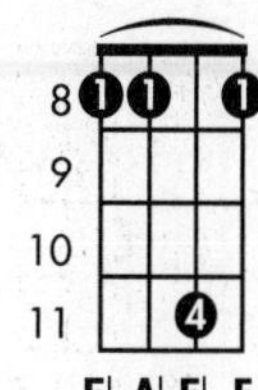

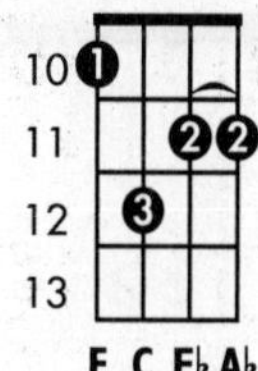

F Minor Seventh Flat Fifth

Fm7(♭5)

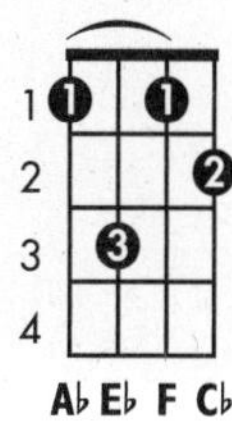

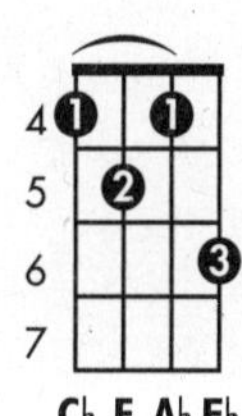

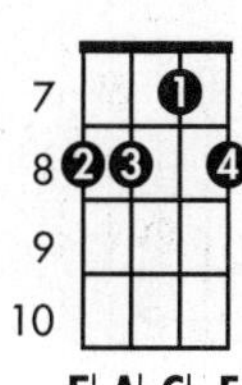

10 11 12 13
F C♭ E♭ A♭

13 14 15 16
A♭ E♭ F C♭

F Diminished Seventh

F°7

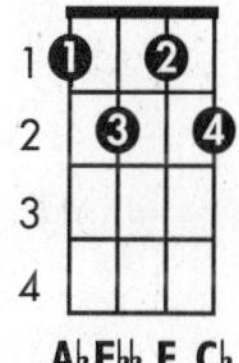

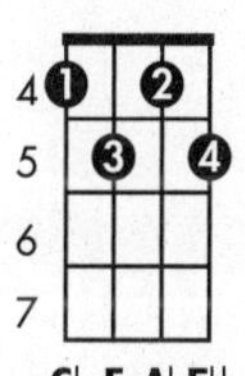

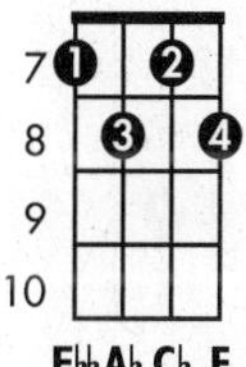

10 11 12 13
F C♭ E♭♭ A♭

13 14 15 16
C♭ F A♭ E♭♭

F Seventh Suspended Fourth

F7sus

Sometimes written **F7sus4**

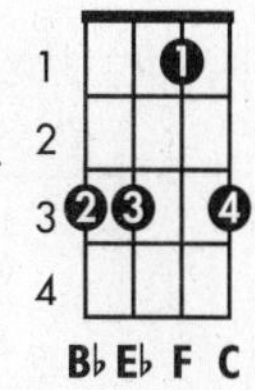

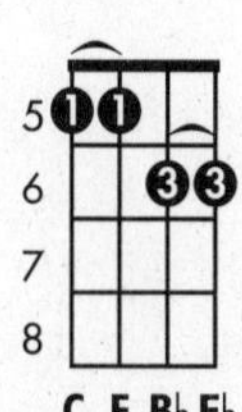

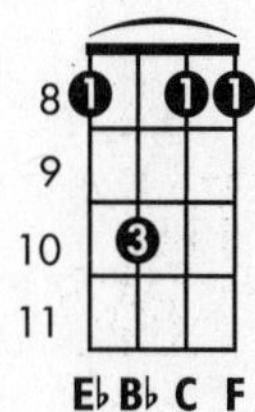

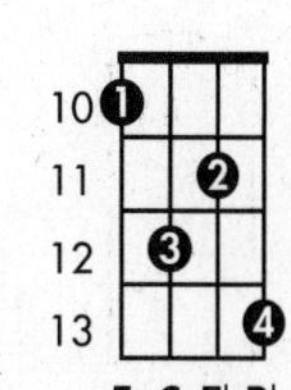

F(add9) — F Major Add Ninth

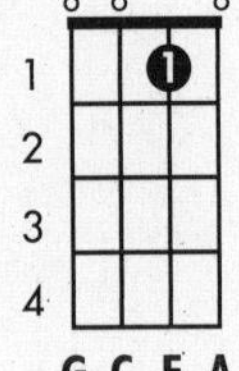

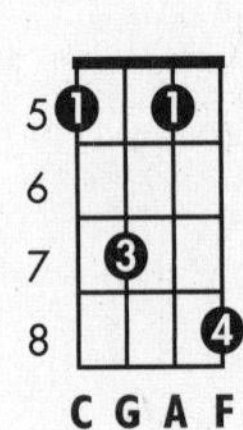

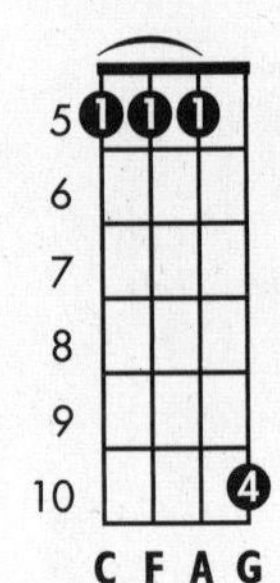

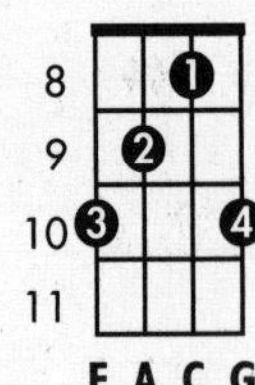

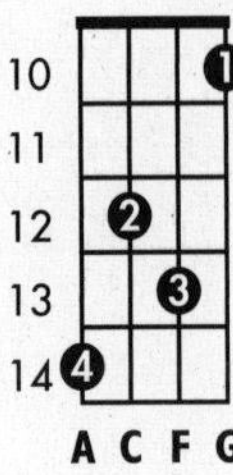

F Major Ninth — Fmaj9

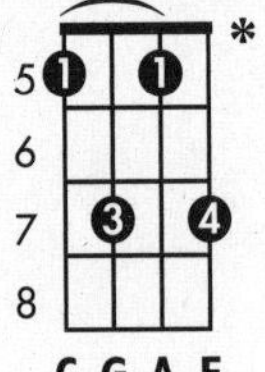

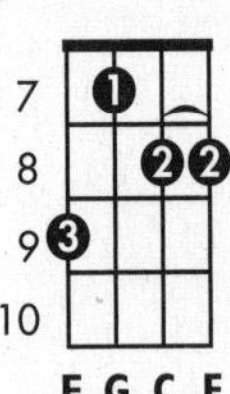

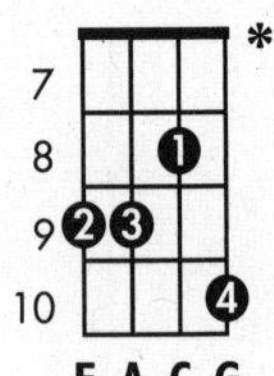

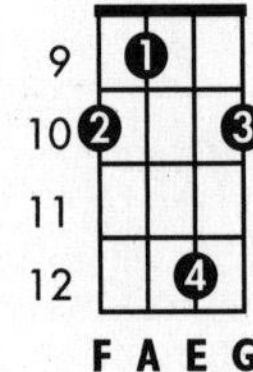

F9 — F Ninth

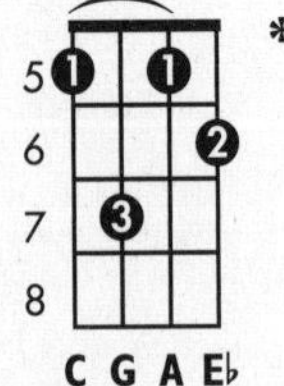

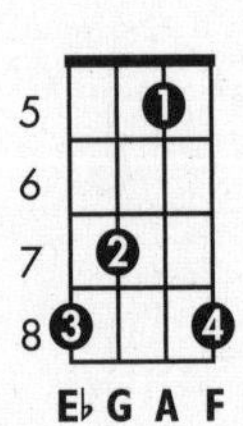

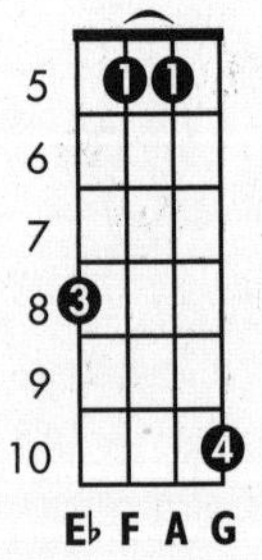

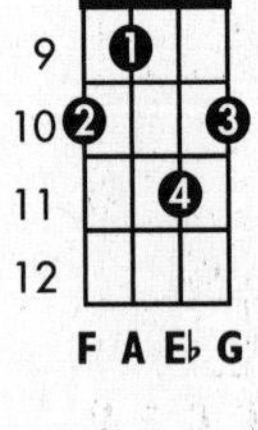

F

Fm9 — F Minor Ninth

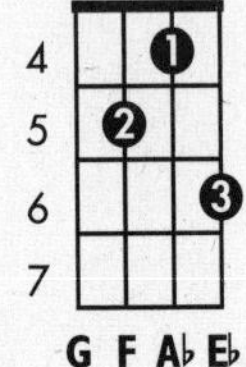

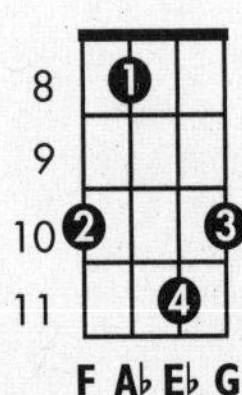

F Sixth Add Ninth

F6/9

Sometimes written F9/6

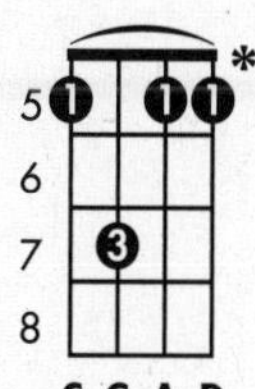

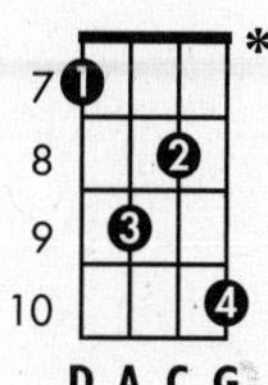

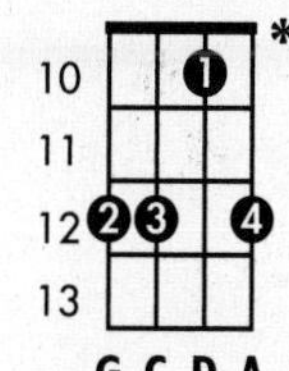

F Minor Sixth Add Ninth

Fm6/9

Sometimes written Fm9/6

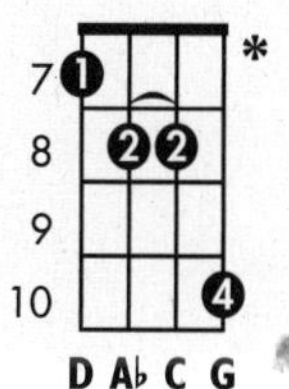

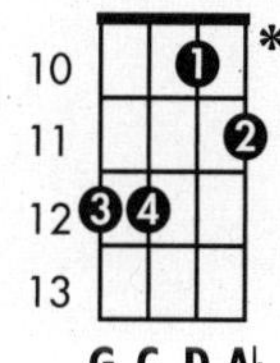

F Minor Major Seventh

Fm(maj7)

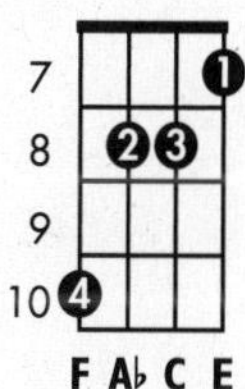

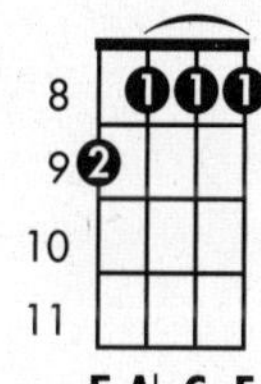

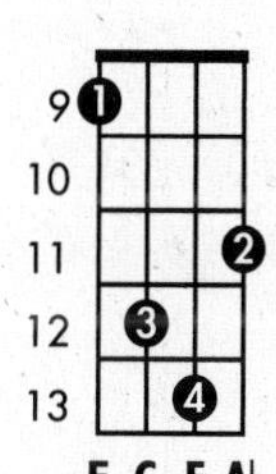

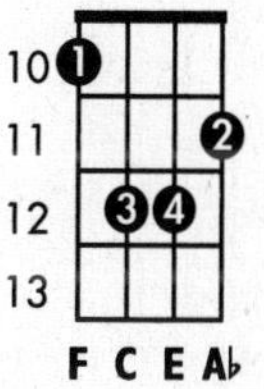

F Minor Ninth Major Seventh

Fm9(maj7)

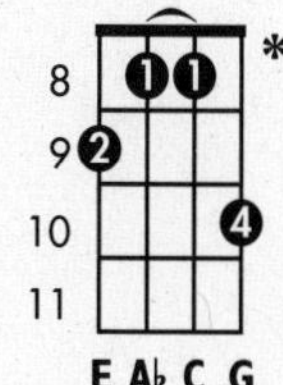

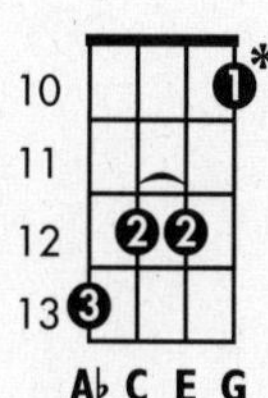

F11 — F Eleventh

Fm11 — F Minor Eleventh

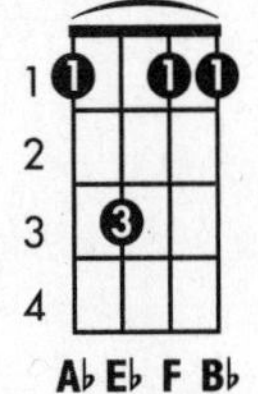

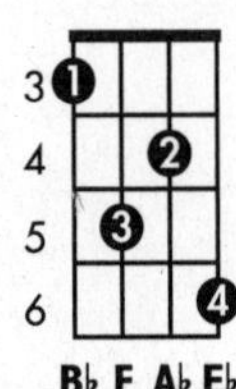

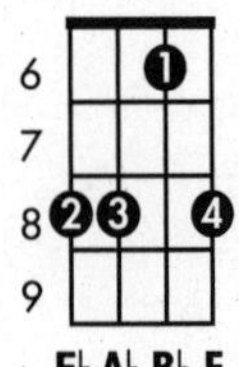

F13 — F Thirteenth

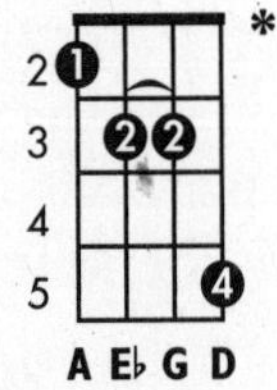

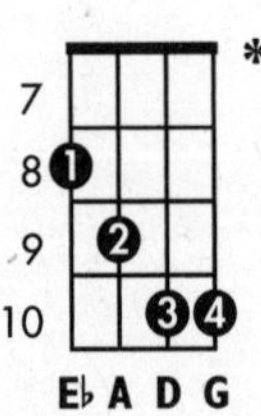

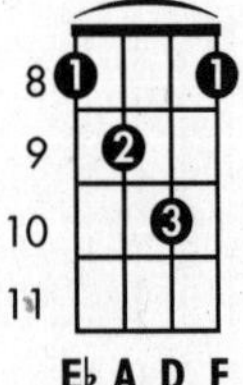

F(♭5) — F Flat Fifth

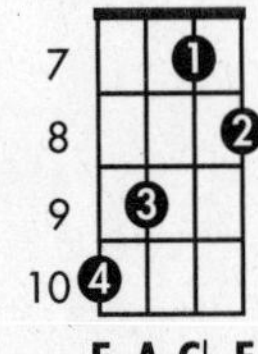

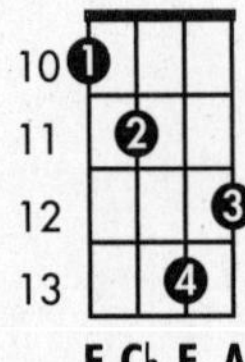

F Seventh Flat Fifth

F7(♭5)

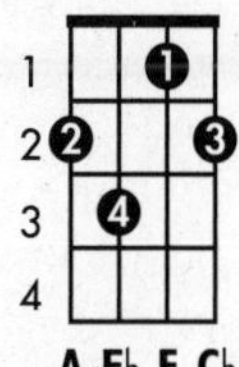

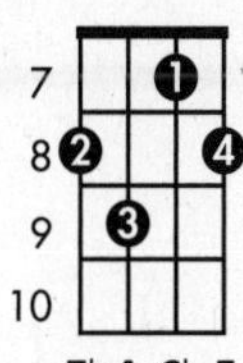

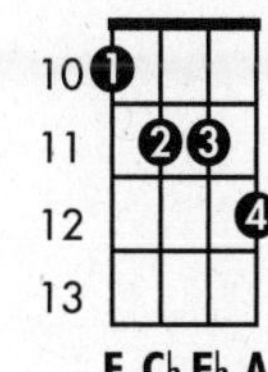

F Seventh Augmented Fifth

F7+

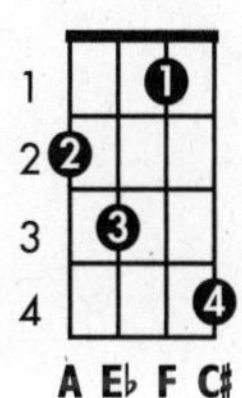

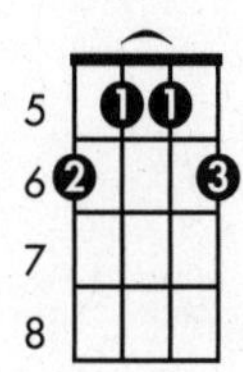

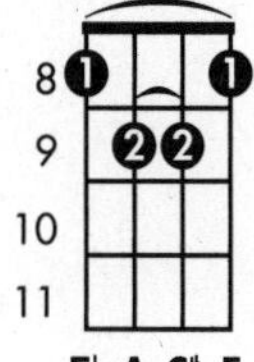

F Major Seventh Flat Fifth

Fmaj7(♭5)

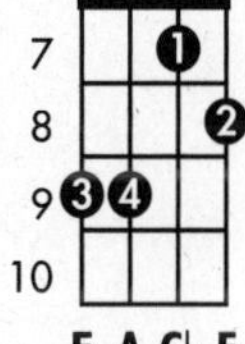

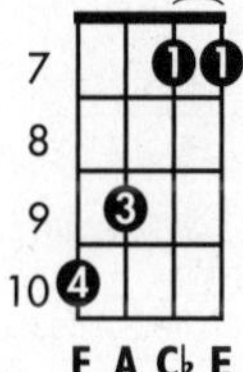

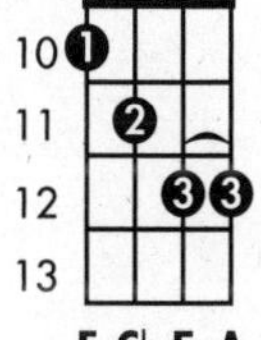

F Seventh Flat Ninth

F7(♭9)

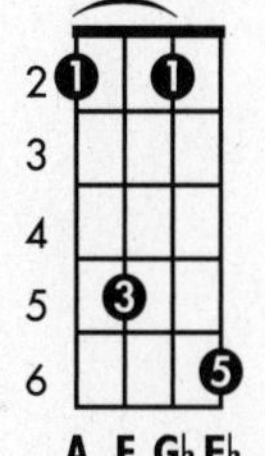

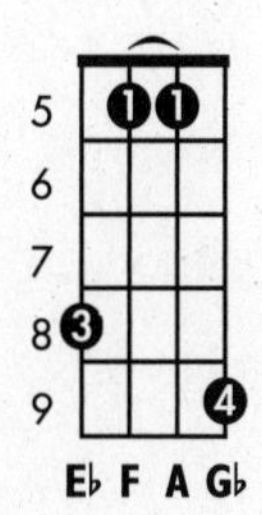

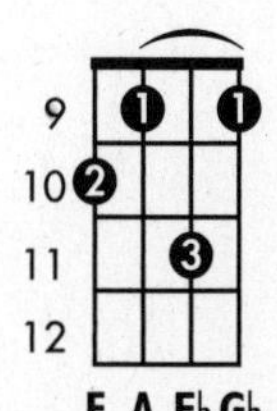

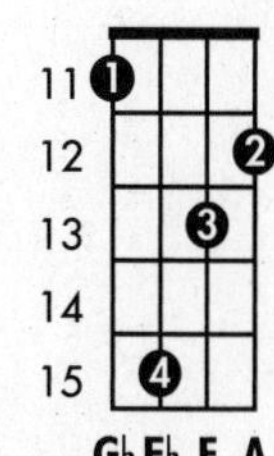

F

F7(♯9) — F Seventh Sharp Ninth

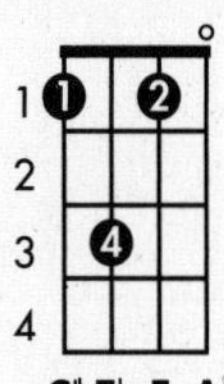

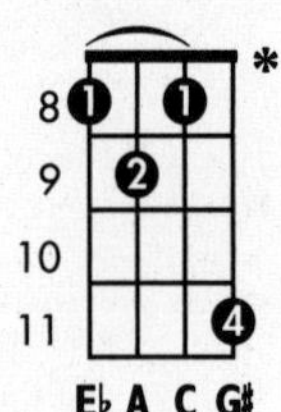

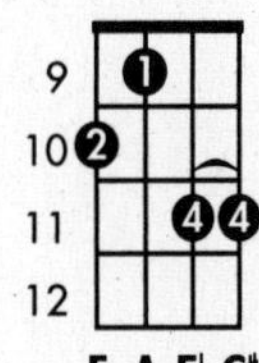

F7+(♭9) — F Seventh Flat Ninth Augmented Fifth

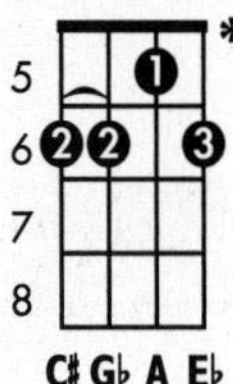

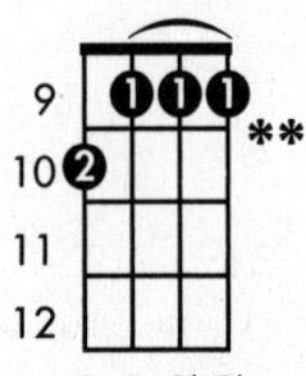

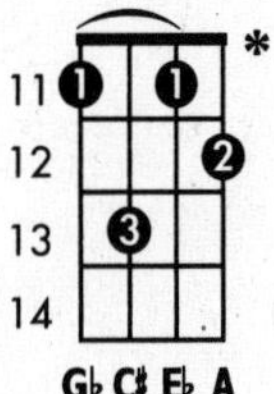

F9+ — F Ninth Augmented Fifth

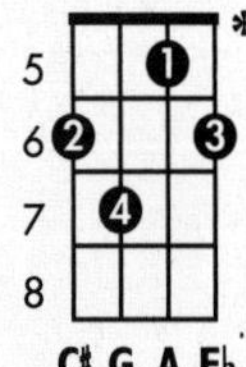

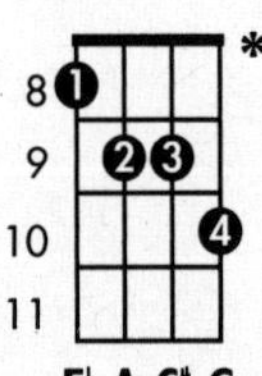

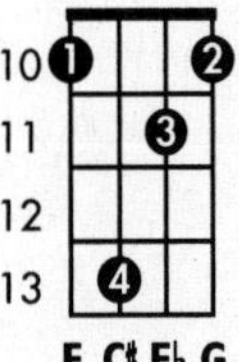

F9(♭5) — F Ninth Flat Fifth

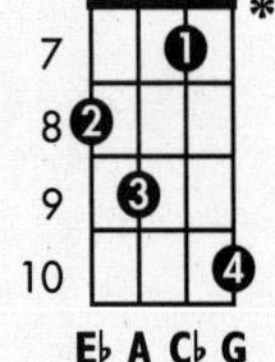

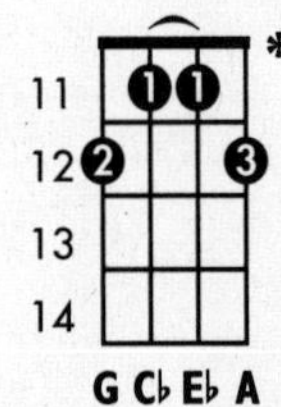

F Ninth Sharp Eleventh

F9(♯11)

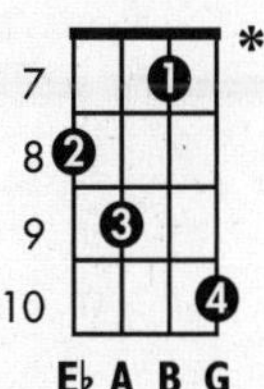

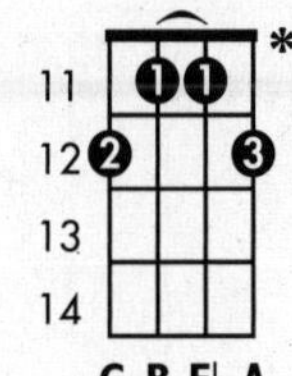

F Thirteenth Flat Ninth

F13(♭9)

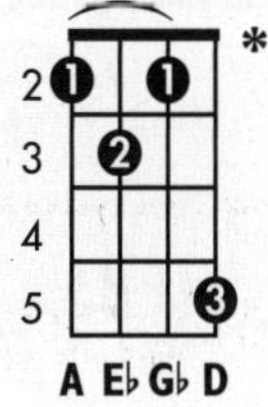

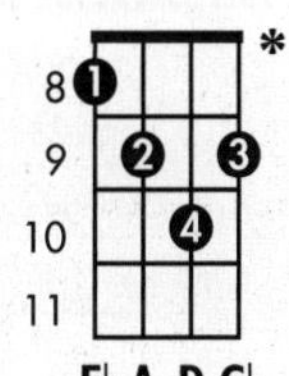

F Thirteenth Flat Ninth Flat Fifth

F13(♭9 ♭5)

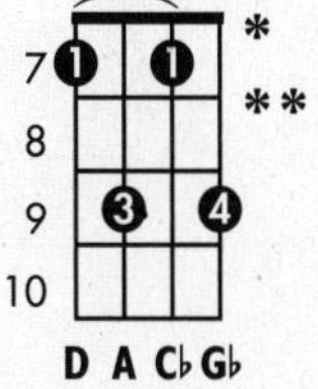

F♯ — F♯ Major

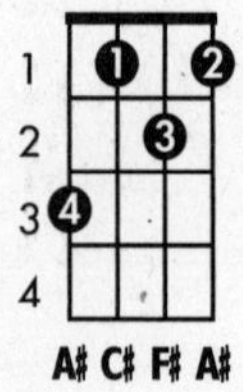

A♯ C♯ F♯ A♯

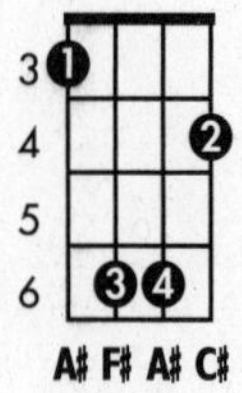

A♯ F♯ A♯ C♯

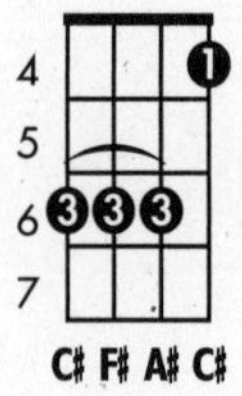

C♯ F♯ A♯ C♯

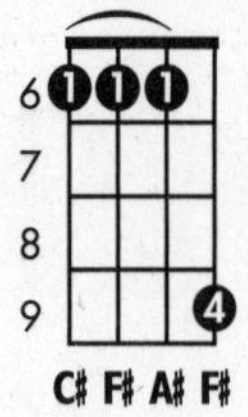

C♯ F♯ A♯ F♯

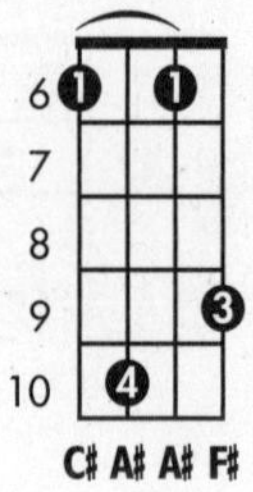

C♯ A♯ A♯ F♯

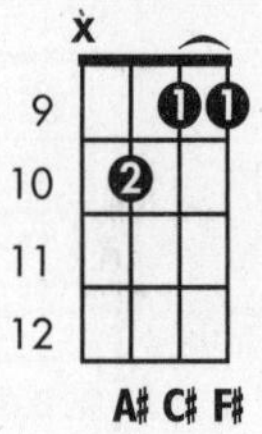

A♯ C♯ F♯

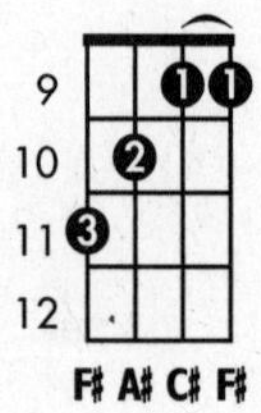

F♯ A♯ C♯ F♯

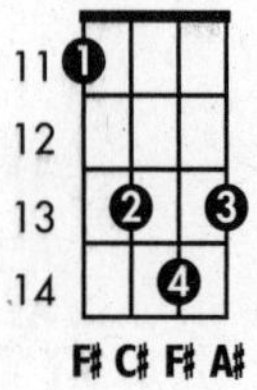

F♯ C♯ F♯ A♯

F♯m — F♯ Minor

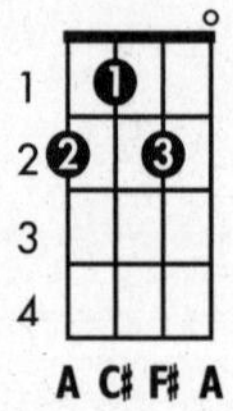

A C♯ F♯ A

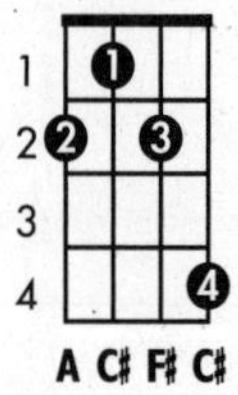

A C♯ F♯ C♯

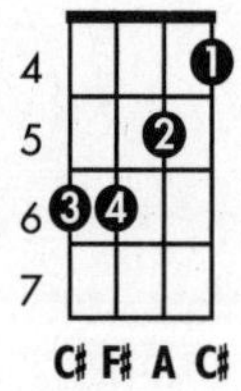

C♯ F♯ A C♯

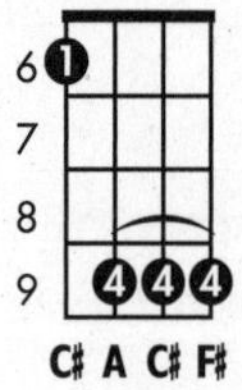

C♯ A C♯ F♯

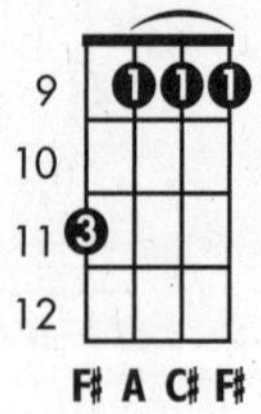

F♯ A C♯ F♯

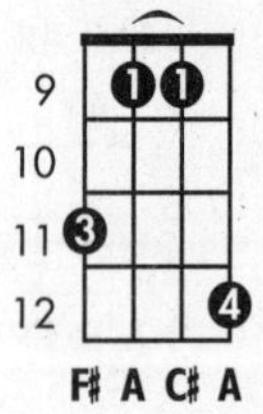

F♯ A C♯ A

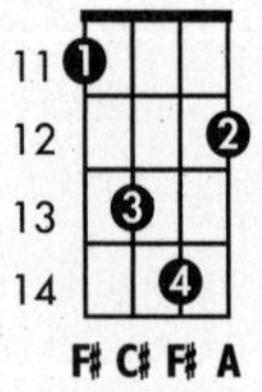

F♯ C♯ F♯ A

F♯° — F♯ Diminished

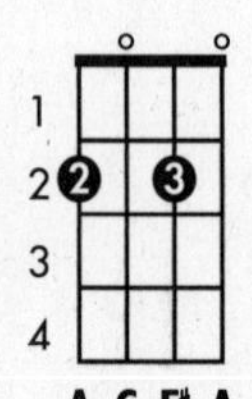

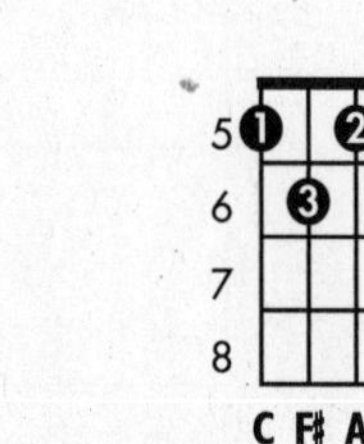

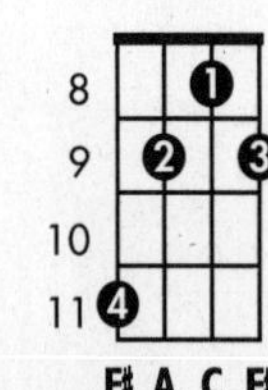

F♯ Augmented

F♯+

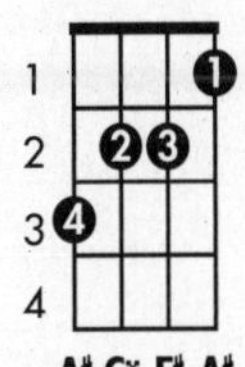
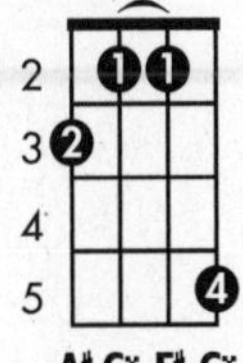
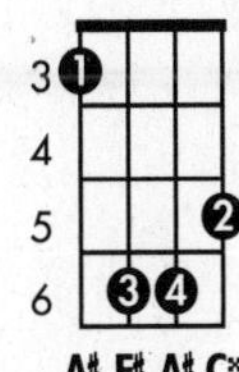
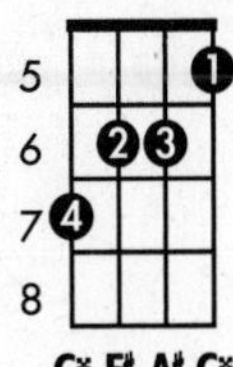
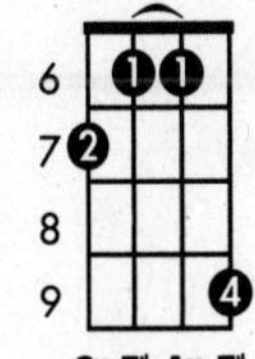
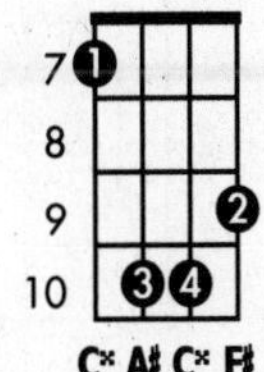
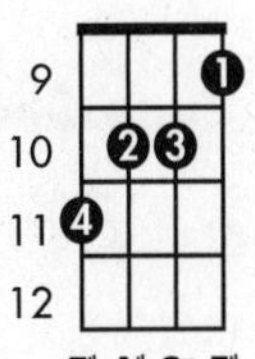
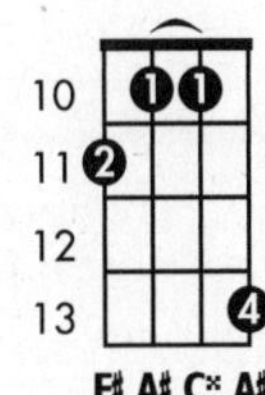
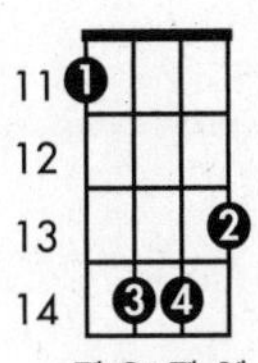

F♯ Fifth

F♯5

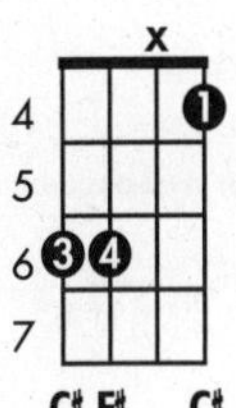
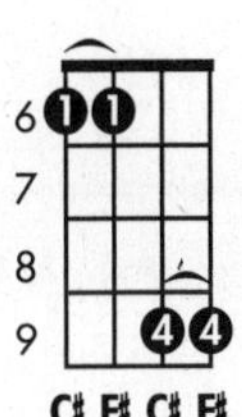
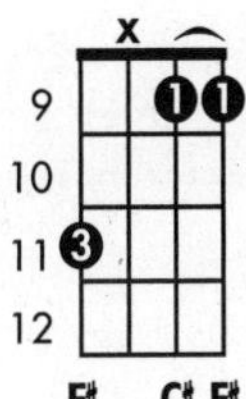
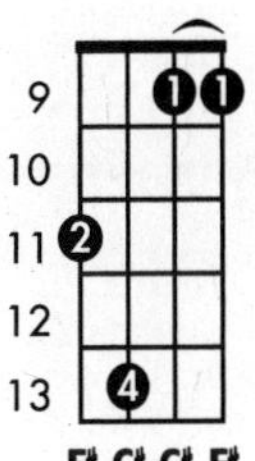

F♯ Major Suspended Fourth

F♯sus

Sometimes written **F♯sus4**

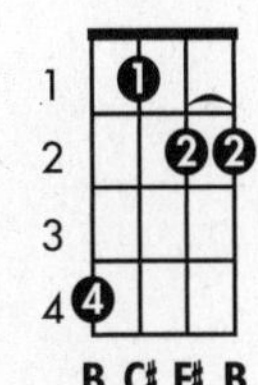
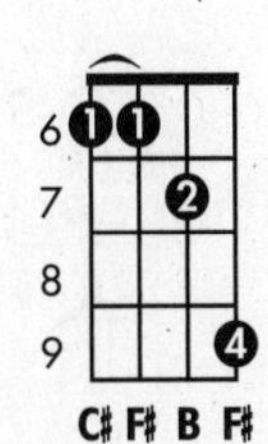
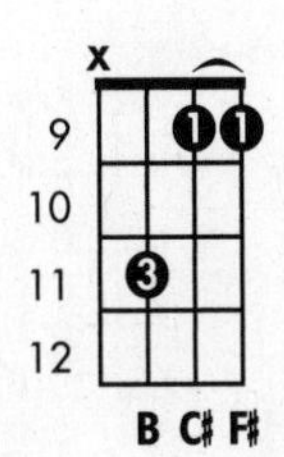
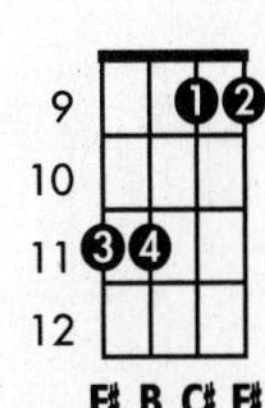
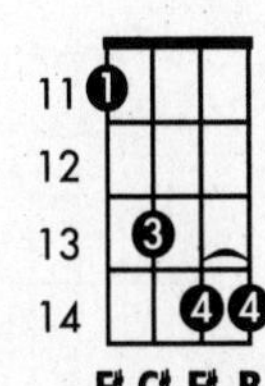

F#6 — F# Major 6th

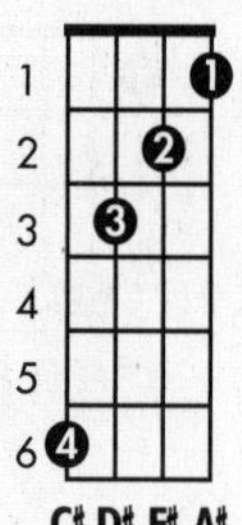

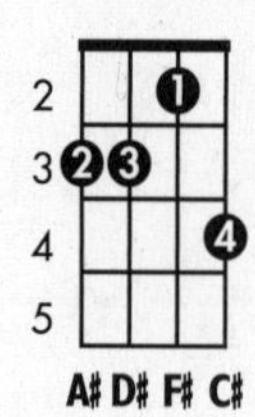

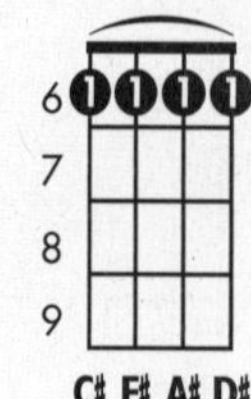

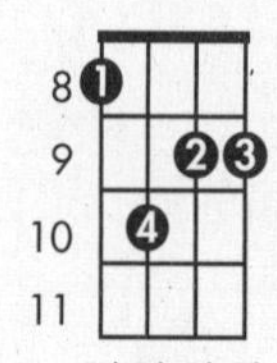

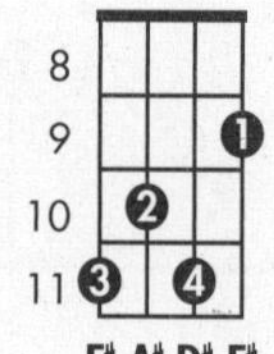

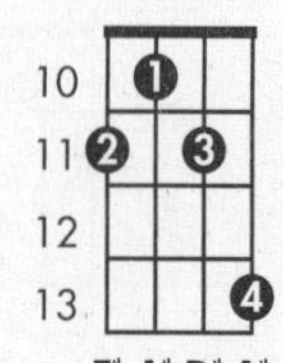

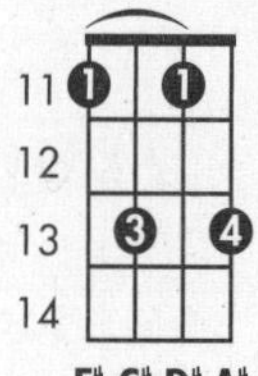

F#m6 — F# Minor Sixth

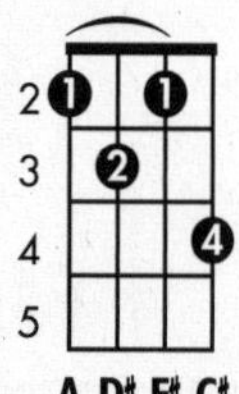

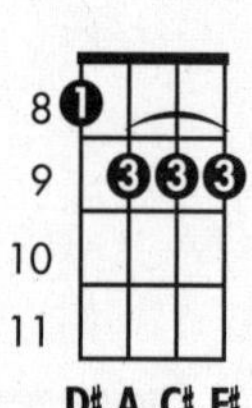

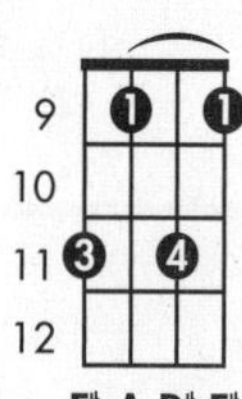

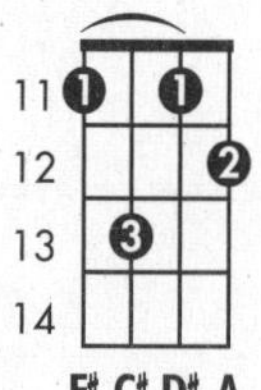

F#maj7 — F# Major Seventh

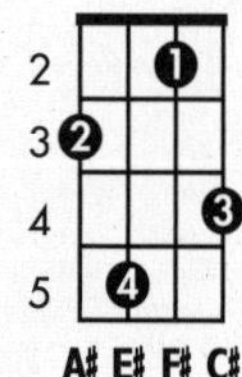

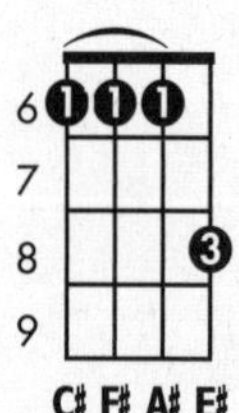

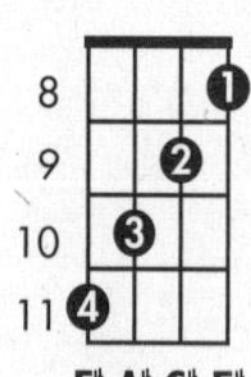

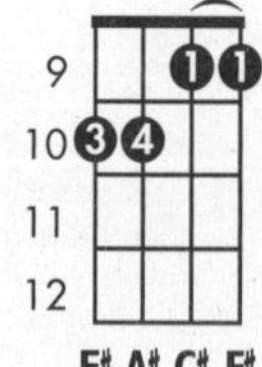

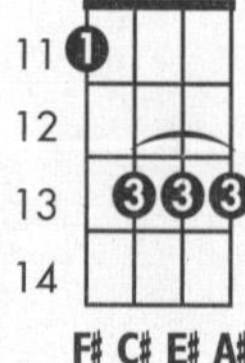

F#7 — F# Seventh

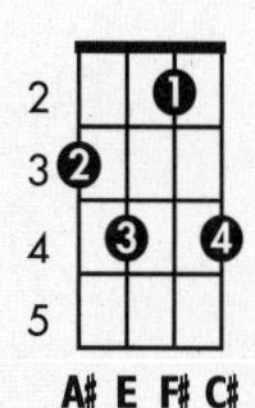

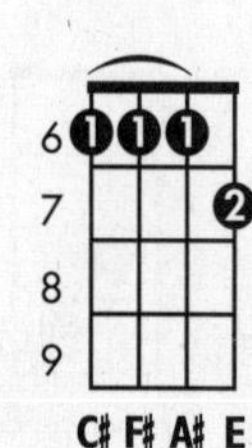

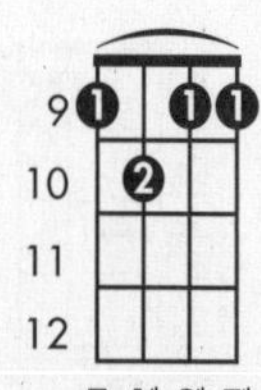

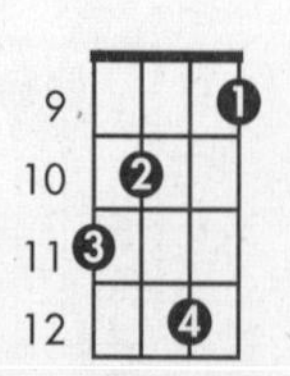

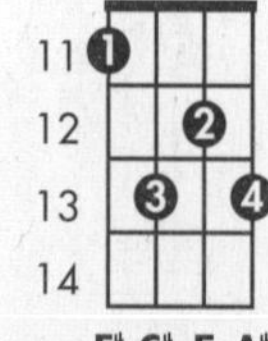

F♯ Minor Seventh

F♯m7

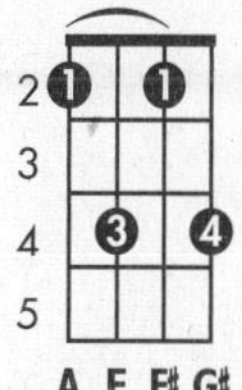

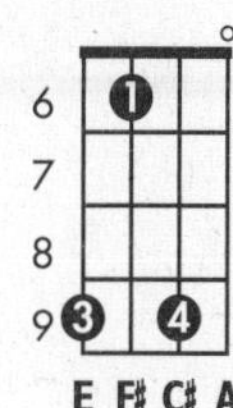
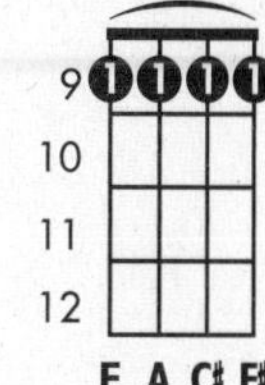
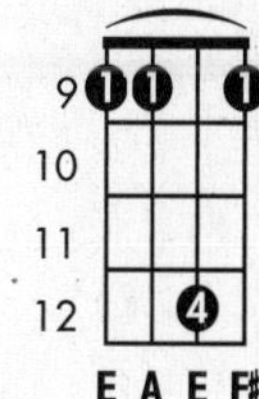

F♯ Minor Seventh Flat Fifth

F♯m7(♭5)

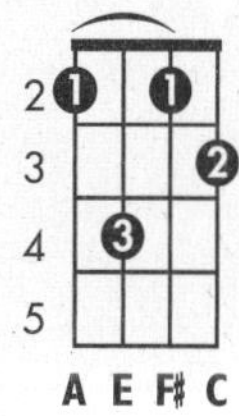
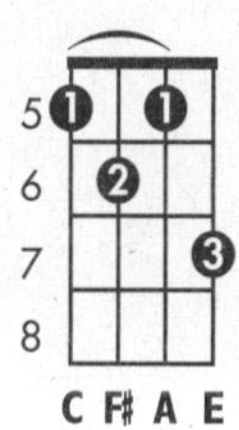
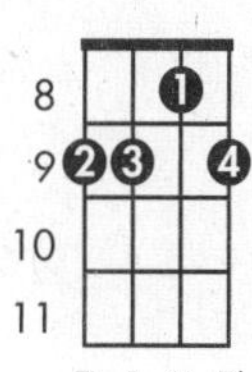
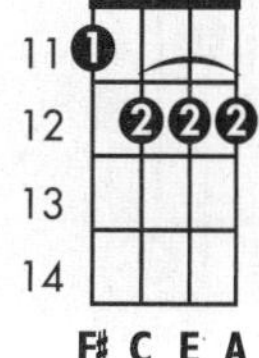

F♯ Diminished Seventh

F♯°7

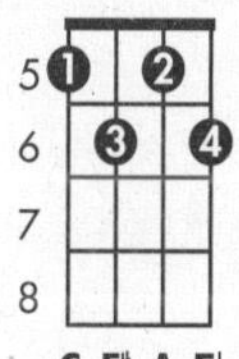
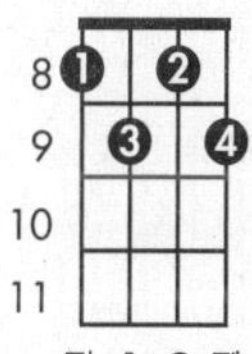
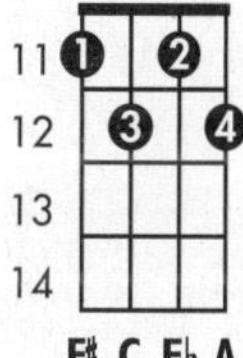
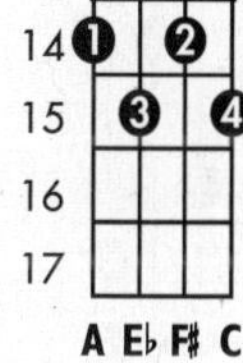

F♯ Seventh Suspended Fourth

F♯7sus

Sometimes written **F♯7sus4**

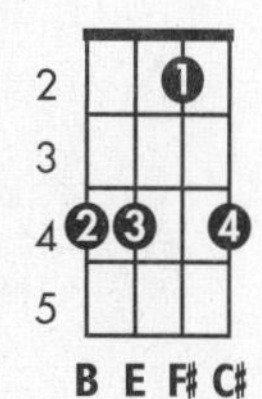
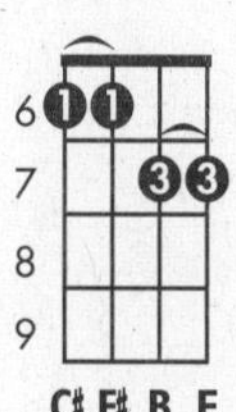
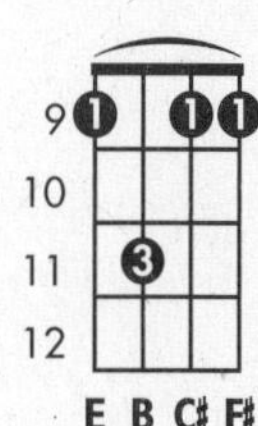
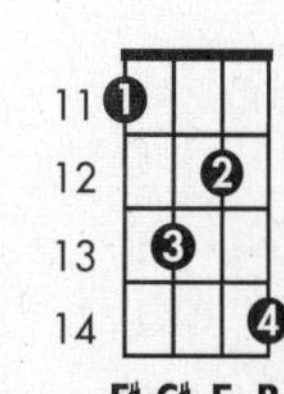

F♯(add9) — F♯ Major Add Ninth

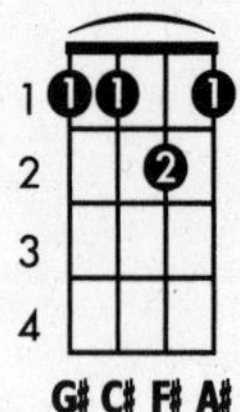
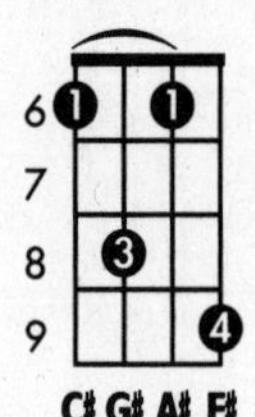
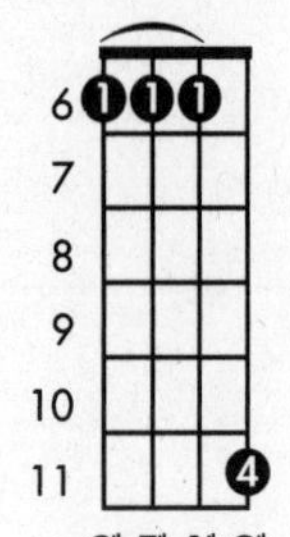
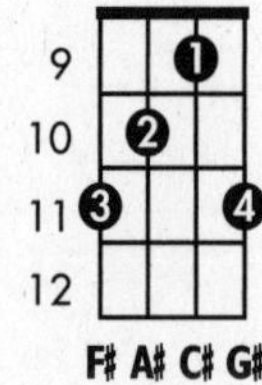
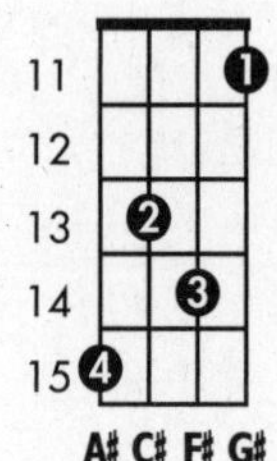

F♯maj9 — F♯ Major Ninth

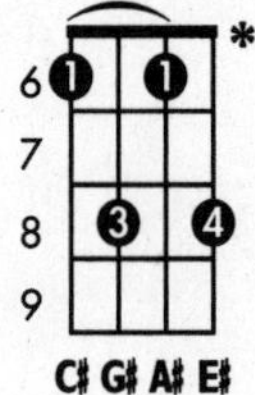
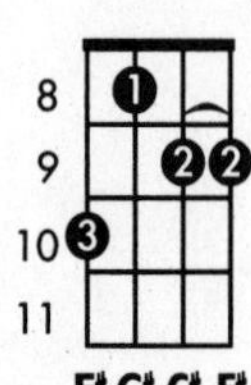
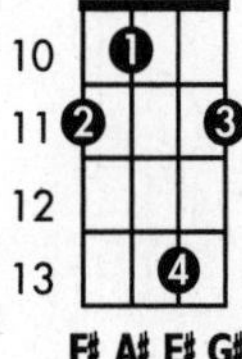

F♯9 — F♯ Ninth

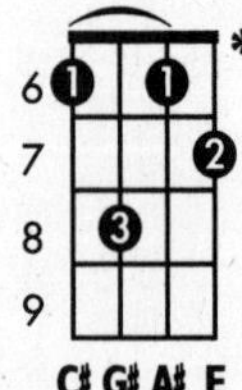
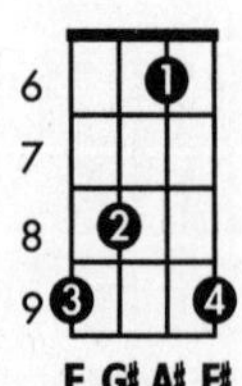
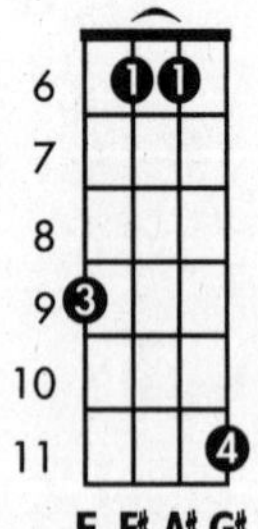
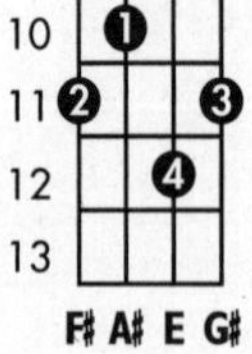

F♯m9 — F♯ Minor Ninth

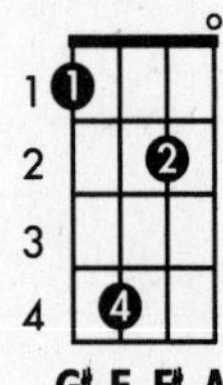
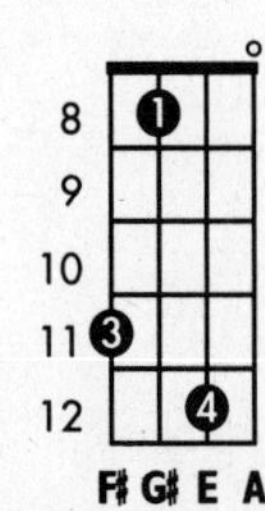
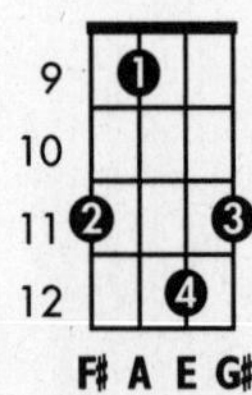

F♯ Sixth Add Ninth

F♯6/9

Sometimes written F♯9/6

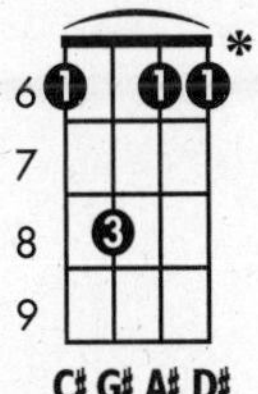

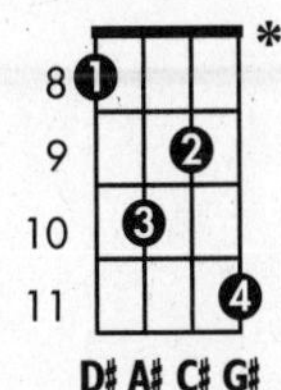

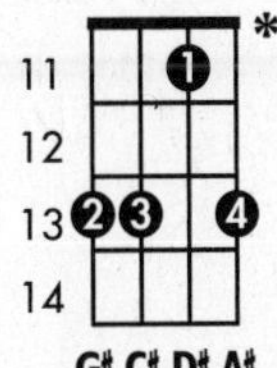

F♯ Minor Sixth Add Ninth

F♯m6/9

Sometimes written F♯m9/6

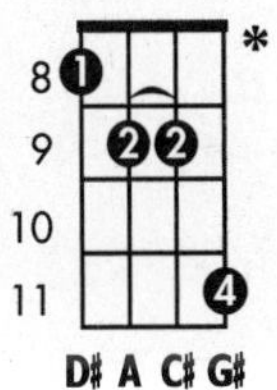

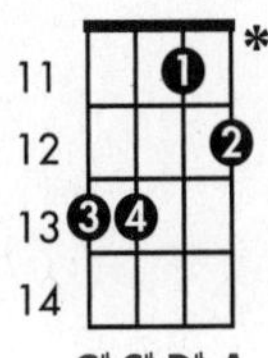

F♯ Minor Major Seventh

F♯m(maj7)

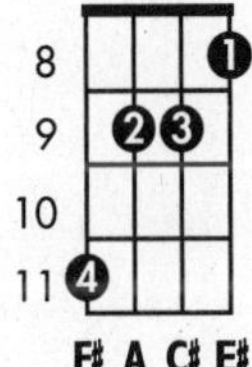

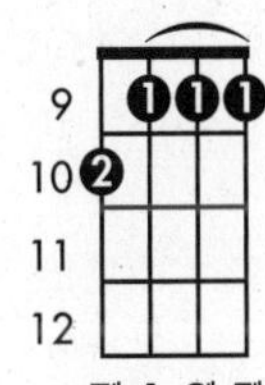

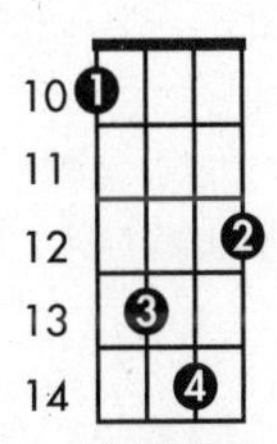

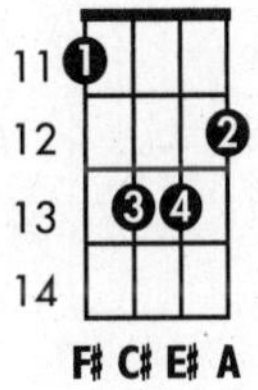

F♯ Minor Ninth Major Seventh

F♯m9(maj7)

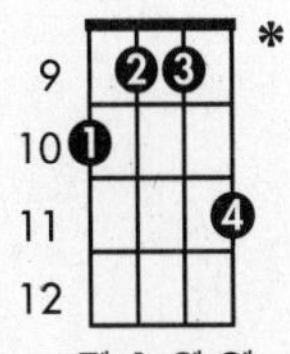

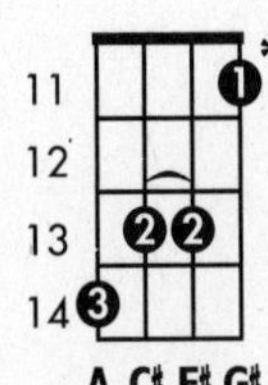

F♯11

F♯ Eleventh

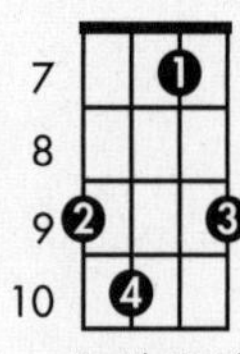

F♯m11

F♯ Minor Eleventh

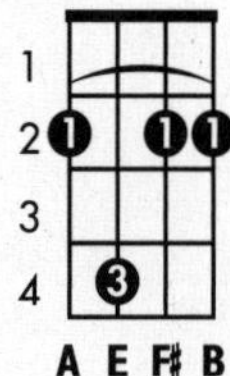

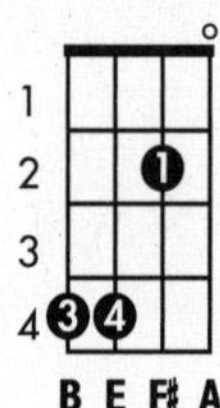

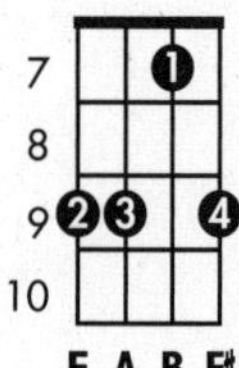

F♯13

F♯ Thirteenth

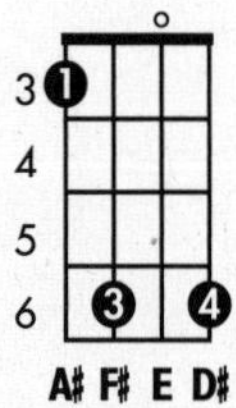

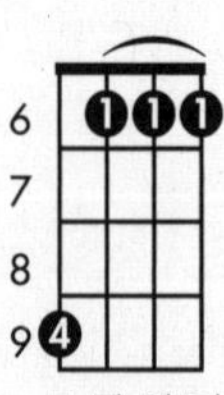

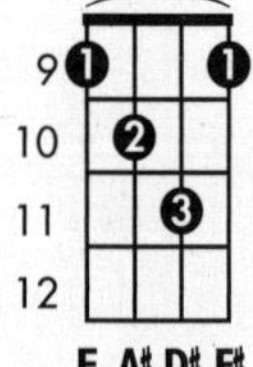

F♯(♭5)

F♯ Flat Fifth

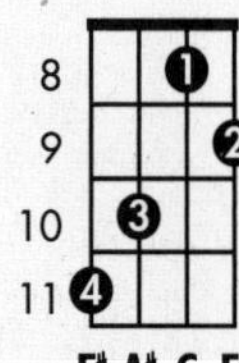

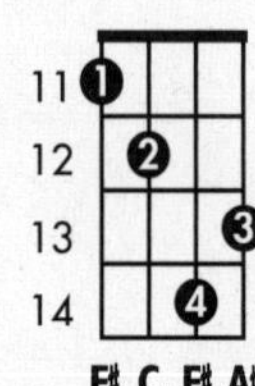

F♯ Seventh Flat Fifth

F♯7(♭5)

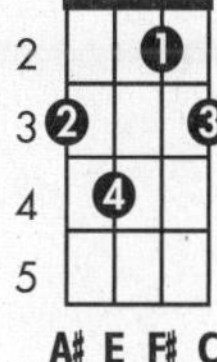

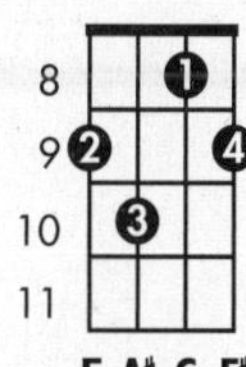

F♯ Seventh Augmented Fifth

F♯7+

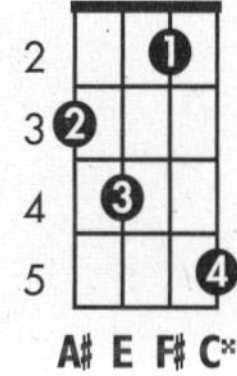

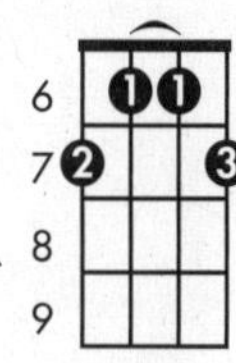

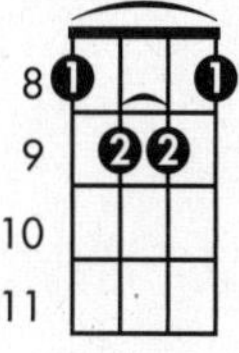

F♯ Major Seventh Flat Fifth

F♯maj7(♭5)

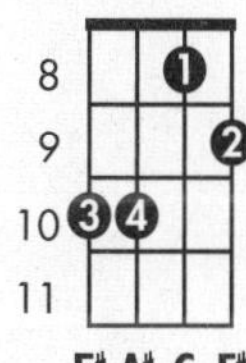

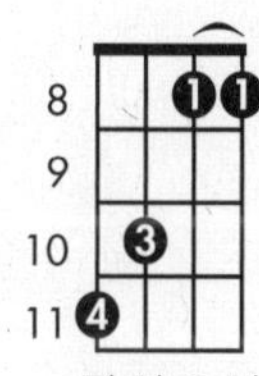

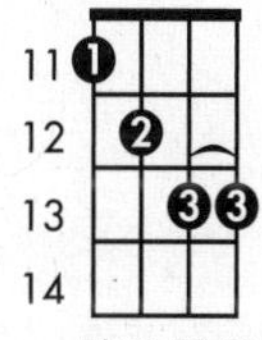

F♯ Seventh Flat Ninth

F♯7(♭9)

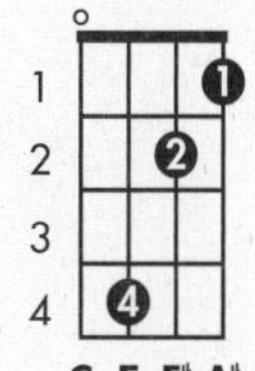

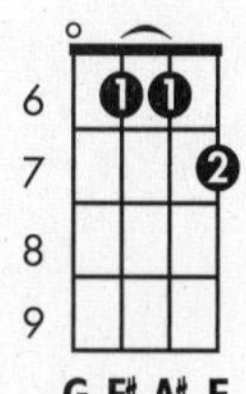

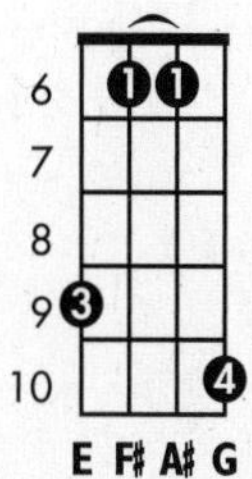

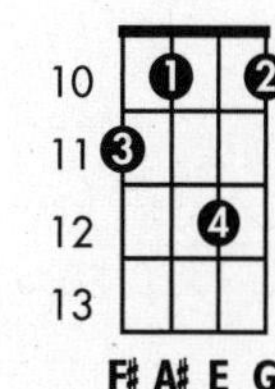

F♯7(♯9) — F♯ Seventh Sharp Ninth

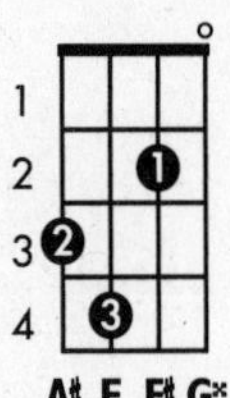

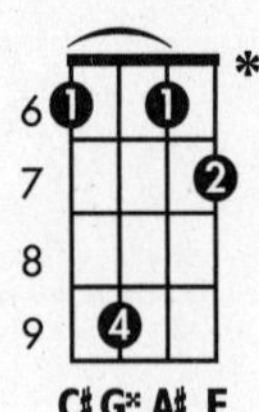

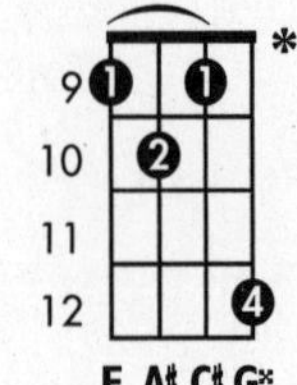

F♯ A♯ E G×

F♯7+(♭9) — F♯ Seventh Flat Ninth Augmented Fifth

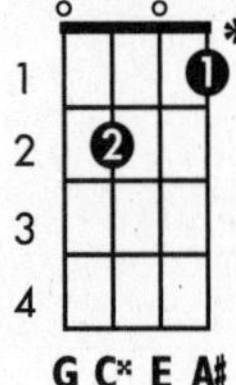

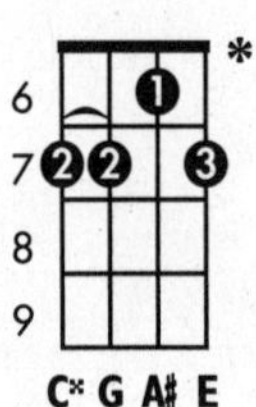

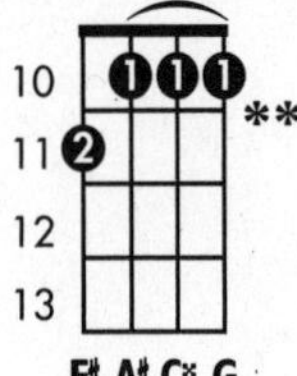

F♯9+ — F♯ Ninth Augmented Fifth

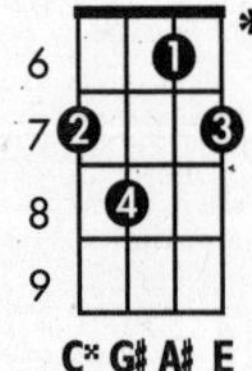

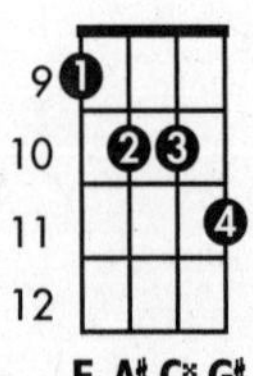

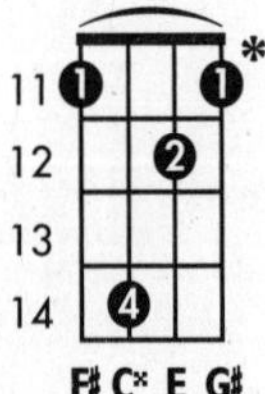

F♯9(♭5) — F♯ Ninth Flat Fifth

F♯

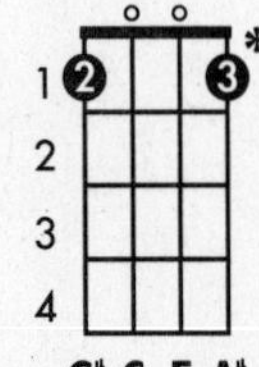

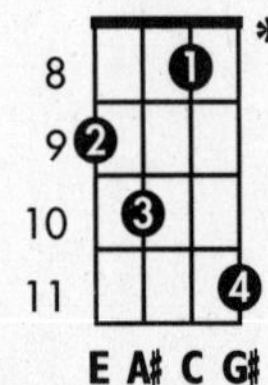

F♯ Ninth Sharp Eleventh

F♯9(♯11)

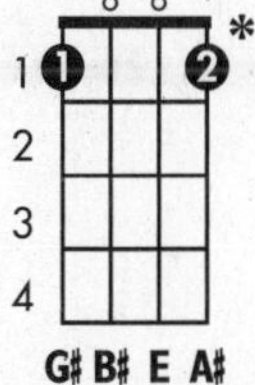

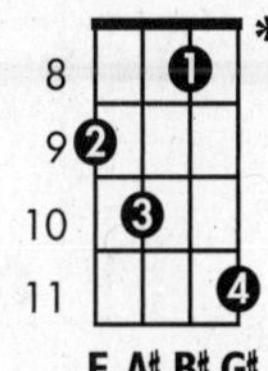

F♯ Thirteenth Flat Ninth

F♯13(♭9)

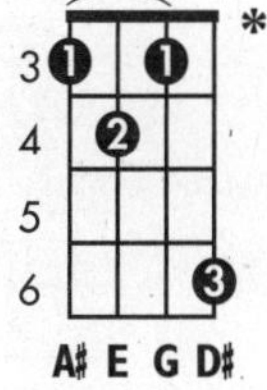

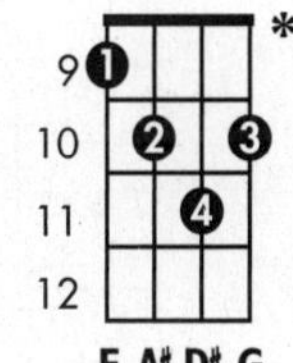

F♯ Thirteenth Flat Ninth Flat Fifth

F♯13(♭9 ♭5)

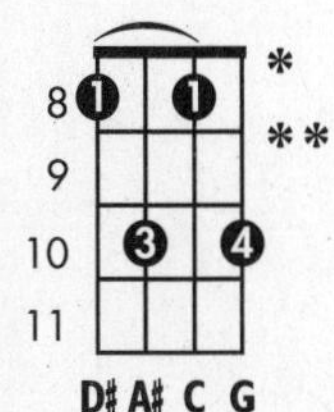

G — G Major

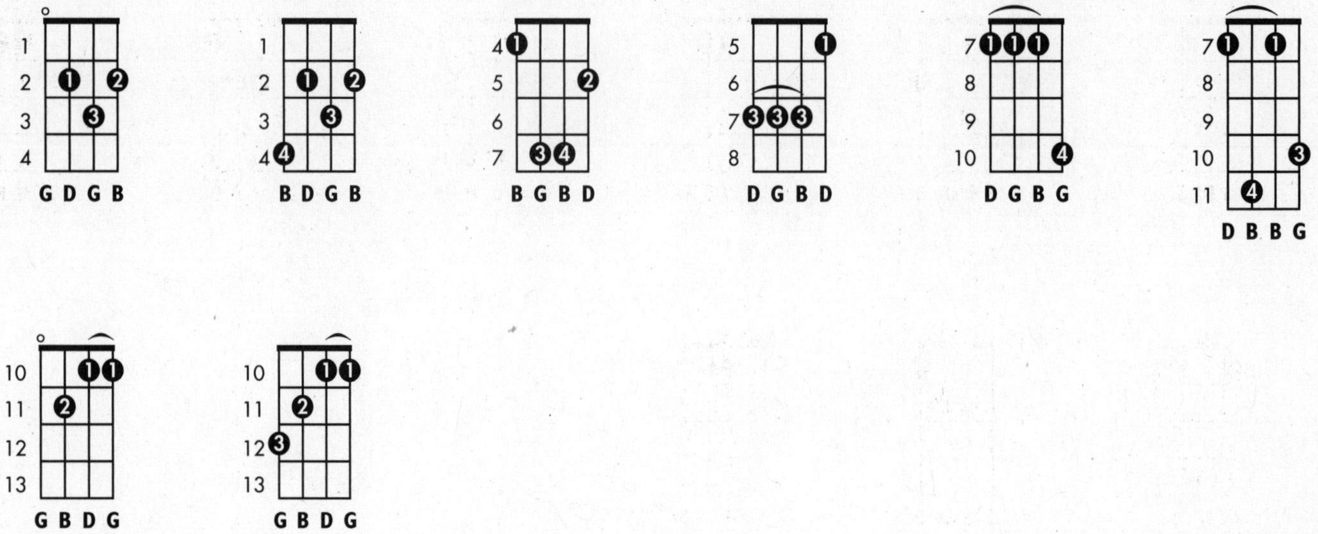

1 2 3 4 — G D G B

1 2 3 4 — B D G B

4 5 6 7 — B G B D

5 6 7 8 — D G B D

7 8 9 10 — D G B G

7 8 9 10 11 — D B B G

10 11 12 13 — G B D G

10 11 12 13 — G B D G

Gm — G Minor

1 2 3 4 — G D G B♭

1 2 3 4 — B♭ D G B♭

2 3 4 5 — B♭ D G D

5 6 7 8 — D G B♭ D

7 8 9 10 — D B♭ D G

10 11 12 13 — G B♭ D G

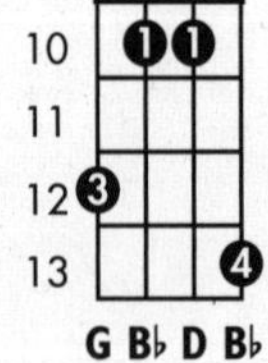

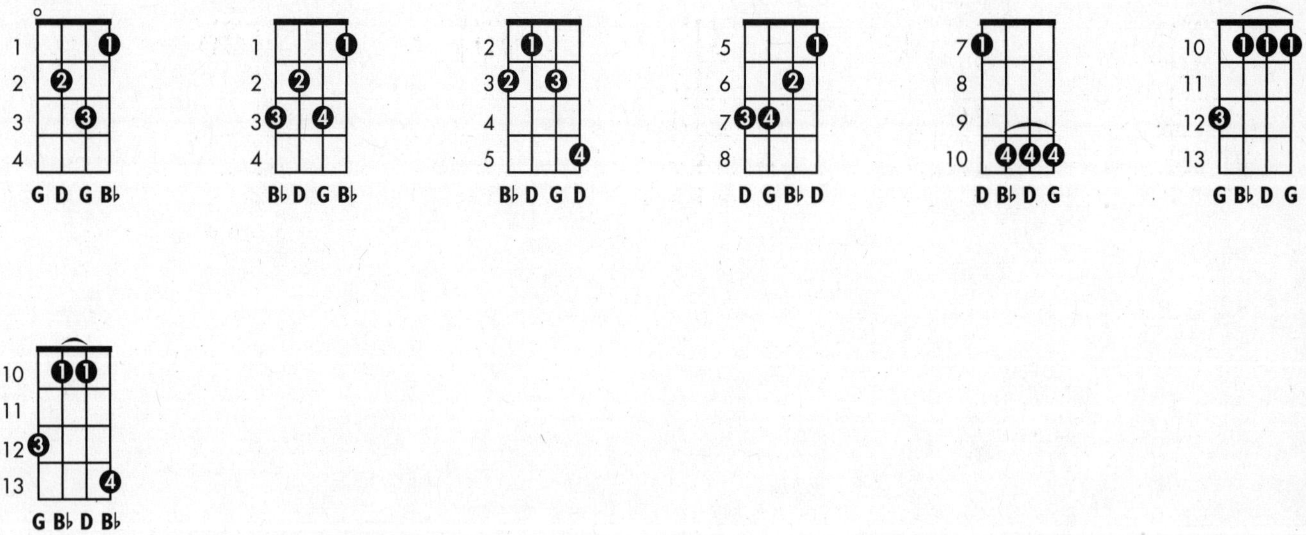

G° — G Diminished

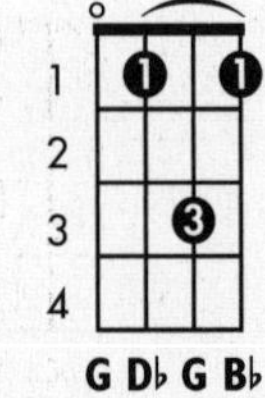

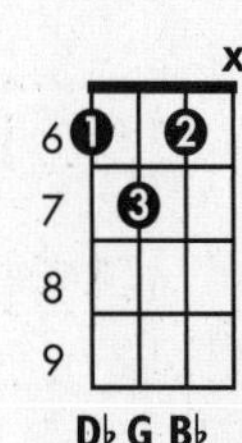

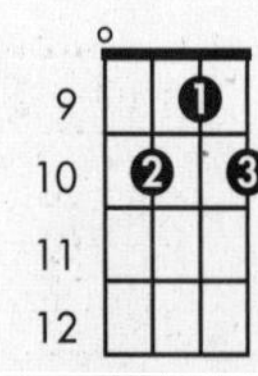

G

G Augmented

G+

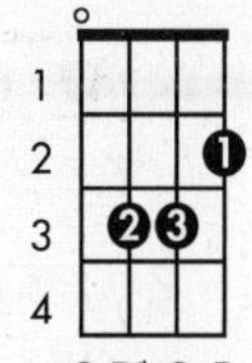

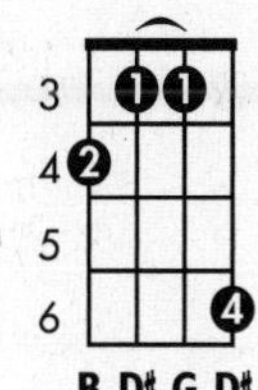
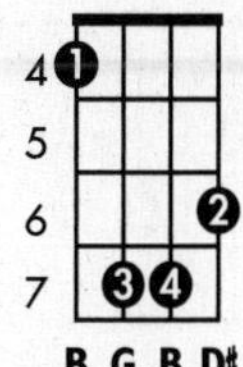
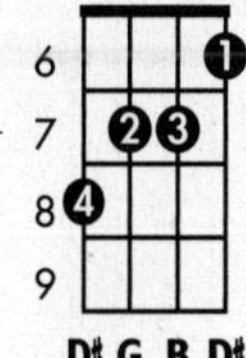
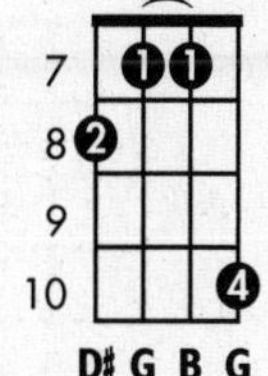
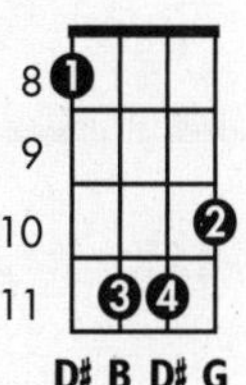
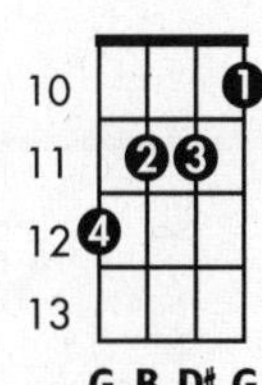
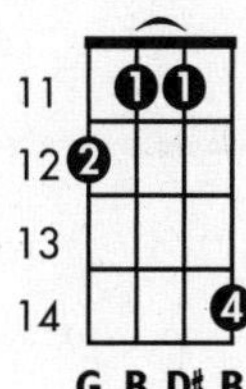

G Fifth

G5

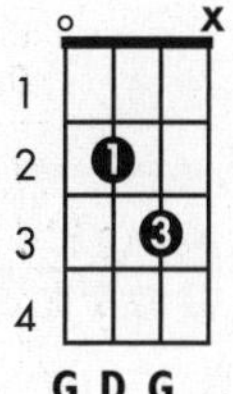
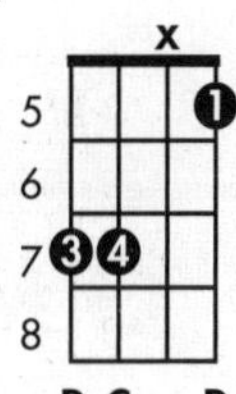
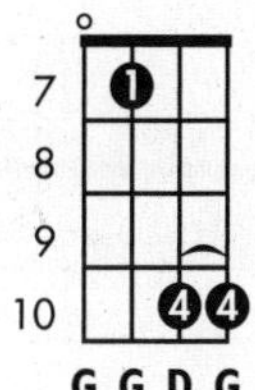
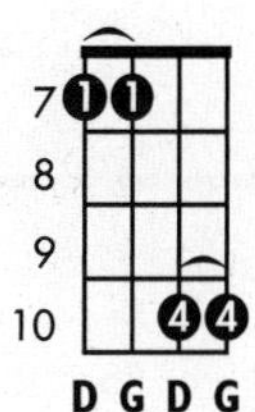
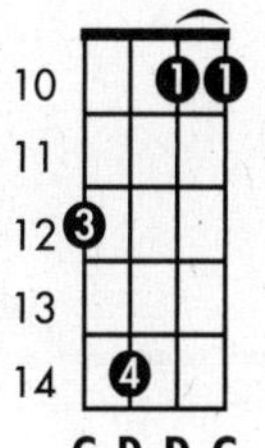

G Major Suspended Fourth

Gsus

Sometimes written **Gsus4**

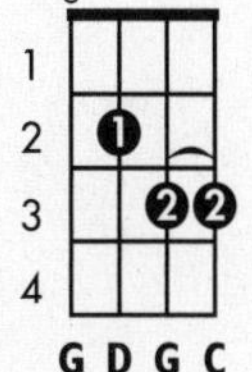
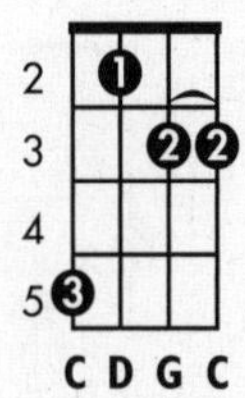
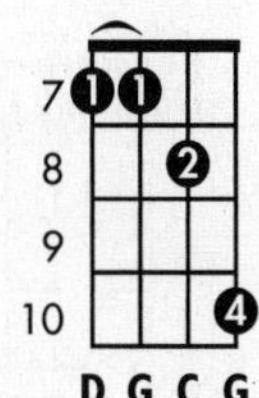
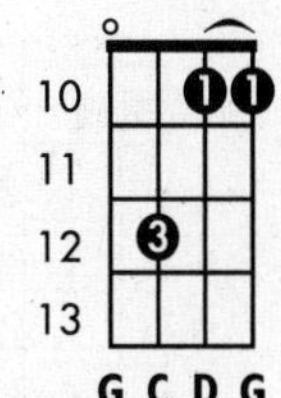
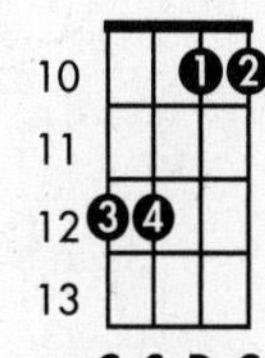
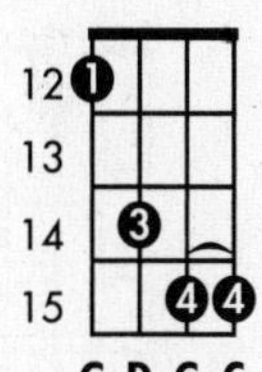

G6 — G Major 6th

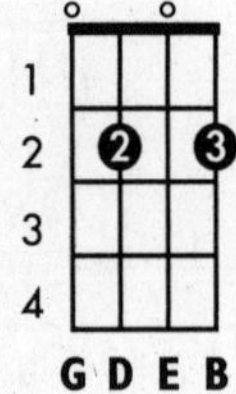

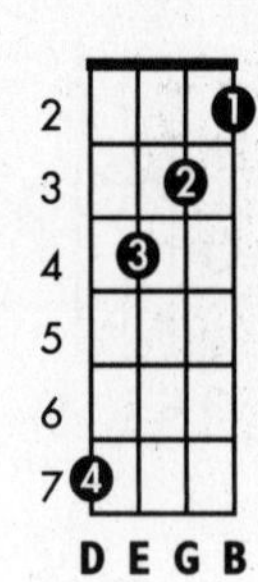

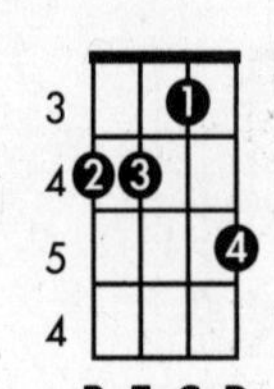

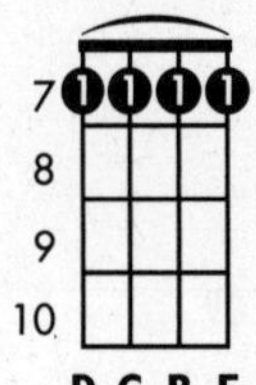

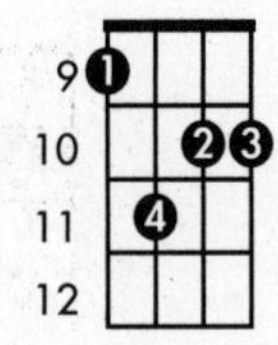

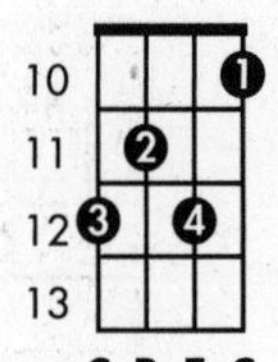

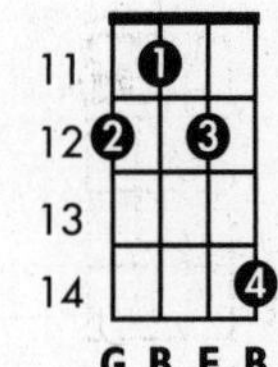

Gm6 — G Minor Sixth

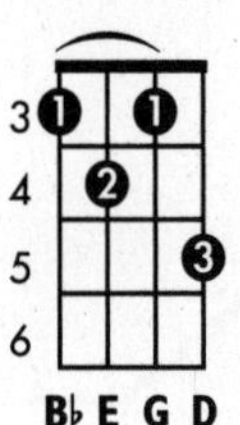

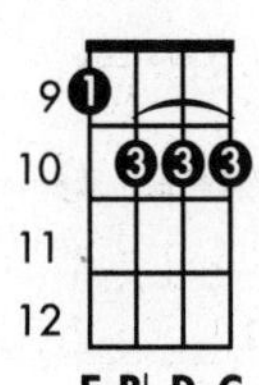

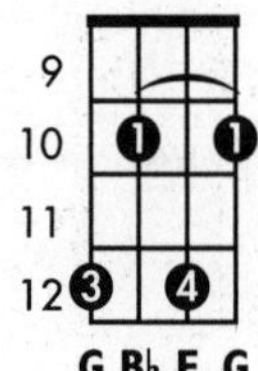

Gmaj7 — G Major Seventh

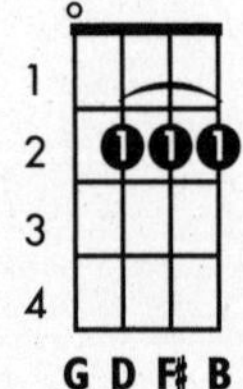

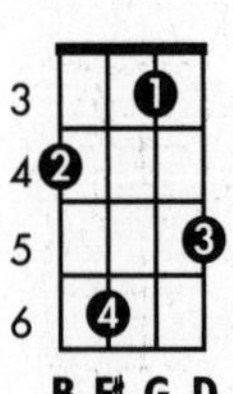

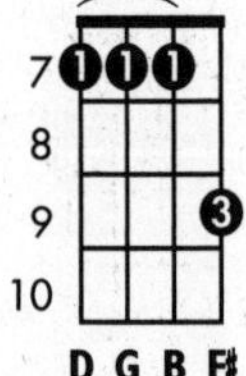

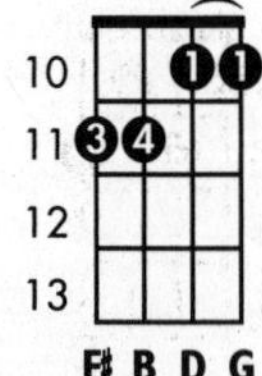

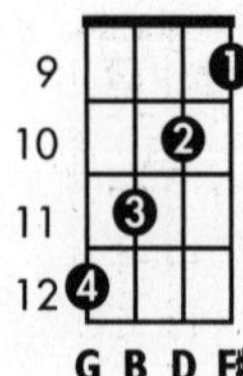

G7 — G Seventh

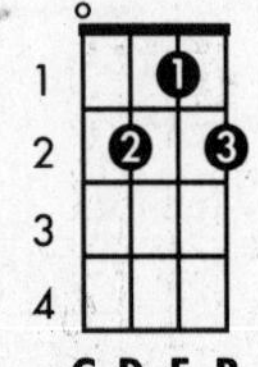

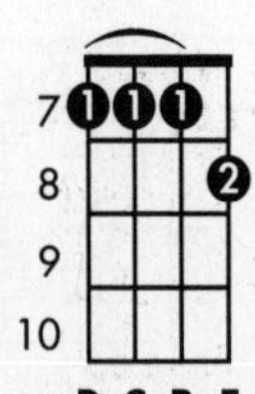

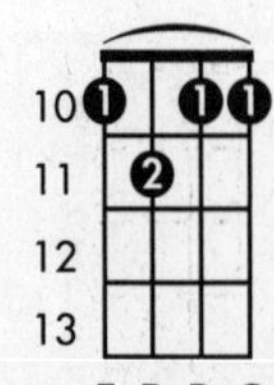

G Minor Seventh — Gm7

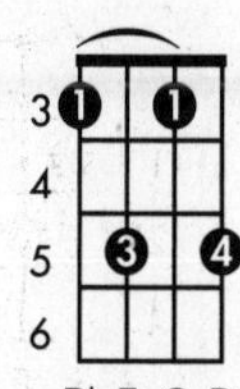

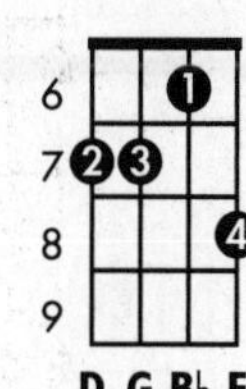

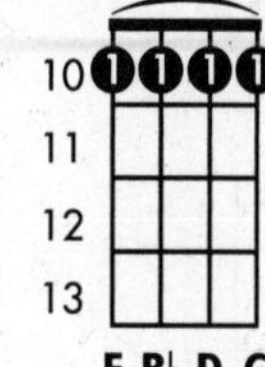

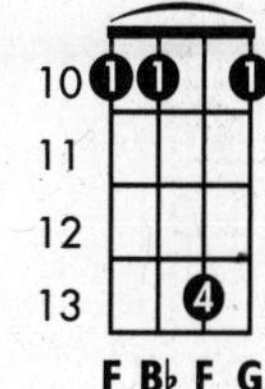

G Minor Seventh Flat Fifth — Gm7(♭5)

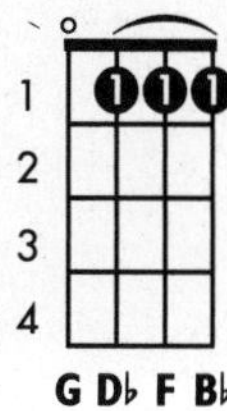

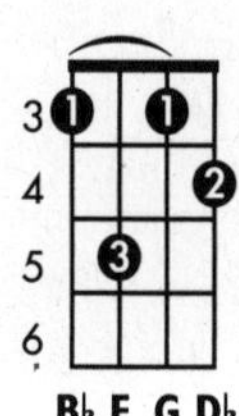

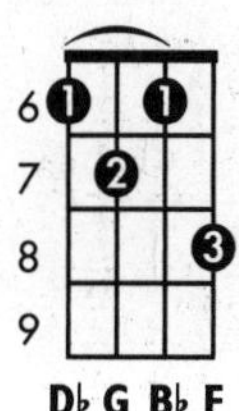

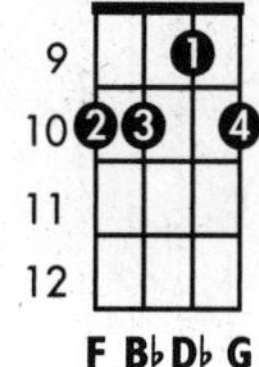

G Diminished Seventh — G°7

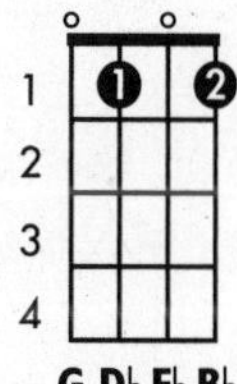

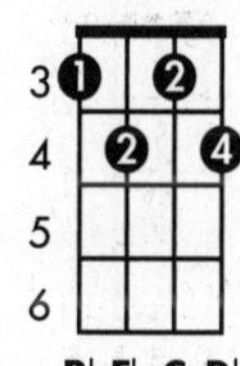

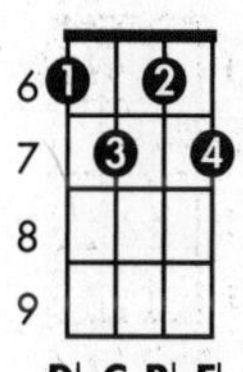

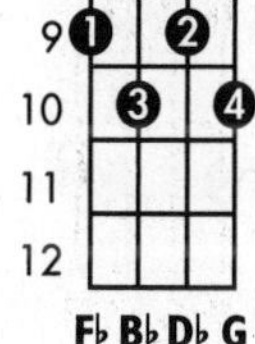

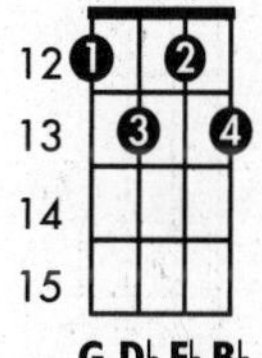

G Seventh Suspended Fourth — G7sus

Sometimes written **G7sus4**

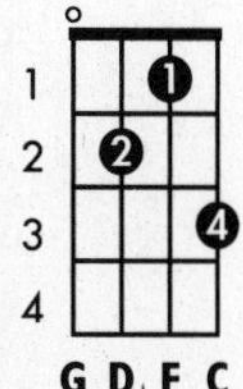

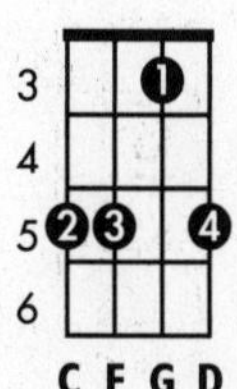

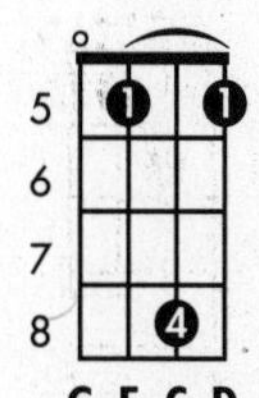

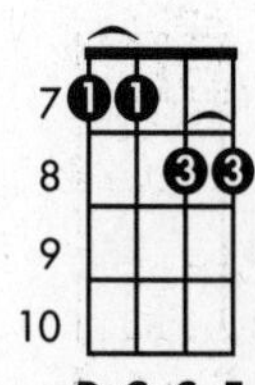

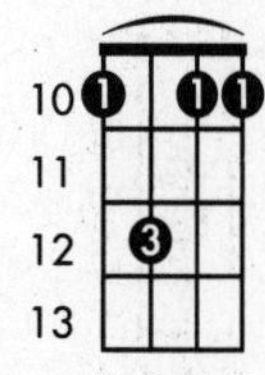

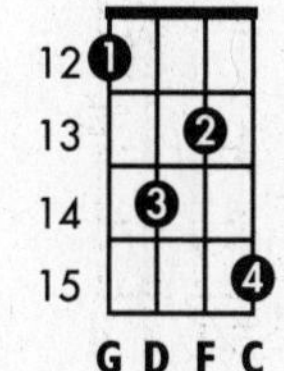

G(add9) — G Major Add Ninth

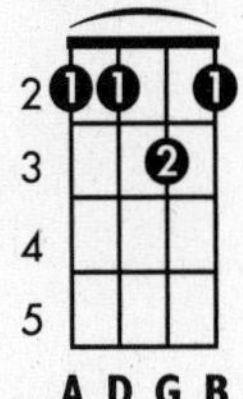

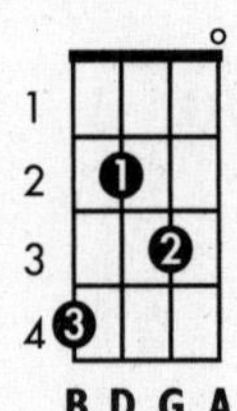

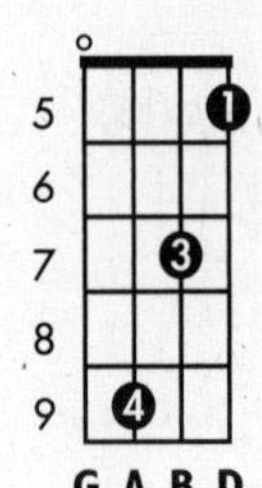

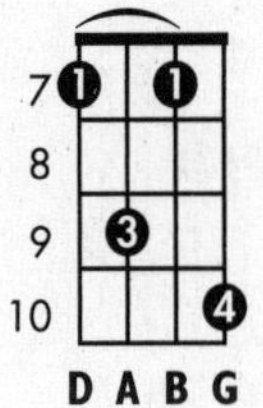

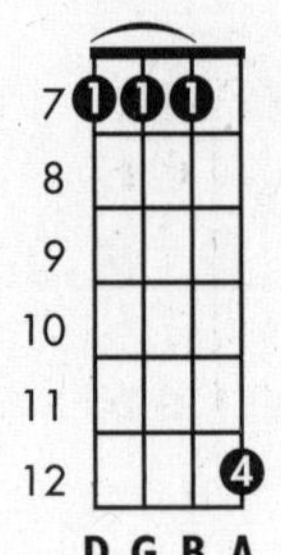

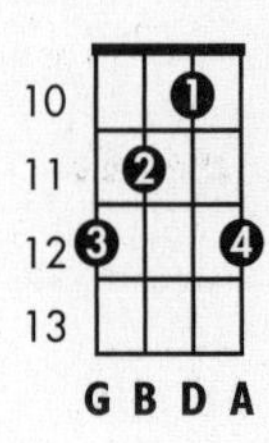

Gmaj9 — G Major Ninth

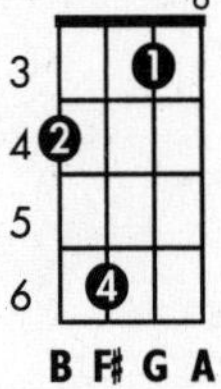

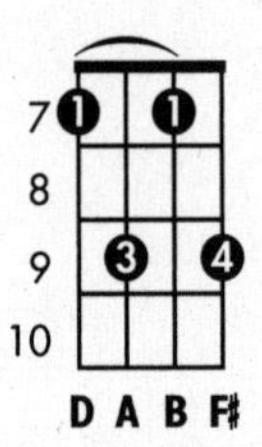

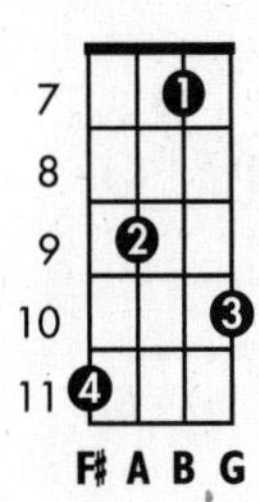

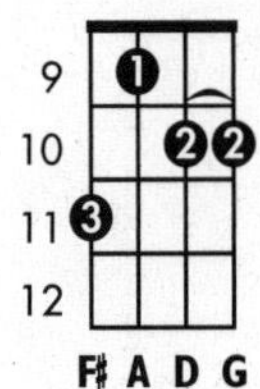

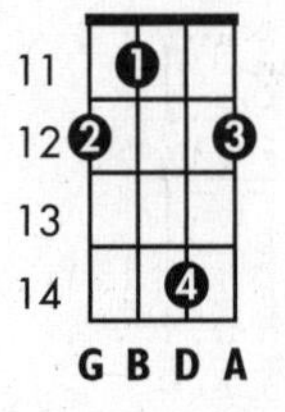

G9 — G Ninth

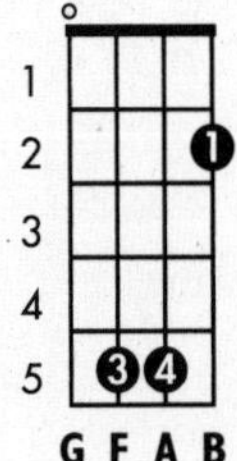

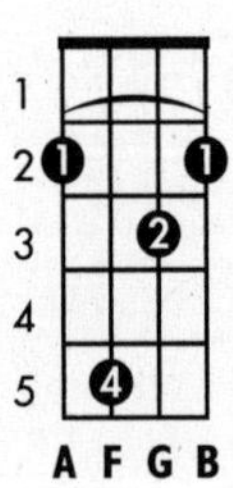

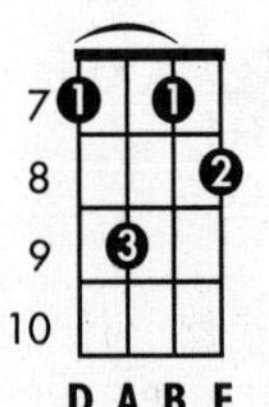

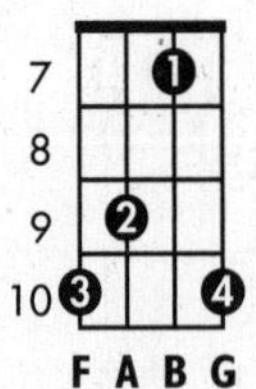

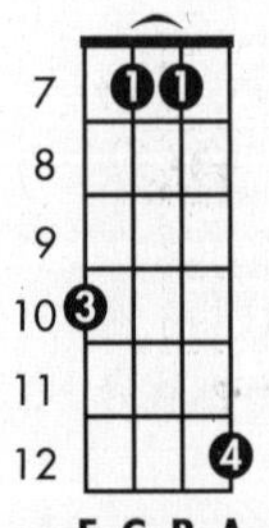

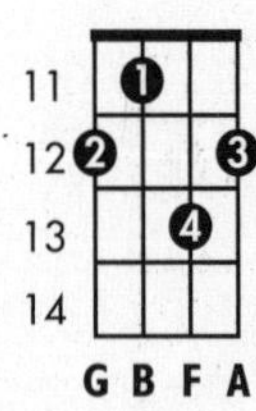

Gm9 — G Minor Ninth

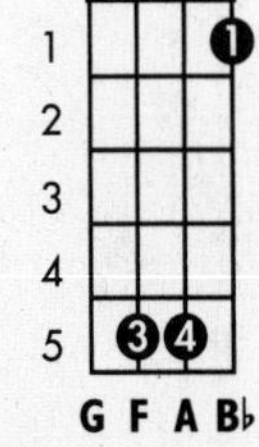

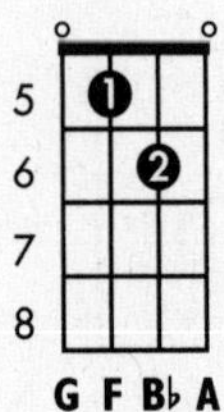

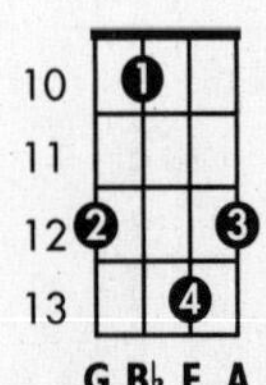

G

G Sixth Add Ninth

G6/9

Sometimes written $G^{9/6}$

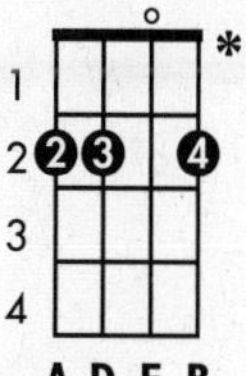

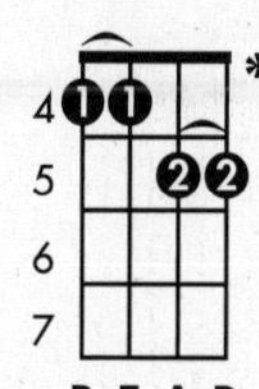

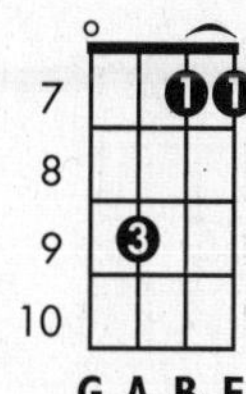

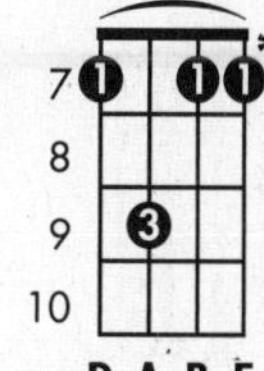

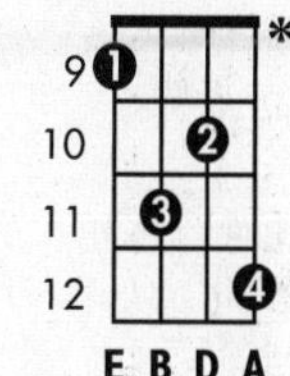

G Minor Sixth Add Ninth

Gm6/9

Sometimes written $Gm^{9/6}$

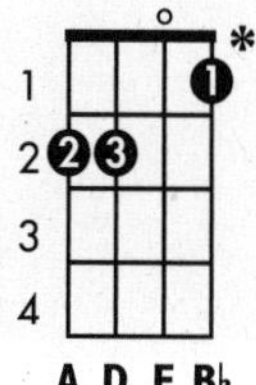

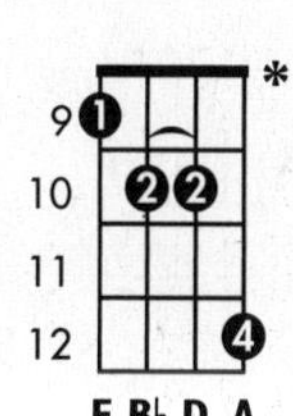

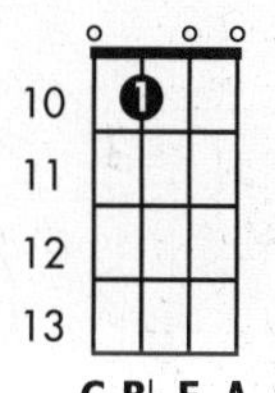

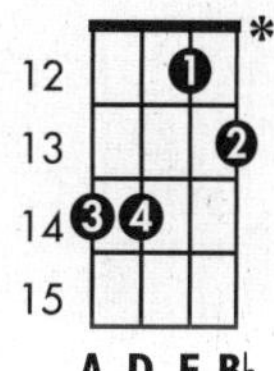

G Minor Major Seventh

Gm(maj7)

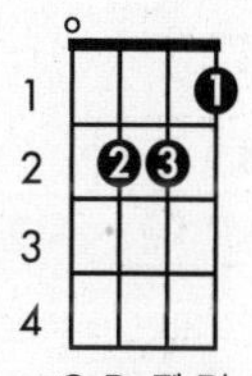

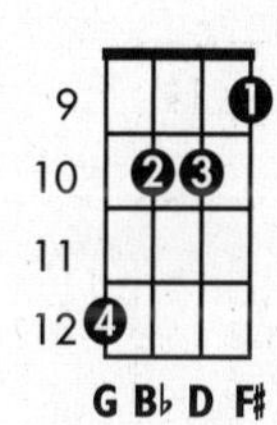

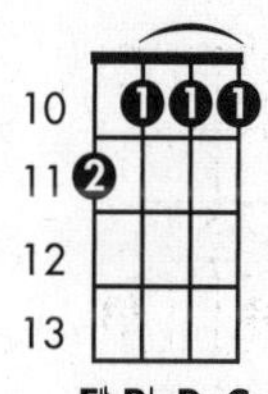

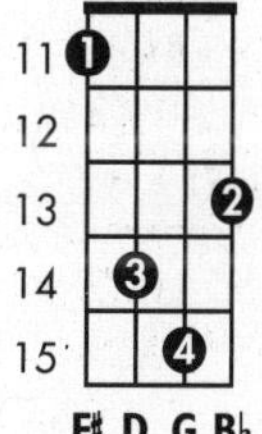

G Minor Ninth Major Seventh

Gm9(maj7)

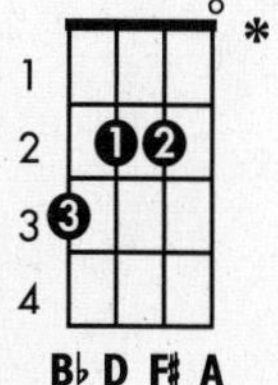

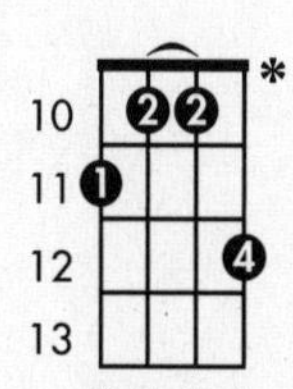

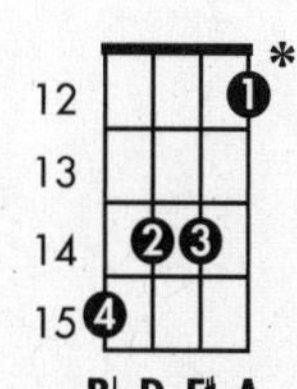

G

G11 — G Eleventh

G C F A

C F G D

C G A F

F B C G

Gm11 — G Minor Eleventh

G C F B♭

B♭ F G C

C G B♭ F

G13 — G Thirteenth

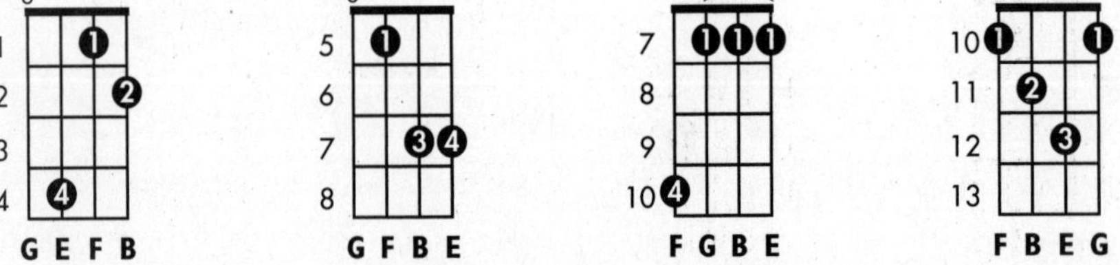

G(♭5) — G Flat Fifth

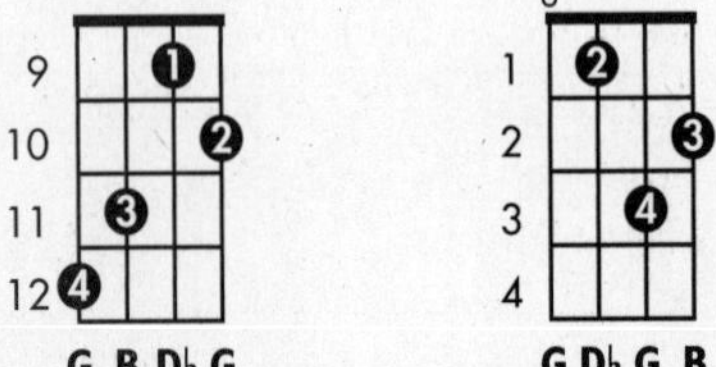

G Seventh Flat Fifth

G7(♭5)

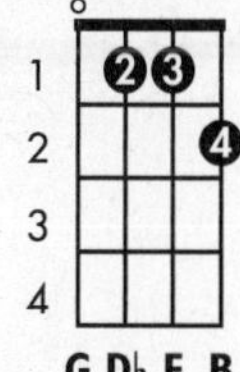

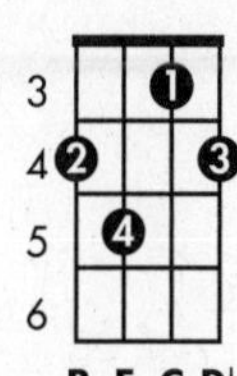

6
7
8
9
D♭ G B F

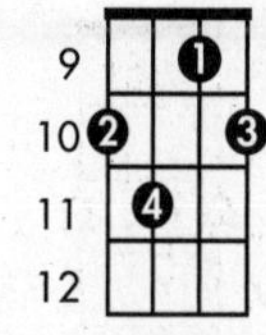

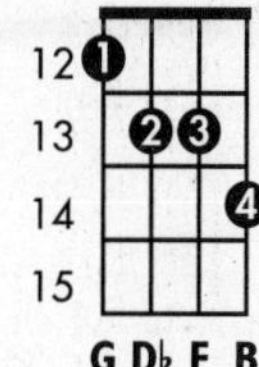

G Seventh Augmented Fifth

G7+

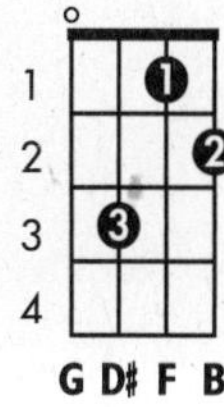

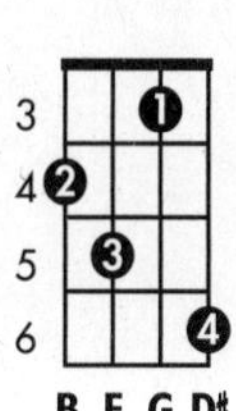

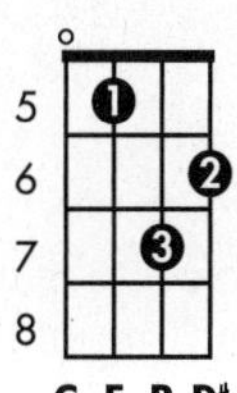

7
8
9
10
D♯ G B F

G Major Seventh Flat Fifth

Gmaj7(♭5)

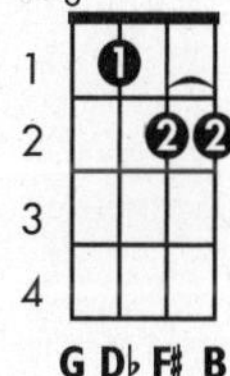

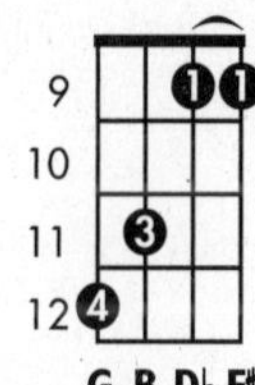

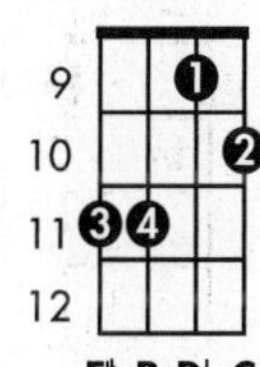

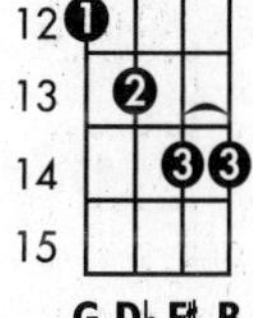

G Seventh Flat Ninth

G7(♭9)

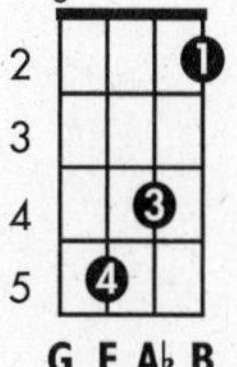

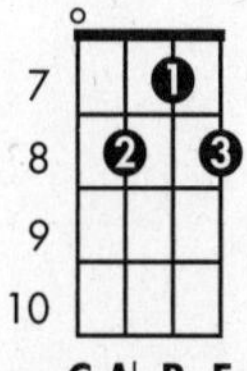

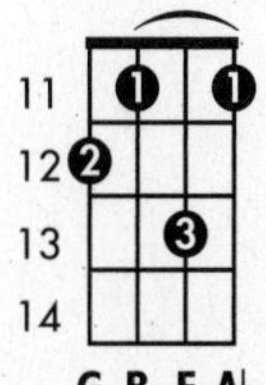

G

G7(♯9) G Seventh Sharp Ninth

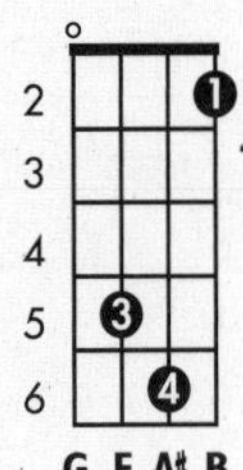

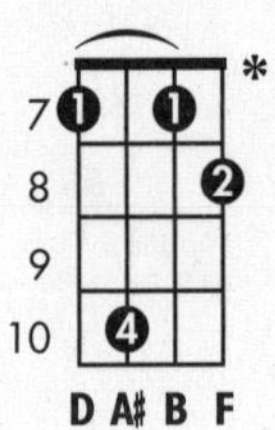

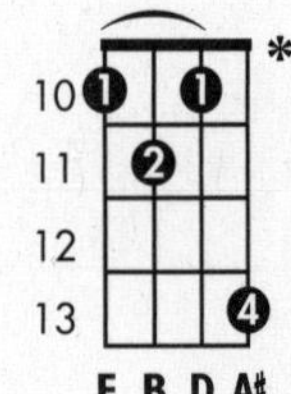

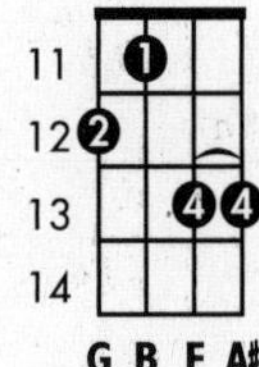

G7+(♭9) G Seventh Flat Ninth Augmented Fifth

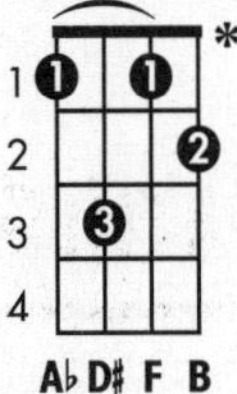

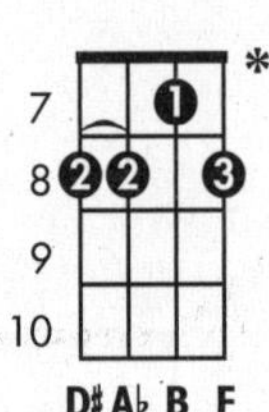

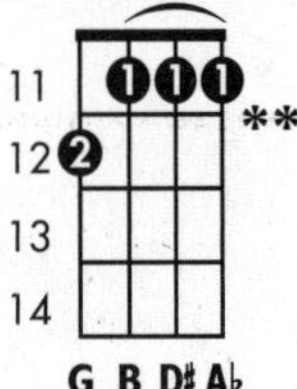

G9+ G Ninth Augmented Fifth

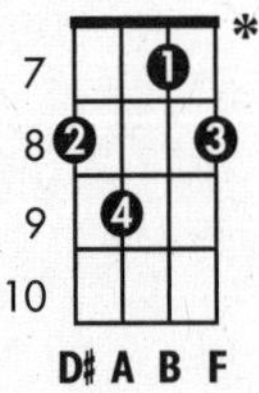

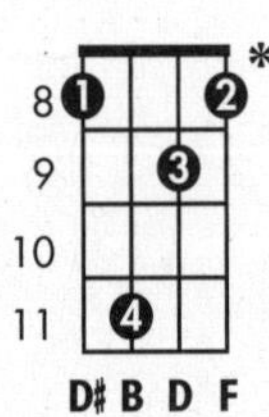

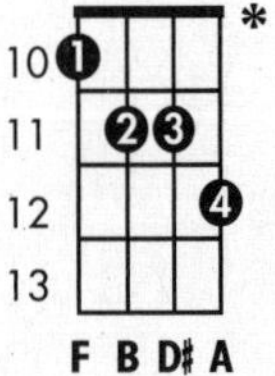

G9(♭5) G Ninth Flat Fifth

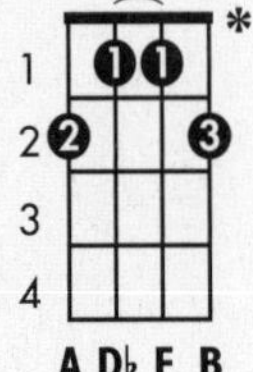

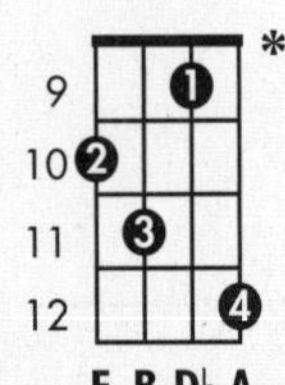

G Ninth Sharp Eleventh
G9(#11)

1 2 3 4
A C# F B

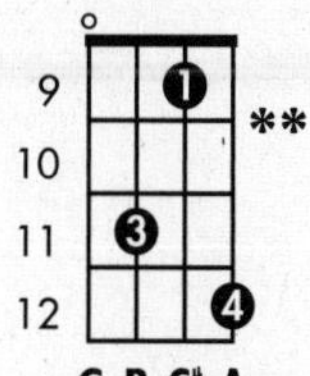

9 10 11 12
F B C# A

G Thirteenth Flat Ninth
G13(♭9)

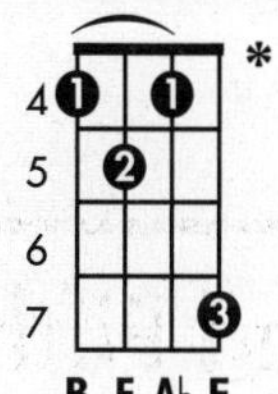

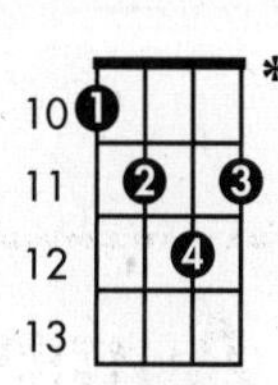

G Thirteenth Flat Ninth Flat Fifth
G13(♭9 ♭5)

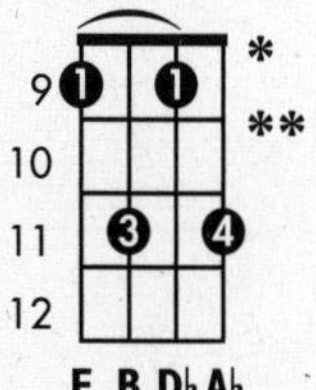

SCALES

Chords are based on scales, so it is important to understand them. A review of the basic theory is available on page 4 of this book. A major scale is W–W–H–W–W–W–H.

Major

W = Whole step
H = Half step

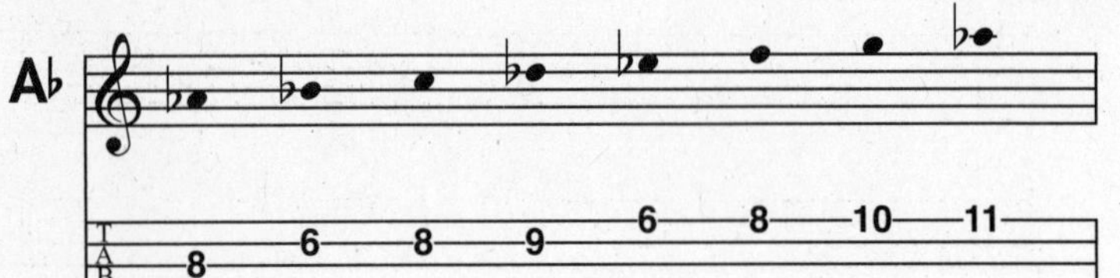

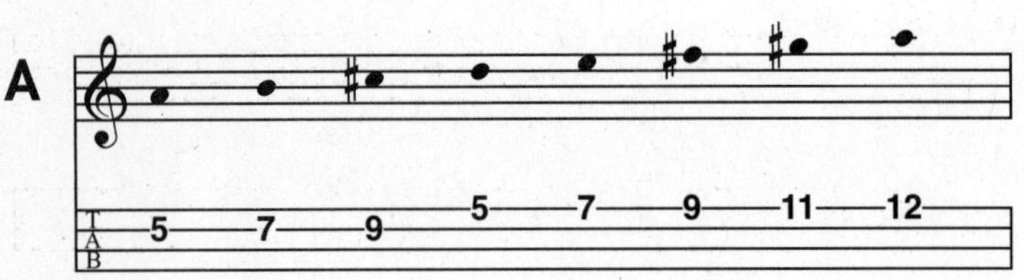

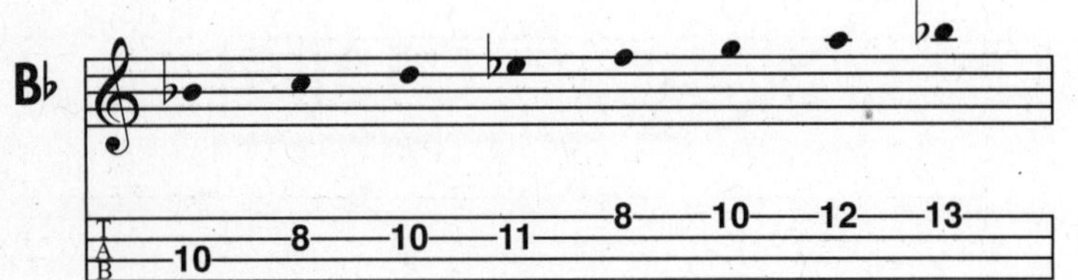

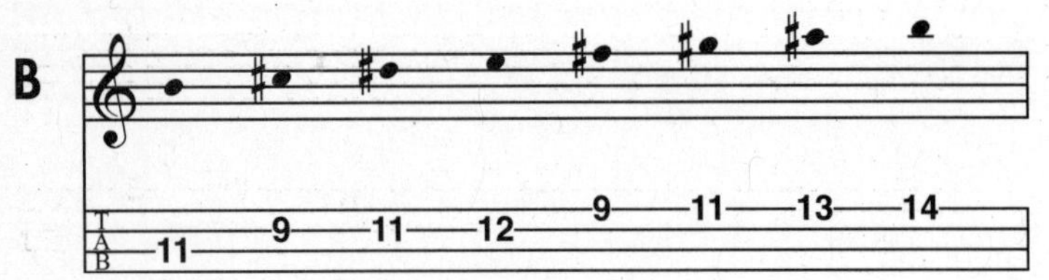

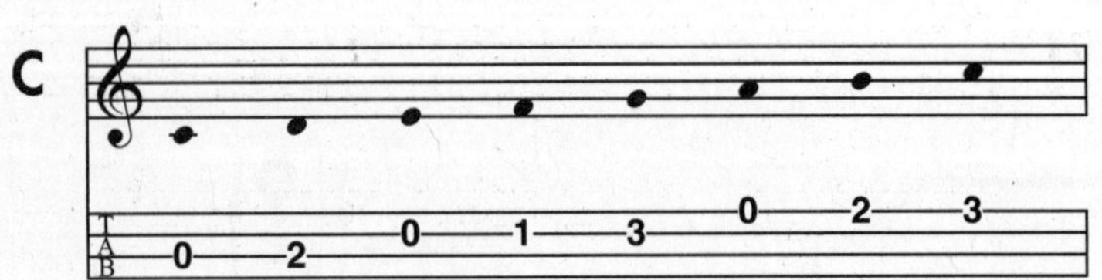

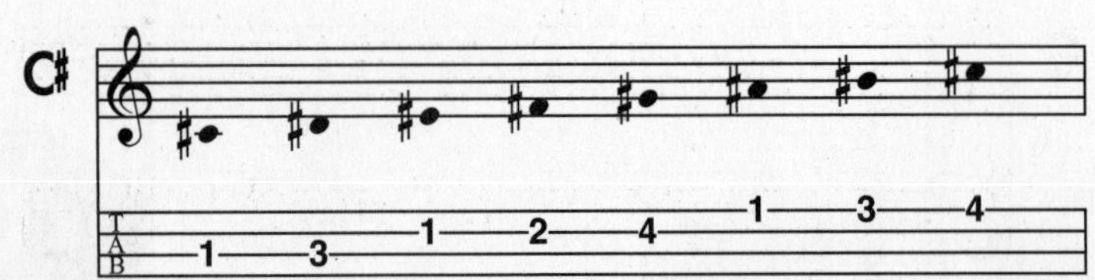

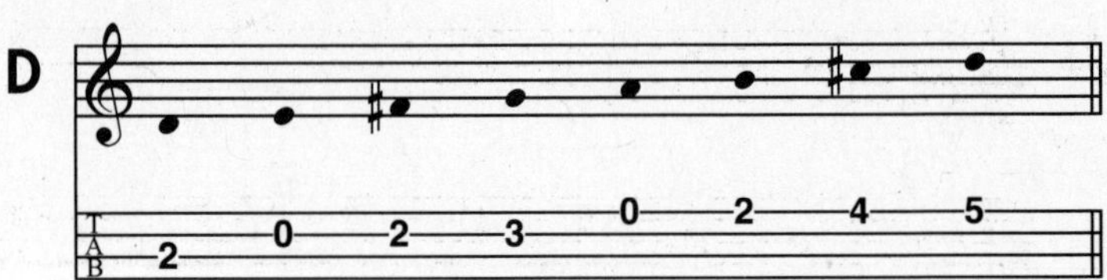

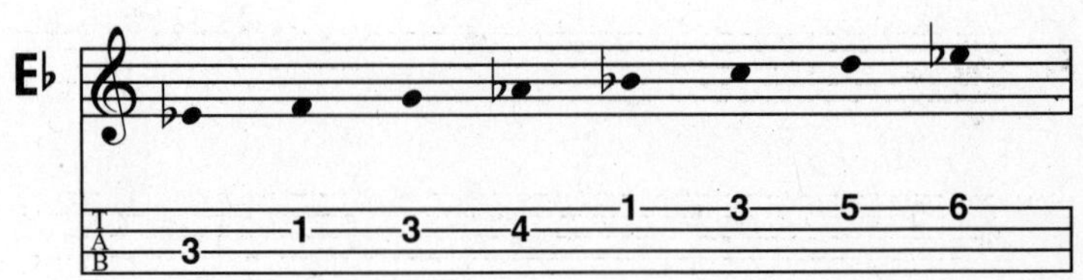

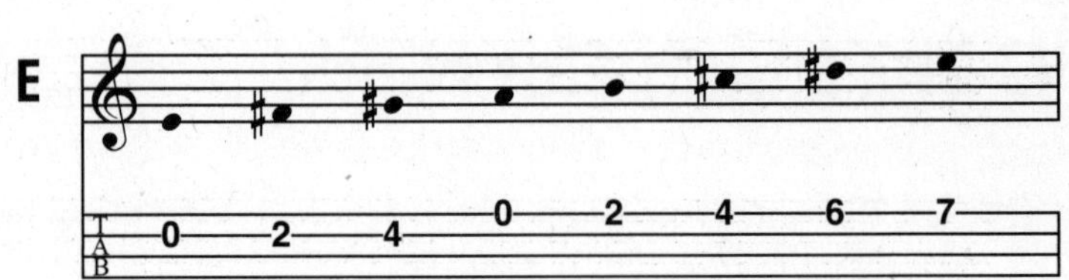

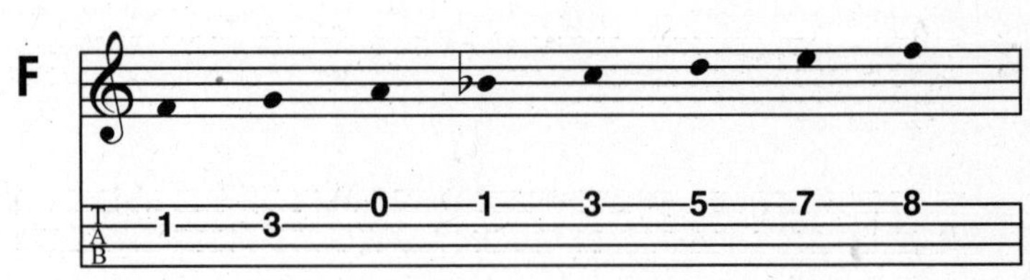

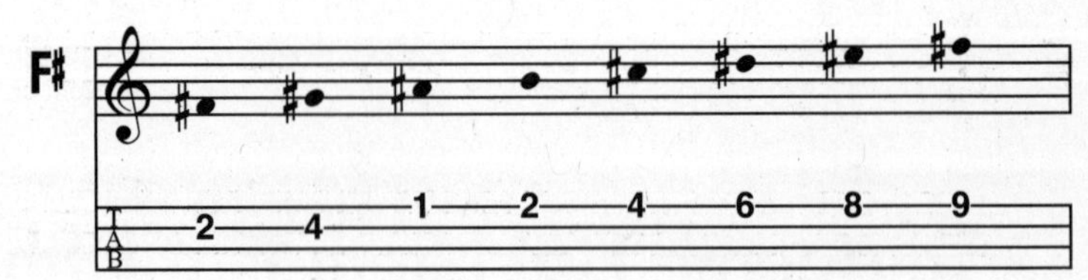

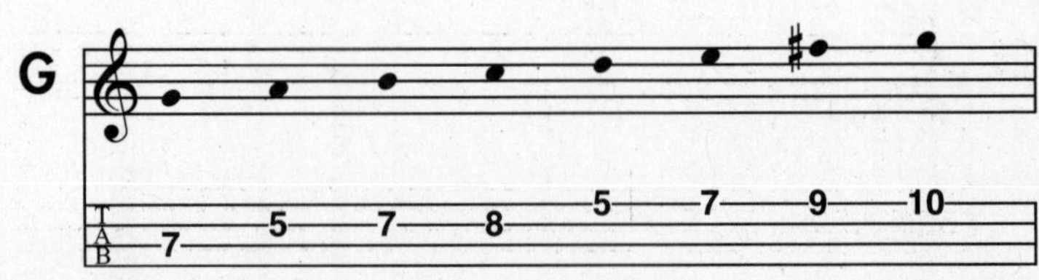

Natural Minor

A natural minor scale is W–H–W–W–H–W–W. Compared to the major scale, it is 1–2–♭3–4–5–♭6–♭7–1.

A♭

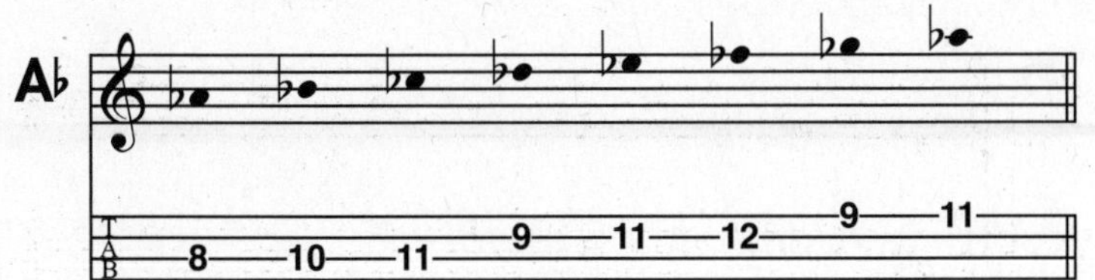

A

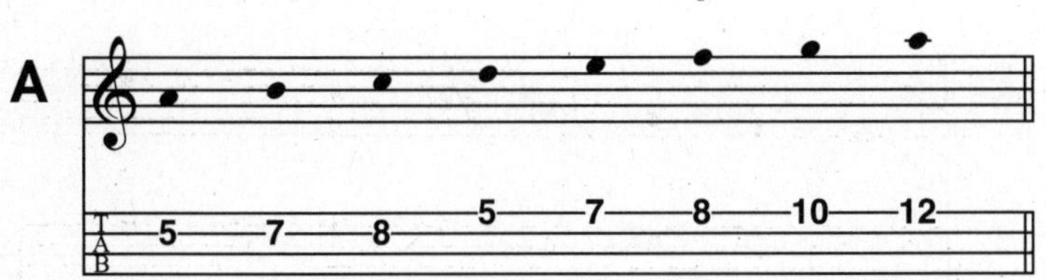

B♭

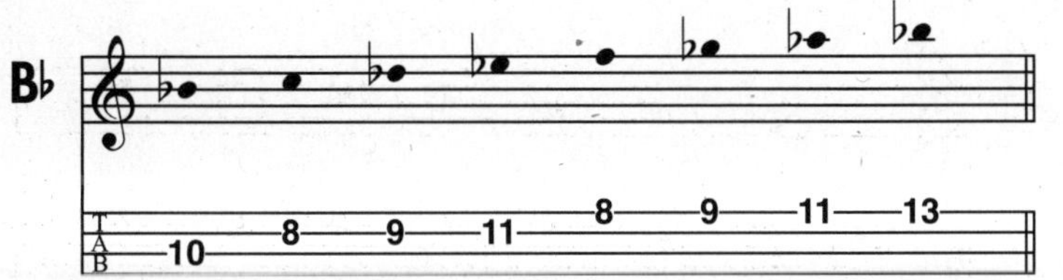

B

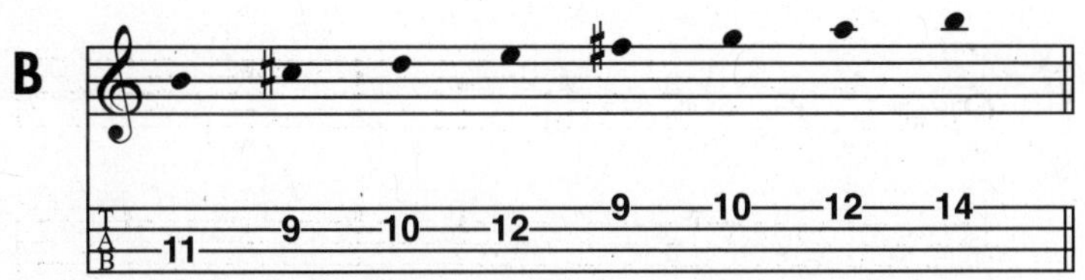

C

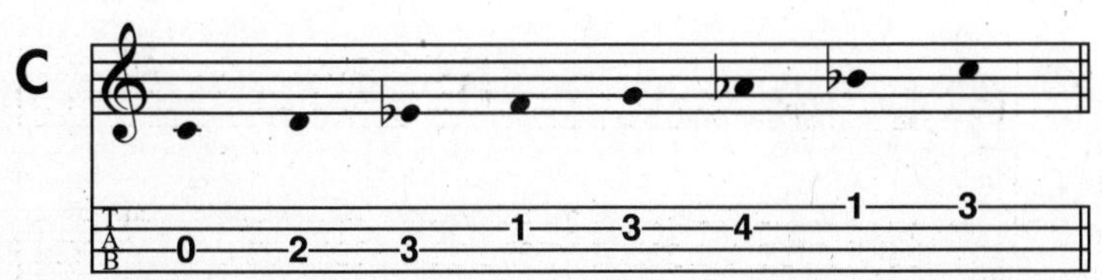

C♯

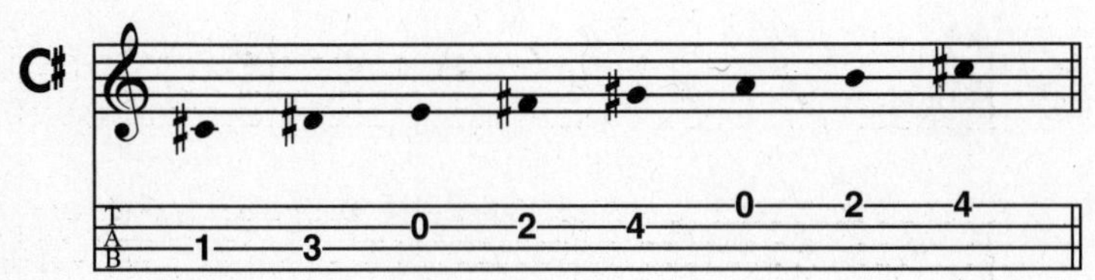

D

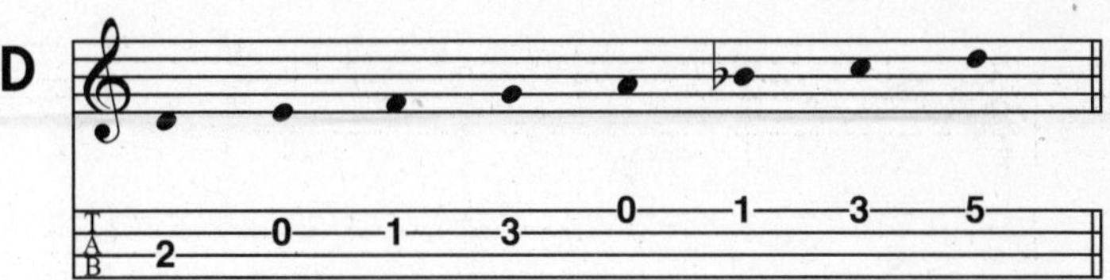

E♭

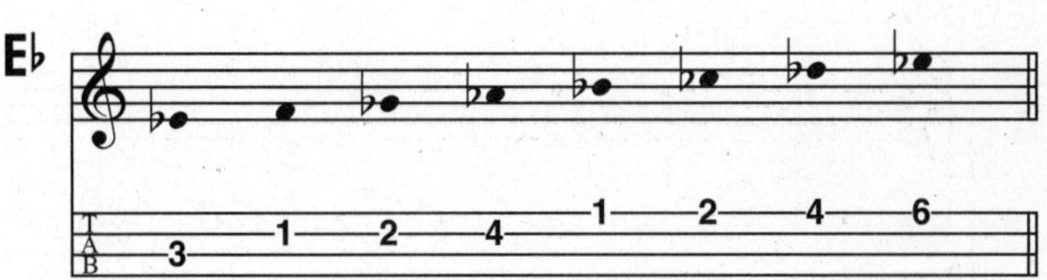

E

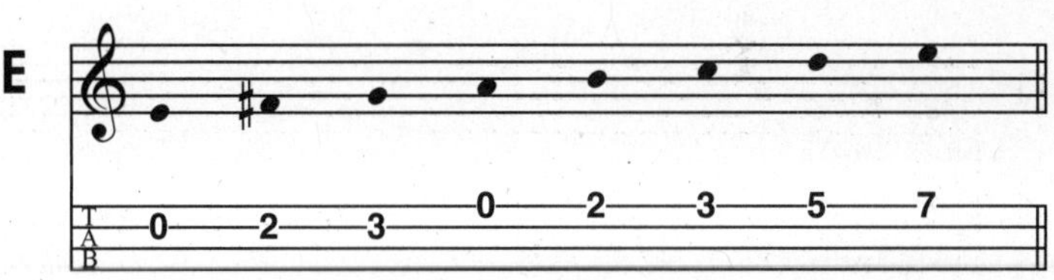

F

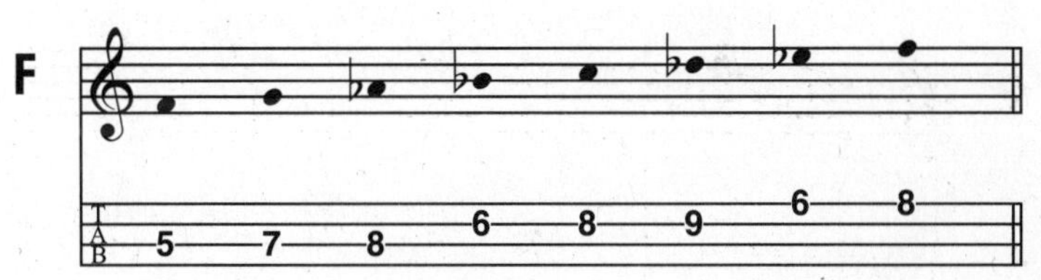

F♯

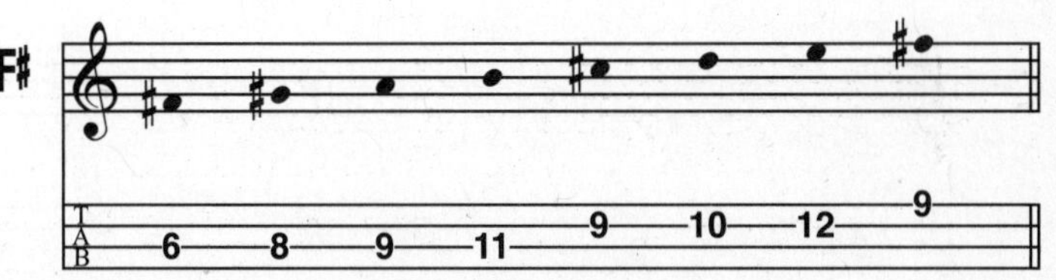

G

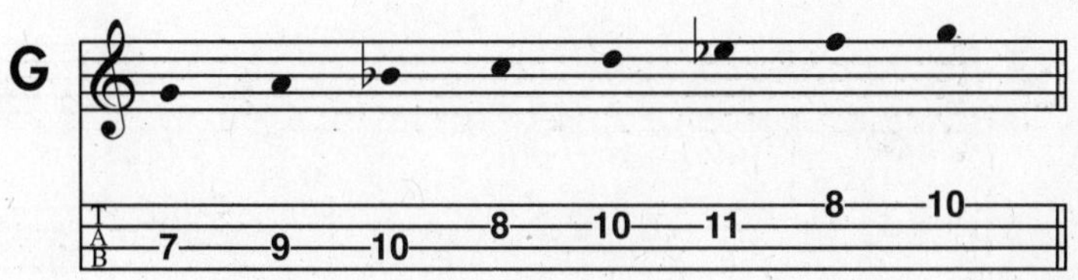

A harmonic minor scale is W–H–W–W–H–W+H–H. Compared to the major scale, it is 1–2–♭3–4–5–♭6–7.

Harmonic Minor

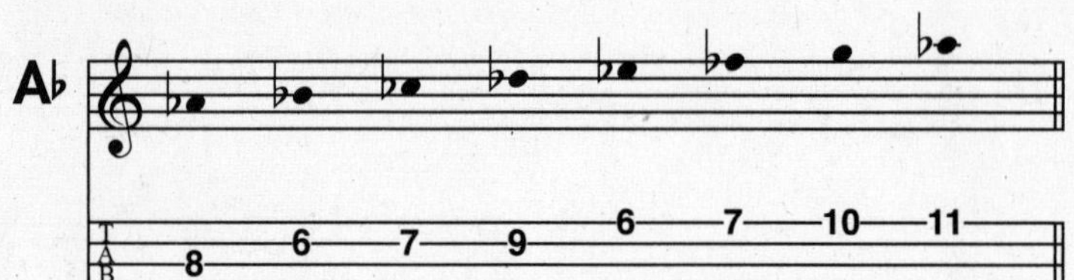

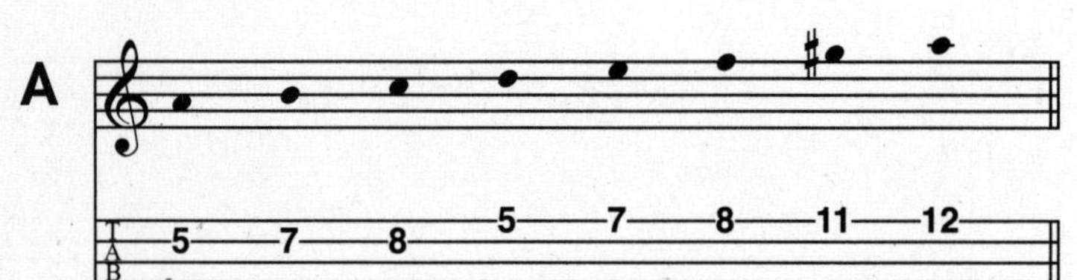

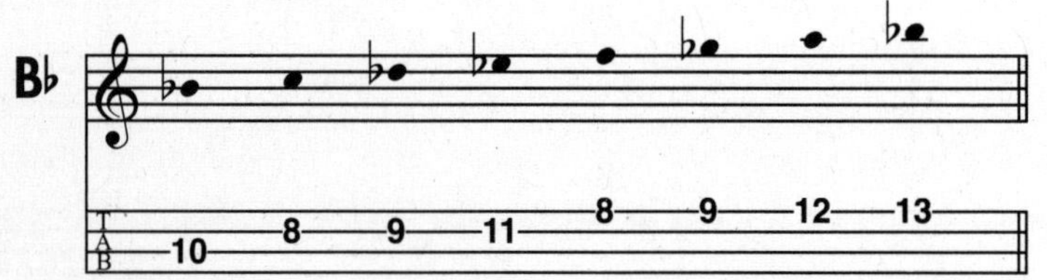

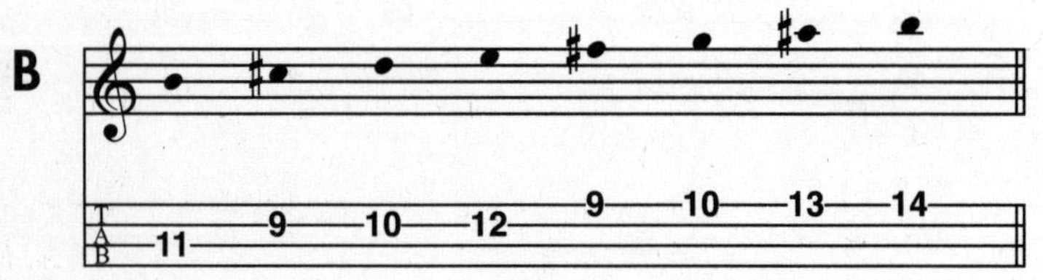

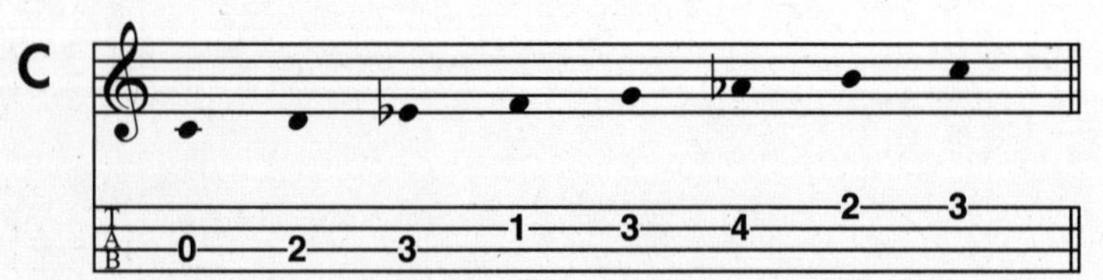

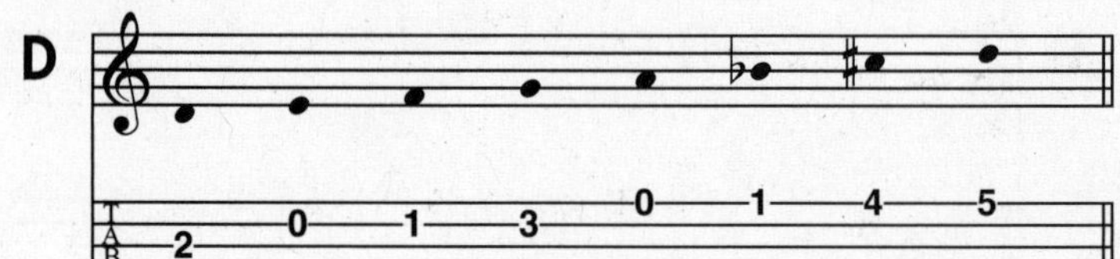

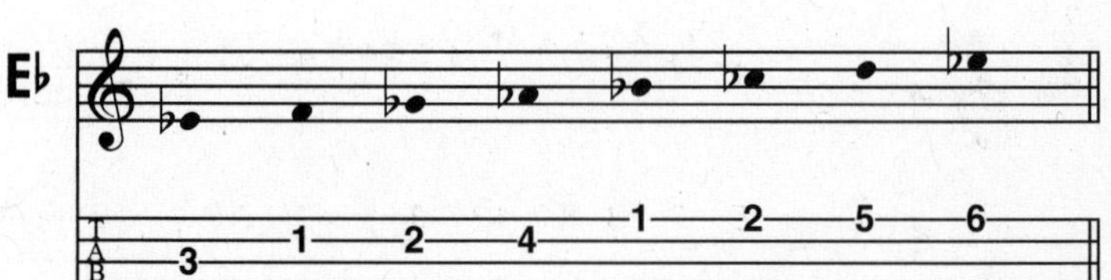

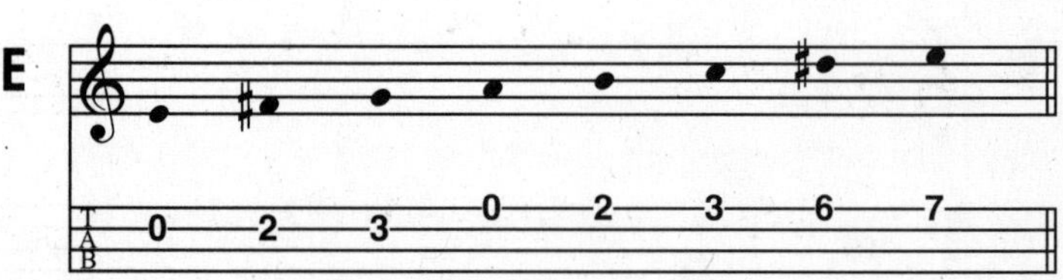

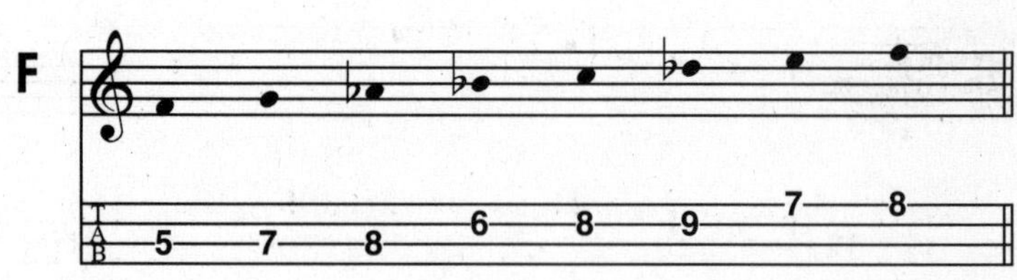

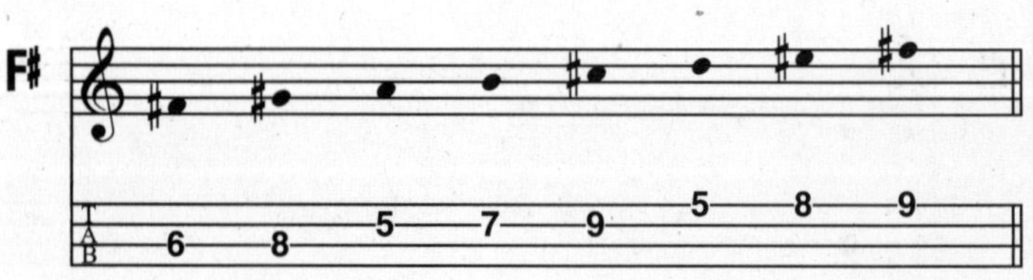

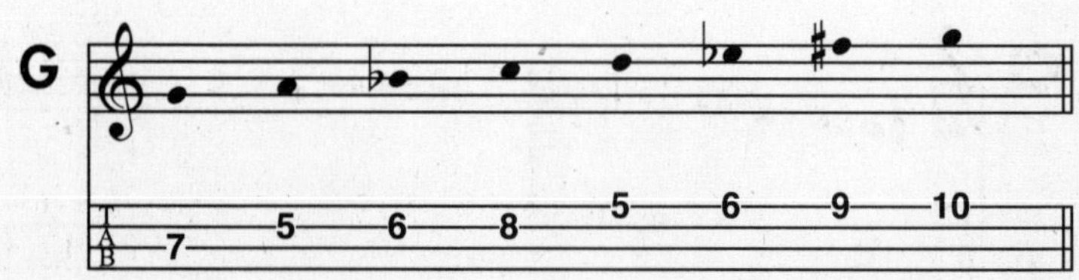